The Football Coaching Bible

American Football Coaches Association

Human Kinetics

Library of Congress Cataloging-in-Publication Data

The football coaching bible / American Football Coaches Association
     p. cm.
Includes bibliographical references (p.   ).
   ISBN 0-7360-4411-6 (Perfect bound)
  1. Football--Coaching.   I. American Football Coaches Association.
  GV956.6 .F68 2002
  796.332'07'7--dc21

                                            2002001185

ISBN: 0-7360-4411-6

Developmental Editor: Cynthia McEntire
Assistant Editors: Carla Zych, Amanda S. Ewing
Copyeditor: Bob Replinger
Proofreader: Kathy Bennet
Permission Manager: Toni Harte
Graphic Designer: Robert Reuther
Graphic Artist: Francine Hamerski
Art and Photo Manager: Carl D. Johnson
Cover Designer: Jack W. Davis
Photographer (cover): Pasadena Tournament of Roses Association®
Illustrator: Mic Greenberg
Printer: Bang Printing

Human Kinetics books are available at special discounts for bulk purchase. Special editions or book excerpts can also be created to specification. For details, contact the Special Sales Manager at Human Kinetics.

Printed in the United States of America 10 9 8 7 6 5 4 3 2 1

Human Kinetics

Web site: www.HumanKinetics.com

United States: Human Kinetics
P.O. Box 5076
Champaign, IL 61825-5076
800-747-4457
e-mail: humank@hkusa.com

Canada: Human Kinetics
475 Devonshire Road Unit 100
Windsor, ON N8Y 2L5
800-465-7301 (in Canada only)
e-mail: orders@hkcanada.com

Europe: Human Kinetics
107 Bradford Road
Stanningley
Leeds LS28 6AT, United Kingdom
+44 (0) 113 255 5665
e-mail: hk@hkeurope.com

Australia: Human Kinetics
57A Price Avenue
Lower Mitcham, South Australia 5062
08 8277 1555
e-mail: liahka@senet.com.au

New Zealand: Human Kinetics
P.O. Box 105-231, Auckland Central
09-523-3462
e-mail: hkp@ihug.co.nz

Contents

PART VI   Game-Winning Strategies 289
Bill Mallory

Introduction

The impact of giving back to the sport we coach cannot be overestimated. We have all been influenced positively by other coaches who took the extra time to add to our own knowledge base. Yes, we compete against one another fiercely each football season, but we are colleagues in our shared concern about the future of our sport.

The Football Coaching Bible is a shining example of how our football coaching community responds when called upon to give back to the profession. Now, I admit to having more than a few doubts when we were game-planning this ambitious publishing project two years before it went into print. But as you'll see in the pages that follow, my concerns were without merit; many of our finest coaches agreed to take part.

In addition to the 27 outstanding coaches who contributed chapters, the book was made possible because of the efforts of six dedicated coordinators—Don Nehlen, Harold "Tubby" Raymond, Bill Curry, Ron Schipper, Dick Tomey, and Bill Mallory—who oversaw each of the respective parts. These men set the standard when it comes to professionalism, service, and commitment to our game.

As you read the book, take note that even the most experienced and successful coaches were also good receivers. By that I mean they remained receptive to the learning opportunities that were offered by other coaches giving back to the game. I encourage you to be an eager recipient as well, and hope you find *The Football Coaching Bible* a valuable addition to your library.

Grant Teaff
AFCA Executive Director

Key to Diagrams

LOS	Line of scrimmage
W	Weakside linebacker, Will linebacker
DE	Defensive end
T	Tackle
M	Middle linebacker, Mike linebacker
S	Strongside linebacker, safety
N	Nose tackle
SS	Strong safety
FS	Free safety
C	Corner (defense)
X	Wide receiver
Z	Z-route receiver
Y	Tight end
HB	Halfback
FB	Fullback
TB	Tailback
○	Offensive player
●	Quarterback
⊕	Center
⊤	Blocking route
↑	Running route
◑	Blocking angle on offensive player
⧧	Handoff

PART I

Professional Duties and Opportunities

Don Nehlen

I grew up in Canton, Ohio, which is a real hotbed for high school football. At an early age, my goal was to be a football player in high school and college and to become a football coach at a major college. During my 42-year coaching career, I was a lucky guy. I was able to coach at all levels—high school and college, as both an assistant coach and a head coach.

Early in my career, I was obsessed with the Xs and Os of this great game. Every chance I had I looked at college and pro film to learn the game. I wanted to know everything about the various offenses and defenses. I felt that the coaches who knew the most about the game would be the winners and the others would be the losers. But as I matured as a coach, I came to realize that the coaching done off the field was as important as the coaching done on the field. I also came to know that the little things in football were just as important as the big things. I soon realized that discipline, conditioning, attitude, commitment, motivation, and morale were more important in winning than the Xs and Os.

This reminiscence brings me to our first four chapters. An alternative title for this section could be "Everything You Always Wanted to Know About Football, Except the Xs and Os."

Grant Teaff, the former great coach at Baylor and the current executive director of the American Football Coaches Association (AFCA), writes about the responsibilities of a coach. He addresses all duties and responsibilities, leaving no stone unturned. While serving as president of the AFCA and working with Grant, it became clear to me that Grant Teaff is the best organizational man in America.

Bo Schembechler writes about motivation as only Bo can. I had the privilege of working for Coach Bo for three years. He was one of the few coaches in America who could tell his team to go to hell and they would look forward to the trip. Bo was a master at having his players and coaches razor sharp at kickoff on Saturday afternoons. Rick Neuheisel, the outstanding young coach of the Washington Huskies, and Jack Harbaugh, the veteran Western Kentucky coach, add their thoughts and wisdom to the chapter.

Fisher DeBerry, the highly respected coach at the Air Force Academy, discusses the moral and ethical issues that coaches face every day. We live in a litigious society; consequently, coaches face more legal issues than ever before. Coach DeBerry discusses the need for a code of conduct and discipline to prevent destructive, antisocial behavior in our football programs.

Jim Tressel, the highly successful coach at Youngstown State who took his magic to Columbus to lead the Ohio State Buckeyes, discusses career decision making in coaching. He talks about leadership, planning, and service to the profession. Jim Tressel, in my opinion, is a star about to shine in the world of coaching. His chapter is a must-read for all coaches.

Responsibilities of a Coach

Grant Teaff

So important and extensive are the responsibilities of a coach that they could easily fill a book. However in the space of this one chapter, I will attempt to highlight the key duties in coaching and convey how imperative it is that current and future coaches dedicate themselves to fulfilling them.

Whether I have expanded the responsibilities far out of proportion or omitted some of the more important ones, this chapter reflects my beliefs about our profession and the responsibilities we shoulder when we accept the title *coach.*

I formed these beliefs as a high school and college athlete, as a coach, and as executive director of the world's largest coaching organization. It is in the latter role—in striving to improve not only myself and my coaching staff, but also the entire football coaching community—that the significance of coaching responsibilities has become especially apparent.

A couple of years ago, I received a telephone call from a young coach who had just become the head coach of a Division I-A institution. He wanted me to talk to his entire staff as they prepared to launch their new football program. My schedule allowed me to accommodate the coach, and my passion for our game and our profession motivated me to seize the opportunity to speak to the new staff and possibly help them with the challenges they were to face.

On the flight to the school, I began to jot down notes and points that I might mention, hoping to help the new staff get off on the right foot. I knew that they were working with an experienced team that had played together and achieved a high level of success. The new staff had a broad range of experience, from graduate assistants just moving into full-time positions to coaches who had been in our profession for many years. They faced a great challenge. I decided that it was important to do the following things from the start:

- Coach positively
- Build trust
- Show unity as a staff
- Become part of the campus and the community
- Build on existing strengths

I paused for a moment, thinking of other things the staff collectively and individually should do. Then I wrote, "Be responsible," to finish the list. Being responsible and accountable is the foundation on which the leader of any enterprise builds success.

Essential Responsibilities for All Coaches

For years the members of the American Football Coaches Association (AFCA) have heard and read my strong beliefs about responsibilities for coaches and members of the organization.

In 1994 I challenged football coaches with the responsibility of professionalism. Personal dress, conduct, and demeanor are the trademarks of a professional. Coaching and teaching is a profession. The coaching profession is a high calling. All coaches have a high profile in their communities, and some are nationally prominent. The language and speech patterns they use are on display for all to observe. The public scrutinizes their personal lives.

Success on the field or the lack of it is what really determines the longevity of coaches. Seldom do administrators and those in authority measure coaches by lives touched and changed. Those whose lives change recognize the contribution of a coach. Therefore I believe the greatest responsibility of a coach is to the athletes who come under his influence every day. Being a role model, teacher, mentor, boss, friend, and sometimes father is an awesome responsibility.

Although they are imposing, do not let the complexity or the challenge of the responsibilities of coaching deter you. Head coach or assistant, college Division 1-A or high school freshman level, we all need to know our responsibilities and live up to them.

Be the Best You Can Be

In 1989, several years before Gordon Wood of Brownwood High School would retire as this nation's winningest high school football coach, he attended a home game at Baylor University. On Friday night, Coach Wood's teams usually defeated an opponent soundly, and on Saturday he would drive to a college football game to learn. Sometimes he might take in two games on a Saturday if they were within his geographical area and if one was played in the afternoon and one at night.

In late September, Baylor University played a night game that resulted in victory. After the game I got a few hours of sleep and returned to Baylor Stadium at 5:00 A.M. to look at the previous night's film, as was my custom before going to the television studio at 6:30 to do my television show. It was pitch dark when I unlocked the front door and walked into the outer lounge area. Out of the corner of my eye, I saw someone lying on the couch in the waiting room. As my eyes adjusted to the light, I realized it was Gordon Wood. I said, "Coach, what in the world are you doing here?"

He replied, "I hope you didn't mind. I spent the night on your couch after the game. I saw some things I wanted to talk to you about, and I knew that you looked at the film early Sunday morning, so I just spent the night and waited on you."

I really don't remember what had caught his eye the night before. That part of the story is immaterial. The important point is that a high school head coach who had already won nine state championships at different high schools, now in the twilight of his coaching career, was making an extraordinary effort to gain some bit of knowledge that he believed would help his team achieve success. *Never* stop improving.

At an AFCA convention just a few years before Don Farout passed away in his 90s, I was a featured speaker. My topic was Baylor's short-yardage offense. At the Coach of the Year reception that night, Coach Farout—who was one of the great innovators in college football at the University of Missouri—walked up to me, pulled out a little notebook, and started reciting from it almost exactly what I had said in the lecture. I said, "Don, you were there at the short-yardage lecture?"

He said, "Oh yeah! I never miss a lecture." Then he said, "I would like to ask you a couple of questions about what you do with the fullback on your lead play."

Courtesy of Chris Hansen

I said, "Don, you haven't coached in nearly 20 years. Why do you still take notes and ask questions?"

Don turned to me, looked me straight in the eye, and said, "Coach, never stop learning."

Be Yourself but Be Willing to Change

When I first came into the coaching profession, Bear Bryant was the standard. I was told many times by men I respected, "Don't try to be Bear Bryant. There is only one Bear Bryant, so be yourself." Frankly, I couldn't have been Bear Bryant if I had wanted to. All the circumstances were different. But I believed that I could learn from Bear Bryant and from others I admired and respected without trying to emulate them.

Coach Bryant had an awesome reputation, and he still does. I observed that although Coach Bryant's personality didn't change that much, he adjusted his philosophy of the game according to the circumstances and the situation. Coach Bryant made an offensive philosophical change when he and his staff came to Texas to visit with Coach Darrell Royal and his staff about the new offense called the wishbone. National championships followed because the Bear was still the Bear, but he was willing to change.

Be Compassionate

I never played for Coach Bryant or had the privilege of coaching for him, but I got to know him through AFCA conventions, at two football games in 1979 and 1980, and by being around him a couple of times on the golf course. When Baylor lost to Alabama in the 1981 Cotton Bowl, our relationship deepened because of the real compassion I saw in him for me. At a joint press conference after the game, it must have been obvious to Coach Bryant that I was down. After we both had answered two or three questions, Coach Bryant leaned over to me and whispered in my left ear in that gravelly voice, "Don't worry yourself about this loss. The important thing was getting here, and remember if anyone criticizes you for losing a bowl game, I am the world champion at losing bowl games." With that he smiled. The loss still hurt, but Coach's compassion made me feel a lot better.

For four or five years in a row after that game, Coach Bryant would call me in early August and ask me to fly to Tuscaloosa on the Sunday before the opening game to speak at a church where he always took his team and coaching staff. Each time I would explain to Coach Bryant, "I just can't take the time away from our team and staff during our preseason preparations." I never did speak for Coach Bryant. After he passed away and I left Baylor for the AFCA, I finally found the time to do the church service. In my heart, I felt that I did it for Coach Bryant.

Be Accountable

Being accountable for your actions and your decisions goes with the leadership role that a coach assumes when he enters the profession. The mindset of accountability requires that you make decisions with forethought, not off the cuff. You should make entirely accurate statements based on the information available. You should teach methods and techniques valid for the application and thoroughly check them for safety. If you are teaching tackling or blocking, the methodology should be clearly within the rules, and more important, safety should be a part of the teaching exercise.

Tackling or blocking with the crown of the helmet is not only illegal but also places the blocker or tackler in jeopardy as well as the player being hit. An accountable coach makes sure his players block and tackle properly.

Be Part of the Solution

In facing the problems of life, coaches should always try to be a part of the solution. For example, a coach has a wonderful opportunity to help eradicate racism in America.

Few places in America are more diverse than the football field. Athletes of all races and creeds become a team, setting common goals and playing with a singular purpose. In 2000, the AFCA initiated a three-year program called "Together We Can," a theme that celebrates diversity on the football field. Every high school, college, and university in America received a poster depicting this theme. Against a beautiful blue sky, hands representing multiple races hold a football high in the air, representing success on the football field achieved by working together. The poster asks the question, "If we can work together in racial harmony on the football field, why can't we in America do the same in the streets, businesses, churches, and government?" The answer is that we can, but we must learn to. Therein lies an important responsibility of the coach. Together we can.

Be Self-Disciplined

Self-discipline is part of almost every aspect of football. How can a coach discipline his players if he is not a disciplined person? Self-discipline has to do with control of your emotions and your decision-making process.

As player in high school I jumped offside during a practice, and my coach blew the play dead. Coach asked me directly if I knew what I had just done. I answered, "I was in the neutral zone illegally."

"What is the cost?" he asked.

I replied, "Five yards."

Then came the penetrating question that I still live with today. "In your wildest imagination, Grant, do you think the official is going to penalize *you* five yards for your lack of discipline? Your poor decision making?"

"No, Coach, the official penalizes the whole team," I responded.

"That's the point," he said. "A lack of self-discipline affects not only the undisciplined one but others as well. Inside the 10-yard line, the cost could be a touchdown, and the loss of a touchdown could cost the district championship, and the loss of the district championship denies play for the state championship." I felt guilty because I jumped offside in practice and cost my school a state championship. The point was not lost on me.

Be a Role Model

Many people in prominent positions do not like to hear the term *role model*. Some high-profile people even deny that they are role models. No matter how vehemently they deny it, they are role models, as we all are. Someone is looking up to each of us right now, emulating what we do and what we say.

In other words, being a role model means that we are influencing those who look up to us with our work and actions. I am who I am today because of the influence of others. First, my family, particularly my mom and dad, influenced me to accept a set of values and standards that have guided me through my entire life, and that I have taught to others. My father's work ethic still has a great influence on my life. I saw him successfully blend commitment to work and devotion to family. Second, my teachers and coaches taught me how to win on and off the football field.

Every coach I encountered—junior high through college—influenced me and affected my life in special ways. Speedy Moffat, my high school coach, taught me the importance of total effort in all that I do. Mule Kaiser taught me self-discipline through his own self-discipline and self-motivation.

In late December of 2000, while walking down a street in New York City, I looked in a storefront window and saw a two-and-a-half foot bronze statue of a little boy in jeans and tennis shoes. As I looked closer at the statue, I realized that the small boy had a football under one arm and a helmet under the other. It occurred to me that the boy was looking for someone to teach him how to play the game and how to live life. He was looking for a coach. He found one that day, as I went into the store and purchased the statue. On the flight back to Waco, I was overcome with a compelling idea to create something for the thousands of men who have coached football and who have profoundly influenced the young people that they coached.

The idea turned into the Plaza of Influence, adjacent to AFCA national headquarters. Anyone who has ever been influenced by a football coach on any level can have the name of that coach permanently engraved on a stone and placed in the Plaza of Influence.

The great thing about positive influence is that it goes on and on. Though many of the coaches who influenced my life are deceased, the power of their influence has gone on through me and will go on through those I have influenced. In this way, the influence will continue.

I penned the poem "A Coach's Influence" while reflecting that, like the boy in the statue, I had looked to someone to teach me how to play the game and to live life and that I had then taught others. The influence continues.

A Coach's Influence

I dreamed a dream, but I had my doubts.
"You can do it," he said. "I'll teach you how."
I tried and tried, he said I should.
I gave it my best, he knew I would.
Lessons taught on the field of strife,
Have been invaluable as I've faced life.
When challenges come my way,
I always think, what would he say?
His inspiring words I hear even now,
"You can do it. I taught you how."
Now others dream and have their doubts.
I say, "You can do it, I'll teach you how."
The influence continues.

Communicate

The most hard-nosed coaches that I had during my high school and college career never used profanity. One coach looked at me and said, "Profanity shows a lack of vocabulary and a lack of respect for the person or persons you are talking to." I determined that day that I would not like it if someone used profanity and that I would therefore try to develop a strong enough vocabulary that I would never use profanity in front of my players. One other note is that use of profanity is a habit. For some people, habits are hard to break.

Use of proper language and the ability to present your ideas has great bearing on advancement in professional life. A leader must be a communicator, and language is an important tool that we use to convey thoughts, ideas, and passion.

Be an Encourager

The scripture in Ecclesiastes says simply that there is a time and a place for everything. Granted, there is certainly a time for constructive criticism and most definitely a time for encouragement. The phrases "keep a thumb on" or "hold a tight rein" illustrate that some people need to be supervised more closely than others and some need to be reined in periodically. A coach can offer encouragement through a word or words, or through gestures, such as a thumbs up, an affirming nod of the head, or even a smile.

Be Above Reproach

The coach's conduct on and off the field should be exemplary. Common sense, sound judgment, and conscious diligence should be your guide. Never put yourself in a compromising position. If an action or gesture could be misinterpreted, don't do it.

Perception is reality to most people. Everyone in your community will know more about your personal life than you can imagine. Many potentially great coaches have lost the chance to pursue their coaching dreams because of poor judgment.

Be Honest

In December 2001, an incident stunned the football coaching world and hopefully other segments of society. George O'Leary, the outstanding head football coach from Georgia Tech University, had just been hired by Notre Dame University. For a coach who had labored so hard for so many years, this opportunity had to be the thrill of a lifetime. Those of us who have known George were excited for him and expected him to do well.

The nation was stunned a few days later when a wire story from South Bend, Indiana, was released to the national media. The first sentence simply read, "George O'Leary resigned as Notre Dame Football Coach five days after being hired, admitting he lied about his academic and athletic background."

Coach O'Leary tried to explain what had happened. "Many years ago, as a young married father, I sought to pursue my dream as a football coach. In seeking employment, I prepared a resume that contained inaccuracies regarding my completion of course work for a masters degree and also my level of participation in football at my Alma Mater. These misstatements were never stricken from my resume or biographical sketch in later years."

Coach O'Leary's statement concluded, "I pray that my experiences will simply be yet another coaching lesson to the youth of this country that we all are accountable for our actions and there can be no double standard."

I was recently interviewed by a sports writer who was measuring the negative effect that this incident had had on Notre Dame, assistant coaches, their families, players, and of course Coach O'Leary and his family. When asked for my opinion, I simply said, "It is a tragedy for all concerned. However I prefer to look at the positive side. Perhaps this can be a great lesson to every young aspiring coach, teacher, or businessperson or to anyone who desires to achieve success in their careers."

A couple of days after this incident, I spoke on the telephone with one of my former players who had also served on my coaching staff. He said, "I thought of all those lectures you used to give us as players and as assistant coaches concerning our honesty—in presenting our university, in dealing with people—and I particularly remember how emphatic you were about being honest with our expense accounts as coaches. I remember you saying that as innocent as an act of dishonesty might be, there will be a time in life when the previous action will be regretted."

George O'Leary is an outstanding coach and a great person. May we all learn from this sad experience.

Specific Responsibilities for Assistant Coaches

Statistics tell us that about half of all assistant coaches aspire to be head coaches. The road to becoming a head coach, however, is slippery. Coaching as an assistant lays the foundation for stepping up to the position where the buck stops, the head job. Assistant coaches have many specific responsibilities. When they master those responsibilities, the door may open to becoming a head coach.

Be Loyal

There is a great difference between being loyal and pretending to be loyal. Loyalty comes from character within and being committed to serving the institution, the head coach, and the system in the capacity in which you are hired. The assistant must make every effort to contribute to the staff and to the team, and to be part of the decision-making process. When the head coach or the staff make a decision, even if it is not the decision the assistant coach wanted, the assistant should back the decision 100 percent.

Although being loyal does not require one to take an oath, every assistant coach should be willing to sign a mental pledge card. If you can't be loyal to an institution, a system, or a head coach, you should quietly look for a place where you can exhibit the required loyalty.

One day while I was an assistant in college, I was having lunch with a well-known member of our staff who had been there for some time. A gentleman from the community came up to our table and addressed the other coach. "You have been around here for a while," he said. "Don't you think it is time for a new head football coach?" The assistant coach just looked up at the supporter and smiled. The supporter turned and walked away, and I thought to myself that the smile was an act of disloyalty. Although it neither confirmed nor denied the statement audibly, silence was an affirmation. Although the question was not addressed to me, my silence gave me a guilty feeling. I should have spoken up in defense of our coach because he was doing a good job and the staff knew it. I should have said so.

Loyalty is not a problem when you are 10-1 or win the championship. Loyalty becomes a challenge when things are not going well and negativism abounds. The assistant coach must guard against acts of disloyalty.

Be Team Minded

To maximize his contribution to a staff, the assistant coach must develop a team mind. In other words, he should think team first. Doing that is not easy because every coach tends to be selfish about the position he is coaching. He wants the best players on his side of the ball. Yes, you should fight for the players that you want. But after the decision is made, even if you didn't get the player you wanted, you need to refocus with a team mind-set.

A motto our staff and players used was, "We don't care who gets the credit as long as the job gets done." If adhered to, that credo lays a foundation for success. The following fable from a monthly publication called *Good Stuff* illustrates my point. A frog asked two geese to take him south with them. At first they resisted; they didn't see how they could do it. Finally the frog suggested that the two geese hold a stick in their beaks and he would hold onto it with his mouth. So off the unlikely threesome went, flying southward over the countryside. It was quite a sight. People looked up and expressed great admiration at this demonstration of creative teamwork. Someone yelled, "It's wonderful. Who was so clever to discover such a fine way to travel?" The frog opened his mouth and said, "It was I," as he plummeted to the ground.

Be a Teacher

In 1994 I wrote a book titled *Coaching in the Classroom*. The premise of that book was simple. The best coaches are teachers, and the best teachers are coaches. Through the years I have always been fascinated by the ability of coaches and teachers to communicate their subject matter to their students or athletes. So I asked everyone I met from all walks of life to describe the best teacher they ever had. The descriptions were similar—a teacher who cared, knew the subject matter, expanded on it, kept a disciplined classroom, and taught self-motivation.

In my own life I found that those after whom I patterned my teaching and coaching had similar traits. All the teachers I admired had high expectations of me. Asking students to develop their best traits, set high goals, and learn basic principles of success is the responsibility of a teacher or coach. A master teacher plans, prepares, and presents. An effective teacher or coach encourages, praises, and shows acceptance and approval because doing so builds self-confidence and esteem. Will Rogers once said, "In order to succeed, you must know what you are doing, like what you are doing, and believe in what you are doing."

Be a Worker

Those who come into the coaching profession should understand the amount of effort and work that it takes to achieve success. Few professionals work harder than coaches do. The time spent during games is insignificant compared with the time required for preparation and practice. Fulfilling the responsibility to counsel and encourage adds more time.

Early on a coach must prioritize his time and find ways to have time with his family. The head coach is responsible for prioritizing time for the staff to make sure that the staff members are achieving the proper balance of time between coaching and family. Then the individual coach is responsible for his own use of time.

Bloom Where Planted

I have long believed that if you do your job and work hard enough, advancement opportunities will take care of themselves. I have never applied for a job. That is unusual, and I recognize that I have been lucky. But my experience points out that if you do a good enough job where you are, folks are going to seek you out. It will happen. Through the years I have had coaches on my staff who spent so much time looking over the fence to see if the grass was greener that they impeded their advancement opportunities.

The second part of my theory is every job should be your life work. The attitude you should have is simple—work as if this is the last job you will ever have. As a coach, you should think of each job as though it is your job for life and then bloom where you are planted.

Be Ethical

The coach must develop a personal set of ethics and then adhere to them. Coaches must abide by the rules and laws of the land as well as the rules that govern our programs, whether they are interscholastic, collegiate, or professional.

The AFCA, founded over 80 years ago, decided early that ethical conduct and behavior was a strong responsibility of any person who called himself a coach. Amos Alonzo Stagg drew up the first football coaching ethics, which the association revised in 1950. In the early 1990s the AFCA updated its Code of Ethics again to fit modern football. Having served as the chairman of the AFCA's ethics committee for 12 years, I can tell you that the road to success is strewn with failed football coaches who developed their own interpretation of the Code of Ethics and ended up sidelined from their coaching goals.

It is your responsibility and obligation to be an ethical person—for the players you teach, for the institution you serve, and for the family you represent. Yes, being ethical costs, sometimes dearly. In the 1980s in the Southwest Conference, unethical behavior and the breaking of NCAA rules were rampant. Many innocent people were hurt. Many coaches were kicked out of the coaching profession, and those who were ethical and did things by the rules suffered in the win-loss column. Those who suffered and were ethical, however, can look back at those times and enjoy a peace that comes with knowing they did things the right way, even if their records are not as favorable as they might have been.

Specific Responsibilities for Head Coaches

A football coach who has worked extremely hard to climb the ladder to reach the pinnacle of being a head coach takes on additional responsibilities.

Set the Example

The members of the staff look up to the head coach as the person to emulate. The head coach has responsibility for the well-being of his players and coaching staff, and further responsibility to the institution and to the alumni to run a successful football program with integrity. He is also responsible for making sure that football finds an appropriate level of emphasis that does not come at the expense of the staff members' families or his own. A successful coach once told me that he had sacrificed his family for football. Coaching success is important, but it's not that important.

Set the Standard

Perhaps the most important responsibility of the head coach is to set the standard for conduct and behavior. Adherence of the head coach to the laws of the land and the rules of the NCAA and the institution is an example for all staff. When student-athletes fail to follow the rules of the game, everyone knows who is ultimately responsible—the head coach. The head coach has the power to see to it that everyone under his charge obeys the rules and the spirit of the rules.

Be a Leader

As a leader, the head football coach has the responsibility of setting the emotional tone for his staff and his team. He must be positive, fair, and decisive. The head coach should exhibit control of his emotions and teach emotional control to his staff and players. The head coach's responsibility is to represent the team and the institution through the media and to represent the goals of his team and coaching staff.

Guard the Family

The extended family of the head coach includes his staff and their families and his players. Being the guardian of the family requires honest evaluation of the time the staff spends away from their families. At Baylor we started staff meetings early in the morning, which allowed coaches to go home after evening practice to spend quality time with their families. Not once did I detect that this approach took away from our preparation, but I did notice that it created a great working environment for our coaching staff.

Another responsibility as guardian of the team is to practice good medicine. Practicing good medicine means that you make sure your team has the best medical personnel, trainers, and emergency plans. Provide education on how to tackle and block properly and how to recognize heat-related symptoms.

We have entered an era in football in which the players' size and speed requires us to be extremely intelligent in working with our medical people. Together we should design drills that effectively train and best protect our athletes. Providing the safest equipment available and developing emergency procedures in case of an accident will lessen the severity of any injury. Coaches at all levels can demonstrate the correct techniques for tackling and blocking. Producing a videotape of the session will allow the coach to play it every so often to remind players of proper techniques.

Nationwide, trainers or medical personnel are now routinely speaking to teams about symptoms of heat injuries. Head coaches are taking the responsibility to tell their teams that although players have to be physically and mentally tough to play the game, they must not hesitate to tell a trainer, coach, or teammate if they do not feel well. If a player notices symptoms in a teammate, he should tell the trainer or a coach. A new day has dawned—the head coach is responsible for ensuring that his program practices good medicine.

The title *coach* should not be taken lightly. Years after coaching my last team, I would rather be called "Coach" than by my name. The title exudes respect—the respect that I had for the coaches who coached me and, I hope, the respect my players had for me. In every war since the Civil War, these words have been heard over and over, "My Coach said . . ." A coach by his words and actions teaches grace under fire and how to overcome adversity. If in reading this chapter, you say, "Wow! Coaching has way too many responsibilities," please remember this: "To whom much is given, much is expected."

Inner Drive and Motivation

Bo Schembechler

Throughout my years as head coach at the University of Michigan, I collected various pieces of literature that reflect the essence of character and success. Never, in my entire career, did I discover a more penetrating insight into the true meaning of motivation than the one contained in this poem:

> I'd rather see a sermon than to hear one any day;
> I'd rather one should walk with me than merely show the way;
> The eye's a better pupil and more willing than the ear;
> Fine counsel is confusing, but examples are always clear.
> And, best of all, the preachers are the men who live their creeds;
> For to see good put in action is what everybody needs.
> I soon can learn to do it, if you'll let me see it done;
> I can see your hands in action, but your tongue too fast may run.
> And the lectures you deliver may be very fine and true,
> But I'd rather get my lesson by observing what you do;
> For I may misunderstand you and the high advice you give;
> But there's no misunderstanding how you act and how you live!

If every coach took a few moments to read those words carefully and digest the message within them, he would walk away with the greatest football lesson there is to learn.

Motivation is the will to do something to the absolute best of one's ability. A motivated man refuses to surrender even when there is nothing left to give. The enormity of the task does not matter. Neither do overwhelming odds against success. An effort may at times fall short of its goal, but a motivated team never allows itself to come up short of effort. Success isn't a case of never making mistakes. It's a case of never giving up after making mistakes. That's motivation!

Ordinary men make promises to achieve excellence. Motivated men are fearless. They take it one step further. They make commitments, and they never compromise. The late Bob Zuppke, who coached the University of Illinois football team for 29 years, once said, "The difference between champions and near champions is the ability to play for something outside of self." That's motivation! No one can achieve lasting success without it.

The responsibility to instill motivation into the hearts and minds of players, trainers, equipment managers, secretaries, and an entire football staff lies in the hands of the head coach and his assistants. They are the mirrors through which the players and all those in the organization will envision themselves. The only foolproof method of imparting motivation that refuses to bend is to paint a living self-portrait of unyielding motivation that everyone understands. Words can't do it. Only actions can.

Don't waste anybody's time talking about motivation—live it! Don't bother looking for motivation hiding somewhere between all those Xs and Os in some fancy playbook; you won't find it there. Don't fool yourself into thinking it comes as easily as some pregame talk. Words are cheap. Motivation is a commodity too precious to take its home there.

The wise coach knows that true motivation comes from within. The successful coach understands how to share that marvelous uncompromising spirit with every member of the football team. People often mistake motivation with the histrionics of a pregame or halftime speech. Normally those kinds of speeches serve only to prove that, given the opportunity, a coach is capable of making as many promises as a double-talking salesman. Speeches are better left to politicians and preachers. Save them for the student pep rallies and the fund-raising affairs.

Sometimes the right words can trigger a player's emotion lying just beneath the surface. But the coach should have planted that emotion in the bellies of everybody on the team a long time ago. A wise old preacher once said, "I'd rather live one good sermon than give a million bad ones." There's no better piece of advice for a football coach.

Motivation is a passion for the game, a passion for life, and a passion for bringing out the best in every person whose life you have the opportunity to touch. A man must commit himself to that degree of passion before he truly earns the title *coach*.

I once read a quote from the great British playwright George Bernard Shaw: "The people who get on in this world are the people who get up and

The Culture of Motivation

Rick Neuheisel

"Some time, Rock, when the team is up against it, when things are wrong and the breaks are beating the boys—tell them to go in there with all they've got and win just one for the Gipper."

These words recounted by Knute Rockne in 1928 became the most famous locker-room speech of our time. Notre Dame went on to defeat Army that afternoon and hence to immortalize both Rockne and George Gipp. Even today, Rockne is held in high esteem as a great motivator.

Most people are not privy to what happens behind the scenes on a football team. They believe that these "made for Hollywood" moments are the essence of motivation. Although every coach would love to deliver that fire-and-brimstone speech for the ages, the real art of motivation is developing a team culture in which passionate play is the norm and commitment to one another is sacred.

Short-term motivation is still valuable. The locker-room speech can get players and coaches to focus on what you deem important. During a season, things always come up that coaches can use to enhance concentration that extra little bit.

Coaches who rely solely on short-term motivation, however, will find themselves reaching for inspiration. The lack of a consistent message will lead to inconsistent play.

To motivate a team to reach its full potential, you must first create a culture. Creating a culture is thus paramount. We attempt to do this by asking three questions at the beginning of every year: Who are we? Where are we going? How are we getting there?

The first question addresses our identity. How do we want people to perceive us, both on and off the field? What do we want our opponents to think about us? The answers to these questions are important because they indicate levels of self-esteem and pride.

The second question helps us set goals. What do we believe we can achieve? Are we willing to shoot for the stars?

Finally, the third question assesses the cost. What are we willing to do to achieve our goals? How much will we give of ourselves and, more important, how much will we commit to others?

Great effort, great attitude, great enthusiasm—we must expect these from all, regardless of circumstance, regardless of adversity. Maintaining long-term motivation depends on closely adhering to our answers to these key questions.

Using long-term motivation each week throughout a season sends a consistent message. We are taking an inventory. Players and coaches alike have to assess their personal commitment to achieving the desired end. Ultimately, when players and coaches can look around a room and know that everybody else is equally committed, you have achieved the culture you set out to establish and motivated your team to its potential.

Rick Neuheisel is the head coach at the University of Washington, where in his second year as head coach his Huskies won the 2001 Rose Bowl, finishing the season 11-1. Before coaching at Washington, Neuheisel coached at the University of Colorado for four years.

look for the circumstances they want, and if they can't find them, make them." That's motivation! Coming from a man who probably never touched a football in his life, that's sage football advice. Of course, it doesn't take a genius to realize that no player ever became good by walking after a ball.

The message is so true. If a coach is unwilling to accept the responsibilities and to meet the demands of such dedication, he'd be wise to turn in his whistle and clipboard and find a job that's measured by a time clock.

A coach cannot instill motivation into any of his players, his assistants, or any other member of the football organization unless he himself is motivated. A coach must live his passion. He must breathe it. Above all, he must conduct himself accordingly, not only on the football field but in every aspect of life. He must be the living image of what each of his players aspires to become. Only then will he have a chance of transferring that motivation to his men.

Motivation is not restricted to the 11 autumn Saturdays when the team plays games. The team must practice it when preparing for each game throughout the season. Motivation must be paramount during off-season conditioning when it's easy to believe that the upcoming season is too far away to worry about. And, most important, motivation must become an integral part of all aspects of life away from the field, where character and morality are the true measures of a man.

A football coach, a firefighter, a lawyer, or a member of any profession brings to the job the exact traits of the person he really is. There's no hiding who the real person is. That's why it is so critical that the head coach possess a moral character so impeccable that he cannot accept anything less from his team and those around him.

The team will reflect what the coach is. The team will believe what the coach believes. How can the coach expect any member of his squad to live by the highest standards if he doesn't apply the same yardstick of judgment to himself? He must radiate his qualities to each member of the organization—assistant coaches, players, trainers, equipment managers, secretaries, every member of the staff. No unit of the team can achieve success without the dedicated effort of the whole.

Motivation doesn't magically start in August when the first footballs are thrown out onto the field. Motivation is a 12-month, 52-week, 24-hour-a-day job. It all starts with the head coach.

If you slice open the belly of motivation, I guarantee you'll find two basic elements—honesty and integrity. No coach, no football player, no person in any occupation will ever become truly successful without embracing each of those qualities with the fury that a football player applies when diving onto a fumbled ball.

The core of coaching is honesty. You can develop a trusting relationship only with people who believe in you, the program, the team, and themselves. A coach must lead his team with truth and honesty to confront the untruth, the half-truths, and all the baloney that others may throw at him.

Dealing with the truth will be tough at times. No coach or player likes to concede that another team may be more physically talented than his own. No one likes to admit that certain mistakes during a critical part of a game resulted in defeat. In the long run, however, I promise that you will be successful with the truth.

The character of a leader, a team, and an entire program depends on honesty from all those involved. You cannot motivate without honesty. You cannot assemble a highly motivated team unless they know you speak the truth. Honesty is the core of coaching.

For 10 years I was privileged to be an assistant coach under Doyt Perry, Ara Parseghian, and Woody Hayes. Those were men of integrity. Those were men of the highest moral standards. Their work ethic was impeccable. Their word was good as gold. Not once in all those years were any of them caught in a lie. Their players merely looked at them to see how to live the right way.

If you live the right way, you'll play the right way. It begins with the head coach. By living the right way, a coach is free to demand the same of his team. Don't ever ask anything of another that you are afraid to do yourself. How can a coach expect his players to develop an enthusiastic attitude if he doesn't have one himself? How can he expect his players to be well disciplined if he himself is not? Players reflect the attitude and motivation of the coach. If you believe in what you're doing and your heart is in your work, you will be able to motivate others to heights they never believed possible. The coach must establish high standards and expect nothing but the best.

A critical aspect of motivation is communication. Only through communication can a coach establish an honest and trusting relationship.

At the end of spring practice I called each player individually into my office. At that time I told them directly what their roles for the following season were going to be. Some were elated. Others had to accept the challenge of developing their skills further if they wanted more playing time. But no player left my office without knowing exactly what I expected of him. Each player could use what he learned as motivation during the summer and as a foundation for what to expect in the fall. Communication, especially with young players, is critical for creating belief in the coach, the team, the program, and most important, themselves.

Team meetings and pregame pep talks are overrated. I prefer one-on-one relationships. They provide the opportunity to establish trust on both sides.

Communication is more than merely exchanging words. Real communication is an art. It takes time. It takes patience. It takes the ability to listen. A coach must learn to accept each player for the individual that he is. A coach must understand that a young man may be reaching out for guidance that he may be unable to get from any other person in his world. That young man may be seeking counsel and direction about something that could affect the rest of his life. That is the exact time when a coach has the opportunity to provide a foundation for motivation. At precisely that time the good coach simply cannot fail.

Throughout my career at the University of Michigan, no player needed an appointment to see me in my office. In or out of season, the door was always open to my players. Whether it was the starting quarterback or a fourth-string walk-on lineman, each young man was welcome to visit me in my office any time, day or night.

My secretary was careful never to disturb me for anything while I was in a meeting—unless one of my players had come to my office to talk. Then all the rules were off. Any time a member of the team wanted to see me, I immediately excused myself from the meeting. Spending time alone with a player in need was more important.

He may have come to talk about an issue that really wasn't significant. For him, however, it may have been the most important thing in the world at the time. He may have had a problem that had nothing to do with football. Maybe he had a problem in school, or maybe something else was bothering him and he needed to talk to someone he could trust. Even if the problem was small, it was big enough for him to come to see me.

Now what if my secretary had told a young man that I was in a meeting and couldn't be disturbed, that he should come back another time? The player had somehow mustered up the courage to see me. Now I had the moral obligation to talk to him. If he had been told to return at another time, he would have walked away with that same problem in his pocket. His trouble might have festered, and who knows whether he would have scraped up the courage to come back again.

If a coach is serious about building character and instilling motivation in the young men under his charge, he must practice being a coach at all times and in every situation. Those men are still impressionable students. Their problems do not always fit the constraints of normal office hours. Each kid is different, though. Each has a level of motivation different from all the others. A method that motivates one may completely stifle another.

All athletes, down deep, want to be challenged. That's why it is so critical for the coach to understand what method of motivation each individual responds to best. Then the coach must act with care and consistency to ensure that each player demands the best from himself so that motivation becomes self-starting.

Motivation takes on a different face in different situations. I have always maintained it is easier to motivate a team after a loss than when things are going well. When your team is on a winning streak and most of the breaks are falling your way, there is a tendency to believe that the good times will never end. If an injury or some other misfortune strikes, a team may not be mentally prepared to overcome adversity.

When we were winning, I was a miserable, persnickety SOB while watching a game film. I spotted minuscule mistakes that normally took a microscope to detect. I always believed that sloppy habits, even in victory, set the table for a crushing defeat. I was far more concerned with instilling proper motivation after a victory than I was after a defeat in which our team expended total effort. Even in victory, a motivated team never accepts lack of effort. Lack of talent is a separate matter. A coach must vociferously approach a lack of effort.

Courtesy of University of Michigan Athletics Archives

Another side of motivation surfaces in the face of injury to key personnel. In our 1984 game against Michigan State, our quarterback, Jim Harbaugh, broke his arm diving for a fumble. As soon as he went down for the ball, I knew we had a problem. Before he got out of the pile, Jim knew he was lost for the rest of the season.

After the game I visited him at the hospital. When I opened the door, the first words out of his mouth were, "Hey, Coach, you aren't going to forget about me, are you?"

I looked him in the eye, knowing that we were going to struggle the rest of the season. "No, Jim," I said. "I'm not going to forget you. We'll be waiting till you get healthy next year and then pick up where you left off."

In our meeting the next day, I told the team we had lost our quarterback for the season and explained exactly what we were up against. They were going to have to strap on their pads a little tighter and fight through adversity. The following week we shut out Northwestern, 31-0. We were outmanned the rest of the way but still managed to win a couple more games on motivation alone. Harbaugh bounced back to lead us to 21 victories over the next two seasons, including one over Nebraska in the 1986 Fiesta Bowl.

In 1973 came the worst experience I ever had in college coaching. Ironically, it was the result of a devastating political decision after our season-ending 10-10 tie with Ohio State rather than anything that occurred on the field. Never in my career did I face a more critical situation regarding the motivation of my team.

The circumstances leading up to the game made it one of the most important contests in the history of both schools. Both teams were undefeated and untied. Both were ranked in the top five in each poll. We were playing the game in Ann Arbor in front of 106,000 people. The Rose Bowl was at stake. No game in college football could have been any more critical. That game was the absolute plum of the entire season.

The game unfolded like a championship boxing match between two highly skilled heavyweights. We traded punches. Everyone but the water boy wound up black and blue. Ohio State scored 10 points in the first half. We tightened our defense to shut them down in the second and came back with 10 points of our own.

On a Buckeye blitz I still see in my mind today, our quarterback, Dennis Franklin, suffered a broken collarbone and had to leave the game. Larry Cipa replaced him and led us down to about the Ohio State 20-yard line, but a last-minute field-goal attempt went astray.

The general consensus was that we would be going to the Rose Bowl, not only because of our performance but also because Ohio State had gone the previous year. At the time, there was a general rule prohibiting back-to-back repeaters from the Big Ten. At the time, the Rose Bowl was the only bowl for which a Big Ten team was eligible.

While walking off the field, Coach Woody Hayes congratulated me on behalf of the team and said we'd be a great representative in Pasadena. Not until I arrived at a Detroit television station to tape my weekly show that evening did I hear what had taken place with the athletic directors from the Big Ten. Because of the injury to Franklin, they voted the Rose Bowl berth to Ohio State.

I was livid. How could a group of old athletic directors vote to take away what my men had won on the field? Franklin was a brilliant quarterback, but what did that vote say about the rest of my men? We had assembled a superb group of players and were still unbeaten. Besides, Cipa was an excellent replacement for Franklin and wound up playing in the National Football League for a couple of seasons. In my judgment, it was an unfair decision.

The next day I had to face my team. Never have I faced a more dejected and disappointed group of young men than that fine 1973 University of Michigan team. It was probably the most difficult talk I ever had to deliver to any team in my whole career. I was highly emotional. I had never seen a coaching staff so dejected and incensed over what they thought was a raw deal. I had to determine how to get them back together quickly so that they could go recruiting with a passion that winter to continue the program we had established.

I told the seniors that they had unknowingly played their last game for the University of Michigan, but that they were able to leave with their heads held high. Those men had left every ounce of effort they had out on the field. Those efforts would pay dividends in the future when the Big Ten finally voted to accept invitations from bowls other than the Rose Bowl.

I knew it would be difficult to motivate the underclassmen to do a good job in school and spring practice in preparation for the 1974 season. I told them that they now must work even harder than before to right what we all considered a major injustice. I refused to let them hangdog over the unfairness of the situation. I promised them that their time would come and told them that they could not allow this grievance to affect the program negatively.

That group came back and won the first 10 games of the following season. On January 1, 1976, Michigan was the first Big Ten team to play in a postseason game other than the Rose Bowl when we played the national champion Oklahoma Sooners in the Orange Bowl.

None of the good that eventually came from that one devastating decision after our 1973 tie with Ohio State could have happened without motivation and total commitment from every person on that squad.

The media will at times criticize every team, every coach, and every player. That comes with the territory, especially with today's emphasis on sports and the extensive network of media outlets. Some of the criticism will be justified. Some of it won't be worth the paper on which the story is written. During times of extreme criticism, I reminded my team that the successful man does not achieve the impossible; he achieves what critics thought was impossible.

When it comes to criticism of the coach, it is critical to remember that he alone understands all the reasons for whatever decision he makes. The head coach knows his squad and the conditions of any situation better than anyone else in the system. A head coach is hired to make all final decisions. Most will produce successful outcomes, but some won't work out the way they were planned. If the coach is truly motivated and dedicated to the program he has put in place, however, he must believe in his decisions as

Motivation Hall of Fame

Courtesy of Joe Imel/Daily News

Jack Harbaugh

Having been associated with two Collegiate Hall of Fame coaches—as a player for Doyt L. Perry of Bowling Green State University from 1957–1961 and as an assistant coach with Bo Schembechler of the University of Michigan from 1973–1979—I have witnessed two of the finest motivators and leaders of football teams. Because I have been coaching for 40 years, I believe I can explain why these two men had the ability to motivate and lead football teams.

Doyt and Bo shared similar motivational skills that made them true leaders even though they possessed different personalities and coaching styles.

First, they were great communicators. They presented a lesson, told a story, delivered a message over time, and developed a powerful style that embedded the message in the player's mind. In the locker room, Bo could bring tears to our eyes with his messages. I believe he could tell the story of "As I Lay Me Down to Sleep" in a way that would make his players break down crying and literally run through the door of a locker room. Doyt, on the other hand, was an off-the-cuff improviser, who during a bad practice might call his team together and say, "This team has no emotion! If Abraham Lincoln rode a bike across this field waving an American flag, you guys would show no emotion!"

Bo and Doyt were honest, truthful, and fair. They demanded honesty from players and coaches in return for a healthy relationship. They never asked anyone to do more than they were willing to do themselves in their professional and personal lives. Neither coach ever had NCAA enforcement problems. Breaking a rule to win meant not winning.

Both men loved to talk sports. They loved the game. They knew the history of football and the coaches who influenced that history. In meetings Bo often talked about how we evolved to a particular offensive or defensive technique, or to whom he had first talked about that technique, or even what Woody's thoughts had been about the technique. Doyt and Bo were often described as stubborn. They were stubborn regarding their principles about how to play the game. They would never compromise fundamentals, blocking, and tackling. Individuals would work hard and play hard, or they would not play. Doyt had a line, "If you won't play hard there is a spot for you on this team—next to me on the sideline!" They developed plans thoroughly and might adjust them, but they would never overhaul them. Both implemented the plans patiently, and because the plans were fundamentally sound, the games came to them.

Both coaches centered their efforts to motivate players on team success. Each time they discussed the roles that players would have to fill to guarantee team victory. When personal accomplishment diverted an athlete's concentration, they would quickly and directly remind him that selfish behavior would not be permitted to disrupt the team focus. Bo and Doyt had the ability to recruit players who responded to their message.

They constantly evaluated their strengths and weaknesses while staying the course and focusing on the goal. They accepted the responsibilities of leadership, and as their careers progressed they thrived on the accountability demanded of them. But they never took themselves so seriously that they could not laugh, reflect, and understand the situations surrounding them. They were always available for their families, their friends, their coaches, and, most important, their men.

Motivation is something that causes a person to act. In my experience, motivation is a daily, minute-to-minute process that draws upon the best mental and physical energies within us. Motivators like Doyt and Bo drew upon those energies from their own principles and values:

- To be honest and fair
- To love competition and the game of football
- To have a plan and execute it with patience and without compromise
- To focus on the team, the team, the team
- To reevaluate oneself constantly
- To accept the responsibility of leadership
- To communicate all of the preceding in a unique style with dignity and humanity

Communicating these values and principles with enthusiasm and sincerity requires personal dedication to a plan executed daily. The success or happiness that ensues for coaches like Doyt and Bo comes from the players and coaches who thank them for the positive influence the message had upon their lives.

Jack Harbaugh, head coach at Western Kentucky University, took his 2000 team to the Division I-AA quarterfinals and finished fifth in the national polls. For the last 10 years under Harbaugh, the Hilltoppers have been placed in the top 20 for both offense and defense, and their rushing offense ranks in the top 10. Harbaugh was awarded the Ohio Valley Conference Coach of the Year in 2000.

---

strongly as he believes in the efforts of his team. Never should the coach allow anyone to dissuade him from following what he believes in his heart is right. The head coach must make decisions in conjunction with his staff. No amount of criticism from the media, alumni, fans, or anyone else should deter him from attempting to reach the goals of his team.

One of the greatest weapons of motivation I carried throughout my career was the confidence my assistants and players had in me regarding criticism from the press. When the press got nasty, they knew the buck stopped with me. They didn't have to worry about any fallout hitting them. That's a tremendous tool of motivation for the team. Don't even consider a head job if you're not prepared to take the heat. A coach must believe in his system on and off the field. He must not allow criticism to throw the program off course.

In the short run, an extraordinarily gifted team can win some games on pure talent alone. Without motivation, though, the team cannot survive the adversities and setbacks that every championship team knows how to conquer. Every good team shares three elements—technical soundness, physical strength, and unflagging motivation. Without this combination, no team can be consistently successful.

At the University of Michigan I was blessed with the complete package. Year after year, every team that took the field was fully equipped with each of those elements. Some teams had more talent than others. Some were so physically strong that we won a few games on sheer strength alone. My primary responsibility, though, was to ensure that each team executed every down as if it were the last they would ever play in a Michigan uniform. That's motivation!

If I had to sacrifice one of those critical three elements, I guarantee you that motivation would be the last to go. That's because a hungry player is a dangerous player. Given just enough talent and the proper strength to do his job, a motivated player can smash a more talented, lackadaisical opponent clear into next week.

In its simplest terms, motivation is the will to do something to the best of one's ability. An effort may sometimes fall short, but the coach never allows a team to come up short of effort. Motivation is a quality we can measure more easily on a football field or in some other sport venue than we can in everyday life. In whatever profession a person chooses to pursue, however, motivation is a powerful force.

No successful coach allows any member of his team to leave that precious treasure on the field when he graduates. The coach must instill within his players the importance of motivation in whatever path of life they choose to follow. Within motivation lie the priceless gifts of honesty and integrity. And it all starts with the head coach!

Professional Conduct

Fisher DeBerry

We are privileged to be able to work in the greatest and most important profession in the world. As coaches we have the responsibility to uphold the ethical standards of our game and of the American Football Coaches Association. The title *coach* carries an awesome responsibility.

When my wife and I were dating, she lived with an elderly lady named Mrs. Mayfield. I will never forget Mrs. Mayfield because she was wise and had a zest for life. When Lu Ann and I would get ready to go to a movie or see friends, she would always say, "Remember who you are," as we left. That comment made a lasting impression on me, and I have often repeated it to my own children. As coaches of the most important resource our nation has—our young people—it behooves us to analyze the example we present every day to the young men who have been entrusted to us. To do so, we must remember who we are.

In many communities across the United States, one of the most well-known and important people in that community is a head coach. Student-athletes deserve the best from us. We can't lose sight of our responsibility to teach them the lessons of life and how to cope with the real world. That is what coaching is all about.

Carrying the title of *coach* is one of the most awesome responsibilities that a person can have in our society. We are responsible for our players' welfare, for seeing that they have the best of everything, for giving them a great competitive experience, and, most important, for seeing that they graduate. These experiences and achievements are more important than having dazzling success on the football field.

Coaching is influencing. Our coaches have all influenced us, and many of us are probably in the coaching profession today because of them. Athletes admire, respect, and look up to us. We have a chance to influence the lives and standards of future generations in a positive way. What an awesome responsibility that is!

I am proud to represent the United States Air Force Academy, a school whose core values are integrity above all, service before self, and excellence in all we do. These core values have made me more conscious of how important integrity is in our profession. Like the academy, our society expects great integrity from our profession. We have a responsibility to be ethical and aboveboard in everything we do and in every decision we make.

At the Air Force Academy, the foundation of our program is family, and we truly care for our brothers. We take great pride in this. We have a saying not to let our brothers down. I believe that the key to successful coaching is to surround yourself with great people of solid character who have positive attitudes.

We have only one rule for our players here at the academy: Do what is right. I believe that our players are mature enough to know what is right and what is wrong. A rule I teach them is that when they have to make a decision whether or not to do something, they should ask themselves, "Will it make our team better?" If so, then do it; if not, don't.

We must be concerned about many issues, and we have a responsibility to talk to the players that have been entrusted to us. Recruiting is one of the biggest issues. Some 18- or 19-year-old prospective players are being told to decommit, that their word doesn't mean anything and that it isn't binding. That

Courtesy of Air Force Media Relations

is one of the worst things we can teach young people, to imply that they need not honor their word. Our word should be the strongest fabric of society.

Second, we must be concerned about teaching our athletes to play hard but fair on the field. That means promoting sportsmanship and safety. We should strongly oppose blocking and tackling techniques that can be dangerous to our players or our opponents. As coaches, we can control that by the way we talk and teach. Coaches must never encourage the use of the face or head or initiating contact with any part of the helmet. We must not tolerate obscene language or gestures that provoke ill will or that demean opponents or game officials.

Today we have an especially pervasive problem and concern. Sports wagering or gambling can jeopardize the integrity of our game. Rates of pathological and problem gambling among college students are three times higher than those in the adult population. Gambling is rampant on college campuses. As coaches, we must be concerned about the welfare of our players and constantly discuss those issues with our teams.

Many of us have clauses in our contracts that state that if we violate the trust of our university or college and the rules of the NCAA, we could be dismissed from our jobs. That is reason enough, along with the personal embarrassment, to do what is right.

We all have compliance directors at our schools. I often tell my coaches that if they don't know whether or not they should do something, in recruiting for example, then they should call the compliance director to verify the correct action. I encourage you to have your compliance director meet with your staff several times a year. Rules and expectations abound, and I can assure you that I learn something new in every session we have with our compliance director.

In recent years, the number of cases of unethical conduct by members of our profession and the number of people who have appeared before the ethics committee has declined steadily. This trend indicates pride in our association and the desire by our membership and coaches to do what is right. All of us are proud of that record, which is a great testament to the attitude and respect that we have for each other. Corporate businesses wish that they had a similar means of policing themselves and had that type of attitude among their employees. We hope that soon no cases will come before the ethics committee in any given year. The accountability we have to each other through our Code of Ethics handbook and the monitoring process we have in place make our profession unique.

A poem I learned through the Fellowship of Christian Athletes many years ago is titled "To Any Athlete." The poem could apply to any coach, player, or parent, but I think it speaks to what our real responsibility is toward each other and our players:

There are little eyes upon you and they're watching night and day,
And there are little ears that quickly take in every word you say.
There are little hands all eager to do anything you do,
And a little boy who's dreaming of the day he'll be like you.

You're the little fellow's idol, you're the wisest of the wise.
In his little mind about you, no suspicions ever arise.
He believes in you devoutly, holds all that you say and do;
He will say and do in your way when he's a grownup like you.

There's a wide-eyed little fellow who believes you're always right,
And his ears are always open, and he watches day and night.
You are setting an example every day in all you do,
For the little boy who's waiting to grow up to be like you.

We all feel intense pressure to win today, but victory outside the rules is not victory at all. I would find it difficult to enjoy a victory or to live with myself afterward if I violated the rules. I remind our players during the season to ask themselves, "If everybody practiced like me, what kind of team would we be?" Coaches could ask themselves a similar question: "If everybody had the attitude toward ethics that I have, what kind of profession and association would we become?" We have a profound responsibility to remember who we are and to recognize that the future of the game depends on each of us.

Few organizations have ever succeeded without an ethical code. Our code makes our profession and association special and the envy of corporate America. Our profession enjoys respect and credibility, and many people watch and scrutinize us every day. This circumstance is a source of pride to all our members. Let me encourage you to adopt the "do what's right" attitude. If we take that approach, we will continue to have the best profession and association in America and our players will become great contributors and citizens. I encourage you to put sportsmanship and ethics first in all you do.

The code and values that the founding fathers of AFCA mandated in 1922 still apply to our profession today. This ongoing commitment to integrity helps explain why college football is the most respected and popular sport in America. We have a responsibility to keep it pure. Fielding Yost, the great former coach of the University of Michigan, said, "Everyone of us here likes to think of men's values coming from intercollegiate athletics and especially football." In my judgment, this prospect hinges entirely on whether or not we have real sportsmanship and ethical standards in our programs.

According to Coach Yost, "The object of all intercollegiate competition should be to result in [the] friendliness, confidence, and goodwill that can never be developed unless you have good sportsmanship and good ethics." That belief was applicable in 1922, and it is still true today. We have the responsibility today as coaches to ensure that our programs follow ethical standards.

In 1927 Coach Yost presented 10 ethical standards that he felt should be a part of each coach's personal code. I ask you to examine each one as it applies to you and your program:

1. To look on one's coaching work as an integral part of the school system with a definite contribution to make to the cause of education
2. To keep in the foreground the fundamental, educational objective of athletic competition and to make other ends subservient to this main purpose
3. To consider the welfare of players of paramount importance and not to tolerate their exploitation for personal or private gain
4. To cultivate the confidence and respect of rival coaches, to look on them as colleagues and friends, and to treat them and talk to them as such
5. To use one's influence to counteract unfounded rumors of questionable practices or violations of rules by opponents
6. To give all reasonable support to the officials in charge of the game
7. To refuse to teach or permit techniques or play contrary to the letter or spirit of the rules
8. To encourage players to respect and accept, without wrangling, the authority and decisions of the officials and to refrain from insulting them or the opponents
9. To discourage illegitimate recruiting, betting on games, and all other practices that tend to commercialize players and deprive them of the character-building opportunities that should be a vital part of football training
10. To be gentlemanly and considerate in victory, undismayed and courageous in defeat

I am confident that if we adhere to these ethical standards suggested by Coach Yost in 1927, our association will continue to be the most ethical association in America. All participants will be better people as a result. We must remember who we are and the responsibilities we have.

Career Decision Making

Jim Tressel

There is much to consider when you contemplate your career path. Seeking fulfillment in a life's work is critical in this ever-changing world and difficult in the highly competitive workplace. Passion and enjoyment for what one does on a daily basis is a gift worth more than gold. We in the coaching profession are blessed to have such a gift.

In order to appreciate this gift, we must be aware of the extraordinary sacrifice that accompanies the enjoyment along the way. Time—our most cherished possession—is the greatest sacrifice of them all. As we build relationships with our young people and develop in them the technical expertise they need in order to succeed, we naturally forfeit inordinate amounts of the personal and family time that is so precious and needed.

In addition, most coaches labor for all or the majority of their careers at financial levels well below what their talents and training could produce. Even so, most of us choose to coach because we believe "There is nothing more valuable or wonderful than the smell of a victorious locker room," as the late, great Coach Bill Maxwell once said.

To have a successful career, a coach must do the following: demonstrate leadership and service, have a plan, work, handle adversity and success, and develop faith and belief.

Leadership Equals Service

Any person who considers taking up this all-important role as a teacher/coach must first recognize that this role is truly a leadership role. Contrary to what some people may think, leadership is an action, not a position, and the primary action of leadership is service.

There will be many instances when one's own needs and desires will be secondary to the needs of the student-athlete being served. First and foremost, we coaches must have a genuine concern for our players. As my father, the late Dr. Lee Tressel, taught us, "They do not care how much you know until they know how much you care!"

In his book *Hotline to Victory,* Coach Woody Hayes states, "The coach must have an intense and continuing interest in the welfare and all-around development of each player." This willingness to be a servant to each and every young person that we are fortunate to coach is the initial commitment that must be made.

A common characteristic of most coaches is that we learn from one another, and at times, borrow from each other. The following characteristics or traits of a leader are ones that I have borrowed from some of the outstanding coaches that I have studied over the years:

- A leader takes risks.
- A leader takes total responsibilities for all of his actions.
- A leader does not judge, he simply evaluates.
- A leader has an aura about him, a sense of impending greatness.
- A leader never quits.

If you have made the decision to lead based on the ideals of taking risks, move on to taking total responsibility.

Have a Plan

After committing to a life of service, it is important to decide next on a plan for the players and yourself that relates to one's whole existence. With an awareness of the time and selflessness required to serve, formulate a blueprint for the personal growth and all-around development of each student. At Ohio State we have a plan called the block O of life.

In 1986, as the staff arrived at Youngstown State University, we sat down and discussed all our past experiences and the many lessons we had learned from countless teachers, coaches, authors, players, and parents. Together we decided on six areas in which we could potentially encourage growth in our players during their careers at YSU: personal/family, spiritual/moral, academics/career, strength/fitness, football family, and caring/giving. We decided that our football program had to integrate all areas of their lives in order give our players a complete experience. As players and coaches gained perspective from this whole-life experience, we believed our success on the field would grow accordingly. Ultimately our desire was for all football family members to reach their full potential in all that they did and all that they were.

The block O of life reflects the areas of development that influence the decisions we make for our coaches and players, decisions that affect their entire being. Necessary for coaching and career decisions as well as program decisions for our players and team is a clear idea of the interests and passions that each individual may have. The goal data that we collect will be revised constantly during a player's and coach's career, as exposed on block O goal sheets (see table 4.1 on page 38). Typically our goal sheet is on 8 1/2 × 14 inch paper so that ample space is given for writing goals, plans, and revisions.

It is our intention that all of the decisions and assistance given to our coaches and players take into consideration the goals of each player, in conjunction with the needs of the families, team, and society. As we go about day-to-day activity, our goal sheets are an important reference for making good decisions.

It is essential that each individual design his own goals and dreams, and that they be specific and measurable. Goals that are truly personal are much more likely to be realized. The plan truly takes shape when the "how" phase of the goal sheet is complete. Our student-athletes need assistance recognizing just what it takes to achieve their goals and dreams, as do we coaches in our career aspirations.

In our society, many people are searching for the fast track to success and self-satisfaction. One of the real challenges we have is to help our young people and our young coaches learn that excellence is a laborious process. Lost in the highlights of successful players, teams, and coaches is the long journey that they traveled to the victory stand—the hours they studied, the training and sacrifices, the setbacks, the comebacks, and their patience.

One-on-one conferences with coaches and players are helpful in crystallizing the plan as to how these goals may be attained. We ask that our people keep their goal sheets in strategic positions so that they can occasionally assess their performances and revise their goals as needed.

TABLE 4.1

Block O of Life Goal Sheet

	General thoughts	Short-term goals	How I will accomplish short-term goals	Dreams	How I will accomplish dreams
Spiritual, ethical	Above all else I realize that my spiritual beliefs and my ethical and moral values will shape my life. I will do what is right.	1. 2. 3.	1. 2. 3.	1. 2. 3.	1. 2. 3.
Academics, degree, career	One of the primary reasons I am at Ohio State is to achieve academically, obtain a valuable degree, and begin a profitable career. My degree will give me choices.	1. 2. 3.	1. 2. 3.	1. 2. 3.	1. 2. 3.
Personal family	The family is the basic social unit of society. My family is important to me in many ways.	1. 2. 3.	1. 2. 3.	1. 2. 3.	1. 2. 3.
Football family	I am part of one of the greatest families known to man. I count on my teammates, and they are counting on me. I will achieve great things for the family.	1. 2. 3.	1. 2. 3.	1. 2. 3.	1. 2. 3.
Physical conditioning	One of the greatest gifts I have is my health. My physical conditioning is a controllable commodity. My conditioning will win for me in the 4th quarter. I will develop lifetime habits.	1. 2. 3.	1. 2. 3.	1. 2. 3.	1. 2. 3.
Caring and giving	My development does not end in the classroom or on the field. How I function as a total person in society is important. I will give back to the community.	1. 2. 3.	1. 2. 3.	1. 2. 3.	1. 2. 3.

Work

Crucial to the understanding needed to make sound decisions in coaching is the understanding of just how much time, effort, and work it really requires. Coaches are among the hardest workers in our society, and clearly the amount of work to make successful progress in this worthy and needed profession is extraordinary!

Both the relationship building and technical components of coaching are ongoing learning processes. As in many roles in our society, the learning, growing, and maturing never cease. The coach must be willing to seek this growth each and every day.

One of the refreshing realities in the coaching profession is the willingness of coaches to share with one another. High school and collegiate coaches from coast to coast open their doors to each other in an effort to promote the game. Numerous magazines, books, journals, videos, and websites contain more knowledge than any of us has time to digest. Clinics are held in every locale so that all coaches have access to them. The dynamic changes that occur each year in our game result from the willingness of coaches to share and the passion of coaches to learn.

As your role on the staff changes, so will the knowledge you need in order to get the job done. No job on the staff is more or less important than any other, but the tools needed for each job are unique, resulting in an autonomy that is fulfilling in its own right.

When considering the ultimate goal of being a head coach, an awareness of the comprehensive nature of this most difficult role is critical. While serving as an assistant coach—under Jim Dennison at the University of Akron, Tom Reed at Miami of Ohio, Dick MacPherson at Syracuse, and Earle Bruce at The Ohio State University—I thought I had all the answers to being a successful head coach. Not until my stellar 2–9 first year as a head coach at YSU did I realize that I had a lot to learn and plenty of work to do.

Handling Adversity and Success

After making the decision to take on the tough task of leadership, completing the plan consisting of goal setting and what it will take, and investing endless hours of work, it is necessary to realize that there will be a variety of outcomes along the way. Some of these will be positive and some will appear to be negative. In either case, it is the reaction to the outcome that ultimately will make or break long-term success and the realization of goals and dreams.

Having the persistence and mental toughness to cope with the difficult times and the humility and level-headedness to handle the good times will be the key. Many of our finest teams and the greatest coaches that I have studied have had the ability to turn setbacks into send-offs for greatness.

In my experience, more has been learned from adverse situations than any number of comfortable, theoretically successful, experiences. Coach Jack Johnson from Pickerington High School in central Ohio shared with students at our Ohio State University Youth Camps a profound illustration of the development from an immature person to a mature person. Coach Johnson explained that the transformation from immaturity to maturity takes place when one possesses humility. The admission of three Fs—fear, faults, and failures—allow an individual to truly be humble and subsequently mature. He related that we all must admit our various fears, but persist, regardless. We must recognize our faults and genuinely work on them. And finally, we must come face-to-face with our failures and proceed in a spirit of growing and learning from them and do better in future opportunities. The maturity to handle adversity and handle success must be a conscious effort, a decision we make, in order to achieve our goals and progress in our careers.

Courtesy of Ohio State Athletics Communications

Faith and Belief

Finally all of our decision making must be fueled by the faith and belief that we will get what our works deserve. Every coaching assignment must be approached as if it were the only job we will ever have and must be treated accordingly.

The finest advice that I ever received about what lies ahead was from Gordon Larson, the athletic director at the University of Akron, in my graduate assistant coaching opportunity. Coach Larson instructed me to keep my mind and my rear-end in the same place! Focus 100 percent on the task at hand, and let the future take care of itself, believing that opportunities will occur if they are deserved. If and when the opportunities do arrive, it is time to reassess goals and dreams and their effects on all phases of being.

As in most occupations, "who" is the key: who you are working with, who you are working for, and who you are competing against. Inevitably relationships determine the level of fulfillment in every situation.

Without question, we are blessed to coach the greatest game known to man at a time in which we are needed the most. We work with many young people who in the future will become world leaders. We can develop these future leaders most effectively by keeping in mind that the most important aspect of leadership is servanthood.

Teaching the ability to set goals and to make the plans and efforts needed to accomplish them will be valuable to our players and our future. Albert Einstein once said, "Concern for man and his fate must always form the chief interest of all technical endeavors. Never forget this in the midst of your diagrams and equations." As long as we keep this in mind, we will make a difference in the world. That is what life is all about.

PART II

Coaching Principles and Priorities

Harold "Tubby" Raymond

When I started my career back in 1949 as head football coach at University High School in Ann Arbor, Michigan, I could hardly fathom the course my football coaching career would take through the next 53 years, up to February 18, 2002, the day I announced my retirement. The three NCAA Division II National Championships and 300 wins in 36 years as head coach at the University of Delaware were certainly rewarding. But even more lasting and richer in memory are the players, coaches, situations, and decisions that made the coaching role so challenging and fulfilling each season.

At all levels of competition, coaches are decision makers. We decide what to emphasize at any given practice, which players play what position, and so on. Some coaches base decisions on insufficient knowledge, a shaky philosophy, and an underdeveloped sense of direction. That's a recipe for failure, inconsistency, and an unsatisfying—if not, short—career.

Most coaches form general ideas as to what is important, how to approach their task, and what steps to take to allow them and their teams to be most successful. The fuzzy, gray areas become clearer with experience.

The best coaches have a highly developed sense of what is right and wrong, have formed solid precepts from which to analyze people and situations, are able to prioritize what is most important, and then gain the support and efforts of their athletes and fellow coaches through their actions. Throughout my career I tried to absorb all I could from other coaches, be they big names or no names. Among those who impacted my approach were Fritz Crisler, my college coach at the University of Michigan, Benny Oosterbaam, and David Nelson, my predecessor at Delaware. I first worked for Harold Westerman at the University of Maine, and he had a great influence on me also. These coaches were special leaders who helped me form a strong foundation for coaching the game.

This section of *The Football Coaching Bible* presents the wisdom of four giants in our sport. In the four chapters that follow, coaches Paterno, Bowden, Osborne, and Holtz share the values and priorities that set the stage for a successful program. Not surprisingly, many of their guiding principles were formed, as mine were, from the great impact of coaching mentors. For Joe, it was Rip Engle; Tom was assistant to Bob Devaney; Lou coached under Woody Hayes.

The careers of these fine coaches illustrate that there are many ways to approach the role of coach. Lou Holtz has been head coach for six colleges and one professional team. Joe Paterno has coached at Penn State for five decades. But believe it or not, they all began by thinking small—first addressing the basics, then forming a consistent plan, and then moving toward short-range goals.

These fine coaches—and all longtime, successful coaches—have something in common. All four chapters highlight the importance of a strong belief system. All four men believe in a higher power than themselves, and their faith helps them keep a sense of perspective as to what is most important. They all view their players and assistant coaches as being more important than they are themselves.

You can sense the resolve each has in his system. Their approaches include the full package, more than just on-field instruction and execution. All four had specific requirements and expectations of coaches and players throughout the program, and none were more demanding of others than they were of themselves.

All four coaches reflect the ability to change, but not just for the sake of change. They had plans that included change. They had to adjust and adapt over the course of time to make their programs the best that they could be.

We have so many great coaches, both past and present, to learn from. Alonzo Stagg, Knute Rockne, Paul Bryant, Eddie Robinson, and thousands of others left a legacy, a history from which to draw. Study the great coaches. Read their books. Seek their counsel. Attend the AFCA convention. Take advantage of all the educational opportunities available, and don't be surprised when ideas come from all sides. I have learned from virtually every player who has played for me and from every coach I have worked with.

Be better prepared to make the difficult challenges and important choices you will face next season. As a head coach or an assistant, at the college or high school level, make the right decisions for your athletes and your program. This section of *The Football Coaching Bible* provides an inside look at the decision-making framework of four of the best decision makers and coaches our game has ever known.

Keeping It Small

Joe Paterno

During a lecture many years ago, Paul "Bear" Bryant talked about the keys to getting prepared for a game. Sitting there among hundreds of other coaches, I was expecting a detailed description of how Coach Bryant readied his offensive, defensive, and kicking units to perform their best each contest. Instead, the wise veteran offered this profound bit of advice. "Whatever you do," he said, "make sure your game plan is a small one." He warned that the worst mistake we coaches make is to develop grand strategies for every unit, down, and distance and fail to become very good at any of them.

Those words of wisdom stuck in my head and still influence how I prepare for every practice and game. They also fit my own way of thinking. Simpler usually is better. People say our uniforms are boring because there are no stars on the helmets or names on the jerseys, but I kind of like them and what they say about the importance of team over individual and the preference for a more austere approach to life.

Coach Bryant's "keep it small" recommendation also applies to handling the highs and lows of coaching. Fans and the media blow the good and bad out of proportion. If you want stability, you need to keep their praise and criticism in perspective.

Coaching Fundamentals

A coach is first a teacher. As a coach, you have a strong impact on the lives of the young people you deal with, second only to the influence of their families and perhaps their churches. Never lose sight of the fact that you are dealing with young people. You are a teacher, and not only do you teach techniques, you teach principles that will help players throughout their lives: discipline, camaraderie, loyalty, trust, and the other intangibles we talk about all the time.

Remember that you are dealing with young, mostly teenage, men who don't really know who they are and aren't sure where they're headed. Sometimes we tell young kids "be a man," but when they look around the inner city, the "man" is the guy with the fancy car who is peddling drugs. So we can't just say things. We need to lead by example. We have to make players understand that if they work hard and do things the right way, they will be better people and will have a better chance of being happy and having successful lives.

Sit down and ask yourself: What do I truly believe about football? What are the things that are important to me? How do I teach those things? Coaching football isn't just a matter of putting plays up on the board. It involves many things. You must determine what football is about and how you believe you can win games based on that orientation. This will affect how you manage and teach practices and handle duties during game day. It will even influence the types of plays you run, who runs those plays, how they run them, and when they run them.

Once you decide what you want to do and the manner in which you plan to do it, it's essential to stick to those principles and goals regardless of what the fans think. Fans will yell at you to throw the ball more, try a different offense, try a different defense, and so on. You cannot react to what the fans want at any given point in the season. You must have enough character and courage to stick with what you have decided is the best for you, your personality, and your coaching philosophy.

You can't copy somebody else. The worst thing young coaches do is try to mimic other people. You are you. You are unique. Find out who you are. Figure out how you can be a successful coach, and then stick with your own style. You can't be your high school coach or college coach. You shouldn't try to be Bud Wilkinson, Bear Bryant, Eddie Robinson, or Joe Paterno. Learn what you can from those people, but use what works best for you.

Your beliefs should be formed early in your career, if not sooner. My fundamental approach to coaching started with my dad, who talked about courage and conviction and integrity. It goes back that far. My high school coach, Zev

Graham, reinforced that. He was a strict disciplinarian. Like the best teachers we all had when we were young, he was the toughest guy around then and is the best-remembered now. Coach Graham was the kind of coach that buddies talk about when they get together years after graduation.

I came to Penn State with only the slightest idea how to coach. I had just graduated from Brown. I did not intend to coach. I intended to be a lawyer, but I needed some money. I watched other people do things and began to form an approach to the game. Head Coach Rick Engle was very good about making me learn for myself. I had to figure things out and form my own way of getting the job done. He didn't try to turn me into a clone of himself.

Inspiring Players to Excel

One of the biggest assets of a coach is the ability to motivate, convince, or sell to people, any way you want to put it. If you can't do that, you aren't going to have much success. You must be able to get a group of people around you and tell them "This is what we are going to do, this is the way we are going to do it, this is what is going to happen. If you do it our way, we are going to have some fun, and it is going to be a great experience." Then you have to constantly reaffirm those things—even when you are losing. "Hey we are a good football team; we just need a break here, a break there. If we just keep hustling, we can do this."

It is a question of sell, sell, sell; of challenging them. People want to be challenged. You talk to them about doing something they can't do. I'm not a guy for signs, but I have one in my office with this quote from Browning: "A man's reach should exceed his grasp or what's a heaven for?"

I try to get kids to say, "We are going to try to be the best, and if we don't quite make it, at least we are going to be better than if we went right down the middle of the pack and didn't make it." You have to excite them all the time.

If they don't buy into it, obviously you've got problems. Then you have to identify some leaders on your team, the kids who really want to succeed, the guys who are willing to pay the price and who will discipline themselves. If you can get five, six, seven, or eight such players on board, they can be your apostles. Through their leadership and encouragement, they might be able to bring along the rest of the squad, and you can go from there.

Selling is an ongoing job and the hardest part of coaching. The minute something goes wrong or you demand something difficult from players, you'll see signs of reluctance, if not resistance. It's easier if you've just won a championship. Players are more prepared to sacrifice because they've seen the payoff. In that case, you can ask players to do things physically and mentally that they never dreamed they could do.

Holding On to a Core Philosophy

A coach should frequently reexamine his tactical approach, whether he is going to run off tackle one way or another, for example. He should be alert to the fact that some teams may be doing things that will make it more difficult to be successful with the old ways. Monitor, reflect, and change minor things all the time, game by game. To me, that is just the method or the means of achieving success within your basic way of playing the game.

But your core beliefs—your philosophy—must be more permanent and broader in scope. I do not change my philosophy. I have a certain concept of what a football coach is all about, what coaching is all about, what my relationship with my squad is all about; I have not changed this view. Yes, I have adapted to the tactical changes that have happened in football over time, but I have not changed my philosophy in 50 years.

Off-the-field changes in society have been more dramatic during that time. Now the biggest problem we face in coaching today's athlete is the environment surrounding sports. There are agents who are looking to make big bucks off the kids, parents who lose perspective of what's important because their kid's name appears in the newspapers, and recruiting gurus with talk shows who claim to be able to identify potential pro prospects when they are high school underclassmen. These folks put the coach in a bind; a kid isn't happy playing tight end when he hears he ought to be a linebacker. Agents talk to kids all the time. Parents are influenced by people in the town they live in.

There is so much exposure. These kids now live in glass jars. You can't protect the kid who makes a slight mistake; it's in all the papers. You have to talk to the kids about temptations. In the old days you had one meeting before you jumped into football. Now you have meetings on sexual abuse, on drinking problems, on agents, on gambling. All those things have created a different type of relationship between coaches and players. It is a whole different world out there. The kids who survive it are really spectacular kids. There is so much temptation.

Once a kid came to me and asked for a day off from practice. When I asked what for, he said he needed to take his girl to get an abortion. I said, "What?!" My first inclination was to throw him out of there. Instead I told him to let me think about it. I talked to a couple people who said, "Joe, it's a different world." He wasn't a key player, so it wouldn't have hurt the team if I threw him off the squad. But in the end I didn't, recognizing that time had marched on and that I needed to either acknowledge that and keep pace or get left behind. This story highlights one of the differences in coaching football today.

Practicing With a Purpose

Practice doesn't make perfect. Perfect practice makes perfect. Every little thing is vital. We tell our kids to pay attention to the little things and the big things will take care of themselves. Every three-step drop, stance, split, and block—whatever move they are supposed to be doing—needs to be done just right. If a player is supposed to set up six yards deep, then he needs to make sure it's six, not five and a half. The little things are important.

Words of Wisdom From a Coaching Mentor

I had the privilege of spending some time at the University of Oklahoma when Bud Wilkinson was having great success there. One day Bud explained coaching to me this way: "Coaching is nothing but doing something over and over to create in practice what is going to happen in a game. And you do it over and over again until a player has learned it by rote." That stuck with me. In other words, what's most important isn't how sharp you are on a blackboard or how impressive your players are in the weight room, but how well you can create in practice what is going to happen in a game. Ever since then, I've tried to give players a great number of repetitions in practice so that their assignments and execution will be automatic in games.

I try to convince players that they either get better or get worse. They don't stay the same. If they are sloppy on the practice field, if they goof around and don't do things right, they are going to come off the field poorer football players. If they go out there with the idea they are going to try to get better and work their tails off, they come off the field better football players. How much better? Who knows, but better than they would be if they did it the other way.

If you were to watch one of our practices, I hope you would leave with the impression that we have a bunch of disciplined kids who hustle on every play, who pay attention to the little things, and who respond to criticism in a good way.

I often tell our kids that the success they have here will probably depend on how well they handle criticism and how well they handle praise. Both can kill a player. He can get sucked in by praise, and he can get beaten down by criticism.

Our coaches work hard, and they are tough and aggressive on the practice field. They don't make excuses for the players. And the players respond. They work hard to do every little thing right every play, to hustle all the time, and to make the maximum effort to get better.

Promoting Discipline

Somebody once said that the difference between the Marine Corps and the other branches of the military—the Army, Air Force, and Navy—is that only the Marine Corps has rules they can enforce. When it comes to establishing guidelines for your team, you start with enforceable rules. It is foolish to have a lot of rules you can't enforce.

We don't have an athletic dormitory on campus. We have players living off campus in apartments, we have players living all over. We have some 40,000 students on campus. I have to start with the idea that the only rules I am going to put in place are the ones I can enforce.

Former Oregon State, UCLA, and Los Angeles Rams coach Tommy Prothro used to say he didn't want any bums, didn't want any boozers, and didn't want any womanizers. He wanted good people who were committed to making the football team and themselves as good as they could. He had few rules and told his players, "I am going to treat you like grown-ups, but I am never going to walk into a bar backwards." His statement reinforces the point that you should establish rules that are enforceable, and refuse to look the other way. If you run across somebody breaking a rule, then there has to be proper punishment for it.

I have found that the best approach to setting guidelines is to meet with 10 to 12 of the team leaders. We sit down once a week to talk. I might indicate that I'm a little worried about a certain area of discipline and seek input from them about how to address it. Sometimes I don't agree with their response, but often they'll suggest something that will work and we'll use it.

At the start of each year I write down the rules and regulations for the season and give each kid a copy. Every player is required to sign his copy before taking part in any team activities. Then players can't come to me later and say they didn't know what the rules were.

You have to sell kids on the idea that the rules are not designed to punish anybody. I emphasize that the regulations are there to give players the opportunity to make us the best football team we can be.

I often use the following scenario to make the point. Imagine playing a football game on a field in which one end zone drops off several hundred feet into an abyss. How much of the field are you going to play on? You are going to play on about 80 yards because when you get to that last 20 you are going to be worried about falling off the cliff. Rules are nothing but a fence

Making a Point

My first year as a head coach, we had a 5-5 record. The first game of my second year, we lost to Navy on the last play of the game. A lot of people thought I was a decent assistant coach but didn't believe I would make it as a head coach. The next game was in Miami against a good club that included future all-pro Ted Hendricks. It was hot. We played some of our young kids, and we came away with an important win.

Afterwards, our charter plane was late returning to the airport, so the team had some time to kill. Many players chose to walk around and look at things. One rule they knew was to never let me see them sitting in a bar during the season. When walking past one of the airport bars, one of the assistant coaches and I spotted our best linebacker and one of our offensive linemen having a couple of beers. They knew they were in trouble. I went in and checked to make sure they were drinking beer, then said "OK, we'll see you when we get back."

When we returned to campus I threw both players off the team. The offensive linebacker was a good player, and he was a great kid and a great student; in fact he went on to become a veterinarian. It was hard, but it was something I felt I had to do. His mom and dad were understandably upset, but I told them, "Look, if I back out of this now, the rest of the kids on the team are not going to buy into the program." That evening when I went to the training table, the team captains said they wanted the linebacker to be reinstated. I said no way. Both former players knew what the rules were; everybody knew what the rules were. I called the team into a meeting room and told them they had a decision to make. They could either leave the team and do whatever they wanted, or they could stick with me and the players who were sick and tired of losing and who were willing to make the sacrifices necessary to be a winning team. Nobody moved. After that we lost one game in four years.

before the cliff. You know exactly how long the field is; you know how wide the field is. That is where you play. You play inside the field. And we will give you every single yard of that field, but no more than that. Inevitably, some players will go over the cliff anyway.

Identifying Positive Player Attributes

In recruiting we look for smart guys, ones who are athletically intelligent. We do not necessarily look for guys who can ace a standardized written test, but we look for players who can read and respond to situations quickly and effectively. We also look for poise and maturity.

We want a kid that we and his teammates can trust. A player has to be able to trust that his teammate is going to do what he is supposed to do in the clutch. It is a character trait that you have to see in kids and try to pull out of them. One thing that bothers me about recruiting these days is that the head coach is allowed to visit a kid only once. It's hard to get a feel for what kind of character a player has in one visit.

When we have a prospect visit campus, I try to sense what he's looking for. Does he want a career? Does he want to make something out of his life? Does he have ambition? Does he have pride? His success on the football field suggests that he's got a work ethic.

A coach can have a positive impact on a kid's pride. We can make him feel good, put him in situations where he will have some success. Conversely, tossing a player into the meat grinder unprepared will only do harm.

One of the biggest mistakes we made at Penn State was an ill-fated attempt to establish toughness in a player. The kid was a big freshman, a highly sought-after prospect from a small school in upstate New York. We all were anxious to see how tough he was, so we put him in a drill against Dave Robinson, who was one of the best players we've ever had at Penn State and who went on to be a first-round draft pick and a great player for the Green Bay Packers. Dave beat the devil out of the kid, and that kid never showed up for another practice. That was just stupid on my part, and it taught me a lesson. Now we put that kind of kid in situations where he can experience some success and build on that. That's one way to develop pride and to get players to feel good about themselves.

A coach can have an impact on many aspects of a player's character and development. If you can push the right buttons and put players in the right environment, you can help bring about some amazing positive changes.

Putting Winning in Perspective

You must sell your kids on doing the best they can and convince them not to worry about winning. Winning will come. If it doesn't come, and you have given it your best shot, hey, that's all you can do.

Sometimes officials have an impact on the game. Sometimes crazy things happen. Sometimes a key player gets injured. There is nothing you can do about those things. Any of them may diminish your team's chances of winning a particular game. But if you and your staff can teach, prepare, and motivate the kids effectively, your players will go out and play as hard as they can. We tell our players not to worry about losing, to just relax and do their best, to enjoy playing.

Now, of course, there are outside forces that can make winning seem like the only thing. A coach can't do anything about the community or the alumni. When a coach tries to please the community by breaking a rule, his career is on a downhill path. You can't ask kids to do certain things and to follow certain rules if you don't do the same. You can't ask players to cheat in certain areas.

Influence players by example. If you get licked, don't go crying about it. When you win, don't go overboard. Tell your athletes to play as well as they can. Teach them to respect the other guy, and hope he plays as well as he can. Encourage them to have a little fun. Hopefully you will win enough games and won't get fired.

Setting Goals

Goals, both individual and team goals, need to be realistic. You can't con players. If you ask them to do something that is far beyond their abilities, you have lost them. I look at a team and think, "Hey, we can be pretty good. We can be competitive." There may be a couple of teams on our schedule that we'll need luck to beat because they are faster than we are, have more depth, more experience, and so on. I talk to the football team as if they are part of my staff. I tell them what I think they can do, which is a judgment call, but that's what I'm getting paid for. I'm supposed to know what's going on out there.

Be realistic with your squad when you communicate the things they need to do in order for the team to be successful. When I first started out as a coach, my goal was for the team to be competitive. A team that is building should start small. They should think: We want other people to respect us. We will see what happens, and as we get better we will set higher goals for ourselves. The better we play, the better we learn techniques, the better we gel as a team, the more confidence we'll have in ourselves. Then we can set goals that go beyond that.

At our current level, with the kind of people we are able to recruit, we should have more difficult goals than that. We aim a little higher. Goals should always be somewhat harder or tougher than the best the players think they can do. Given our accomplishments and our level of talent, it isn't appropriate to tell the team, "OK, we can win four games, we can win five games, we can win seven games, but the main thing is let's get better. Let's be a better team this week than we were last week. Let's be a better team next week then we are this week." Those are the kinds of goals you should set at first and use until your team has reached a certain level of play.

Now my goals for our team are simple: we want to be the best football team in the country. That is what we are going to aim for. We are going to reach for a national championship.

When a coach wins a championship, he has to find other ways to motivate players the following season. His goals must relate to the things that he believes are most important for making his team the best it can be, and he must have confidence that accomplishing those goals will result in a similar degree of success, in terms of the win-loss record, to what the team achieved the previous year.

Remember that each player is different and has his own job to do. I could put an offensive guard against Warren Sapp that could not block Sapp very well, and I could put the same offensive guard against someone else and he might kick the devil out of him.

I've never been an individual grade kind of guy. I don't care how many tackles somebody makes. Our position coaches use grades as a more objective yardstick of performance. That way, when a kid wants to know why he graded low, the coach can point to the play in which he didn't go across the field to make the tackle or to something else he wasn't physically able to do. The kid can't deny it when there is a specific record, and the coach can say, "I've noted three plays that you loafed on" or "You've hustled on only every other play."

But I've stayed away from grades because kids who may not grade well are often the ones who make the big plays or allow others to make plays. Do you bench a kid who is crucial to your team's success because he doesn't get high enough grades?

Making Tactical Adjustments

My preference would be to always run the football. In the past, when we emphasized the running game, people called our offensive approach "vanilla." But it's important to adjust to the talents of your squad and to what the other guy is doing.

In 1994 we were a great offensive team, although we weren't that great defensively. We were able to win 15 or 16 games despite that imbalance, which shows how strong our offense really was. But usually we strive to stop the opponent with our defense, force him to kick and execute well on special teams, and then take care of the football on offense. When one unit—offense, defense, or kicking—is less effective, you have to take a few more chances, as we did on offense in 1994.

People aren't as patient offensively as I like to be, and I'm less patient myself. Modern defenses have forced us to be less patient. Many teams have different defensive philosophies from a few years ago. Now you see much more man on the corners and eight guys in the box. That makes it very difficult to run the football. Defenses have put so many people in there to block the running game that they have forced us to throw the football.

You have to change if the other guy makes you change. Unless you have a super football team, you cannot dictate the way the game is being played today. There are too many good coaches, and you have to be smart enough to analyze what is going on. If your wideouts can't beat their corners and you can't throw the football, the defense will put eight guys in the box, and you'll have a tough day. On the other hand, if you can play eight guys in the box and your wideouts can handle their corners, you'll have a standoff. It's cat and mouse.

Gauging Success

Most of us feel that we could have done a better job in specific situations. I know I always do. I always second-guess myself. The sense of accomplishment comes when you look at your team at the end of the year and see improvement, when the squad as a whole is playing about as well as you think it can play. If you can do that, then you have done a good job, regardless of how many games you won or lost.

Maybe that's one reason I've always loved playoffs. I think if you are a good coach and a good teacher, your team will get better as the year goes on. At the end of the year, you might be good enough to build up to your best performance and make a name for yourself, as some lower-ranked basketball teams do in the postseason tournament.

It's important and rewarding to look at your team as the season progresses and to be able to say, "Hey, they are playing smarter. They are getting better. They are more cohesive. They don't do dumb things." When that is the case, the kids will play with greater enthusiasm and practice hard because they sense their improvement, too. I don't know how else to judge it.

Singling out one season as being the most successful or satisfying doesn't interest me. I have a rule: Be careful when you praise somebody, because ordinarily when you give something to somebody you take something away from somebody else.

I have been asked many times who is the greatest player I have ever coached. I always bite my lip because I know if I mention so and so, 10 other guys will think, "How come he didn't mention me?"

I have had a lot of great football teams, not in the sense that they were all national champions, but in terms of how much better they were at the end of the season than at the start. When that happens, you and your coaching staff can say you've done your jobs well.

Staying Motivated

First, you need to be a competitor. You have to love competition. Coaching is an all day profession. Every minute you must want to be around your football team, preparing for the next game or next season. As I sit here writing this, I am anxious to start work on some things to get our football program ready for next season.

Second, you have to love being around young people and seeing them improve. The drama of the game is energizing, and the sight of the kids at the end of practice grabbing hands is amazingly fulfilling. You have to really enjoy young people and feel deep down that you can have an impact on their lives. I treasure the experiences I have had with young people. Many parents have said to me, "It has been great to be a part of the Penn State football program. My kid is so much better and has learned so much." That's what keeps me going.

Staying True to You

Bobby Bowden

In football coaching, it is tempting to try to copy great and successful coaches. When you see a certain offensive or defensive scheme work, notice a team handling something well on special teams, or hear about a new practice drill, you start thinking, "Hey, we could be better next season if we used that." Maybe you could improve, but remember that you can't and shouldn't try to be someone other than who you are.

Coaching role models can be a positive influence; I've benefited from many of them. When I started in football in Alabama, the big name was Bob Neyland at Tennessee. Everybody I played for and coached with used Bob Neyland's stuff. Bear Bryant was another role model, great on fundamentals. Of course I followed Bobby Dodd of Georgia Tech and Joe Paterno at Penn State. I learned so much from all of them and many others. But I never tried to coach like them. Their approaches worked because they orchestrated them. I had to create my own way.

All of those coaches had "it." They had the goods. But that isn't always enough. You can have the goods and still not win.

The Right Mix

Coaching involves mixing a whole lot of things together in a certain way for a particular coach and program. Scheduling, weather, athletes, injuries, facilities, and so on come into play. So, too, do the expertise, experience, and individual characteristics of the coaching staff.

Every coach has his own personality, his own way of handling things. I have seen coaches who approach their roles in a different way than I would, do a good job and be successful. Every coach has to do what he thinks is right in the way he thinks it ought to be done.

Look for the right job, the right fit, but be careful not to judge a program on past history alone. Some jobs that look like losing propositions actually may just need the right man. Consider Steve Spurrier at Florida. Florida had never won a Southeastern Conference Championship. They had never won a national championship. Steve was the perfect fit. He stepped in there and won six conference championships and a national championship. He was the guy with the goods, and he landed at the right school for him.

I have known some great coaches who coached at schools where they didn't have a chance to win. A 5-5 record would be considered a very good year. But take the same coach and put him at Oklahoma, Alabama, or Florida State, and he might have a great year every year. What makes any coach successful is having what it takes and being at the right school.

If you haven't thought about this before, do so. Take stock of your preferences, principles, strengths, weaknesses, and all the things that define you as a person and coach. Get input from colleagues and perhaps former players who know you well. Ask for their objective evaluations. Have respected football minds analyze how you are managing things from technical and tactical standpoints. Recall past events that have shaped your outlook, attitude, and lifestyle. All this can be helpful in understanding both how you are being perceived by others—which impacts how they respond to you—and how you might improve.

Coaching Roots

People always comment on my use of gadget plays and the element of surprise. Yes, I have always done that, although I don't do it as much now as I used to. A lot of it comes from my personality and the culture in which I was raised.

I was the runt of the litter, always the smallest guy out there. I was fast and quick but little, so when we played touch football I would have to devise ways to try to beat the other guy. A lot of times, a reverse pass or something tricky gave me an edge. That was a big part of my initial experience in football.

In 1943 when I was 13 years old, I contracted rheumatic fever and was bedridden for six months. For a young athlete who grew up in the shadow of Legion Field, this period of inactivity in the hospital and another full year of confined recuperation was especially frustrating. It was a year of staying in my room with no television, no video games, no computer, none of today's modern distractions or means of communication. It was just me and my radio.

I mostly listened to news accounts of World War II. I spent hours each day soaking up reports on the war, imagining the battles being fought at sites across Europe. I listened to a play-by-play of World War II for a year, imagining in my mind's eye the look of every place, the terrain of the battle-field, the army units marching, and the sounds and smells of the war. I had a pretty good map in my head of the key locations in Europe, and I even began to learn which generals were leading which units.

I've never lost my fascination for World War II, and I still read about it as much I can. Listening to those radio accounts and reading books and other sources about the big battles certainly shaped my coaching approach. The war and my repeated experience as the underdog because of my small size played significant, defining roles in my tactical approach to battles on the football field.

The underdog role carried over into my first head-coaching job at a jun-ior college in Georgia. We had to schedule a lot of senior colleges that had better, bigger, stronger athletes. We had to run reverses, fake punt passes, and things like that. Although we were outmanned, we were pretty suc-cessful. Later on, despite not being the favorite in many of our contests, we were able to achieve records of 31-6 at Samford from 1959 to 1962, and 42-26 at West Virginia from 1970 to 1975.

I brought that underdog attitude with me into major college football. The situation at Florida State was pretty bleak when we started. My first year,

we began 0-4 and were playing seven pure freshmen. After three seasons, we were within a game of playing for the na-tional championship. We used our share of surprises to win by deception games we couldn't win with power or speed at that point. But when we improved in the mid 1980s, we didn't try to trick people so much. The better you are, the less you have to use tricks. I did it to survive when I was younger.

I still love to spring the ele-ment of surprise on an oppo-nent. We go into every game with a trick play, but we might go five games before using it. I love having that option in my back pocket for catching the opposition off guard. That's just

© Mark Friedman/SportsChrome USA

61

my personality. Winning is the greatest feeling there is in coaching, but I probably get the most satisfaction out of putting in the strategies and watching them play out.

Coaching Priorities

A coach must have his priorities in life in order, and football cannot be the top priority. In my opinion, God is first, family is second, and other people are third. Around fourth, football comes in. To me, football is a way to make a living. Fortunately, God has given me the talent to coach. I feel that I am doing what God wants me to do when I coach. If I lose, I am not going to cut my wrist. I'm not going to go get drunk. I'm not going to go home and beat my wife. Other things are more important. A coach who is not careful, who puts all his eggs in the football basket, will not have a strong enough support system to withstand a terrible year.

Three of my four sons went into coaching. They had an advantage over other coaches in that they saw me lose big games and they saw me win a national championship. They saw the good and the bad. When they went into coaching, they were aware of its pitfalls and highlights. They had experienced firsthand the benefit of making God and family the top priorities. The football coaching graveyard is full of guys who made football their god.

Appeal of Coaching

Why did I get into coaching and stick with it? Well, winning is nice, but day in and day out, the thing I like most is dealing with the kids. I like coaching players. I also like the closeness and camaraderie of the coaching staff.

I enjoy putting my team on display and trying to beat a coach who is pretty doggone good. I get excited when we play against somebody who is heavily favored. I get much more worked up over that kind of game than if we are playing somebody we are heavily favored to beat.

I have been as low and as high as a coach can get. Whatever inspired me back in 1953 when I first started coaching kept me going through the '60s, '70s, and '80s. Whatever it is, it's still there. It's still burning.

I admit that it has helped to have won so much in the latter part of my career. At my age, I couldn't go through a 2-11 season. Well, I might get through one, but I wouldn't go through two. I have always felt that even if we did have a terrible year, I wouldn't want to hang it up. I would want to see if I could bring it back the next year. If I couldn't, then I think it would be time for me to get out. It would be time for me to turn the program over to a younger guy. As I have gotten older, being successful has helped me stay in the game.

Even so, every coach sometimes questions whether it's all worth it: the long hours, the criticism, the pressure. I've asked myself many times, "Bobby, are you doing the right thing? Look at all these people who are writing you bad letters. You don't have to put up with this. Why not go work in real estate with your daddy or something?" I always eventually answer, "No, I would rather coach than do anything else."

So here I am, a football coach in his 70s with 21 grandchildren. The things that drew me to coaching are the same things that keep me coaching. Whatever they are, I haven't lost them. I still get excited about each year—about spring practice, about recruiting, about everything.

Coaching Fundamentals

Perhaps one reason I've remained a football coach all these years is that I sincerely believe football can develop character. As leader of the program, the coach needs to model the kind of behavior he expects his players to embrace and exhibit, starting with what I consider the three fundamentals in coaching: honesty, loyalty, and compassion.

The first is honesty. Be honest with the players you coach, the coaches you work with, the people within your school or university. It all starts there. If there is dishonesty between the coach and others, everything else will eventually break down.

Loyalty is number two. Again that means loyalty to your players, to the people you coach with, and to your administrators and the people above you. I tell my coaches, we must be loyal to each other, we must be loyal to our players, we must be loyal to our athletic director, and we must be loyal to our president and to our university.

We've been fortunate to have had little turnover in our coaching staff over the years. Some coaches have left to take head-coaching jobs, but few have left for what might be considered lateral moves. Our players also have demonstrated a great deal of loyalty, both current players and former athletes. That strong bond is important when things get tough, and the coach sets the example for that.

The third essential quality in coaching is compassion for those you work with and for your players. Compassion is very important. You really must feel for your players and not simply use them to get ahead.

The need to be concerned about each player's well-being was driven home to me early in my career. When I first started coaching, I coached with a man who had been coaching since the early 1930s. He believed that there was no such as thing as an injury. If a kid got hurt, he didn't accept it. "That's OK, son, we'll tape it up. Go in anyway," was his attitude. The fact is that players do get hurt, and they do feel pain. Each player is somebody's son. Keep that in mind as you work with your team. There is such a thing as an injury. If a player is hurt, he is hurt, and you'd better not abuse him.

Flexible But Firm

I have been coaching for nearly 50 years. Times have certainly changed. I have gotten older and, I hope, a little wiser. I've become more lenient, which I think is a plus rather than a minus. As a young coach, I would take a player off the field for blinking his eye wrong. Now I don't do that. Through the years I have become more tolerant. Tolerance comes with maturity.

Most of us coaches had a fit back in the 1960s and early 1970s when players started growing beards and mustaches and wearing their hair long. We were sure that facial hair and hair sticking out from under the helmet simply could not be tolerated. When you stand back and think about how many national championships the nice, crew-cut wearing, clean-shaven boys at Army and Navy have won, hair doesn't seem to be the most important issue. Sure we have some standards about facial hair and hair length, but we don't make our players shave every day or check that their hair does not touch their shirt collars.

We allow a lot of things now that we didn't allow when I started coaching. Some things I don't agree with but have allowed because times change. If you don't keep up with the changes, you might wind up looking for another job.

You have to keep up with the times and be prepared to bend, but you don't have to sacrifice your ideals to new trends. Your moral and ethical standards should stay solid, as should your core coaching beliefs.

My feelings about this go back to the approach Jim Carlen had at West Virginia when I coached there. Jim's thinking was to have as few rules as possible, but to enforce them. Why develop a 70-page rulebook if it is filled with things you can't do anything about? Cut it down to the essential rules, but then abide by them.

If a kid wants to jump up and down and holler after he makes a touchdown—which is what they do in the pros and everywhere else—as long as he's not taunting the opponent, I'm a little more lenient.

Coaching today's players is like holding a bird in your hand. Grip the bird too tight, and you will squeeze him to death. Hold the bird with too loose a grip, and he'll fly away. You have to determine the proper firmness for each situation at that point in time.

In 1953 when I got my first coaching job, if you told a kid what to do, he did it without question. "Son, do this," was all you had to say. Nowadays, that doesn't work. Some players might accept what you say, but most of them weren't raised to take instruction without asking why they can't do it another way and what's in it for them.

I try to explain that this is what we need to do and this is why, this is how it will benefit you and will make you a better player and a better person. You have to tell your players what you are going to do and why. The days of saying, "Hey, this is the way we are going to do it. If you don't like it, too bad," are over.

Identifying Players

When we recruit, the first thing we look for is physical ability of the highest quality. We look for players who can play Notre Dame, Florida, Miami, and Alabama. That is the caliber of athlete we have to have. A player must measure up in terms of size, strength, speed, and so on.

That doesn't mean we totally dismiss a smaller player who has a big heart. Dexter Carter was a tiny 160-pound back from Baxley, Georgia, who was bound and determined he was going to be a starting running back for the Seminoles his freshman year. Only one problem: we already had Sammie Smith—who stood 6 foot 2, weighed 225 pounds, and had world-class speed—and another back who was our leading rusher the season before. Dexter's determination pushed him into the lineup. He started five games for us as a freshman and went on to become a first-round draft pick.

If we see the athletic ability we want in a player, we go to his school and talk with his advisor. We check his academic records to make sure that the prospect will be accepted by our admissions department. We only want athletes who have the potential to graduate. We pass the player's transcript to our registrar, who determines whether he has the academic background and aptitude to compete in the classroom and graduate. If the registrar says no, we won't recruit him.

Third is character. We try to find out everything about the player's character from his coach, his family, and his guidance counselors at school. We want a player who is dependable and accountable. If he has a history of problems, we drop him right then.

Building character in today's social climate is especially tough. Many players come from broken, malfunctioning homes, with no father figure to provide discipline or set a positive example. If players aren't going to develop discipline and character at home, where are they going to get it? The church would be the next option, but that's an alternative kids from troubled homes rarely turn to.

The next best place for discipline and character development might just be a football field. Football requires sacrifice. You can't play football if you are selfish. You can't play football if you are not a team man. You can't play football unless you love your teammates. Many aspects of building a winning football team are bound to help build character as well. That doesn't mean players are going to be angels, but we have seen positive personal growth in many players who started with little discipline and left with academic degrees and a winning attitude that made them successful in their careers and lives.

I am forthright about these three attributes—athletic ability, academic standing, and character—when I talk to prospects and their families. If we are making a home visit, then the athlete almost certainly has athletic ability. If we have any concerns about his schoolwork or attitude, I might say something like, "Son, I'm not worried about your football. I have already seen you play, and you've got what we are looking for in football. What you need to work on are these other things. You simply have to pick up your grades, or we cannot recruit you." I'll encourage him in that way, and make the point to his parents at the same time.

Some kids are no problem. They are always aboveboard. In the case of the borderline player, the one on the bubble, we tell him exactly what he must do to earn a scholarship. Then I talk to him about his character. The big thing I usually always talk about is being careful about who he runs around with. I tell him not to run around with bad characters. He won't lift them up; they will take him down.

You can't play football unless you are disciplined, so discipline is a big part of character. I also include morality. A kid has to have some kind of ethical base in order to make good choices.

Charlie Ward had it when he came here. Charlie's father was a coach and his mother was a schoolteacher. Charlie had six brothers and sisters. His family saw to it that he was disciplined at home. He was taught to be honest and accountable. Athletes like Charlie are fun to coach. Chris Weinke was much the same way.

Setting Priorities for Players

Athletes like Charlie Ward and Chris Weinke, who have team-first perspectives, are rare these days. Most kids think, "I, me, my, mine, what can you do for me?" That kind of outlook destroys a football squad. Football is a team sport, and the team must take priority over the individual. That doesn't mean you don't use a superior athlete's talents to the utmost. It simply means that you fit his abilities into the kind of attack that is going to be most successful for the team.

With our kids, we stress playing a role. We tell them: If you are the tailback, your job is to gain yards and try to score a touchdown when you carry the ball. Depending on the play called, you may be asked to block or catch a pass. Don't worry about statistics. Play your role. Don't say, "But, coach, I only got in the game for 10 plays." That's all right; that was your role. If you are a substitute who didn't get into a game, accept your role and be ready to go next practice. I don't want to get a call from Mom, asking, "How come you didn't put in my son?" Your number may not always get called, but you have a role and your day will come.

It's team—T-E-A-M! It's not I. It's the WE-formation, not the I-formation. Everything is we, us, ours. When I talk to my team, togetherness is the emphasis. We can't accomplish anything great in this sport as individuals; we can be a great team.

Managing Personnel

I try to build around our offensive and defensive talent. You have to accentuate what your players do best. The respective and collective talents of our players dictate our style of play.

For example, let's say we've got a quarterback who can throw the heck out of the ball but he can't run. We have to put him in the pocket and protect him so that he has time to throw. We don't ask him to run. If we have another quarterback who is a great runner but can't throw very well, we're going to run the option. I'm going to put in running plays so he can become an extra running back. There is no sense in making him try to use a pro passing attack. If I've got a great receiver, I find a way to get him the ball.

Defensively, if we are big and strong but not very fast, we need to contain everything, keep the ball inside, and surround the offense because we can't catch them. If we have great speed but are not very big, we have to play inside and chase the ball outside where we can catch it. All those factors affect your style of play.

Final Advice

Whatever coaching job you get—at the junior high, high school, college, or any other level—work at it like it's the last job you will ever have. Work every day as if it is the last day you will ever work. Some guys are always looking ahead. The grass always looks greener. Do the best job you can wherever you are, as if you are going to be there forever. Good things will happen if you do the best you can.

You never really know what kind of job you're doing until you finish your career and have time to look back. People mean well when they tell me to look at what we've accomplished, but I don't believe in looking back. I've got another game next year; I've got another season ahead of me. I'm scared to look back. The challenges are ahead of me, and that's where I have to look.

A coach who has had a great year needs to watch out for complacency. That's the biggest enemy of a successful team. For 14 years in a row, we were ranked among the top four teams in the nation. Each year our biggest enemy was complacency. When everything is going well, watch out. I start off every year telling the coaching staff and players that we can't be complacent. If we rest on what we did before, then we are going to fall. You cannot let up.

Don't look back. I don't ever look back at a job well done. I don't even know if I have done a good job. Even in 1999 when we were undefeated, ranked number one in the country every week of the year, and were about as successful as a team can get, my focus was the future. You can't live off what you did last season. When I reflect, it is only to review my priorities—What did I stand for? Did I make a positive difference?

When you get into coaching, you have to realize that everybody can't win. When two teams play, one is going to lose. You have to accept that, and you have to know how to lose. It is easy to win. It is easy to be gracious when you win, although some coaches abuse the role of the winner. Losing is difficult, but you need to be able to handle the losses or you aren't going to make it. Coaching would really be easy if everybody won, but it doesn't work that way. Anytime a team goes 10-0, another team somewhere goes 0-10.

If you really want to know if you have done a good job, after a game or after the season, look at yourself in the mirror and ask, "Did I do the best I could?" If you can say yes, the job has been well done.

Leading Your Team

Tom Osborne

A common vision and mission are necessary to get any group to perform at the highest level. A team with a strong desire to achieve specific, shared goals plays with a much greater sense of purpose and energy. Positive, goal-directed behavior also tends to be much more disciplined, which means fewer attitude problems and off-the-field rule transgressions.

Before you can implement effective goal setting with a team, you first must establish basic principles within the football program's culture. Foremost among these are honesty, loyalty, and work ethic.

Honesty, Loyalty, and Work Ethic

If your players ever feel that you have lied to them, deceived them, or manipulated them, they are not going to trust you. And a good team has to have a great deal of trust. So, if you promise a guy that he is going to play and then you don't play him, or if you bring a player into your program by doing something illegal, you have not only broken the trust, you've severely harmed your team.

Honesty works both ways. If a player told me something, I believed it. But if I found that he had deceived me, my trust in him would be lost. So make honesty a priority, right from the start, and—for the good of the program—allow no exceptions.

I never wanted to be in the position of bringing a player thousands of miles from home and then using him as a pawn. Players who make a commitment to the program should be given your unwavering loyalty. If a player gets hurt or has a family crisis or just needs help with off-the-field situations that aren't going well for him, you need to be there to support him.

I took heat on occasion for being loyal to my players. But I believe that my decisions and actions backed up what I had preached about loyalty, and the athletes appreciated that. If you treat people with loyalty and you care about them, you are going to get loyalty in return. The same is true of the coaching staff. If you are loyal to the other coaches in your program, then you have a good chance of them being loyal to you in return.

Consider the case of Turner Gill, our starting quarterback in the early and mid 1980s. Turner had played only one year as quarterback in high school and was a little bit of an unknown quantity at that position. Because he was a multidimensional athlete and we had never had an African-American quarterback at Nebraska, some people told him that he would never play quarterback as a Cornhusker. Apparently he trusted me enough to believe that I would play him at quarterback as I said I would. In return for being treated fairly, he demonstrated his loyalty though his great effort and performance on the field and his model behavior as a leader of our team off the field.

Any worthwhile goal will require considerable effort to achieve. A sound work ethic doesn't guarantee victory, but it does give your program a chance to accomplish great things. The coach is the model for the kind of initiative and diligence that goal achievement requires.

Coaching is not a job for lazy people. Your staff and players aren't going to pay any greater price than you do. If you ask your players to show up for off-season workouts but never come around and don't express much interest in them, then don't expect a lot of effort from the team.

Now, work needs to be kept in proper perspective. Hard work can be counterproductive if it produces overuse injuries, extra high levels of tension, and staleness in the second half of the season. At Nebraska we didn't work on Sunday morning. I encouraged the coaches to spend time with their families and go to church. We didn't do anything with our players on Sundays, even before the NCAA passed rules that limited the number of hours you could practice each week. We simply felt that it was critical that players get at least one complete day a week away from football.

No specific schedule is the best, but I worked with the coaches on Sunday night and Monday night, and we tried to finish up by 10:00 P.M. those nights. We usually started at 7:00 A.M. Monday through Friday, so Monday was our longest day in the office. On Tuesday, Wednesday, and Thursday nights, everybody went home after practice. Although I took film home with me and worked some at night, I always felt the staff was more effective and energetic if we stayed away from 20-hour days and seven workdays a week. At some point, an extended schedule becomes self-defeating.

We tried to make practices concise and sharp and not lengthy. We averaged about an hour and a half per practice, with two hours being the maximum. That way we felt we could maintain a good tempo, a good pace. We aimed for quality over quantity. If you drag practice out, then people start practicing at a lower performance level and at a pace you don't want to see in a game.

We also tried to introduce a bit of fun. I made sure that we did not create an overly intense environment in which players were continually being chewed out or belittled. I don't believe in humiliation or tearing a player down through personal attacks. It is important to correct a player and teach him how to do things right, but it is also

Courtesy of University of Nebraska

important not to do anything that would demean him and challenge his value or worth as a person. When negative and personal attacks start happening, football gets old awfully quick.

Treating Players Right

Once you have laid the foundation for trust, loyalty, and hard work, goals become much more attainable. It is important to maintain the group's enthusiasm in striving to reach the goals you have set.

I came to Nebraska as a graduate assistant coach in 1962 when Bob Devaney became the head coach. Prior to that year, Nebraska had won two or three games a season for several years. In Bob's first season, we went 9-2. When I asked players to describe the major differences between the 1962 season and the year before, they pointed out that practices were much shorter and that the coach seemed to believe in them and had made playing football fun again. The same players who had been so unsuccessful the year before were thriving because of a different, more positive atmosphere.

Since then I have made a point of interacting with the players, knowing their names, and being willing to kid around a little bit with them. Sure, you want their respect and you demand effort from them, but you don't need a militaristic atmosphere in which people shake in their boots during every practice and game. Coach Devaney could be really intense sometimes, but 10 minutes later he'd be joking around, putting his arm around the player that he had just chewed out.

Here is another piece of advice about how to treat players: praise in public, criticize in private. Give players public recognition for the things they do well. If you have to correct them or chew them out for something really serious, call them into your office.

Turning the Corner

Just as the program had a breakthrough season in 1962, we turned a big corner in 1991. We had incurred discipline problems of various sorts for a few years, and rule violations and the resulting penalties had begun to add up. Within the team, some players felt that certain rule violators were let off easy while others were penalized too harshly. We not only had to deal with the difficult task of meting out equitable punishment, we had to do so in a manner that all players perceived as fair.

Looking for a better way to handle these matters, we started something called the Unity Council in 1991. The council consisted of two players elected from each segment of the team—the defensive backs elected two people, the offensive line elected two, the running backs elected two, and so on. We had a total of 16 people on the council.

I told the council I wanted them to do two things to get started. First I wanted them to consult with a sport psychologist we had hired and with one or two assistant coaches, and write out a code of discipline that made sense to them. This would give the players a sense of ownership, rather than having them feel that the coach was imposing an arbitrary or unfair system of discipline on them.

They came up with a five-point penalty system. Each player started off with zero, a clean slate. Any player who reached five points was suspended. For every class a player missed, he received a point. If he missed five classes, he was not allowed to play the next week. Missing practice was a three-point violation; missing a team meeting resulted in a two-point penalty. So if a player missed a practice and a meeting, he didn't play. A misdemeanor offense was worth four points. Any type of serious legal conviction meant five points and an automatic suspension.

Once a player reached three points, he had to go in front of the Unity Council. The council would call out his violations, such as missing classes, practice, and so on. That peer pressure was important. Players couldn't hide their transgressions from their teammates, and the council made sure the offending player knew he was letting the team down by his actions.

Once a player got to four points, he would have to come and see me. At that point, I would usually notify his folks that he was on the ropes and in danger of being suspended. Once a player got to five points, I suspended him. I had the option of making the suspension permanent or limiting it to a specified number of games if he met some stringent guidelines to get back into the team's good graces. The type of suspension depended on what the violation was, and I usually took the recommendation of the Unity Council.

This approach was helpful in eliminating discipline problems and their consequences. Players knew the price that would have to be paid for missing class and goofing off in other ways. When a guy appeared frequently in front of the Unity Council, his teammates would recognize that he had a problem and would talk to him and do what they could to straighten him up themselves.

Another thing the Unity Council did was to bring to my attention anything that the players saw as interfering with the well-being or mission of the team—the food on the training table, the equipment manager's attitude, and so on. The council provided players with a forum to voice concerns about the little stuff that tends to build up, the kinds of things I might not normally hear. Once we knew where the problems were, we would try to address the things that we thought were hurting the team.

The Unity Council helped us get everyone on the same page both in terms of discipline and direction. In short, it made goal setting and goal achieving possible.

Social Forces That Can Stymie Goals

No coach can isolate his program from the social milieu of the community. Today a coach must be more aware than ever of how family and financial factors, as well as media scrutiny, can derail a program.

Since 1962 when I first started coaching, the family structure in the United States has changed significantly. Back in the early 1960s, the out-of-wedlock birthrate was 5 percent; today it is 33 percent. Back in the early 1960s it was rare to find someone who wasn't living with both biological parents. Today nearly one-half of our young people grow up without both biological parents. As a coach, you need to be prepared to work with kids who probably have more emotional baggage than you did when you were growing up. Their family foundations are not as stable, so your program needs to provide some of the missing structure.

There also has been a big increase in monetary pressure. This pressure exists not only at the college level, where you have agents talking to athletes about signing for 7 to 10 million dollars and encouraging them to declare for the draft early, but also at the high school level, where boosters with financial clout influence decisions made by school boards concerning the athletic department. Such occurrences were rare back in the 1960s. When they surface in a program and change the way even one individual is thinking or behaving, financial pressures can become a cancer that eats away at the fabric holding the team together.

Now the media isn't just interested in what you do on Friday night or Saturday afternoon. They want to know everything about every player and coach, and they often look much harder for the bad than the good. This additional media scrutiny of coaches and players can be distracting if you let it be. Keep your focus and your team's focus on what you do, and don't let the media intervene. Be cordial and cooperative, but don't allow the media to make it more difficult to achieve your goals.

Philosophical and Ethical Issues

Perhaps the biggest pressure felt in modern football is the pressure to win. Everyone wants to be the champion at the end of the season, though obviously that isn't possible.

Yes, winning is important. You can't completely remove it from the equation, though sometimes you might wish that you could. We didn't emphasize winning as much we talked about playing well. We thought that if we played well and did certain things in a game, winning would take care of itself. If we played well and the other team had more talent and played better, there wasn't anything we could do about it.

John Wooden never talked to his players about winning. I tried not to do that either. Did we have aspirations for winning the conference or even the national title in our goals some years? Yes, but these outcome goals were not given nearly as much attention as the process or performance goals that we set.

Unfortunately, the only standards many people use to evaluate effectiveness are the win/loss record and personal popularity. Many tremendous coaches haven't won as many games as other lesser coaches. Maybe the talent level was poor, but the players had a positive experience, grew individually, and excelled academically. Too little credit is awarded coaches for those types of achievements.

So I always tried—and I suggest that you try—to be intrinsically motivated. Remind yourself every day what's most important, and keep the broad view in mind. Winning is what you and your administration define it to be. It's essential that you understand each other clearly on that point.

In addition to deciding how much winning will be emphasized in your program, you also need to establish ethical standards that every athlete and staff member will follow. It is important that you work at a school where you feel comfortable and for an individual who shares your ethical outlook. Never put yourself in a position in which you will be forced to violate your principles.

For instance, if the head coach uses a lot of profanity, mistreats players, or does devious things such as trying to scout an opponent's practice, you have every right to step away from the situation. You should never take that kind of job just to move up the ranks. Make sure that there is a fairly good philosophical fit.

To do that, you need to form a clear coaching philosophy and a clear personal philosophy. Every year we would meet as a staff to write down our coaching philosophy. We didn't just stick to something that had been written five years ago; we rewrote it every year. That way everybody knew what the staff felt was important. We wrote down an offensive philosophy and a defense philosophy. Were we going to be an attacking defense or a bend but don't break defense? Would we play man-to-man or zone? Were we a running team, an option team, a route back team? Did we want to play multiple sets? Our philosophies for offense and defense became pretty detailed and specific, and we spelled out the details for special teams. It is important that everyone have a clear understanding of the head coach's personal philosophy as well as the offensive and defensive philosophies of the team.

If you decide to take a job, then be absolutely loyal to the coach and the administration that hired you. Don't undercut, and don't bad-mouth. Such actions are not only very destructive to the program, but they will follow you your entire career.

The Potential to Influence

Tom Landry once said that in all his years as a professional coach he had never seen a player change his character. As head coach of the Dallas Cowboys, Tom rarely dealt with anyone younger than 22. Character is likely to be more defined at that stage than it is when we college and high school coaches begin work with a player.

Coaches have a tremendous role in shaping who their players become, especially those who coach junior high and high school players. The breakdown of the family in our culture—to the point where there are approximately 18 million fatherless children in our country today—makes the coach's role even more important. A coach today has a very influential position within the school system and the community. You can use that power positively or negatively. If you don't care about your players, if you use intimidation tactics and are dishonest with them, then you will play a destructive role in your young athletes' lives. And the younger the player is, the worse the damage can be.

The old adage that a team takes on the personality of its coach is often true. Even in the college-age athletes we coached, we saw significant changes during their four years in the program. Examples of their growth would crop up all the time. For instance, in postgame press conferences players would sometimes repeat things that we coaches had said during the week. They weren't consciously trying to parrot us or make us feel good, they had assimilated what we had told them.

Although I liked seeing players learn and grow as athletes, I liked seeing them grow as people even more. As they got an education, their personalities and character emerged.

Irving Fryar was a very talented player when he arrived on campus, but he was emotional, and his performance was similarly up and down. Toward the end of his career at Nebraska and during his highly successful pro career, Irving realigned himself spiritually and blossomed into a really outstanding person.

The Goal-Setting Process

Some of my successful methods for establishing desired behaviors and outcomes I learned through education, but most I learned through first-hand experience. For a more technical description of goal setting, refer to chapter 5 in my book *Faith in the Game* (Bantam Doubleday Dell, 2000).

The goals you set must be consistent with and must emphasize your philosophy. Your overall coaching philosophy is important and so are its components, but when setting goals you must start with the team philosophy for each area of the game and then move into specific goals.

Our offensive philosophy was that we were going to be a run-oriented team. In our part of the country, we had harsh weather and a lot of wind. We felt that we were not likely to have 11 Saturdays a year in which we could throw the ball, so we wanted to be a good running team. We planned to run options and multiple sets, to do some shifting, and so on.

We then set a goal to average six yards per rushing attempt. We also wanted to set the stage for longer gains on the ground, so we established a goal of having more than 100 knockdowns—instances of knocking players off their feet at the point of attack as well as downfield—during the course of a ball game. Since we placed a high value on ball possession, we aimed to have no more than one turnover per game. We made sure that all 10 to 12 offensive goals fit our offensive philosophy.

We did the same for defense and the kicking game. We set a series of specific goals for each area, a practice many people don't think about and might not consider as important as we did.

Every Monday after a game, we would show the game film and review how well we met our goals. As the screen showed the game action, we would indicate on the blackboard how well the players achieved their goals. Achieving 10 out of 12 goals meant that we had played really well; accomplishing only 3 out of 12 goals meant that we hadn't played very well, regardless of whether or not we won the game. There were games we won by 50 points but were not proud of, and there were a few games we lost but felt good about having played really well.

I tried to emphasize that we could control execution and effort in meeting our goals. For example, one of our kickoff coverage goals was to keep the opponent from advancing the ball beyond the 23-yard line. Although that may not seem like much, and although kick coverage isn't something that people think a lot about, there is a huge difference between having your opponent start on his own 20 and having him start from the 35. The scoring percentage almost triples with that 15 yards. Little things like that were important to our success. The most important thing, though, was that our players bought into the concept, and not just for the kickoff coverage. We tried intensely to meet that goal.

Since most goals are short-term, they can change a lot depending on the twists and turns of a given season. A coach like Steve Spurrier, who is committed to his passing game, may not change certain goals—such as completion percentage, yards per catch, sacks allowed, and so on—but the majority of goals a coach sets will be short-term, determined on a practice-by-practice or game-by-game basis.

We set long-term goals as well. During the last eight or nine years that I coached, I asked each player before the start of the season to write down, in order, the five most important things that he wanted the team to accomplish that year. We compiled the responses from all 150 players, and ranked them from highest to lowest. Usually we'd adopt the top seven or eight goals on the list. It is important to emphasize that I wasn't setting these goals, the players were.

It seemed that when the players set the goals, we performed better and met more of them. They set goals such as winning a national championship, going undefeated during the regular season, having no mediocre performances (determined, perhaps, by how many specific game goals were met), having no off-the-field incidents that embarrassed the team, and maintaining a grade point average of 3.0 or better. Their goals were a blend of outcome and behavior-related aims.

The 1994 season was one of the most satisfying years of my coaching career. Unfortunately our superb starting quarterback, Tommy Frazier, suffered from blood clots and was benched for much of the year. His backup, Brook Berringer, stepped in and led us to eight straight wins. We went on to beat Miami in the Orange Bowl on their home field to finish the season undefeated. We probably got more out of that team's collective talent than any team we ever had. Perhaps not coincidentally, that team was one of the most close-knit groups I have ever coached.

We enjoyed a great deal of success the last several years at Nebraska, after we implemented this goal-setting process. We also had outstanding athletes, so some might question whether it's a chicken or egg type of thing. But I believe that if you set goals with your team, players will perform better on the field, be a more cohesive unit, and develop more quickly and positively as individuals off the field. You have the important responsibility of leading them.

Pursuing Your Vision

Lou Holtz

The school administrators can hire you to be the head football coach, but they cannot appoint you as the leader. They can give you the title, they can give you the position, but they cannot make you a leader.

The players and assistant coaches have to select you as the leader. To assume leadership of a football team, you have to have a vision of where you want to go and a plan for how to get there. People will follow someone who has a clear vision and a well-thought-out plan. The key is to retain faith in your approach, even when things aren't going well.

I had a vision and a plan when I took the head-coaching job at South Carolina, but nobody followed or believed in them at first. We stuck with it, even after we went 0-11 my first year. Although the players weren't entirely on board that first season, I believed that the vision could become reality. I had great confidence in the plan because it had worked before. By the second year, we were ranked 19th in the country. By the third year, we rose to 13th.

I have inherited nonwinning programs six times in my coaching career. In each case, we went to a bowl game by the second year. Success starts with having a vision of where you want to go and a plan to make it happen.

Convincing Players

At the first meeting in a new program, I tell players, "You did not pick me, and I understand that. If you had your choice of a head football coach, I would have been the last guy you would have chosen. But what is important for you to understand is that I chose you. I knew you were here and I still chose to come here, and I am going to do everything I can to see that you have an opportunity to win as soon as possible."

I want to impress on team members that they are not adopted children. I don't look at them as my recruits or my predecessor's recruits. They are members of the university and players for the school. I treat them as such and will do everything I can to see that they win quickly. For seniors, I do everything I can to see that they leave on a winning note, go to a bowl game, and get the most out of their final season of college competition.

In every game the coach must ask, "Am I giving my players a chance to win?" If you are giving them the best opportunity to be successful as a group, then you are doing your job. That is the bare minimum your players should expect of you. You do your team a disservice if you don't give them the opportunity to perform to their collective potential.

You will be able to tell that the team is on board by observing the extent to which players adhere to what you are trying to do. But whether players buy into the program or philosophy the first year is not important. Sometimes they believe everything you say the first year; sometimes they believe nothing. But if you are persistent, and if you are correct, eventually they will buy into your way of thinking.

Emphasize your philosophy rather than bombarding players with a lot of rules or regulations. If they buy into your philosophy, they will behave in a manner that allows the program to achieve your objectives. They won't try to cut corners.

Everybody's philosophy is a little bit different. I am more of a team-oriented coach than a star-oriented coach. No one player is more important than the overall welfare of the team. Each of us has to be personally responsible, and I don't allow slacking off.

From that broad philosophical perspective, we established three rules that form the whole basis of our program:

1. Do what's right, and avoid what's wrong. If you have any doubt, get out the Bible.
2. Do everything to the very best of your ability, and don't accept anything less than the best you are capable of being in every area of your life. I certainly won't.
3. Follow the golden rule, and treat other people as you would like to be treated. That is essential.

We ask three questions of everyone in our program: Can I trust him? Is he committed to excellence? Does he care about others? The answers to these questions are absolutely critical. By following the three rules, players can improve their self-image, increase their self-confidence, and become contributing members of the team.

My first year, the players didn't buy this idea. Eventually they earned my trust. They grew more committed, demonstrated by the increase in their overall grade point average from 2.1 to over 2.6. Now players live up to the concept of personal accountability and take responsibility for their actions. This shows up in many areas, from the weight room during winter conditioning to the classroom during academic sessions.

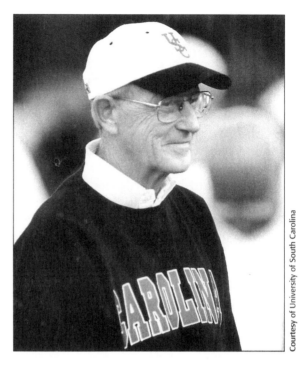

Courtesy of University of South Carolina

If there is a problem, someone is likely to let us know. We might get a phone call about a player creating a problem in the dining hall. We address problems immediately and make it clear that such behavior will not be tolerated again. If the offender won't change his conduct, I won't live with it. Since I'm not leaving the program, he will have to leave.

A guy who can be trusted, is committed to excellence, and cares about the team is a potential player in our program. Even if he's not the most talented athlete, he has a chance to compete for us if he has the right mind-set.

Plugging Players Into the Program

If an athlete meets the prerequisites for attitude and behavior, we evaluate his physical abilities. Certainly, anyone we recruit is going to have some athletic talent. As the coach, I will be able to use that talent to help us win. Maybe he won't be a star or a starter, but if he has the desire and character we look for and will do what's right to be the best in everything he does, then I need to be smart enough to find a way to make him succeed.

Don't be afraid to move players to different positions, especially if their speed is somewhat of a liability in one spot but could be an asset in another. One note of caution: If a player absolutely can't play a position, you will never be successful moving him. A good football player will be able to play the position he's assigned, but he might become a great player if you move him to a position at which he can make the most of his speed.

When we encounter a player who has all the other attributes we're looking for but is not working to his potential at his current position, we know that it can only be because he lacks the speed to be a great player in that position. If speed is the only thing he is lacking, we try to move him to another position, one in which the speed he has will be an asset.

When I went to Notre Dame, we moved Frank Stams, who had marginal speed for a fullback, to defensive end. Andy Heck and Tom Rehder both had marginal speed as tight ends but excellent speed as offensive tackles. Linebacker Chris Zorich had so-so speed for a linebacker but great speed for middle guard. After our first year at South Carolina, we moved Antione Nesmith from running back to free safety because of his leadership and toughness. His speed as a running back was average for his position, but it was a great advantage on the defensive side of the ball. During the 2001 season, we moved Jermaine Lemon from strong safety to linebacker, and he excelled at the new position.

A Hidden Gem

One day a physician in Ohio called me about an athlete in his state, Ryan Brewer, who was a good football player but was not being recruited by many schools. He had won a lot of honors in Ohio, including being named Ohio High School Player of the 1990s by *Ohio Prep Magazine* and the state's Mr. Football in 1998. But he was a 5-foot-9-inch running back who didn't have great speed, and few big-time college programs were interested in him.

At the doctor's prompting, I called Ryan. Ryan said, "I want to play major college football, and I want to play for you." I had been at South Carolina only for about a week and needed players badly, so we made a commitment to him without even looking at his film.

What appeared to be a long shot has turned up aces. Ryan was named MVP of the Outback Bowl his sophomore year, amassing 214 all-purpose yards and contributing at running back, receiver, and punt returner. This is a guy nobody recruited. He didn't have a major college scholarship offer. But if you want an example of attitude, character, and work habits, Ryan is it.

Discovering untapped talent can happen only if you keep an open mind. Athletes who have less God-given ability or are small in stature may well play beyond expectations. Players who have great talent but lack desire or integrity may come up short. Do not make judgements on the basis of who's the flashiest or who appears to have the most potential, but rather who will produce.

Speed is a major factor, but the player's overall talent and ability—whether he can throw, whether he can catch, and so on—are also important. We look closely at every player, judging for ourselves where he can contribute most to the team. Don't just accept the fact that he'll be a wide receiver because that's the position he has played in the past.

No matter where you are coaching or at what level, you must use the talent you have to the fullest. Here at South Carolina, we have used the shotgun a lot. We spread out. We throw so much because that is what we have to do to win. We could not win if we tried to outmuscle or out-tough teams. We just aren't big enough, strong enough, quick enough, or good enough to compete with many teams in the Southeastern Conference by going toe-to-toe. Opening the field and using our speed to the fullest has helped us offset whatever shortcomings we have.

Setting Standards and Goals

At this point in my career, there is nothing I can do in coaching that I haven't done before, from winning the national championship to being awarded individual honors. What keeps me coaching at this point isn't the prospect of titles or personal achievements, but rather the satisfaction of seeing young people change their lives for the better through their participation in our program. Here at South Carolina, it has been very rewarding to see our players improve off the field as well as on the field.

The coach has an obligation to develop players as citizens, not necessarily by preaching or forcing a code of behavior on them, but by the way he acts, by setting the example. Our players see that my faith is of great importance to me. They know that the standards of conduct I expect of them are established according to the principles of that faith and the imperatives for becoming part of a successful football team. Athletes who participate in our program soon learn that we are not going to compromise our expectations of their behavior. Over time, they learn to set high standards in all that they do, never settling for less.

This is a constant battle. We live in a selfish, undisciplined society. Many people worry too much about being popular and lower their standards to appeal to certain people. I don't believe in lowering standards. I believe in showing people how to reach higher standards.

If a particular student's standard in a class is to get a C but the professor's standard is to have dedicated students who want to get As, that student might think that the professor is totally unfair. I run into trouble when my players' expectations and standards for themselves are not as high as my expectations and standards for them. I teach players that throughout life they will run into people whose expectations are greater than their expectations of themselves. I almost always think that my players are capable of doing more than they believe they can do.

Many people talk about their rights and privileges. I'm one of those old-fashioned people who still talk about obligations and responsibilities. That's why, when it comes to goals, I provide guidance, but the players set them. I want players to embrace the level of performance we expect them to achieve. We make it clear that it won't be easy. Players must be committed to striving for that high level, or they won't succeed.

Over the years, team goals for a particular season have included one or more of the following: to win a national championship; to be conference champions; to rank in the top 10 at the end of the year; to win a bowl game; to have a winning season. We may not achieve all those goals in a given season, but our minimum goal is always to have a winning record.

We give out few individual awards. Players vote on most valuable player and one other award at the end of the season, but to me the important thing is to have winning team performances. If we win 8 out of 11 football games, each player gets a beautiful plaque that has his picture on it. Engraved on the plaque is something like, "You have proven to us conclusively that you are a winner on and off the field by your performance." That is the highest award a player can get in our program.

When we went 0-11, I still gave out three plaques to deserving players because I didn't want them to think that their efforts and performances were those of losers. They weren't. If everybody else had played like they did, we would have won our share of games.

On Mondays I announce the winning players of the week, those who gave their very best and who contributed the most to the team. That acknowledgement is important to the players. The reward is something simple like a candy bar, but it's a tangible way to recognize deserving players in front of their teammates.

Handling Adversity

After being named head coach at North Carolina State, I was highly disappointed over my lack of success in signing players to join our program. I showed up at a coaches' convention in Chicago feeling down and sorry for myself. When I arrived at the hotel, I saw former Temple and Navy coach Wayne Hardin in the lobby. Wayne said he wanted to buy me a drink.

Soon he picked up on my low mood. Instead of consoling me or commiserating with me, Wayne asked, "Lou, are you the best coach in the country?" I felt about two inches tall at the time, so I looked at Wayne with a bewildered expression and said, "Goodness gracious, no! I want to be one of the best coaches, but I'm not even in the top 100." He responded, "Then you ought to resign! N.C. State hired you because they thought you were the best coach in the country, and you ought believe it, or you ought to leave."

I decided that if North Carolina State was dumb enough to hire me, I was going to be dumb enough to believe that I was the correct man for the job. Years later, I appreciate the wisdom of Wayne's advice all the more.

It's easy to slide into a negative attitude. Once a media organization covered me during a game. After reviewing the tape, my first comment was, "Why didn't you include more positive comments that I made during the game? Everything seemed so negative." They responded, "Well, Coach, you didn't make many positive comments." I listened to the tape again, and they were right. I had become negative without even realizing it.

Constantly reexamine what you are doing, how you are doing it, and what you believe. When you see negativity creeping in, extinguish it fast. That sounds much easier than it is sometimes, especially when the deck seems to be stacked against you.

During my first year at South Carolina, my wife had her second major cancer surgery, my son Skip almost died, and my mother died the Friday before we played Florida. On a recruiting trip, we stopped at Lady's Island (S.C.) Airport so I could visit a prospective player. The plane needed some fuel, so the pilot told me he was going to fly up to Hilton Head for fuel while I visited the athlete. During that 11-mile flight to refuel, the plane crashed. One pilot was killed and the other seriously injured. All my suitcases and materials were on the airplane, and the manifest indicated that I was, too.

We lost every single football game we played that year. Everyone kept telling me that I was too old, that the game had passed me by.

If you are going to coach or play this game, you are going to get knocked down. You are going to have disappointments. How well you handle them depends on your attitude.

Keep Attacking

At Notre Dame, we took over a program that was at the bottom. People said we couldn't win there, but for nine straight years we went to a major January bowl: Sugar, Cotton, Orange, or Fiesta. We competed for national championships. My last two years, our records were 9-2 and 8-3. Out of the five losses, three occurred in overtime and two resulted from a missed extra point during the game. Losing five games in two years at Notre Dame gets to you. I had thought I was tired of coaching. I wasn't. I was tired of maintaining.

That's just me. I suppose my philosophy is much like General George Patton's in that respect. I don't want to hold the same position day after day, week after week, season after season. I want to attack day and night. I just don't enjoy coaching any other way.

Perhaps that is why I have moved on to new positions and new challenges throughout my career rather than staying at one school decade after decade, like the great Eddie Robinson. All the college coaching positions

I've had—William & Mary, N.C. State, Arkansas, Minnesota, Notre Dame, and South Carolina—have been enjoyable in their own way.

Be Fearless

The one job I took that I approached fearing that I might fail was the New York Jets head-coaching position in 1976. Perhaps it isn't surprising that I resigned only eight months later with a 3-10 record.

I should have heeded the advice of Wayne Woodrow Hayes, one of the best coaches ever. Woody was a great disciplinarian, but he also was a great teacher of fundamentals. He preached simplicity. He approached the game as if it were the military, as Patton would do.

One of the most valuable pearls of wisdom I ever received came from Woody. He advised me to respect the challenges of the job and the opponent, but not to worry about what lies ahead or how great anyone else may be. Focus on running the program the very best way you possibly can. Don't fixate on what you don't have, use the talents and abilities you do have.

One of the main reasons I came back into coaching—besides the fact that my wife encouraged me to do so, and the challenge of the South Carolina position—was the great encouragement I received from former players. At least 100 players from seasons past called me and told me to go back into coaching.

Even more gratifying were their expressions of appreciation. They told me how much they had learned about working hard and being committed, traits they took with them into every aspect of their lives. Then they'd boast about a promotion at work or something they had done for their community, their families, and so on.

I take very seriously the coach's role of preparing athletes to lead successful lives. I don't coach only football, I coach life. I try to draw analogies between what happens in football and what will happen in life. I try to prepare players for success. That is what makes coaching satisfying at this stage of my career.

PART III

Program Building and Management

Bill Curry

In August 1955 I reported to my first football training camp. I had not the vaguest notion of what I was getting into or why. I had never watched an entire football game. I had no visions of greatness, no football heroes. I cannot tell you exactly what prompted my being there.

I can tell you that my life was never the same. I had been discovered by the greatest team sport ever devised. For the last 47 years I have been consumed by a challenge that demands every ounce of a man's courage every day. Through no merit of my own I have been part of some of the greatest football teams of all time. That is not important.

What is important is that we preserve the attributes of our great teams. We must teach all who will listen the value system of a game that is a microcosm of the human experience. People around the globe should understand what the game demands of those who desire to be champions. We need to show them the one sport in which *every* player needs *every* teammate on *every* play just to survive. The world we all depend on is in a desperate struggle between those who would build and those who would destroy. Perhaps our sport, with its millions of ardent followers, can provide a metaphor for all that is good about shared values and building community. Perhaps we can make a difference well beyond the victories on the field and in the classroom.

Presumptuous? I think not. Those of us who have lived in the trenches of football recognize a common bond that links all races, religions, and political persuasions. We respect leaders, and we know what they look like. We especially respect leaders who function with purpose and presence of mind, who are calm when all hell is breaking loose, who are brave when their necks are in the noose, who are not intimidated when the enemy is talented and elusive, who care not that the alumni are rampaging. We respect them, and we follow them. We want to be like them. We want to win with them and for them. We will lay it on the line for them. We learn how to follow, how to lead. We learn *community*.

That football huddle is a metaphor for our culture—imperfect like all metaphors but nonetheless a microcosm. In the huddle are a bunch of folks who are black, brown, white, red, yellow, liberal, conservative, Muslim, Jewish, Christian, Buddhist, and Hindu. We are slim, fat, short, tall, fast, and slow. We are analytical folks and impulsive folks. We have some of the finest men on earth, and heaven knows we have a few rounders. We have been through the fires of Bobby Dodd, Vince Lombardi, Don Shula, and other coaches who know exactly how to extract every ounce of our energy. People see all that, and it resonates with them. They crave it. They take it, and us, into their hearts.

The young men who earn a place in the huddle have experienced the miracle of *team*. The training-camp experience is unbelievable—day after day, week after week, two-a-day practices in the heat, often in 14 pounds of equipment. Many drop out, remove themselves, or suffer injury. Numbers thin, and everybody thinks about quitting—everybody.

Those who stay have the opportunity to participate in the ultimate team sport. The fact that someone of my limited ability could be a part of the game, could hike the ball to Bart Starr and John Unitas, could get in some monster's way for three seconds, and could be accepted as part of the team speaks volumes to the common man. We learn, ever so slowly, that our differences do not matter in the huddle. When we trudge in after each interminable workout, we realize that the sweat smells just about the same on everybody. When we get busted in the mouth, the blood that trickles is the same color on everyone. Everybody is tired. Everybody is hurt.

In the midst of this process a miracle occurs. Men who have been raised to hate each other's guts become brothers. I have seen racists reformed. I have seen the most unlikely hugs after victories or losses. I have seen inner-city kids invite country boys to their homes for Thanksgiving dinner. I have seen the invitations accepted, and reciprocated, thus changing parents' lives. Our players become brothers for life. This is what America is supposed to be, could be, might be—in our best dreams.

In their essence, good football programs are shared values. They are *community*. Great programs that flourish year after year are synergistic marvels that produce far more than victories and high graduation rates. Each one forces accountability, respect for all ethnic, racial, and gender groups. Each one teaches the necessity of mutual dependence and unselfishness. These eternal values stand out in the midst of a quick-fix society.

We selected five coaches to explain the fundamentals of such programs, asking each to describe the foundation of his institution's remarkable success. Bill Snyder, Larry Kehres, Dick Foster, George Curry, and Mack Brown took the job seriously, sharing the details of the grueling process required to build a solid underpinning. From high school to Division I-A, the basics revolve around the core values of integrity, education, mutual respect, and winning. Although there are similarities in those areas among programs at different levels, coaches from each rung on the ladder address the eccentricities of each level.

We are fortunate to have such outstanding men as contributors. They represent the thousands upon thousands of fine women and men who have given their lives to the noble pursuit of coaching. It is our fervent hope that their work will be a lasting inspiration to all who give so selflessly to the young people of the world.

Building and Sustaining a Division I Program

Bill Snyder

Some people believe that building a program and sustaining a program are two separate topics, and many think that sustaining success is the more difficult task. That may be true in some programs, but at Kansas State we feel that we have met both challenges in the same manner, using the same principles and values.

I can speak only of those Division I programs that I have been involved with, at North Texas State University and the University of Iowa, both under the leadership of Hayden Fry, and through 12 seasons at Kansas State University.

I doubt that we at Kansas State have the answers for everyone. Many have asked, and our response has always been that we have no secrets and that achieving success doesn't go much beyond people, effort, values, and principles. Most coaches understand that. In many respects, however, we had to push these fundamentals to the limit to get the Kansas State University program on track.

No one can relate to the position our university was in 13 years ago. Kansas State was the losingest program in the history of college football (299-509-41 over a period of 93 years). Ours was the only program at that time to have lost more than 500 games. Attendance did not meet NCAA standards for remaining a Division I-A program. The board of regents considered dropping into Division II athletics or dropping football altogether. Facilities had gone unaltered for over 20 years and did not resemble even the modest facilities of many Division II programs. Perhaps the most disturbing aspect was the prevailing attitude that the program could not succeed and was a deterrent to the success of the university. We found a complacency (with the exception of a few) unlike any we had seen anywhere before. Over the previous 43 years the program ranked last in both total offense and total defense. Kansas State football stood alone at the top of the then media-based bottom 10 printed each week along with the top 10.

The lack of success was not due to a lack of quality coaches. Indeed, many excellent head coaches and assistant coaches had coached here during those years. They were far better coaches than I—Mike Ahearn, Pappy Waldorf, Charles Bachman, Z.G. Clevenger, Vince Gibson, and Jim Dickey, to name a few. These capable men had many fine assistants who now serve as assistants or head coaches in highly successful programs across the country. As Mitch Holthus, former voice of the Wildcats (and present voice of the Kansas City Chiefs), put it, Kansas State was accustomed to being "oh-for-autumn." To many people, bringing success to almost any program (downtrodden or not) is a matter of money, facilities, recruiting, and hard work. I don't argue that, but Kansas State, because of its uniqueness, may be an exception to the rule. We needed to do more.

Getting Involved in the Community

One of the first major issues for our program was people. We needed people who could and would positively affect the program. In a few instances, those people were in place waiting to move forward—president Jon Wefald and his staff, athletic director Steve Miller, a few eager alums who wouldn't give up, a few members of the support staff, and about 13,000 fans who were extremely loyal to Kansas State football. I knew the program could succeed with the loyalty and never-say-die attitude exhibited by these people. There just weren't enough of them.

To move the program into a positive light, we approached every group that could provide support. No group was too insignificant. We spent time with faculty members, sent them informational letters on a regular basis, brought them into our mentoring program, and invited the deans of our nine colleges to be our guests on our television show and in our suite on game day. We assigned a coach to call each dean of each college on a regular basis to exchange information about our program and theirs. Like most college coaches, we went out on campus to speak to faculty and student groups, but we didn't just beg for their support. We shared with them the values and principles of our program and how those principles could fit them and their programs. We detailed how we would be involved in improving their experience at Kansas State.

We got involved with student groups—the Black Student Union, the Student Senate, and sorority and fraternity groups—presenting programs and activities for and with them. We committed ourselves to raising money for a monumental new library project and campaigned for necessary increases in faculty salaries. We made every attempt to make each group feel important, wanted, and needed in our program.

We went into the community, again not just to solicit support but also to explain how we intended to support them. We described our values and principles so that they would understand that we respected the community. We explained that we wanted to stand side by side with the community, not stand above it, to help promote continued progress for Manhattan. Our players and coaches became involved with virtually every local charity and project. We took players into the five retirement centers to spend quality time with the elderly people who were without family and friends to visit them. Boys' Club, Girls' Club, food and Christmas programs for the needy, Special Olympics, Junior Wildcat organization, and so on—our players and coaches did it all, and the community in return has supported our football program in unbelievable ways.

In the early 1990s a major flood uprooted households in a large residential area in Manhattan. Our players and coaches dropped everything and spent several days filling, lifting, and moving sandbags to build levees that eventually saved many homes. It is all about caring. Show others that you care about them, and they will care about you and your program.

We created several youth programs in the local school district that allowed our players to do group mentoring with virtually every local elementary and middle school student. Our players did one-on-one mentoring with select high school students, those considered high-risk from troubled pasts and difficult home lives. We brought these youngsters into our program, put them on behavior contracts, and allowed them to participate with our players in activities and our daily routine. Our players and coaches taught the values that were at the core of our program.

We felt it was important that the university, the community, and the state recognize our program and our players as being caring and compassionate, representing quality values and principles. We strived to gain the respect of our new constituency, and we achieved our goal. All of the programs are still in place, as is the mutual respect.

Changing Player Attitudes

All this led to a change in the attitude toward our football program. Most significant was the attitude of our players, none of whom had ever played in a victory at the Division I level. We coaches met with all the parting seniors in December that first year (1988), just after I accepted the position. The 22 players who had completed their eligibility were good young men who cared and craved success, but the lack of it had tamped them down.

They spoke of how the constant losing had negatively affected their classroom work and curtailed their enjoyment of the college experience. We quickly learned that the returning student-athletes in the program felt the same way. How could we change that? We needed not only a plan but also a set of values and principles to guide each of us toward success in all facets of our lives. We established "16 Wildcat Goals for Success," a set of intrinsic values that would establish the foundation for success (figure 9.1).

We did not intend to establish lofty goals that we could not reach. We wanted to establish goals that each player and coach had complete control over obtaining. Our players needed to see something positive happen. They needed to have some successes come their way, regardless of how small those successes might seem. At the time, we had just 47 players on scholarship (which contributed to the uniqueness of our program). The NCAA limit was 95. We were using less than 50 percent of the permissible scholarships.

One of the goals for our players was for them to find a way every day to improve as people, as students, and as football athletes. Accomplishing that really isn't hard, and our players learned that they could do it. We weren't judging them on the scoreboard but on their fundamentals and techniques. We tried to put each of them in a position on the practice field where they could experience daily successes. Every day after practice we went through the locker room and asked each player how he had improved that day.

In time, each had a positive response almost every day. They could feel the improvement, and they could see it on videotape even though it didn't show on the scoreboard. In fact, our first season (1989) ended with a 1-10 record. But their attitudes had changed. They realized that they had improved and that they would continue to do so.

Our program has stayed on that path—gradual improvement year in and year out, with a plateau or setback from time to time, since that 1-10 year. We progressed to eight consecutive 9-win seasons and four consecutive 11-win seasons.

At the close of that initial season, we knew we were going to succeed. Our players and coaches began to believe that when we achieved those 16 goals for success, we would indeed have success on the field and in other areas of our lives. To this day, we send notes to the players on the teams of the early 1990s reminding them that although they were not here for the bowl games and the accolades, they were responsible for establishing the foundation, setting the bricks that support the program today. When we built our indoor practice facility, we placed a monument in the foyer with names of all those players.

Make a commitment.

Be unselfish.

Create unity—come together as never before.

Improve every day as a player, person, and student.

Be tough.

Be self-disciplined—do it right, don't accept less.

Give great effort.

Be enthusiastic.

Eliminate mistakes—don't beat yourself.

Never give up.

Don't accept losing.

Permit no self-limitations—expect more of yourself.

Expect to win.

Be consistent.

Develop leadership.

Be responsible.

Figure 9.1 The values expressed in the 16 Wildcat Goals for Success provide the foundation for success in football and in life.

Pushing for Improvement

Although it is a simple idea, the principle of self-improvement has been as valuable to our success as any other concept. We ask players and coaches to find a way each day to become just a little bit better in each priority in their lives. We suggest that a player's priorities should be his faith, his family, and becoming the best person, best student, and best football athlete he can possibly be. We realize that it is not difficult to find a way to make a little improvement in each area each day of our lives. Over a period of a week; a month; a year; two, three, or four years; each member of our program can become successful in each of those priorities. Collectively, over that same period, we can become a much improved football team and program in each of those areas.

Because our players have seen this take place throughout the past decade, they trust the concept. They did not see this program suddenly emerge to great success. They participated in gradual, step-by-step, year-by-year growth, obtaining a little more success each year. We did, however, experience setbacks, which without a solid foundation and great perseverance could have restricted the eventual success of our program. Sticking with our plan and refusing to give up or to compromise our values has been vital to our progress. We all have a plan, and each in its own way is probably the right one for our particular situation, but it is easy when we fall on hard times to lose sight of what we knew to be the right way. Perseverance has served us well.

The priorities of faith, family, and being the best person, best student, and best football athlete possible are also significant in our goal-achievement process. As in most athletic programs, goals become a yearly point of focus. We believe strongly in the method we use to achieve what is important for us. We ask our players to assess honestly what is important to them and to establish their goals (individual and team) based on those priorities. That is the easy part. Second, and crucial, is to have a well-conceived plan (a step-by-step process) that directs us toward the achievement of each goal. As coaches, we must provide direction to players in developing the plan. The third and final step is simply the Nike slogan "Just do it." At that point the values of hard work and persistence enter the picture.

We use the same process to determine the objectives that we coaches must achieve to continue the success of our program. We establish these objectives through an honest assessment of each individual, each position, and each unit in the program. Once we recognize strengths and weaknesses, our priorities and objectives become clear. We can then establish a well-thought-out plan that, if followed closely, diligently, and with great effort, will produce the successful achievement of the objectives we established.

We often hear of the present-day arms race in football facilities. We never intended to create a Taj Mahal at Kansas State, but construction has been progressing continuously throughout our tenure. Private funding from special and intelligent people who would not invest in a dying cause has paid for all of it except our recent stadium expansion. The significance of the construction of a new weight room, new locker rooms, an academic learning center, players' lounges, a new indoor practice facility, and so on was that players each year saw that we were holding true to our pledge, thus increasing their trust in the system. Although we couldn't afford to do it all at once, I am not sure we would have done so even if it had been possible. Our players were inspired by seeing something special being done for them each year. As Quentin Neujahr, a four-year starter and six-year NFL veteran, stated, "It wasn't so much the new facilities as it was the concept that we learned to trust what we were told was the truth." We have not changed our approach.

Recruiting and Evaluation

In those early years our approach to recruiting centered around a realistic understanding that we were not in position to compete for the young men that Nebraska, Oklahoma, Colorado, and other high-profile programs were after.

What was important to us was evaluation (nothing has changed). We pursued young student-athletes who would fit what we were all about. We felt that to compete for the blue-chip athlete and to finish second was a waste of time, effort, and money that we could better use working with student-athletes whom others might have referred to as second-level athletes. We were going to have to fall back on them sooner or later, so we went there first. We merely wanted to improve our talent pool and do it with good young people.

We all get caught up in the high-profile athlete and rightfully so, but I can recall the incredible number of players who entered our program at Kansas State and at the University of Iowa in the 1980s as walk-ons and became all-conference, all-American, and NFL players. Good fortune has much to do with that, but then so does the ability to evaluate not only the physical and athletic future of an athlete but his intrinsic values as well. If a young man can meet our 16 goals for success, I am certain he can play successfully for Kansas State. Don't overlook the intangibles. We believe that quality people who truly care and who want to be in your program are eventually the ones who give you greater opportunities to succeed.

We believe that we should promote what we have at Kansas State, not criticize what exists somewhere else. No one knows our program like we do, and no one knows other programs like those who are there.

Kansas State, like all other schools, has some special attributes, not just in our football program but also in our faculty, administration, education, community and campus life, and fan support. Young student-athletes select schools for a variety of reasons, some appropriate and some perhaps not. We therefore attempt to emphasize everything we have at Kansas State and in Manhattan that may be or may become important to a young man and his family. Honesty is important in our recruiting process. We want a young man here because he wants to be here, not because we twisted his arm or because we told him only what he wanted to hear. It boils down to wanting players to trust our program while they are with us. If they find our program different from what we led them to believe, they immediately lose trust in our staff and our program.

Laying the Foundation for Success

In football, just as in business or in any aspect of life, sustained success relies on building a sound foundation from the outset. Building a program on solid ground (in cement, not sand) allows for future success. Pursuing shortcuts to quick successes may be tempting, but most of us recognize that these methods produce short-lived successes that can jeopardize the future

of a program. We build a solid foundation through strict adherence to a well-thought-out set of principles that represent a value system we strongly believe in.

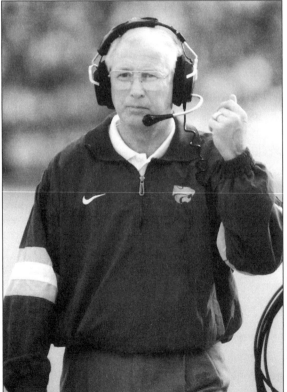

Building the foundation begins with the basic principle of surrounding yourself with great people. I have been fortunate in my lifetime to be associated with many outstanding people. We ask our players to associate themselves with people who want to help make their lives better. Convincing young student-athletes how valuable this basic principle is in their development as a person and an athlete is as important as anything we do in a leadership role. Learning to seek out such people is a key factor not only for players but for all those connected with the program. Important, too, is understanding that learning from others is an ongoing process. A level of expectation exists with every program in the country. The leadership of our program places great demands and expectations on everyone within the scope of the program. We attempt to raise the level of self-expectations and to prevent players and others in the program from placing limitations on their ability to achieve success. We see it as a compliment that we believe they can do more.

Only by expecting more of myself can I ask others to expect more of themselves. Just as we ask a quarterback to anticipate receivers coming open, we attempt to anticipate problems. Trust that they will frequently occur. Expect them but don't be discouraged by them. Address them with the knowledge that you can solve every problem, no matter how complex.

We regularly address the values of responsibility and accountability, as I am certain most programs do. Everyone in a successful program must be accountable for both success and failure (winning and losing). Everyone wants to accept responsibility for a program's success, but few are willing to accept the same degree of responsibility for failure. We hold everyone—players, coaches, support staff—accountable for their responsibilities. Players are responsible for their behavior, academic success, health, and effort, and coaches are responsible for their players. This approach has been important to us and to our players. Because most programs now have many support-staff members, the responsibility for the different areas of a young man's life is decentralized. When communication breaks down, problems can easily develop. Although we have all the support staff we need to help young people in each area of life, the ultimate responsibility lies with the coaching staff. Players and coaches must understand that.

Accountability should encompass demonstrating responsibility, expecting and demanding that people successfully complete tasks on time, and providing consequences when people fail to meet goals. We encourage each member of our program to seek additional responsibilities. Those who do are normally the ones who move forward, having put themselves in position to have greater success.

Obviously, mutual commitment is essential to continued success. We maintain constant dialogue with coaches, staff, and players to promote commitment. Involvement is an important element of our program. We work diligently to get as many people as possible actively involved in our program. Those who are with you won't be against you. Building support takes time and effort, and many overlook it. We are actively involved with community and university projects that allow us to work with and for community members, faculty, students, and administration. We periodically send newsletters to faculty, community leaders, and parents describing all aspects of our program, the academic achievements of our players, and the players' involvement with community programs to assist local youth and the elderly. Our coaches are also responsible for calling the parents of each of their players each month to share information about our program and the progress of their sons.

We have mentioned priorities several times. Maintaining success often centers on staying up with basic but changing priorities within the program (or any other facet of life). Our approach is to understand and promote what is important within the program. If a priority is important, make it so. If not, don't waste time with it. We believe that you can excel at what you emphasize.

Another principle in which we place faith is caring for players without losing sight of the tremendous role that discipline plays in their lives. Players must know that you care about them, that your compassion for them and their present and future well-being on and off the field is not just lip service but a genuine desire to be meaningful in their personal development. This commitment falls on deaf ears if coaches do not hold players accountable.

Young coaches often want to become best friends with the players they coach, divorcing themselves from maintaining the discipline needed to promote doing things right for fear of losing acceptance from the players. I believe football student-athletes benefit from knowing that even though coaches place great demands on them, they will not be asked to do anything not in their best interests. They must know that although we are demanding, we care about them not just as football athletes but as people and students.

We ask our coaching staff to schedule weekly conferences with each of their players and to open up those meetings to areas of the player's life outside football. I meet twice a year with each player in the program to discuss his academic progress, chosen career field, family, and any other aspect of his personal life he wishes to discuss. Listening becomes a valuable ingredient in showing young men that you care. Provide them time to understand that they are important to you. Your interest in their nonfootball lives helps them understand that they are more than just a football tool to you.

Making Good Decisions

We have helped our players feel some ownership of the program by allowing them to make decisions about important issues within the program. We operate under the premise that the program is theirs and that they have the responsibility to make decisions that will allow them to be proud of the program. We then expect them to be accountable for their actions as those actions relate to their decisions. This approach has helped our players believe that the team is truly theirs and to accept more responsibility for it. It is important to convey to young people that discipline is not personal, that they should focus on the lesson to be learned, not the tone. We have made the players here aware of the purpose of discipline. As a result, they are capable of sorting through the issues they confront without feeling as though the criticism is directed at them personally.

Recognize that decision making is a process. When making a decision that relates to the Kansas State University football program, we always ask a simple question: if we chose to do this, would it help our program become better? If the answer is no, we won't do it. We promote the same process within the program. We have been fortunate that the young people in this program have made few poor personal and behavioral decisions. As we all know, when any member of a program makes a poor decision, the result may prove detrimental to all. Inappropriate behavior normally receives national exposure and interrupts a team's focus on the task at hand.

In an attempt to promote appropriate decision making, we encourage each young man in our program to follow a process, one I learned from Hayden Fry. When a player must make a decision, we ask him to take 10 seconds to step back and ask a simple question (again based on his priorities): if I chose to do this, would it help me with my faith, my family, or my goal to become a better person, better student, or better football athlete? If the answer is yes, we suggest that the player do it with all the enthusiasm he has. If the answer is no, then the players should ask why in the world he would want to do it. This simple process can guide a player toward making the correct decisions. My point is that most people, let alone young people, do not have a method by which they make business or personal decisions. If you can provide them with the experience of using a process, they will eventually realize its value.

Stress the Fundamentals

If you believe in building a solid foundation brick by brick, then you probably believe in fundamentals and repetition. We do. The fundamentals of athletic ability and the game of football are vital ingredients of success. We have never strayed from that concept. As we have become a better program and a more polished team, we continually remind ourselves to go back to basics. Don't stray from what has allowed you to improve, the fundamentals and techniques of execution and teaching. Players in our program know that a good portion of their practice time will be devoted to learning the techniques of their position, and coaches know that we will spend a great deal of time addressing the fundamentals of teaching and motivating young people.

Acquiring and properly executing skills requires repetition. Learning requires repetition. Have a plan, continue to repeat it, and you will improve as a player, a coach, and a program.

This discussion leads to the skill of organization. The time demands of coaching and playing this game are so immense that it is virtually impossible to succeed without detailed planning, precise organization, and attention to all aspects of the program. Well-organized programs and people breed confidence. Disorganization breeds confusion.

The players and coaches in our program have normally appreciated the organization and its attention to detail even though it places additional burdens on them at times. Program members should know exactly what to expect, when to expect it, and exactly what they are responsible for.

Demonstrating and Teaching Leadership

Developing leadership from within is inherent to our profession. A major contributing factor lies in the desire and willingness of players and coaches in the program to provide positive and effective leadership, guidance, and direction. We have spent an inordinate amount of time discussing player leadership. Many think that leadership is a gift. We believe that players can and must develop leadership. Our answer to the need for leadership is not merely to appoint leaders and let them do their thing, but to cultivate and teach the principles of leadership to those who possess the values that are essential to becoming successful people. We discuss these principles on a daily basis, identifying prospects and methods of teaching leadership. Assigning leadership projects for players and coaches has been instrumental in the development of quality leaders. Often a young man wants to lead but doesn't know how and has no experience to draw from. We determine where there is a need and how a potential leader might address the issue to provide the desired result. We then assign the player to the task and provide him with appropriate direction so that he can gain the experience of leading. This is the first step in cultivating and developing quality leadership. Our process has been instrumental in developing leaders who are successful not only in our program but also in other areas of life. Our method has also helped us cultivate younger players for future leadership roles in the program.

In our haste to complete our daily tasks, we often overlook tremendous opportunities to guide and direct young people. A valuable principle for us has always been to seek out, identify, and accept the opportunity to do just that. The opportunity to counsel young people is always available, but the window of opportunity for each individual is often narrow. When we identify it, we must seize it. Counseling need not always be a response to problems. Of course, we confront problem issues, but we also face pure issues on a regular basis. We talk on a basic, goal-oriented level. How do we get from where we are to where we want to be? Again, this process shows the young man that you have an investment in his life, which in turn brings him to a greater investment in you and the program.

Setbacks or momentary failures always happen as we strive to succeed. In this highly competitive sport with its monumental expectations, many feel the need to find fault and attach blame for setbacks or failures. You can improve the continuity and unity of your program if you are able to deflect that criticism from your players and coaches to yourself. Egos sometimes prevent programs from maintaining success. As a program succeeds, more people want more credit. A selfless program, although ideal, is extremely hard to come by. I believe that it is in your best interest as a head coach to shoulder the blame publicly when something goes wrong and to pass on the credit for success to players, coaches, and staff members. Humility goes a long way in defusing problems that petty jealousy and oversized egos can create.

Be where you are. As a young coach in the initial years of my career, I was what I would call half in and half out—partially committed to the program I was in and partially committed to moving up the ladder. The problem was that I wasn't doing justice to the program I was in. I soon realized that all would be better served if I tried being where I was, providing a 100-percent commitment to the program I was in and letting the chips fall where they may. All of us have had the desire to succeed at the highest possible level, to advance from assistant coach to coordinator to head coach, from high school to college to pro. Whatever your ambition, you will have a better chance of attaining it by making a full-time commitment to where you are. You will be more successful there, which will eventually enhance your opportunities. They will seek you. The program you are in will become more successful because of your commitment. Commitment, loyalty, or whatever you call it creates the stability and continuity within a program that promotes lasting success even during difficult times.

We have always placed tremendous emphasis on not taking anything for granted, not the smallest of items. Focusing on details is not an easy task. It requires constant daily attention. It is easy to allow things to slide, to not give enough attention to detail, to take for granted that someone will complete a task and that everything will work out because it always has. Nothing erodes a program more than complacency, taking an issue for granted, and not completing assignments on time. Players and coaches alike can fall into that mode. To us, a poor practice is a poor practice, and if we allow it to happen, we will only promote more poor practices. Not preparing thoroughly for what you must teach your players because you have done it so many times before will eventually affect their performance. Many items require attention each day, so unless you provide constant supervision with a true sense of urgency, you and your program will fall further and further behind the curve.

In closing, let me remind you that Kansas State is unique. What has been the right direction for us may not be correct for others. But we believe that the values and principles expressed in this chapter apply to virtually every organization, athletic or otherwise. These principles and values are matters that we completely control. Most significant has been the desire of each of our players and coaches to believe in and trust the system. It has worked for them. In 1989 *Sports Illustrated* printed an article titled "Futility U," describing the state of our program. Five years later, the same writer revisited Kansas State and wrote a follow-up article claiming that we had made "the greatest turnaround in college football history." I appreciate that some people believe that. But more important, I appreciate the players, coaches, support staff, fans, faculty, and administration who believe and trust in the values and principles of this program. They have given us the opportunity to maintain a degree of success in which they can all take pride.

Building and Sustaining a Divisional College Program

Larry Kehres

Building and maintaining a successful divisional college football program can be explained systematically as a five-phase process. Phase one is the identification of the purpose, mission, and goals, which guide all intercollegiate football programs. Phase two involves the selection and retention of quality individuals to compose all aspects of the program, that is, the football family. The third phase is the use of human-relation skills, particularly communication and motivation, which are critical to team building. Phase four is the development of a teaching-learning style for the staff that will help the team execute a system of football in a highly efficient manner. The fifth phase is the ability to hone problem-solving and problem-prevention skills to battle the tendency to self-destruct. This five-part process is not sequential; it is imperative to manage these five processes simultaneously. You could view the phases as spokes of a wheel. Each spoke equally maintains the strength of the wheel.

Identifying the Mission

The purpose, mission, and goals that guide intercollegiate football serve to point a direction for us all. They chart a course and create boundaries. They provide the skeleton, the frame on which we build. Your vision of the completed program allows for your unique beliefs, values, and style to complete the work, thus creating a football program that is right for your players, your institution, and you. Your program shares a foundation with all others, but it may be like no other because of the finish you apply to the completed form.

We can easily find sources of purpose and mission. Our national organization defines the purpose of intercollegiate athletics. The National Collegiate Athletic Association (NCAA) states that "competitive athletics programs of member institutions are designed to be a vital part of the educational system" and that "the athlete is an integral part of the student body." These statements clearly portray the football player as a student-athlete whose educational experience is our primary concern. The nonscholarship regulations of Division III football serve to keep this basic purpose in our minds. The principles of student-athlete welfare, outlined in the NCAA Division III manual, are another source of direction. Specifically, principle 2.2.4 tells us that each member institution has the responsibility to establish and maintain an environment that fosters a positive relationship between the student-athlete and coach. Principle 2.2.5 states that each member institution has the responsibility to ensure that coaches and administrators exhibit fairness, openness, and honesty in their relationships with student-athletes. Remember that individuals with wisdom, experience, and a love of intercollegiate athletics have written these principles for our use.

Another source of direction is the American Football Coaches Association (AFCA). AFCA has provided a Code of Ethics for football coaches. Article one details the coach's mission in terms of his responsibilities to players. Article two explains responsibilities to the institution, and article three discusses the coach's responsibility to the rules of the game. Coaches at any level can find direction and purpose in the fundamental guidance provided by the Code of Ethics. The code can provide an answer to virtually any question and clarify cloudy issues. No better reference exists. If a coach must make a major decision and he is uncertain of the possible ramifications of the decision, the Code of Ethics is there. Use it! Share its wisdom and guidance with young men entering the profession. The great coaches who have served AFCA as members of the ethics committee have performed an invaluable service by writing this code. We honor their dedication to our profession by following the precepts they have given us.

Our institutions help chart our goals by defining an institutional mission. As football coaches, we must study this mission and use our football program as an educational tool that contributes to the fulfillment of the institution's mission. My institution has a mission in part to "prepare students for meaningful work, fulfilling lives, and responsible citizenship." A player committed to improving his team by improving himself is learning a lesson in the significance of meaningful work. Men who bond into lifelong friends by experiencing the thrill of complete dedication to a goal are certainly preparing for fulfillment in their postcollegiate relationships. As family and community members, these men will prove worthy of trust and commitment. Responsibility for self and to teammates is excellent preparation for responsible citizenship in the larger community. Can the great game of football contribute to the educational experience of students? You had better believe it, because it is an enormous part of your job!

Conference affiliations are a source of great rivalries in our game, rivalries that often evoke strong emotions. From this passion to succeed against long-time worthy opponents comes the source of inspiration for many coaches. These annually renewed conference games provide a wonderful opportunity for teachable moments. The lesson for players is that healthy respect for an opponent is far more valuable than disdain and contempt. The concept of respect is inherent in the principles of sportsmanship. Teach your players to respect their opponents; learned well, this lesson actually increases your chances of success.

Student-athletes can help identify goals. Listen to them. Give players the opportunity to articulate their individual goals. Allow players to meet as a group to discuss team goals. A player in a group discussion instigated the first mention of a national championship during my coaching career. The player asked why the coaches had never mentioned the subject. The obvious answer was that the coaches were fearful of stating such a bold goal. Once the topic was on the table, several players quickly joined in and supported the teammate who first broached the subject. Listen carefully to your players. They are good men.

Finally, each head coach must stamp his identity and his vision of purpose and mission into his football program. He must personalize the program, make it his, in a manner of speaking. In doing so, a coach must seek to find the fine line between intimidating the team with unrealistic expectations and setting his sights short of where his men can go. Good luck!

Building the Football Family

The second concept in building and maintaining a successful divisional football program lies in the selection and retention of quality personnel—players, coaches, and support staff. Think carefully about the type of players that you want to bring into your program. Nothing you do will be more important to your success than recruiting players. Sure, in Division III we do not have athletic scholarships to offer. What real difference does this make? More players play Division III football than Division I football. Young men want to play football, and we recruit them to do just that.

The admissions director of our institution identifies the academic requirements for admission. Recognize that the collective administrative hierarchy of the institution establishes these standards. Respect the decisions of the admissions director and support the efforts of this individual to achieve the goals of the admissions department. It is shortsighted to think that a particular athlete, if admitted, can turn your program around. If an athlete is rejected for admission, find another. Whining and complaining to others about the selectivity of the admissions director will not help your program contribute to the mission of your institution. Complaining can make you look like you are not concerned with the academic integrity of the institution. Avoid this trap!

Aside from academic requirements, what will you look for in a candidate for your football program? Let me suggest three traits: look for good men, men with a passion for football, and men who are determined to achieve their academic potential. Young men know what we mean when we tell them we are looking for good men. They stare back with understanding in their eyes. *Good* is a simple word to understand. Passion for

football is more difficult to express to a prospect. Passion for football is all about feelings and emotions—strong feelings and emotions. A young man who possesses this passion knows that he has what I want. He senses he has the feelings I am trying to verbalize. He often nods in agreement as I speak. I want this man! Ask a young man if he plans to achieve his academic potential. Ask him what his academic potential is. Explore with him the possibility that his potential may lie beyond his current vision. Explain that the process of higher education is designed to widen horizons, to arouse curiosity, and that limits may expand far beyond what we can imagine. Challenge him! Convince young men that you can help them. Of course, you must be able to deliver

Courtesy of Mount Union College

on this promise. Tell a prospect how he can help the football program. Clarify for the prospect that your program offers a win-win situation.

Look for assistant coaches who are experienced, intelligent, creative, tireless, unselfish, sharing, caring, daring, and who will work cheap. Seriously, in Division III football a good emphasis for forming a staff involves the concept of balance. Balance offense and defense, youth and experience, conservatism and risk taking. In short, create diversity within your staff. Division III staffs are usually a mix of a few full-time coaches, teachers with high school coaching experience, and young men entering the profession as part-timers. You have the opportunity as head coach to establish a sense of purpose and oneness from an assembly of individuals. Achieving this is both a tremendous challenge and a good opportunity to practice for the challenge of uniting your players into a unit, a team. Communicate with and motivate your staff. Lead and serve them. Think of your years as an assistant coach and do the things that you wanted the head coach to do for you. Make your staff happy!

What inspires you? Do you have a source of inspiration in your life? If not, look for one. Find a way to lift your spirits. Seek a source of refreshment and energy. Reading, listening to tapes, spending quiet and introspective time alone, or attending meetings might serve you well. A successful coach told me that he found meaning and inspiration in listening to tapes in his car during recruiting trips. Rather than listening to the radio, he listened to messages regarding the power of positive thinking. Players can be a great source of inspiration to me. I look at the work they will do to have a chance to be successful football players, and I marvel. They truly inspire me. To inspire others, you must experience the joy that inspiration can bring you. Seek it.

Developing Relationships

The third idea in building a successful college divisional football program is the development of human-relation skills. Know your place in the administrative hierarchy of the athletic program and know how the athletic program fits within the administrative framework of the institution. Be knowledgeable about the goals and purposes of the constituency of the institution. Seek respect from the faculty and administration by directing your football program in a manner that helps to accomplish the mission of your institution.

Relate to the total football family by both leading and serving. Lead your staff and players by example. Serve them with humility and grace. Be specific in your expectations so that your staff and players can evaluate their performance precisely. Allow each staff member to handle significant responsibilities so that each can feel the sense of accomplishment that so strongly motivates people to do their best.

Serve the staff. Provide each member with a clear understanding of his relationship to you and other staff. Help each with professional development. Provide ideas to help with growth and professional advancement. Share in the joy felt by a member of your staff who takes a job in Division I football. Make a habit of doing little things to show each staff member how much you appreciate his efforts. Complimentary notes, thank-you cards, a soda, a walk, a pat on the back—these small gestures can be effective forms of recognition. And lobby for your deserving staff members at contract time. Financial rewards are a great form of recognition!

Bring the family members of your staff together. Include families of the support staff. Share the social dimension of life through cookouts, picnics, dinners, and golf outings. Allow for interactions as often as time permits. Get together after games at the home of one of the coaches. Relax and enjoy each other's company. Make trips to games an enjoyable experience for each coach's family. Division III teams make few lengthy trips, but even one-night stays can be enjoyable. Players enjoy relating to the children of the staff. Older coaches often are like grandparents to the children of the younger staff members. Allowing your football family to interact on a trip will not diminish the focus of the team. In fact, the interaction may relieve the tension and anxiety that hinder performance. Build the concept of family. Don't be a party pooper!

Share your team with others. Allow the cheerleaders to attend important social functions, such as banquets held before playoff games. Have student trainers and student equipment managers attend team sessions when you discuss nonfootball topics. Distribute praise to everyone involved in the successful completion of a game or a trip. Share the team and the good times with those around the periphery of the program, and they will be there to support you and the players during the hard times. Study the principles of effective communication. Learn to be a focused listener.

Allow your players the opportunity to speak to you. Of course, chosen representatives often speak for the team. But you must hear each individual if you are to have complete communication with your team. Perhaps you can best hear what players have to say by giving them a chance to write their thoughts and goals. Constantly strive to encourage players to express their thoughts. Open-door policies work only if players enter. Go find your players and talk on their turf.

Study the science of behavioral psychology. Study it again. Understand the principles of motivation. Your task is to develop and control the behavior of players. The behavior of your players in football, academics, and social life will determine your success as a coach. Do not depend on your personal experiences to provide you with the knowledge necessary to develop and control behavior. Rely on science and empirical evidence. Search for proven and effective methods of teaching and motivating. Know what strategies and techniques will work to help your players succeed athletically, academically, and socially. Do not underestimate the power of praise and recognition. Your players want to get on the playing field! How hard will a good man who is passionate about football work to have the opportunity for a few plays in a game? Find the answer to that question. Although we do not have athletic scholarships in Division III, the principles of motivation do not change.

Teaching the System

Phase four in building and maintaining a successful divisional college football program is the development of a teaching-learning philosophy or style that will enable your players to execute a system of football in an efficient manner. Your philosophy and beliefs about learning are vitally important. Can you accept the premise that if players are not learning, then coaches must not be coaching effectively? Your staff must be students of learning and measure their ability as teachers by the performance of the players. If the progress of players is too slow, look for different teaching strategies. A tremendous sense of accomplishment results from working hard to find a teaching strategy that proves effective in a problematic situation. The point is that we often barely scratch the surface of proven learning theory.

Create a positive environment for your team. Without an athletic scholarship, student-athletes may question themselves about committing so much time to football. Academic demands can be tiresome. We must give continual reinforcement for appropriate effort by our players. Encourage your assistant coaches to have a ratio of four positive interactions with players for every corrective or negative interaction. Develop and maintain an atmosphere that fosters learning. Prepare your team to expect to succeed. They will start to contribute to the upbeat environment by encouraging one another.

Coaches must be flexible in their approach to players. Determine each man's hot buttons. Reach out to each player. Avoid the frustration that comes with using labels. Let your staff know that you do not like to hear phrases like "he's too lazy," "he can't learn," or "he's too slow." Find a way to teach each player. Do not accept the notion that a player cannot improve. Do not allow a talented athlete to languish on the bench because "he can't learn." Explore the research of behavioral science. Find a way!

Other chapters in this book cover offensive and defensive systems of football. I encourage you to identify and refine your system by using all the creativity and imagination you can muster. Think and draw. Draw and think. Use your own ideas. Trust yourself. Remember your days on the playground when you drew your own plays in the dirt. Football is a game that rewards creative thinking. The college game features a tremendous variety of successful offensive and defensive schemes. Be an innovator!

Solving and Preventing Problems

Phase five is the ability to hone problem-solving and problem-prevention skills. You must establish a framework for order and organization. All members of the football family need assistance from the head coach in making critical decisions about behavior.

Many outstanding coaches have recommended a priority system of God and faith first, family and academics second, and football third. That prescription works for us. Suppose a player has a family member who selects a fall football Saturday for a wedding. What should the player do, attend the wedding or his game? If family matters are a higher priority than football, then the player should attend the wedding. This exact situation has occurred several times, and we have encouraged players to attend the wedding. By establishing a precedent, future decisions of this type become free of anguish and consternation. Give examples to your players of how they must establish priorities in their lives. Teach them to be appropriately dedicated to their teammates.

Academic demands on student-athletes can be a source of problems for players and coaches. At times, players must be late for practice because of classes and labs. Meetings with professors often occur in the afternoon when the professor has time to spend quality minutes with the student. Do not allow these academic requirements to create tension and anxiety in your players. Work with your players to see that they have a fair schedule for their major. Help them plan for efficient study opportunities. Review with them the techniques for effective listening and note-taking in class. Insist on promptness for all football-related activities so that players will form the habit of promptness. Do all the simple things in your power to assist the academic development of your players. Remember to refer student-athletes to the specialists on your campus. Being football coaches does not make us experts in all areas. Use the resources of your institution to the benefit of your players. Remember the basic purpose and mission of the institution and help to achieve that mission.

Discuss problems that former players are dealing with. Tell of both successful outcomes and failures. Ask the men to identify problems they see their classmates experiencing. Often they will tell you of problems they are experiencing themselves. Listen carefully for hints about problems so that you can work for solutions before things get out of hand.

The abuse of alcohol is a problem that just won't go away. What will you do about this issue? How will you deal with this question when establishing team policies? Start by examining your own lifestyle. What decision have you made regarding this issue for yourself and your family? Your beliefs and values will help shape the position you take. Help your institution enforce institutional policy, and then look in the mirror as you plan your approach with your players. There are no easy answers. Seek help from above.

Allow your players to make choices. They must practice at decision making before they become effective decision makers. Give your men this opportunity. Of course, the coach must lead on some critical issues, but we have many opportunities to allow our players to make decisions for themselves. Guide the decision-making process but give your men the satisfaction of participating in the process. Consensus can prevent problems.

Identify team rules clearly and enforce consequences of rule-breaking behavior immediately. Be fair and consistent. Do not create problems in handling rules enforcement. The enforcement of penalties for rules violations must serve to deter future rules violations.

How much will you change during your career as a head coach? How much change has occurred from your high school and college playing days until now? Work to view the athletic and educational experience of your players from their perspective. Analyze the effect societal differences might have on the views of an 18-year-old today as contrasted with an 18-year-old 25 years ago. Learn to be sensitive to different values. Refrain from the notion that being disciplined has narrow definitional boundaries. Prevent problems through understanding, tolerance, and compromise. Recognize that you are not always right.

Summary

Success can be as difficult to explain as failure. It is dangerous to think you know the answers. Coaching football is a dynamic whirlwind because the problems we face change constantly. Stand steady in this ever-changing complex by establishing a foundation on which you will build your career. Remember the song about the wise man who built his house on the rock. Identify the values, ethics, and principles that will guide you. Write them down and share them with your staff and players. Identify yourself and stand tall.

Be consistent in your daily approach to your staff and players. Let them know what you expect from them. An edgy, jumpy, anxiety-ridden, fearful group of players and coaches will struggle. Perfection is out of reach, and all of us lose our temper. Recognize that your weaknesses make you human. Apologize if you have acted foolishly. Your staff and players will respect you for your honesty.

Accept what you cannot change. Our institutions of higher education are designed to stand the tests of time. Change often occurs slowly, following reflection, committee analysis, and much open dialogue. You may grow impatient when you believe institutional regulations and policies hinder the success of your team. Recognize that you have to be part of your institutional team if your institutional leaders are to hear you. You must earn respect before you can command attention to your thoughts and ideas regarding the need for change. Commit to your job long term if you want to be an institutional leader among the faculty and staff. If your goal is to move up to a better position quickly, then pick your first Division III position where the key elements for success are in place. In Division III football coaching, patience is a virtue. Learn from your failures. Study the reasons for your losses. This process has been of great benefit to me.

Following a national championship semifinal loss, a reporter once asked me, "How does it feel to gain 600 yards, not punt, and still lose?" I stared at the statistical summary of the contest in shock! My team had done precisely that! We had gained over 600 yards and never punted the ball away, yet we had lost the game and the opportunity to go to the Stagg Bowl. How could this have happened? I had no answer for the young reporter, so he pressed on and asked what I could do to prevent that circumstance from occurring in the future. I wanted to tell him to get lost! The defeat was not my fault! I had just witnessed a great performance by my team. The only problem was the darn scoreboard. I wanted to blame bad luck and even worse weather. But good luck and good weather were not the answer to preventing that type of thing from happening in the future. That loss caused more introspection and self-analysis than any other event in my career. My team was unable to score in the red zone because we had an incomplete red-zone offensive attack. My offensive coordinator, me, had done a poor job. That man, me, who I wanted to believe had done everything he could to give his team a chance to win, had messed up. I often wish some of my early teams could come back and play again so that I could coach them better. Learn from your failures so that you do not repeat them. That adage is undeniably true.

Look for the humor and joy present in each day with your players. They want to be able to like you, and they want you to like them. Winning can never take the place of friendship. We enjoy success only when we share it.

Building and Sustaining a Junior College Program

Dick Foster

I was a junior college head football coach for 16 years and won national championships at both Fort Scott Junior College and Coffeyville Community College in Kansas. Those two colleges and the situations surrounding my hiring at each were different, but I was able to be successful in both settings.

Although every job presents distinct challenges to a head coach, I believe that the following truths are the foundation on which a coach can build a successful junior college program anywhere in the country.

To be successful as a head coach, you must first be well organized and know how to use your time. Many coaches fail because they do not understand time management. I am convinced that you will be no more effective at any facet of your coaching job than you are at organizing and managing your time.

A special thank-you goes to Helen Rigdon, Jack McNickle, and Tony Jimenez for helping me prepare and present this chapter. I would like to thank the AFCA for allowing me to share with you what I learned as a head coach in junior college football.

Second, recruiting is the most important part of any college athletic program, and you cannot be truly successful unless you master the ins and outs of the recruiting process.

Third, in junior college football you do not have the luxury of slowly building a good program. You must field a decent team the first year or two, or you could find yourself out of a job.

Fourth, facilities are crucial to the recruiting process, and it is easier to prepare your team when you have good facilities. It took 25 years of work and planning to take Coffeyville Community College from owning no football facilities whatsoever to having the best junior college facilities in the country. But we were successful in the intervening time. Do not let the lack of first-class facilities discourage you. Be positive about what you have to work with!

Finally, a coach cannot drown himself in complaining about what he does not have. Early in my junior college coaching career, I learned that great lesson. A coach must be proud of and positive about the things he has. This positive philosophy influences the players as well as the rest of the coaching staff.

This chapter describes how I came to realize the truth of those statements and details the steps I took to build success in my years at the helm of top-notch junior college football teams. Rest assured, without full understanding and knowledge of these matters, you will find it difficult, if not impossible, to reach success at the junior college level.

Fort Scott

Before I became a head junior college coach, I spent two years as an assistant coach at Grain Valley High School in Missouri and 12 years as head coach at Platte City High School, also in Missouri. The last 6 of those years, I was also the high school principal.

I became head coach at Fort Scott Junior College in Kansas in late July of 1969 and was head coach for two football seasons. When I went to Fort Scott, the Greyhounds had just come off a great season. Charlie Cowdrey, the previous head coach, was a friend of mine from the days we had coached high school football teams against each other in northwest Missouri. Charlie was joining Dan Devine's staff at the University of Missouri and didn't resign his position at Fort Scott until July 1, 1969. Because he knew he was going to the University of Missouri, he had not recruited many freshmen, but he left a strong nucleus of sophomores.

When I finally got the job in late July, besides not having many freshmen, we had no coaching staff, no dorms for players to live in, and no meal service. I faced four major areas of concern:

1. Rerecruiting the sophomores to be sure that they were coming back

2. Finding assistant coaches

3. Finding housing for players to live in during the school year

4. Most important, recruiting freshmen players

I had three weeks to do all this.

Following a successful coaching staff is always tough. In his three years at Fort Scott, Coach Cowdrey had been highly successful. He helped me a good deal with the sophomore players, but I still had to sell myself to them. I learned early in my coaching career never to tell a player in the recruiting process something you cannot back up. You are better off listening to what a player has to say than making promises you cannot keep. First impressions are important, so you need to know as much about an individual as you can before you talk or visit with him.

In 1969 most two-year colleges in Kansas had only one or two assistant coaches. My biggest break was being able to convince Bob Shores, who had coached there before and was in student services at the college, to continue to help me. As a college counselor, Bob understood the personalities of the players and what it took to persuade them to play hard. He also understood the faculty and all the problems that we had to overcome to be successful. The college had hired a psychology instructor who came to the afternoon practices as an assistant coach, but because he taught a full load he was unable to attend the meetings and film study. During that time, coaches had to perform these duties themselves. I personally believe that it is important for a coach to teach classes at a junior college but not a full load. Football players often see their coaches in a different light as instructors, and this is important. Being on the faculty also helps the coaches get to know other faculty members and become comfortable in working with them. Coaches on my staff had to be good instructors and accept the responsibilities. I strongly believe that coaching is teaching. If an assistant coach cannot teach well, then he cannot coach well.

Finding housing for players was the toughest part of my job. I had no experience with that undertaking. The people of Fort Scott did not consider football players to be good tenants. In the Kansas Junior College Conference at the time, each school had a squad of 40 players, and only 10 could be from out of state. Scholarships were for tuition and books only. Students had to pay for their own room or apartment and meals. Players paid their expenses through government work-study programs, student loans, and part-time jobs. I spent much of my time calling on people to help find homes for these players. Some of the sophomores helped me find places.

As I look back on my career, I feel that recruiting was my strongest area. I was able to find the right players for our program. At every level, the people who have the greatest success are those who recruit student-athletes who can be successful in the program. I have seen too many coaches recruit players who cannot be successful in their programs. The better the quality of your players, the better you will be as a coach.

I had my most successful year of recruiting during the only year I recruited at Fort Scott. I did all the recruiting, and not one prospective recruit visited the Fort Scott campus. At that time Fort Scott Junior College only had two buildings, no residence halls, no athletic facilities, and little tradition. But with only eight returning sophomores in my second year as head coach, we were 10-0 and won the 1970 national junior college championship. I would not want to go through that type of situation again. I was fortunate that Fort Scott High had turned out some excellent players. Twelve of the 40 players on our final roster were from southeast Kansas.

Boosters are important in developing your program. Jim Hammer was a strong University of Missouri alumnus who helped me with the players that Missouri placed in the program. He was well thought of in the community and helped persuade community boosters to donate money for scholarships. He also introduced me to Charlie Grover, a University of Kansas alumnus. I was thus able to bring in some players that Pepper Rodgers, head coach at the University of Kansas, would place at Fort Scott. In every community, a coach needs to find people like Jim and Charlie who can help with booster clubs and fund-raising, two important parts of any junior college program. People outside the college are as important as assistant coaches are.

After my staff and I had completed those four areas in only three weeks, the players arrived, and we set to the task of coaching, molding, and developing these young men into a team. We won our first 2 games, lost the next 2, and then went on to win 17 straight games over the remainder of that season and the next. In my first year at Fort Scott, I did nothing about meetings, offense, defense, and special teams. We did not have time for specialized areas. Coach Shores coached the defense the way he wanted, and I coached the offense. I am sorry to say we did not spend much time on special teams.

Because of time constraints, I did not spend much time raising money for scholarships or working with our booster club. I was fortunate to have good help from my community coaches. Doing a good job in the classroom, and organizing and coaching the team took up all my time. Like many coaches, I spent more than a few nights sleeping in my office for a couple of hours.

After my second season at Fort Scott, during which we went 10-0 and won the national championship by defeating Mesa, Arizona, in the Shrine Bowl, I left to work on Don Fambrough's staff as a freshman coach at the University of Kansas. The next four years gave me the opportunity to work with some of the best coaches in college football. I also had a chance to reevaluate myself as a head coach to determine how I could do a better job.

Coffeyville Community College

In February 1975 I took the head-coaching job at Coffeyville Community College, also in Kansas. By this time, I was much better prepared to be a head coach at the junior college level. I had a different experience there than I did at Fort Scott, even though the two junior colleges are in the same conference and only 100 miles apart.

Coffeyville had great success after World War II and throughout the 1960s. But in the eight years before I arrived, they had won only 29 games while losing 48 under four different coaches. Attendance at home games had declined to less than 500 people per game.

I knew Dr. Russell Graham, the president at Coffeyville. He had spoken with me several times about how he would like to rebuild the program and return to the glory days of winning and playing before big crowds. I highlighted the areas that I knew would have to be addressed to put the program back on top.

To have a chance, the head coach must be in complete control of the entire football program, and he must have commitment and support from the administration, board of trustees, faculty, and community. He must be able to organize and be actively involved in many specific areas:

- Recruiting program (heart and soul of the program)
- Assistant coaches
- Support staff
- Facilities
- Scholarship money and ticket sales
- Publicity—newspapers, radio, and TV
- Game programs, press guides, newsletters to boosters and prospective players
- Plan to involve faculty and staff with football program
- Speaking opportunities with civic groups, churches, social clubs, and area high schools
- Local and county government
- Fellowship of Christian Athletes on campus
- Youth football program
- Football, weight, and speed camps
- Off-season and summer school
- High school football clinics
- Former lettermen's association, alumni support programs
- Booster club
- Study hall and tutoring program

The situation at Coffeyville in February of 1975 was completely different than the one I had experienced at Fort Scott. I had an entire spring and summer to build the program. I had time to do many of the things I did not have time to accomplish at Fort Scott. I also had experience this time—two years of coaching junior college football in the always tough Jayhawk Conference. I knew that the administration desired a good football program. They gave me full control of the program, an arrangement they had not offered to previous coaches.

Assistant coaches are vital to a football program. I was able to bring two coaches from the University of Kansas with me. Mike Sweatman had been a full-time coach at KU and became our defensive coordinator. Pat Henderson was a graduate assistant at KU and coached the secondary. I retained Charlie Hampton, who was on the former staff, as the offensive-line coach. I felt it was important to have a coach on staff who knew and understood the system. I also had Nolan Luhn, who had played five years for the Green Bay Packers, as our receiver coach.

We had some excellent players that first season, but the high quality and experience of the coaching staff allowed us to outcoach several opponents. If I made one contribution to junior college football in the state of Kansas, it was to bring in highly qualified coaches. The other colleges had one or two

Courtesy of Dick Foster

assistants whom the administration had hired to perform other duties first and coach second. After 1975 other colleges started developing their staffs to be equivalent to Coffeyville's.

I understood that assistant coaches were much like players. They were going to come to Coffeyville, learn while coaching, and then move on to better jobs. I had over 30 assistant coaches go through Coffeyville in the 14 years I was head coach.

When I started in 1975, all three of my assistant coaches taught 8 to 10 credit hours and were either head coaches or assistant coaches for other sports on campus. When I left, I had arranged it so that my assistants were still teaching half loads but had no coaching duties beyond football.

Today in the Jayhawk Conference, most teams have four or five full-time assistant coaches along with graduate assistants who live in the residence halls. Each year 40 to 50 players in the conference sign Division I scholarships. I believe that the quality of assistant coaches is what has allowed teams from the Jayhawk Conference to win so many national championships.

Support staff is always important to any successful program. When I started at Coffeyville, I had no support staff. The football staff handled its own correspondence and other office duties. We had no trainers or equipment managers. Over the years, I developed and implemented a system that included a full-time secretary, a trainer on staff, and an equipment manager.

I was fortunate to have had great support from members of the board of trustees at Coffeyville. Dr. Herb George and Maurice Weinberg were strong supporters of the athletic programs. They understood the value of strong athletic programs, especially football. Other supporters of football on the board included David Dennis and, most recently, Dickie Rolls. The college president is also important. Over the years, I have learned that a college president who wants a strong football program will do the things required to achieve a goal of being the best in the conference. Dr. Dan Kinney was one of the best junior college presidents that a football coach could wish for. A week never went by that Dr. Kinney did not call or stop by my office to ask what he could do to improve the program. Having the support of both the college president and board of trustees is an important part of building and sustaining a quality football program.

Facilities are crucial to the recruiting process. Having good facilities also makes it much easier to prepare your team. During my first two years at Coffeyville, we had no practice facilities. We were never on a marked field except on Saturday nights. We had no weight room. At that time the college did not own any athletic facility, so we used the high school and city facilities. Coffeyville now has the best football facilities of any junior college in the country, a result of 25 years of planning and hard work.

After we went 11-0 that first season, I visited with the president of the college to see what we could do about acquiring some facilities of our own.

President Graham said, "You have gone 11-0. Why do you need facilities?" At that point, however, we started forming a plan to develop the best facilities in the country.

Raising scholarship money and increasing ticket sales are two significant parts of the head-coaching duties in junior college football. I knew when I took over the head-coaching job at Coffeyville that these were major areas of concern. We needed to organize a new plan. I started by speaking to civic organizations, churches, social clubs, and area high schools about the importance they, the fans, would play in developing a winning program. I told anyone who would listen that if they did their part, we could again win the conference championship, go to bowl games, and play for the national championship. I realized that four other coaches in the past eight years had told them the same thing. Nevertheless, our campaign became the talk of the community. I believe that many people came to our first game to see if what I had been talking about all spring and summer was true.

In junior college ball you do not have the luxury of having several years to build a good program. Unless you have a decent team the first year or two, you can soon find yourself out of a job. I told the community we would fill our stadium for the first home game. The stadium held 5,000. I went to the two main grocery stores in town and asked them to give away tickets with each $10 purchase. Five thousand fans attended that first game. I knew that if we won, the fans would return and begin buying tickets for the home games. After that first big win, everyone jumped on the bandwagon. The secret to building attendance is promoting during the off-season and getting the community excited about football. Then when the season rolls around, the crowd is there to support their team. People ask me what would have happened if we had not won that first game and gone on to an 11-0 season. I tell them I did not worry about that—I knew we would win.

Recruiting

Recruiting is the most important part of every college program. Through my experience at Coffeyville, I identified four elements that are important in a sound recruiting program.

First, what resources are available for you to run the entire recruiting program? You must be sure that you spend every dollar wisely and gain a good return for the investment. Second, how many coaches can you have on the road? Do you plan to recruit by area or by position? We always had three assistant coaches on the road to recruit the major areas in Kansas. I personally took care of all the out-of-state recruiting. I would also take the top 10 to 15 players in Kansas and spend as much time as I could with the young men and their families. Third, on-campus visits are important. Finally, the overall organization of the year-round recruiting program is crucial to the total process. You must spend some time each day of the year on recruiting.

Steps for Recruiting Student-Athletes

1. Contact high school coaches a year in advance to make your prospect list.
2. Visit schools for film, academic assessment, and character evaluation during the spring.
3. Mail information to students starting in July, before their senior year.
4. Make telephone calls during the summer, fall, and during recruiting season in December and January.
5. Visit the high schools to set up campus visits. Write letters to high school coaches and parents.
6. Invite the student-athlete for an on-campus visit.
7. Visit the student-athlete's home.
8. Sign the student-athlete.
9. Arrange for publicity after signing the student-athlete.
10. Follow up with phone calls by the recruiting coach, position coach, and head coach until the player arrives at camp in the fall.

Out-of-State Recruiting

The out-of-state recruiting process was the backbone of each recruiting class. We had to do this over the telephone because we did not have the budget to go off campus or bring in prospects for campus visits.

The list of prospects comes from the college and university coaches you work with during the recruiting process. The process is a two-way street; you have players in your program that these coaches want to bring into their programs, and they help you with players who need to attend junior college.

During my 14 years at Coffeyville, we had a few players who were signed and placed in our program by major university programs. One was Mike Rozier, who had signed with the University of Nebraska. Mike was a great player for the Ravens. He transferred to Nebraska his sophomore year, was an all-American, and won the Heisman Trophy his senior year. We had over 30 young men who played in our program and went on to play in the NFL; few were placed at Coffeyville by major university programs. Over the years I became acquainted with many college and high school coaches across the country who would help me attract the right players into our program. These coaches knew that the players would build a solid foundation in academics, work out in a good off-season weight program, and receive discipline both on and off the field. All are important prerequisites for a young man to be successful on the next level.

You should also strive to place all your sophomores in programs where they can be successful. I personally spent much time in this endeavor. A student-athlete placed in the wrong school does nothing for the reputation of junior college head coach.

Student-Athlete On-Campus Visits

The on-campus visit is one of the most important parts of the recruiting process. In junior college you have to allow a student-athlete to visit your campus any time he can make the visit. We liked to have them come on weekends if they were making an overnight visit.

Local prospects came in for midweek visits, which gave them an opportunity to see what classes and campus were like during a normal school day. The staff worked extra hard to get the parents to attend the official visit with their sons so that they could see the emphasis we placed on academics. A typical recruiting visit began with a welcome to campus. The head coach met the prospects and established a rapport. We introduced the prospects to the staff and faculty. Then we distributed and discussed the itinerary with the prospects and their parents so that they knew what to expect. After all the prospects had arrived, we divided them into two groups. One group toured the football complex and went over the off-season weight and conditioning program with the strength and conditioning coach and other assistant coaches. The other group stayed with the head coach and viewed the highlight tape from the previous season. The two groups would then switch, and we would repeat the process. After this the prospects had academic advisement followed by special events and functions they attended with their student hosts. They then met with their respective position coaches.

The head coach discussed with the entire group how the academic process worked at the college. We held this meeting in the Learning Resource Center. Assistant coaches worked with the staff and faculty who were there, setting them up to work with small groups of prospects. Later we divided the large group into smaller groups of three or four student-athletes. The student-athletes met with the faculty who taught in their fields of study. The faculty explained the academic process and helped the student-athletes fill out a sample schedule of classes they might take. The fact that the college faculty members were there made the prospect and his parents aware of the caring that the college as a whole had for the success of its students.

The week after the visit, we sent a copy of the sample schedule to the parents who were unable to attend. We offered a four-semester schedule or a three-semester, two-summer schedule to meet the different graduation or transfer needs of the student-athletes. Following the academic meeting, representatives from Student Services met with the student-athletes and discussed residence halls, cafeteria, medical insurance, telephone, cable, student life, computer labs, and other areas of campus living. A coach or a host from the Admissions Office then led the student-athletes on a campus tour featuring visits to the Student Union, Arts and Sciences and Occupational Buildings, athletic facilities (game and practice), recreational areas, residence halls (if possible, prospects stayed in a residence hall during their visit), the cafeteria, computer labs, the student medical facility, TV-media area, and high-interest areas in the community such as the local medical center. If the prospect was highly sought after, we introduced community leaders and boosters to him. Giving a prospect the opportunity to see and visit with many current students of the college is always helpful, but be aware that a person may occasionally say something that will damage the chances of getting a certain prospect.

An important aspect of the on-campus visit is the correct selection of the student host, usually a player, for the prospect. The football staff did not always take the time to make an appropriate match between the host and the prospect. To help the student host with his duties, the coaching staff can prepare the host by organizing events for the host and prospect to do together, giving the host an information sheet on the prospect in advance, and being sure that the host follows up the visit with a telephone call and letter to his prospect.

Normally, we scheduled campus visits around special events on campus such as home basketball games, dances, concerts, drama productions, or intramural championships. If nothing was scheduled, the coaches tried to schedule a pick-up basketball game with some of the assistant coaches playing to keep it under control and to further develop relationships.

We discouraged off-campus activities, such as parties. Activities such as these can lose more good prospects than they gain. When the student-athletes are off campus during their visit, too many factors are beyond the coaches' control.

The position meeting is an essential part of the on-campus visit. The position coach will be the person coaching the prospect if he signs. The coach discusses techniques and strategies of the prospect's position. If possible, the position coach meets with the prospect's head coach and parents. Strong relationships must be forged during the recruiting process. The more position recruiting you do, the better your chance of signing the prospect.

Getting the Community Behind Your Program

Having the press and radio behind you can help promote your program. I was lucky because we had a good daily newspaper, the *Coffeyville Journal,* and a radio station, KGGF, that thoroughly supported the Red Raven football program. I could go to either medium at any time for support. The first two or three years the college did not have a WATS telephone line, so I went to the radio station about 8:00 each night to call prospects. The station ran promotions all the time. They hosted the coach's show and broadcast our games, home and away. Each Wednesday the newspaper ran a half page on our Players of the Week. On Friday they ran a pregame story, and on Sunday morning a half-page story appeared about the game that had been played the night before.

In the early 1980s the college had a TV station that hosted a playback about the previous week's game and the weekly coach's show during the season. We developed a preseason press guide and an excellent game program, which won some national awards over the years. We made some money for our scholarship program and did a great job of selling advertising in the program not only to the people of Coffeyville but to people all across the state of Kansas.

We sent a newsletter to boosters twice each month, and later I developed a newsletter to send to prospects. We put together a four-page informational newsletter, called the *Red Raven Preview,* which we sent each month to prospects for six months before national signing day. Once our Lettermen's Association was formed, we sent the *Red Raven Preview* to them as well.

We developed a program to make the faculty and staff a vital part of our football program. I spent much time visiting personally with each faculty member, asking for his or her help and support. Because all the coaches taught classes and because we required our players to attend class, act respectfully, and be the best students they could be, the faculty appreciated our efforts.

I made it a point for every assistant coach to develop a friendship with other faculty members on the staff. We asked many of these instructors to monitor the grades of student-athletes to see if any of them needed additional help after classes. After recruiting season ended, I hosted a big get-together at my home to show our appreciation to the staff and faculty of the college for everything they had done for the football program that past year.

Meeting with local and county government officials helped sell our program. I assured these officials that we were bringing quality student-athletes into the city. If any of the players got into trouble, the officials knew how to contact me and they knew that I would support them. In the early 1980s we became one of the first junior college programs to do drug testing. Making this decision was tough for me, but after studying it for about a year, we put the policy into effect. I was able to accomplish this task only because I had the county court system help me administer the policy. The local judges felt it was important and worthwhile for the players and community.

I also started a drug-education program for our student-athletes at the college and taught the class during the spring semester. I was involved on the state level, which enabled me to bring in speakers for the course. The program was so successful that the college officials requested that we open it up to the entire student body.

In the spring of 1976 we started a Fellowship of Christian Athletes (FCA) program on campus for all students. Once our program was up and running, we offered to help the local high school with their chapter. Because I lived in the Kansas City area for many years, the Kansas City Chiefs influenced me a great deal. Lamar Hunt, the Chiefs' owner, formed the Huddle Club, of which my children were members. I started a similar program with the Coffeyville Little League football program. Our players and coaching staff hosted a clinic early in the fall for the Little League players. We gave them T-shirts, which would get them into Ravens games, and the Little League teams played during halftime at one of the home games. This project was another factor in our attendance success because the parents would naturally attend games with their children.

We always built up a game that we thought might not draw a large crowd. We tried to have a special event at halftime of each home game to draw more people.

In my first year at Coffeyville I started a football camp, which was a great recruiting tool. Having high school players and their coaches spend a week in Coffeyville also gave the community a boost. In the 14 years we held the camp, over 2,000 young people visited our campus. Any time you can draw people to your campus, you benefit recruiting.

In May we always held a high school coaches clinic. The speakers at this program were four-year college coaches and top high school coaches. This was our way of saying thank you to the high school coaches we dealt with during the recruiting season. At one time we hosted these clinics in the Wichita, Kansas City, and Topeka areas, which were our major recruiting spots.

The Red Raven Booster Club was developed to raise money for scholarships and help support the football program. One of the main projects I started my first year at Coffeyville was our host family program. Mrs. B.J. Pendleton, an instructor, college cheer squad sponsor, and the top Red Raven supporter of all time, arranged to have a host family for players each weekend. Players would go out after church on Sundays, have dinner, and be back into a home and family situation for a while each week. This arrangement gave our players a weekly home-cooked meal, helped them deal with homesickness, and gave them an opportunity to meet people in the community. The players rotated so that everyone involved in the program met all the players. The players and the host families started friendships that will last a lifetime.

Ensuring Academic Success for Your Players

Of all the programs I developed at Coffeyville, the most successful was the study hall and tutoring program. Being a former high school principal, I had experience in organizing a quality study-hall program. When the NCAA put academic standards into effect, I met with our president and worked on developing a program to help the student-athletes prepare themselves to attend an NCAA school. We developed a model program that our entire college would later use.

I worked with Linda Ellison, an instructor in the developmental education department. We put together a study-hall and tutoring program that was as good as any in the country. Our coaching staff did the entire academic advisement for the players, and we held study hall three nights every week from 7:30 to 9:00 in the Learning Resource Center. A football coach always monitored study hall, and I personally monitored it on Monday and Wednesday nights.

Each Thursday night for the first 16 weeks of the fall semester, we taught a course in freshman orientation. Our first coaching staff developed a curriculum guide that offered information and advice that would help a freshman student-athlete adjust to being away from home and attending college. One coach was in charge of this program, and we brought in different speakers each week from the campus and community.

The study-hall program used football peer tutors to help with study groups and one-on-one sessions with the student-athletes. Ms. Ellison selected top sophomore football tutors based on their GPAs, attendance in class, and their compatibility with other players. Using peer tutoring not only helped our student-athletes become better students but also developed leadership in our football program. One important but often overlooked area is personally coaching your student-athletes. A coach must have the ability to communicate and connect with his players. He must spend a lot of time off the field talking to and coaching players one-on-one. Coaches must get to know each player as an individual, not just a football player. In turn, the player will come to know the coach as a person, not just as his coach. Spend as much time as possible off the field meeting with your players individually.

Off-Season Program and Summer School

The Ravens' year-round off-season program has played a vital role in sustaining our football program over the years. All the coaches took an active role in developing our players during the off-season. One of the assistant coaches became the head coach during the off-season program. I personally did not have the time during recruiting to oversee the weight conditioning. I did not hire assistant coaches unless they had a strong background and a burning desire to work in the weight room. The Ravens have a 9,600-square-foot weight room with all new equipment to develop the players further during the all-important off-season.

Summer school was always a key part of my success with the program. Most of our players attended classes in the morning and then worked out for three hours in the afternoon during June. This process helped the incoming freshman adjust to college life and learn our system in the classroom, in study hall, and in the weight room.

Mission Statement and Philosophy

Each year our coaching staff started our fall meeting by developing a mission statement and philosophy for the season. We worked on several areas:

1. Model sound character. We discussed in detail loyalty, work ethic, professionalism in all areas, integrity, and respect for staff, players, administration, faculty, secretaries, trainers, and managers.

2. Believe. We wanted to have a vision of what was possible, to believe in the total program, and to exhibit positive behavior and attitude. Out staff wanted to be confident, to show team unity (we before I), and demonstrate accountability to God, the college, the administration, the coaching staff, and the players.

3. Develop. Our coaches set goals to develop each player to his highest level and to grow professionally as a staff.

Anyone who might come into contact with our players—coaches, grad assistants, secretaries, trainers, managers, and filmers—honored this mission statement. We wanted everyone involved to understand our position on all issues that might come up during a season.

In late November, before we started bringing recruits on campus in December and January, the coaching staff met to discuss what we wanted to accomplish during the upcoming recruiting season. After spring or summer workouts, I had the players write down five team goals they wanted the team to accomplish in the upcoming season. Our staff compiled these goals and then met with the entire team to divulge them. Here are the goals my last Coffeyville football team established in 1988:

1. Win the conference championship.
2. Go to a postseason bowl game.
3. Win the national championship.
4. Demonstrate unity.
5. Have no off-field incidents.
6. Play one game at a time.
7. Be the most physically and mentally prepared team in the country.
8. Earn a team GPA of 2.75 or higher.
9. Get sophomores placed in good four-year programs.
10. Have fun and enjoy teammates.

In Retrospect

One final area of importance is the coaches' wives and families. I was fortunate that my wife Karen understood and excelled in her role of being a mother to our seven children and a counselor to the assistant coaches' wives and the players who came by our home. Coaches' wives must be special people to be able to deal with the ups and downs of a coach's career. What success I have achieved in this life goes back to my wife. I do wish I had taken more time to enjoy my seven children. One of my sons, Skip, played for me in 1979–80 and came back to Coffeyville to coach in 1985. In 1989 he took over the reins as the Ravens head coach when I went to the University of Oklahoma. In 1990 he led the Ravens to the national championship. At that point I went from being a Coffeyville legend to being Skip's dad, and that is how I wanted it. When I retired from OU, I moved back to Coffeyville and helped him coach for three years. For 26 years a Foster has coached the Coffeyville Community College Red Ravens.

Skip often says, "Instead of Dad and me going fishing or playing golf, we would kick back and talk about football." Now that I am retired, I can enjoy my grandchildren and all their activities.

After retiring from the University of Oklahoma in 1997, I moved back to Coffeyville and started the Lettermen's Association, made up of the former players at Coffeyville Community College. I had always wanted to pursue this project while I was a head coach, but I lacked the time. We started a hall of fame in 1998, and we have an annual banquet at homecoming and a golf day. We send out four newsletters each year. The organization now has 150 members. We try to get former players to return to campus throughout the year. A number of these lettermen donated to the campaign for the new locker room and training and weight facility that was built in 1999.

I was able to be successful for 16 years as a head coach because of my wife and family, the players, the assistant coaches, the faculty and administration, and the support staff of a secretary, trainers, managers, and filmers. But perhaps the most important contributors were the many fans who helped to build two of the finest programs in junior college football.

Building and Sustaining a High School Program

George Curry

I have been involved in football since I was four years old. I've spent 53 years of my life around the game as a manager, player, and coach. The one constant in all my years of coaching is my philosophy.

My philosophy of coaching centers around three factors—mental development, physical development, and career development. I believe that I can take a ninth-grade youngster and in four years make him physically and mentally stronger and direct him into a productive career.

Physical development is the first area of concern. I ask players to put in four times as many hours as our opponents do. As a result, they are four times stronger and four times more confident. A strong, well-conditioned athlete is a confident athlete. My players have always been the strongest in the league. They put up tremendous numbers in the weight room, and their physical prowess shows on the field. Developing a strong, well-conditioned athlete is something we work hard at and take pride in.

I also stress mental toughness on a daily basis from the time the athlete steps into the football program. I challenge, push, discipline, and motivate players to achieve more than they believe they are capable of achieving.

I like to create some anxiety every day in all our activities—practice, strength training, games, and so forth. You can prepare a youngster for stressful situations by creating pressure. I want our athletes to be able to look anxiety and pressure right in the eye and confidently conquer them. This attitude is a learned behavior. Coaches can't be soft and easy on their players. They must coach mental toughness. This mental toughness will carry a person through his entire life. We must get everything out of that athlete our way.

Career perspective is something I've always believed is more important than any championship. I tell my athletes, "Your brains will always take you further than your legs." Simply put, we demand academic commitment, personal accountability, and short- and long-term goal setting. We want our players always to know where they are going. We tell our players to use football as a means to an end, not as an end in itself. Our players must pass 24 credits to graduate from high school. They can't cut class; they can't take academics lightly. We put academics first!

We live in a competitive, often cruel, world. I believe that my hard-nosed philosophy prepares an athlete to deal with the difficulties of life. These three areas—mental development, physical development, and career development—will never change. Times may change, but what I feel is good for youngsters will always be the same. Work hard and good things will happen.

Foundation

No matter what you're building, you must start with a strong foundation. All successful Fortune 500 companies were built with a strong foundation. The same is true with all sports franchises that win consistently. During my first year at Berwick High School, I built a strong foundation. That was my chief goal as a young coach four decades ago.

To build a strong foundation, I had to come up with a great plan. I concentrated on four areas: attract players into the program, get the faculty involved and behind the program, gain the support of the community, and do whatever it takes to get parents behind the program. I knew it would take not only a lot of energy on my part but also my best marketing skills. I had to get everyone in the community excited. The previous two coaches did not have winning records. In the decade before my arrival at Berwick High School, the football team had only three winning seasons. I was the ninth coach in 25 years. I knew I had a tough job ahead of me, but I also knew the people wanted a winner. Berwick is, was, and always has been a football-crazy town. I tried to capitalize on the theme "Together we all can get it done."

Increasing the Numbers

I immediately set out to recruit every youngster in the school district. My goal was to get 90 players out for football my first year. Here is how I did it.

First, I went to each elementary school and personally spoke to every young male student in every building. I did my best to motivate these youngsters. I invited them to practices, games, and the weightlifting program. I let them know that although they were too young at the time, the BHS football program was theirs. I told each one that together we could put Berwick on the map. I encouraged them to carry on the tradition their grandfathers, fathers, uncles, and cousins had built. I challenged them to become involved and to keep producing winners.

I challenged each varsity player to get five junior high students involved in the junior high program. If 50 varsity players each persuaded at least two youngsters to come out for football, we would have 100 junior high players. I had everyone in town help boost our numbers. I had police officers, clergymen, businesspersons, alumni, coaches, and players talking to the young men in the towns of Berwick and Nescopeck.

The campaign worked. I had nearly 100 varsity players out for the team my first year. We also had approximately 110 junior high boys out for the junior high team that year. Another 200 youngsters in our community played youth (Pop Warner) football. All together, we had over 400 young men playing football in Berwick. Even if 50 or 60 dropped out, we had well over 300 youngsters ready and willing to give us the strong feeder system we needed to win consistently.

Courtesy of George Curry

I've always said, "You win with numbers." If you have a great number of youngsters coming up from the junior high program year in and year out, you have a strong foundation. You never rebuild; you reload. I've always said to each oncoming class, "It's now your turn to win."

Gaining Faculty Support

After recruiting the youngsters, my next goal was to get the faculty and administration behind the program. I assured them that we could win without jeopardizing academics. I reminded the school board, administration, and faculty that football took place after school and I would do my best to ensure that players were students first. I had formal and informal meetings with the faculty and administrators to present my philosophy on the student-athlete.

I also asked the teachers and administrators to let me know immediately if they had problems with any of my players. I would not tolerate cutting classes, tardiness, insubordination, or poor attitude in the classroom. If a player got in trouble in the classroom for any reason, he would be punished twice—once by the vice principal and once by me.

I believe that the faculty bought my philosophy. They came to the games, and I involved many of them as clock timers, chain-gang members, ticket sellers and collectors, stadium ushers, game filmers, and announcers. I even gave them Berwick football sweaters they could wear on game day. We began rebuilding faculty unity with the football program. I gave the faculty what they wanted, a strong academic commitment, and they gave me what I wanted, support. This relationship went a long way toward building a strong foundation.

Reaching Out to the Community

The third area I concentrated on was the business community and media. I figured the best way to get the community behind me was to become part of it. I had football motivation signs put in business windows. I sold stadium advertisements. I showed film of the previous game at a different business each week. Our announcer read ads over the public-address system during timeouts. We worked out a deal with businesses to sponsor the Player of the Game.

Another goal was to get the media behind the program. I did what I could to get my own radio and TV show. By doing this I was able to stroke the business community and gain their support. It's amazing how you can market your program when you have radio and TV as a means of communication. The more exposure you get, the more visible your football program becomes. Marketing football is like marketing a big movie.

The media can make or break a beginning coach. I needed the media to help me market my product—the sport of football. I had media day before the season. I invited all the newspapers (local and national), television stations (ABC, CBS, NBC, and FOX), radio stations, parents, family, friends, and fans. We offered player photos and player interviews. I had media packets that included all the information the media needed (position, stats, height, weight, speed, and so on). I included a small gift for each media member—a pen, hat, bumper sticker, or something similar. I worked hard to get the media behind our program.

Working effectively with the media is part of building a strong foundation. The best marketing plans will not go anywhere if you don't have the means to inform the public.

I'll never forget my first game as the head football coach at Berwick. We opened at home against West Scranton High School. I spent so much time publicizing our program in the off-season that people who hadn't been to a high school game in years showed up for this one. They wanted to see what the new coach was all about, to see if Curry could coach as well as he could promote. We packed the stadium with approximately 10,000 people, far above its seating capacity of 7,200. We won big—39-0. That was the beginning of the program. We caught fire, and we never looked back. The foundation was set!

Involving Parents

The last block in the strong foundation was to get the parents involved. Parents have a tremendous effect on their children. I felt I should meet them and talk about the role that parents should play in building champions. Show me a great player, and I'll show you a parent who let the coach work with the youngster. Parents must accept the coach's philosophy and support the coach at every step. Figure 12.1 is an example of a preseason letter I sent to each parent.

I tell the parents, "If you aren't with me, don't let your son play." I also go over the team rules with parents. I send a copy of these rules to each parent along with my preseason letter:

1. Drinking and smoking are not allowed. Violation will lead to demotion or suspension.

2. Use of drugs will cause immediate dismissal from the squad. No second chances. Players suspected of taking steroids may be asked to submit to a urine test. Failure to do so means you are dropped from the squad.

3. Curfew will be 10:00 P.M. on weeknights (including Sunday evenings). On game nights, players are under parents' curfew.

4. Long and unruly hair will be cut. We stress safety, and shorter hair means a better-fitting helmet. Furthermore, you're football players, not fashion plates. Also, no athlete is allowed to wear earrings. Aside from it being illegal in high school football in the state of Pennsylvania, when I played in the late 1950s and early 1960s, only girls wore earrings.

5. All pads must be worn on the field unless players are told otherwise. Helmet must be on while walking out to the field.

6. Players must report ready to go at least 10 minutes before practice begins.

7. No practice, no play. Any player missing practice must report to practice and watch if he can't physically participate. The only exception is a doctor's excuse or if a coach excuses you. If a player fails to call the field personally by 7:30 A.M., his equipment will be collected.

8. All injuries must be reported and taken care of by either the team physician or the trainer. It's up to the players to get healthy.

9. Jealousy and egomania are not tolerated on our squad. Again, it can lead to a demotion or suspension. United we stand, divided we fall.

10. Crying and bellyaching to Mommy and Daddy will not be tolerated. If a player has any questions, he should confront one of the coaching staff with the problem. Crying to Mommy and Daddy will not help you make the team. It will only get you demoted or fired. Don't be a baby; win your job by hard work and dedication, not crying.

11. Watch your comments concerning our team. Don't talk football strategy off the field. Some people carry information to other teams. All comments involving our squad should be in the best interest of the team. Also, don't assassinate the character of any of your teammates.

12. Publicity is only one man's opinion. Don't be swayed by newspaper articles. Also, don't play for publicity or glory. If any of our players gets publicity, feel as if you're part of it. Again, don't become jealous.

13. Fighting among teammates will not be tolerated. We must stick together if we're to become champions. Understand each other's differences and show respect for one another.

14. Talking back or sassing coaches will not be tolerated. It could lead to a demotion or firing. Be coachable. It shows that you're disciplined.

15. No football player is allowed to participate in other sports (wrestling, basketball, baseball) during the season. Each player must finish the season or he will be released to participate in the other sport (his letter will be forfeited). Show character. Be dedicated to your teammates, yourself, and your coaches. Finish what you start.

16. Keep up your grades. It's up to you to maintain your grades and remain eligible. Grow up and establish good educational priorities. Good grades and good football ability mean scholarships.

17. Stealing will definitely not be tolerated. All equipment must be handed in. Good teams don't steal. Stealing will lead to dismissal from the team!

18. Foul and obscene language will not be tolerated in the locker room, showers, bus, field, or anywhere else. We don't need filthy-mouthed athletes ruining the champion image.

19. Horseplay in the locker rooms, buses, or elsewhere will not be tolerated. You're here to play football, not be a clown.

20. All gridders are encouraged to attend church on Sundays (or whenever your religion dictates). Great athletes are strong in faith.

21. All players are responsible for keeping their lockers and the area around their lockers clean.

22. No awards (jackets, rings, etc.) will be presented to players who do not make two-thirds of the practices. Exception: a starter or potential letter winner who incurs an injury that ends his season.

23. If any player is declared ineligible because of absence (20 days or more in the previous semester), he will not be allowed to participate because he is ineligible for the first marking period.

24. Injured players, out for the year, will ride on bus two!

25. Lockers will be assigned to each athlete. Respect other people's property.

26. Any rules not mentioned here or later rules are a coaching prerogative. These may relate to locker supervision, attitude, bus travel, shirts and ties, and so on. Punishment for rule violations is at the discretion of the coaching staff: dismissal, game suspension, extra conditioning within reason, verbal chastisement. Winners do not abuse the rules!

I explain to players and parents that they can find my team rules in the Bible, although they may be worded differently. My rules are nothing more than a set of laws that helps a player discipline himself to be a better person. Parents have supported my team rules, because the rules made their job as parents easier. I assured parents that their sons would be better people coming out of our program. Good parents can help any coach in building a strong foundation.

My first years as a football coach were critical to ensuring long-term success. Once we laid the groundwork and built a strong foundation, Berwick became a state and national power that ranked with the elite.

Dear Parent,

Coaching is becoming tougher and tougher, so I'm sending this communication to all parents of my players. The purpose of this letter is two-fold. First, I would like to ask you for your support for the upcoming football season. Second, I'd like to explain to you a little about our program.

My coaching staff and I have spent many hours with your son since our last game. We constantly try to improve each player in the six areas necessary to make the starting team. Those areas are strength, quickness and speed, size, knowledge of our system, hitting ability and toughness, and attitude. We have had most of our players involved in the following activities: weightlifting for strength, seven-on-sevens and running drills for agility, spring football clinics and daily films at the field for knowledge, individual instruction, summer football drills, and skill development by position.

Some players did nothing to prepare themselves, while others worked extremely hard. I am showing you, as a parent, the criteria for making the Bulldog football team. I am asking for your help and encouragement with your son. All parents think their son is a star, which is only human. Realistically, only 11 players can be offensive starters and only 11 can be defensive starters. You must encourage, not complain; motivate, not agitate; and be a team parent, not a selfish parent.

Regardless of the outcome of our season (wins and losses), your son will be a better person if we offer proper guidance. My experience (47 years as a player and coach) has taught me this. When negative parental influence is greater than the coaches' and team's philosophy, the player (if he doesn't quit) becomes a complainer for the rest of his life. He begins to rationalize, criticize, and seek excuses why he didn't or isn't playing. Let us, as supportive parents, prevent this. Keep in mind the real purpose of why your son is playing—to become a better person. Most of you know how we run

Figure 12.1 Sample preseason letter.

our program. We demand discipline, teamwork, sacrifice, and total commitment.

If you, as a parent, cannot handle the ups and downs your son will go through in our program, don't allow him to play. We will all be better off that way—parents won't have any problems, and the young man won't have any problems.

Your positive guidance regarding football will certainly help put your son on the right track in life. He'll be better able to cope with his future bosses, company policies, his future wife, civil laws, and other institutions of authority. Football is not for everyone. It takes a special type of young man to play this violent game. Parental influence is vital. The great players I've coached, besides having talent, have had good parental influence.

In conclusion, I want to thank you for taking the time to read about our philosophy and to consider ideas that may help you as a parent. In my years as a head football coach, the majority of parents have been super as supportive football parents. I'm certainly looking forward to coaching your son. I know I'll make him a better person.

Yours kindly,

George Curry
Head Football Coach

P.S. Here are the six criteria and the grading scale we use in determining starters:

1. Strength in five major lifts 1-2-3-4-5-6-7-8-9-10
2. Quickness and speed 1-2-3-4-5-6-7-8-9-10
3. Size (if position dictates) 1-2-3-4-5-6-7-8-9-10
4. Knowledge of the game 1-2-3-4-5-6-7-8-9-10
5. Toughness and hitting ability 1-2-3-4-5-6-7-8-9-10
6. Attitude 1-2-3-4-5-6-7-8-9-10

Ten Don'ts

I ask parents of my players to observe 10 don'ts if they want their sons to be successful:

1. Don't try to live your life through your son. You had your chance to be young. Let your youngster do his thing. Don't force football or any sport down his throat.

2. Don't be negative with your son. It rubs off. If you complain about why your son isn't in the starting lineup, he will do the same. Be positive. Motivate and encourage your son.

3. Don't be unrealistic. The good Lord gave all of us certain abilities. Accept your son as he is. We would all like to be big, tall, handsome, intelligent, and strong, but it doesn't happen that way. Accept what the Lord blessed you with and go on with your life. Make the best of it. It's the same in football—someone may be bigger, faster, tougher, or smarter. Know your son's limitations and encourage him to make the best of it. Accept his role on the team.

4. Don't knock the coaching staff. How can you expect your son to perform to his fullest if all he hears from you about the coach is negative? The coach represents authority. You will give your youngster the wrong message if you ridicule the coach or his teachers. Support the coach's rules, philosophies, playbook, and so on.

5. Don't be envious of other players. Treat each player as if he were your son. Don't dislike a player because you don't like his parents.

6. Don't be a know-it-all. Coaches work with youngsters 12 months of the year. They spend many hours with these youngsters in situations that their parents may never see. In some cases, coaches know more about the player than the parents do. Don't exert pressure on your son by telling him things he shouldn't have to hear. Be a good role model. Let the coaches coach.

7. Don't be an absent parent. Monitor your son's grades. Insist that your son study and earn good grades. If you put academics first, you son will be more successful.

8. Don't neglect your son's social activities. Monitor his friends, hangouts, girlfriend, curfew, language, rules, and so on. Talk to your son about drugs, alcohol, and tobacco use. Encourage your son to make the right choices. If you don't communicate well in these areas, the wrong people may influence your son.

9. Don't be selfish. Don't use football for the wrong reasons. Don't push your son to play for a scholarship. Doing so pressures him unduly. If he is good enough, he will earn a scholarship. Let him play because he loves the game.

10. Don't baby your son. Sever the umbilical cord. It's a tough world out there. Let him begin preparing for it by not babying him. Let the coaches push your son. Let the coaches make him tougher mentally by challenging him. A youngster can learn mental toughness regardless of whether he plays.

Developing a Championship Coaching Staff

To be consistently successful, you must hire, teach, develop, and trust the right people. Show me a good football program on any level, and I'll show you a good coaching staff. To build a solid foundation, you must have a strong coaching staff.

When I was hired, one of the first things I asked for was the authority to hire my coaches. I didn't want the school board giving me coaches I didn't want. Many coaches are politically appointed and forced on the head coach. Berwick High School allowed me to pick my coaches. I immediately began interviews, background reference checks, and meetings to pick my staff.

I expect my coaches to observe 10 commandments. First, treat the coaching staff with respect, dignity, and professionalism. They're adults, not kids. Motivate them, don't agitate them. Educate them, don't demean them. Set goals with them, not by yourself. Involve them. Use their energy (five is better than one) and their strengths. Listen to their suggestions. Don't blow them off or they'll never offer you their true feelings. Be honest and up front, not phony. Make them feel worthwhile.

Second, treat every youngster as if he were your own. Motivate players. Get in their heads. Get everything you can out of them. Teach them, don't holler at them. Tear them down only to build them up again. Discipline them, set your rules, and don't compromise. Be consistent, not wishy-washy. Be honest with players even if it seems unfair. Be fair. Communicate often and well with your players; let them know where they stand. Get maximum effort by setting goals. Make them all feel worthwhile and important.

Third, cooperate with administrators, teachers, and other supporters. Be enthusiastic about all phases of the educational programs within the school. Support all programs. Perform all administrative directives with enthusiasm. Work closely with the faculty. Make the maintenance staff feel as if they're part of your program; get them on your side.

Fourth, work well with coaches from other teams. Always be professional. Be up front and honest in dealing with fellow coaches, in film exchange, for example. Never publicly humiliate another coach or his program. Help kids in other programs—we're in this for the kids. Promote all student-athletes. Work together for the betterment of the game and the profession. Shake hands with opponents after the game. Don't intentionally run up the score on an opponent. Have a philosophy (the four-touchdown rule). Don't be envious of other programs. Build your program up to be a winner rather than tear winners down. Don't find fault with the programs of other coaches, don't give excuses for your program, and don't point the finger of blame. Don't offer excuses before, during, or after games about why you lost or why you will lose.

Fifth, be honest and up front with parents. Have a preseason meeting with parents to present the philosophy and rules of your program. Prepare handouts. Work on good communication with your players' parents. Tell them exactly where their youngsters stand. Don't lie to them. Educate parents about how you select the starting team. Have concrete facts and prepare a list of criteria you use to pick the starting lineup. Help parents understand their role.

Sixth, be humble. Be a "we" person, not an "I" person. Avoid one-upmanship. Give others credit. Give your opponents credit. Don't blow your own horn. If you're good, others will blow it for you. Don't be paranoid. You can't function if you feel that the world is against you. Be humble in victory and show character in defeat. Don't embarrass your school, town, team, or family by having an attitude. Great coaches and programs don't do any of this. Don't try to be someone else, be yourself. Don't blame the players. Shoulder the blame.

Seventh, be open, honest, humble, and sincere when dealing with the media. Think before you speak. Anticipate questions and prepare answers. In planned interviews, ask what questions you'll be asked—be prepared. Don't take interviews in the heat of battle. Remember, everyone reads what you say to the press, and you're responsible for what comes out of your mouth. Prepare everything from delivery to substance. Paint a good picture of yourself. You need the media behind you and your program. Don't alienate them with an antimedia attitude. They may not like your program, a game, or a call, but they'll respect you and in the end will treat you with dignity. If you have difficulty dealing with the media, assign a coach or team spokesperson who is good at media relations.

Eighth, grow professionally. Develop a great work ethic. Attend clinics and seminars. Have one-on-one miniclinics with coaches from good programs. Work college football camps to learn from other coaches. Read books and listen to tapes to learn all you can about the psychology of the game. Learn about motivation, organization, preparation, and the intangibles. Study film on opponents' offenses and defenses. Try to understand their systems as you well as you know your own. Attend college spring practices. Meet with people smarter than you and pick their brains.

Ninth, be a motivator. Think about the best teachers and the most successful people you've been around. What do they do or have that motivated you? Know what makes people tick. Know the psychology of the athlete. To understand the psychology of a person, you must know what motivation is. Teach motivation to everyone—players, parents, managers.

Finally, lead by example. Work hard and live right.

I want my assistants to know what I expect of them. They know from day one what coaching in Berwick is all about. It's not about money and prestige, although both come with the job. It's about commitment, loyalty, trust, and teaching youngsters to meet their full potential.

I've been fortunate to have a staff that possesses those intangibles. My coaches are good, smart men who know and understand the Berwick way. Of the 12 coaches on my staff, 10 played for me. They know the Curry system, psyche, and work ethic, and the importance of the game in Berwick. This staff, which handles the entire program from 7th to 12th grade, is one of the oldest, longest-lasting coaching football staffs in Pennsylvania. Four of my coaches have been with me for over 25 years. Eight of them have been with me for more than 20 years. All the coaches on my staff have been with me for over 10 years. I picked the right people. We get along well, and we believe in one another. My coaches are loyal to me and trust each other.

During our first meeting at the start of a new season, I hand out a list of coaching duties and responsibilities to my staff. I expect my coaches to be willing to work seven days per week throughout the entire season, from August until the last game. They need to be available for two-a-day practices from 8:30 to 11:15 A.M. and from 5:00 to 8:00 P.M. During the regular season and playoffs they need to be available at the following times:

- Monday through Thursday from 3:00 to 6:30 or 7:00 P.M. for practice.
- Saturdays for junior varsity (JV) practice.
- Every weekend if possible for scouting. Each coach will scout because he, in many cases, runs the scouting offense or defense.
- Sunday evening 6:00 P.M. for the weekly coaches' meeting.

Coaching football involves a total time commitment. If a coach's lifestyle changes to the point that he cannot make that commitment, he should give up his position. Coaching football involves sacrifices at the expense of one's family, friends, extra business affairs, and social life. To coach properly involves total commitment. My coaches need to be willing to work hard.

Coaching assignments vary by grade. For the seventh- and eighth-grade team, we have an offensive coach, a defensive coach, and an assistant coach. The ninth-grade team has an offensive coach and a defensive coach. For the varsity team, I am the head coach, and three defensive coaches and two offensive coaches work under me.

All coaches scout whenever I schedule them to do so. They must report to all meetings on time, sober, and with a pencil and paper. Assistants do not speak to the press or media unless I authorize it. We follow one philosophy and use one PR head.

I have specific expectations about how the coaches should handle players. I require them to

- treat all players with respect;
- set personal differences aside and be fair;
- coach youngsters as if they were their sons;

- teach the game by being teachers, not screamers;
- be patient with the younger players;
- build self-esteem in every player by making him feel that he is worth something;
- keep open good lines of communication, let every player know where he stands, and encourage him to move up; and
- try to play as many youngsters as possible in JV and junior high games.

Safety is an essential element in any football philosophy. I remind coaches to make sure that we have a signed physical form on file for all players. Players must wear all equipment on full-scale practice days. They must always wear helmets on the field, even when walking on or off the practice or game fields. We report all injuries to a doctor or a trainer (who will report to the doctor), and we treat injuries as well as we can until proper professional help is available. Coaches should try to prevent personal mismatches when doing live drills (for example, a 210-pound youngster versus a 110-pound youngster). Before doing anything, coaches teach tackling technique and emphasize tackling without using the head. Coaches must insist on water breaks during hot, humid days. I tell my coaches not to run the kids into the ground. All players must be properly equipped with good-fitting NOCSE sealed equipment, not their personal equipment.

Winning With Xs and Os

An old saying among coaches is that "You win with talent." John McKay once said, "Give me a great tailback, and I'll show you a great coach." He's correct. On a high school level, however, I believe you win more games with Xs and Os than you do with talent. But don't get me wrong; it's easier to win with great talent.

In my opinion, one of the main reasons for our 344 wins is our playbook. To win consistently, your system must help you win games you aren't supposed to win. Much of our success comes from adapting my system to the talent I have. You don't always have big offensive linemen, a great tailback, or a great quarterback. You must look at the players you have and go from there.

I've looked at the 27 championship teams I've been associated with and noticed that we've won with different styles. For example, the 1971 conference championship team was a passing team that included a talented Division I quarterback, one back, and a wide-open passing attack. The 1977 Eastern Conference championship team was an I-formation running team featuring a 2,000-yard rusher. In 1978 we won the conference championship with two 1,000-yard rushers, but the 1981 Eastern Conference championship team and the 1982 conference championship team were predominantly passing teams featuring Division I quarterbacks. The 1983 national champions featured a balanced attack with a Division I quarterback and a Division I fullback. The 1984, 1985, and 1986 conference championship teams were predominantly running teams, but the 1988 state championship team was predominantly a passing team. In 1992 we were national champions with a balanced passing and running attack that featured Division I players at quarterback, wide receiver, and fullback. From 1994 to 1997 we reigned as state champions. We had a balanced attack in 1994 and 1995, and a predominantly running attack in 1996 and 1997, built around a Division I fullback in 1996 and a big offensive line featuring two Division I linemen in 1997.

When I had a great quarterback, I built the offense around him. I expanded the playbook to allow his talents to take us to a title. When we were blessed with big linemen and a great fullback or tailback, we ran the football down our opponent's throat. At times I had only three championship-type linemen, and I wound up flopping those three guys all the way to a state championship (1997). We took advantage of our best linemen to get the matchups we wanted. Our other linemen, who were only sophomores, simply weren't ready for prime time yet.

You do what gives you an advantage. Football comes down to a chess game. You want to win most of the matchups every game. This is what we mean by the Xs and Os.

You can win games in two ways. You either outtalent and outmuscle your opponent because you have all the big, fast studs, or you outfox, outplot, and outmaneuver your opponent because you have a system that your opponents can't prepare for in one week. The wide-open multiplicity in our playbook accounts for 75 percent of our wins. I may run 35 or 40 formations a game.

Every team we played over the years made Berwick their game of the year. Our opponents work long and hard preparing to stop us. It hasn't happened often. Our system provides an answer for most situations.

Defensively, we've been a 50 defense for my entire 34 years as a head coach. I run more 4-3 defenses lately against spread offenses, but I believe in the 50 front when we play a two-back team. Besides great players, all great defenses have one thing in common—they're unpredictable. We don't sit in one defense two plays in a row. We move constantly—stemming, shifting, disguising coverages—to confuse our opponents. In high school football you have 25 seconds to run a play, but the opponent really has only about 5 to 7 seconds to recognize what defense we're in. Because of our shifting, stemming, and jumping around, the offensive linemen have only 2 or 3 seconds to recognize what we're doing and then try to block us. We thus dictate play, causing opposing teams to become vanilla on offense.

Great programs master the Xs and Os. They know what has to be done in given situations. We have become an outstanding game-day program because the system rarely fails us.

Communication Is the Key to Victory

Communication is the ability to convey one's intentions, ideas, and facts to others. This sounds like an easy thing to do, but it isn't. How many times a day does a parent say, "These kids just don't listen"? How many times a day does a teacher, boss, spouse, or member of the clergy say the same thing? I believe that communication skills and motivational ability go hand in hand. They're the same. Show me a good motivator, and I'll show you a great communicator.

Coaching football is more motivation and mental ability than it is Xs and Os. A coach could be knowledgeable, work hard, and devote his entire life to the game and still not win if he can't persuade people to listen and respond.

I believe in working with the psychological part of the game. We as a staff talk a good deal about how to get the most out of each youngster. I want players to know and understand motivation. I share material with my staff on motivating people. I insist that they read it and learn how it will help get the most out of our players. How many coaches take the time to go over each player individually and study his background? Is this player an only child? The first born? The middle or last born? Does he come from a two-parent family? No parents? Foster parents?

We call this a psychological profile. I want to know everything there is to know about my players because I can use it to motivate them. For example, did you know that first-born children are more extrinsically motivated than middle-born children? Did you know that children born in the middle are more intrinsically motivated? Did you know that studies have shown that children from broken homes have much lower self-esteem than children from two-parent homes? Coaches should spend more time on this part of the game. Some great material is out there. Learn from big business—they're always looking for the psychological edge.

Many psychological factors go with each youngster. A coach should learn how to reach the unreachable kid. Over the years I've found the hot button on many players because I looked into his psychological makeup. These players went on to be productive, successful people. I persuaded that athlete to listen to me because I found his hot button. Communication and motivation have been a big reason for our success at Berwick. Our players respond. Coaching is getting the most out of your talent. To me, that means it's more psychological than physical.

My dad used to tell me, "If you can communicate, I don't care what walk of life you pursue, you'll be highly successful." The best salespeople, managers, members of the clergy, doctors, administrators, and teachers are excellent communicators. And the best communicators are the best motivators. The two abilities go hand in hand.

Coaches who have great communication skills are successful. A coach must deal each day with many groups of people—media, parents, administrators, teachers, maintenance staff, and, most important, players.

Oh, and he must deal with booster clubs, which can be his biggest challenge. My experience has taught me that even after several years of harmony between the booster club and coaches, problems can occur. A booster club member or members will find an ax to grind over some issue—a player-related concern, a personality difference between parents and a coach, or a difference of opinion on how to raise or spend the booster club's money.

The purpose of a booster club should be to help the football program financially by buying equipment necessary to run a top-notch in-season and out-of-season program. The club might pay for banquets, hats, T-shirts, sweatshirts, championship jackets, and trophies. Funds might pay for camps, college visits, or weightlifting equipment. The booster club should work for and with the coach, and should not interfere or be contrary in any way to the coach's philosophy. In other words, the coach runs the program; the booster club does not run the coach. Booster clubs however, often become too powerful. They become a political faction and try to run the coach by taking control of the school board. The result is that the club loses sight of its basic function and purpose. The club goes beyond its initial intent and tries to pressure the coach into playing certain kids, throwing more, running more, winning more, and so on.

Problems often begin when a few booster club members begin fighting with each other over an issue. Before you know it the coach is in the middle of the controversy. This is a no-win situation for the coach. Coaches must be prepared to deal with these problems because they can crop up in any program. Adversity often tests a coach's communication skills. Sometimes a coach must communicate harshly. Communication is the key to victory, on or off the field.

The Big Three

Coaches often preach commitment, leadership, and work ethic. Every coach talks about these intangibles, and winning programs have them. With our success, our football team became the envy of everyone—the media, other programs, other towns. Administrators viewed our popularity as power, and power struggles developed. Attacks that come with success often bring a team closer together. I've seen the effect that success has had on our team, and Berwick players rise to the occasion! I've been in the game almost 35 years and have never seen stronger commitment on the part of our players.

These guys want to win more than ever. The attitude to do whatever it takes prevails in our program from top to bottom.

I break the season down into three phases: the off-season from December to May, the spring season from May to August 10, and the in-season from August 13 to December 8.

I'm fortunate to have an outstanding strength coach, my son, who brought a great strength program and youthful exuberance to our program. Here's what we expect of our players in our off-season weightlifting and strength program. We lift four days per week, between 6:30 and 8:00 A.M. or between 2:30 and 6:30 P.M. A youngster has a choice. If one of our players is involved in another sport that takes place after school, he'll lift early in the morning. Many of our athletes lift in both sessions. This goes on year round.

The Berwick kids put in the hours in the weight room. When you have over 100 youngsters lifting weights on a daily basis, that is championship commitment. We've had to expand our weight-training facilities on three occasions since I've been in Berwick, and we've outgrown our most recent expansion. We are one of the strongest teams in the state year in and year out. Each player in our offensive line on the 1995 team could bench press over 400 pounds, and one lineman benched 500 pounds. *Bigger-Faster-Stronger* magazine documented this achievement.

This commitment in the off-season becomes contagious. Everyone gets involved. Players link winning with commitment. This commitment goes a long way in overcoming the envy of the critics. Twenty-six youngsters on our current team bench press over 300 pounds, and 11 of them bench over 350 pounds. We have 15 players power cleaning over 300 pounds. Commitment on the part of our athletes brings about a terrific work ethic.

I preach two sayings all the time: "You win championships with championship people" and "If you work hard, good things will happen to you." These maxims are all about commitment. Our off-season is a lot of hard work.

During spring we continue to lift and begin going outside to work on skill development. I run a number of minicamps. We have a chance to do a lot of teaching. Our youngsters look forward to camps after being cooped up in a field house all winter. We also visit spring football practice at various colleges. I take our players to Penn State, Pittsburgh, Army, Temple, Virginia Tech, and other schools so that they can see what college players are learning at their positions. The visits motivate our players to work toward winding up on one of those campuses.

Every Wednesday throughout the year we work on plyometrics and speed training. Attendance at these sessions is tremendous. I'm sure that winning has a lot to do with this, but the sessions are a priority for our players. We also get into seven-on-seven summer passing games from June to August. We may have 12 or 13 games. These sessions help the players learn their routes, and they get into great condition.

We break lifting into four nine-week cycles, and we strength test players after each cycle. We also speed test at the beginning and end of the summer. During the off-season a Berwick football player puts 25 hours a week into some aspect of the program, which adds up to over 1,000 hours of off-season preparation by the time the season starts. Again, this requires commitment and a work ethic.

When players spend over 1,000 hours together in an off-season strength and conditioning program, leaders emerge. Guys start taking charge in the weight room. A leader is a guy who can move people in a positive direction. Everyday I see our young men doing that—pushing and challenging each other. This is leadership happening in the purest sense of the word. To maintain a consistent winner, you must have leadership. My staff and I must be good leaders, and our players must step up and take charge as well.

I recently met with my team on an annual fund-raising project. We work the Pocono 500 race to help raise money for our team. I asked the seniors to get me 100 people (minimum) from the junior and senior high program to work for three days at the racetrack. Working this event requires a significant effort. Our players leave at 4:30 or 5:00 A.M. and arrive back in Berwick late at night. The seniors took charge. We filled two busloads of players and made a lot of money for the program. Leadership stepped up. Your team is only as good as the senior leadership. Commitment, work ethic, and leadership have been so good over the past two decades that nothing can pull our team apart.

Paying the Price of Success

Earlier in this chapter I talked about how to build a successful program. Now that we've been on top for over three decades, some people have turned on us. Some want to see the big monster fall. Many sportswriters made a name for themselves by attacking me and my program. School board members turned on us, perhaps because the tremendous success we've had overshadows other good things happening in the school district.

From 1994 to 1998 we won four straight state titles and earned a national title in 1995, but I was one vote away from being fired. We had a school board that had four votes against anything I asked for. That school board voted five to four to expand our new field house, which was to be done at no cost. I got the Local 55 Bricklayers Union to come in along with a former player's parents to build us a state-of-the-art strength-training facility. Four board members voted against this, a freebie. We have a chance to receive a state-of-the-art scoreboard in our stadium free of charge, a donation from our local bottling company. The same four board members tabled it, yet they accepted the same offer for a new scoreboard for the high school gymnasium.

I could cite many more examples of how things change when you're on top. I feel that the opposition we face is because of envy, a form of hate. People hate for many reasons, some justifiable. Envy is hate for the wrong reason. We work hard, we're committed, we're disciplined, we're good role models, and yes, we're successful. People have no reason to hate us.

Successful programs have a way of overcoming the negatives hurled at them. I know that hostility has motivated our team to work harder. I've been called a crook and a cheat. People have said that I recruit, that my players don't go to class. People on the inside know better. We are the only football team in our area that drug tests. Nearly 80 percent of our players go on to college after graduation. Our players have earned millions of dollars in football scholarships. We average approximately $400,000 in football scholarships every year. People have trouble accepting that success.

To win consistently, you must be mentally tough. No program anywhere in any sport has won for three decades without being hammered. The key is knowing how to handle success. I'm sure there is a plan for that; great programs have a plan for everything.

Coaching high school sports today is tough. Coaches are under the microscope. Schools are finding it difficult to find coaches. Whether you are a rookie or a veteran, you're constantly under the gun. I've seen great high school coaches with 200 or more wins get fired. No matter what your record is, you are at the mercy of the school board. If five voters line up against you, you're history.

How do you deal with this? How does a coach survive? How does a perennial winner deal with the problems associated with winning? How does a losing coach survive? My best advice is this—simply concentrate on coaching your players. When it comes right down to it, you need only the players, your assistants, the field, and a football. That's all you really need to do your job. If people want to cause problems, avoid them. Most of my problems during my years as a head coach have been with adults, not kids. Coaches should concentrate on the people they need.

The things I needed to build a championship program may not be what you need to maintain a championship program. Times have changed; family values have changed. To win consistently, coaches must change. Growth never ceases in this profession. Your philosophy should remain the same, but professional growth and persistence will keep you on top.

13

Promoting Your Program

Mack Brown

Let me say from the start that this is not the gospel according to Mack Brown. I had many teachers. My granddad, Jelly Watson, was the winningest high school coach in middle Tennessee history. They named the stadium after him. In almost 30 years of coaching, including 18 as a head coach, I have been fortunate to work with many great people. I learned something from each of them.

What I will cover in this chapter are principles that I have found to be true. I'll talk about some ways I've found to promote a program. I have been a head coach at four schools. The challenges are unique at each place, but the basic methods are the same. These ideas are time tested, and I think you'll find that they will work for you if you stick with them.

Let me say that when I talk about promotion, I am not talking about gimmicks and giveaways. I am talking about building relationships because that is where true promotion begins. I will talk about what I will call the *I*'s of Texas, and you can make them fit your own program.

Make a Good Impression

The first *I* is *impress*. It's curious how we react to that word. It's fine to try to "make a good impression," but we are being critical when we say, "He is just trying to impress people." In any case, if you want people to believe in you and your program, set out to impress them. If you don't believe in yourself, how can you expect someone else to believe in you? I am not talking here about being cocky. I am talking about being self-assured, showing people from the outset that you know exactly what you are doing. We often call it walking with a swagger.

Most of all, however, you need to show them who you really are and what you are going to stand for in your program. I have been a head coach at Appalachian State, Tulane, North Carolina, and Texas, and although the schools were different, all of them believed strongly in academics. So I told people that our goal was to win championships with nice kids who graduate. Saying that was easy because that's what I believe in. When you become a coach, you have to ask yourself what kind of program and what kind of school you want to work with. If you don't believe in what you are doing or in the type of people you are working with, you have no chance to succeed as a coach.

In the beginning, the impression you make will dictate what kind of staff you are able to build. The impression you have left will determine the support you get from your administration. I have been fortunate to work with some outstanding athletics administrators: Jim Garner at Appalachian State, Wright Waters at Tulane, John Swofford at North Carolina, and DeLoss Dodds at Texas. At Texas, DeLoss allowed us to hire the best staff possible because he believed in what we were trying to do.

Courtesy of University of Texas

Obviously, the most important group when it comes to the impression you make will be your players. First, you work with the players you have at your school. Most of the time when you take over a program, the players you inherit will have bruised feelings. If the previous staff left, the players feel abandoned. If the previous staff was fired, the players are likely to be hurt and angry. The first thing you should do is put your arms around them and let them know it is a new beginning. Every guy has a new chance.

When we came to Texas, John Mackovic and his staff had struggled to a 4-7 season in 1997. The media and the fans had beaten up the staff and the kids. We told the players that we didn't intend to rebuild; we aimed to win now. We owed it to the seniors. That attitude opened the way to a 9-3 season. Our approach weighed heavily in the decision of Ricky Williams, who set a number of all-time NCAA career records, to come back for his senior season. Ricky needed to hear that we were committed to winning that season. He won the Heisman Trophy, and we were the 1999 Southwestern Bell Cotton Bowl champs. If Ricky hadn't been impressed with what we were trying to do, our start at Texas would have been much more difficult.

The second part of the player equation, obviously, is recruiting. We needed to build bridges with high school coaches, and we needed to let recruits know what we planned to do at Texas. We did that by establishing trust, communication, and respect. Those three things will carry you a long way in anything you do, but if you want to impress somebody, there is no better way than to radiate those three virtues.

The impression you make bridges into every one of the many publics you touch as a coach—the faculty, fans, parents, alumni, media, and so on. This is an area in which you can help yourself. A head coach should not have to make streamers or spirit posters, but he can speak to fans and use every method available to get the story of his program out there. Depending on where you coach, you may need to speak at every opportunity you can to promote your program. When I went to North Carolina the football program was down, and we needed to create interest. In our first year I spoke over 70 times.

People want their head coach to be visible, and you should accept that responsibility. At Texas we speak to Longhorn clubs around the state in the off-season and take advantage of the new technology of the Internet to open a whole new way of communicating with our publics. But you have to be careful with how you mange your time.

Greg Davis, our offensive coordinator and once my successor as the head coach at Tulane, says that the difference between being a head coach and being an assistant is that an assistant makes suggestions and a head coach makes decisions. Besides being the decision maker, a head coach must be many things to many people.

I once heard Johnny Majors, who was the head coach at Tennessee, say that the difference in coaching in a high-profile job like Tennessee compared with coaching at Pittsburgh (where he also had great success) was that at Pittsburgh you were the head coach in the fall. At Tennessee you were the head coach 12 months a year. The image you create from the impression you leave will determine your success in every area of your job.

Dare to Imagine

The second *I* is *imagine.* From the time you become a coach, imagine what you want your program to look like and then, when your opportunity comes, use every asset you have to make it happen. In sport we call that visualizing. Before a game we encourage our kids to visualize themselves in a winning locker room and to think about how that would feel. That's what I mean by figuring out what you want and then going to get it.

When we came to Texas, we were fortunate that the stadium and the football facility were undergoing extensive remodeling. The timing was perfect. We were able to design everything, from the locker room to the trophy room to the player lounge to the weight room, to follow the image we wanted to create.

We were lucky in that we had just finished helping design a facility at North Carolina. My wife, Sally, is a real-estate developer with a degree in architecture. She helped a lot by talking to our players about what they would like where in our building. We built it so that the academic center, the meeting rooms, the training room, and the strength and conditioning room were all centrally located to the dressing room. In our decorations we tapped the rich history of Texas. We put up walls of photos of great moments and planned a path to the game field that went past plaques of the all-Americans. We put up a set of longhorns for the players to touch to represent the pride of those who earned those awards.

Everything we did in the building touched one of three areas—recruits, players, and the Texas tradition. When you enter the elevator, you hear "Texas Taps," our fight song, on the way up and "The Eyes of Texas," our alma mater, on the way down. We wanted to be sure that recruits and everyone else always knew that they were at Texas.

We follow the same idea with every publication and printed item, whether it is a card we send out or a poster we give out. We have a unique mascot, and people around the world know our emblem of the longhorn head. You can create your own image with such things. Some people have changed their school insignia for that purpose. You want something that is distinctly yours.

As I mentioned earlier, the newest and largest opportunity today in promotion is the Internet. At Texas we were among the first programs to start our own Web site. In the summer of 2001 we redesigned it completely. After launching the new site in August, we had over 3.8 million hits in the first three weeks. We use that site for daily practice updates and a weekly interview. We almost feel as if we're having a chat with every one of our fans.

The media is still a tremendous part of any promotion you do because they can reach so many people. But the advertising situation in many cities has diluted the opportunity to buy time to talk about your message. In a city the size of Austin, one radio commercial soon becomes cost prohibitive, and it is impossible to reach a target audience. The media has always been a conduit to the public. Now, through the Internet, the public is coming directly to us, and we can answer their questions and tell our side of a story daily.

Imagine the relationship you want to have with high school coaches and then put a plan in place to achieve that. In Texas 1,200 high schools have football teams. The first phone call I made when I got to Austin—on the way to our first press conference—was to Eddie Joseph, the executive director of the Texas High School Coaches Association. My roots were in high school coaching, and I knew that if we were to succeed in the state we would need to have an excellent relationship with those coaches. We had done the same thing in North Carolina and Louisiana.

To do that, we opened our program to them. We started a clinic that draws over 1,000 coaches each spring. We invited them to practice and to our games. Our staff attends the annual coaches' school each summer. Our participation is not just for show. We attend the panels and lectures along with the high school coaches. We have learned a lot from those sessions. They constantly give us new ideas, and this fits perfectly with the idea of imagining.

Each season we begin with a different theme for the team. The first year we felt we needed to reemphasize the fact that winning didn't come easy, so we took a theme of "Practice winning every day." That premise wasn't just about practicing to win a game. It was entirely about image—the image you project to others and the image you have of yourself. Winning every day meant going to class every day, taking care of business every day, and of course, practicing better each day.

The following year we wanted to stress a commitment to winning, so we used WIT—"Whatever it takes." That too was about self-image. The theme spoke to what we needed to accomplish to be a successful team, and we included a WIT chart that gave a tangible rating to what we had accomplished.

In the season of 2001 many people were talking about winning the national championship before the season. We talked a lot about taking each game at a time, but every kid who ever plays the game dreams of winning it all. Our slogan became "Live your dream," so we tried to make the high expectations a positive and put it out there. We gave each player a dream catcher, an old Indian charm made of feathers and webbing. The idea is that the dream catcher traps the bad dreams and lets the good dreams come through.

We have been at places with big budgets, like the one we have at Texas, and at places with smaller budgets. Whatever your resources allow you to do, you can do it with class. The most important lesson you can learn, however, is that you don't have to do everything yourself. Use your staff to help create an image you want, and do everything in your power within the rules to reach your goals. A vivid imagination is a good thing.

Strive to Involve

That's where our third *I* comes in—*involve.* In our early years at North Carolina, we were going through a particularly tough time, and I called my wife and said I just wanted to quit. She said to wait at least until lunch, and we would talk about it.

When I got home our good friend Dick Coop, an outstanding sports psychologist, was there. He gave me two good pieces of advice. The first was not to make any decision if I was angry, tired, or confused. I was all three. The second was to figure out the parts of my job that I did well and enjoyed doing and separate those from the parts that I was not as effective with but on which I spent more time than I should. He suggested that I spend more time on the things I enjoyed doing and delegate the rest to others.

When it comes to promoting a program, that may be the most important thing a coach can learn. You can't do it by yourself. Involving others—from the student body, to your staff, to the fan base—is where the heart of promoting a program lies.

First, hire good people and put them to work to help your coaches. At Texas we have a tremendous photography department, and we use their photos in displays and publications. Nothing tells your story like a great picture. Nothing attracts attention in your offices like a photo of a memorable moment. Whether black and white or color (color obviously is more striking, but it depends on your budget), photos decorate your offices like nothing else. With modern technology, large blowups are not that expensive. Change the photos regularly. Seeing photos of themselves in the offices will excite your kids, and fans relate to the photos as well. Out-of-date images, however, don't serve either purpose.

Staying up to date is also important with things like action highlights for callers to hear when they are placed on hold when calling your office. The telephone, by the way, is a great promotional tool. During the season, we have everybody who answers the phone in our offices respond, "Texas Longhorn football beat . . ." whoever it is we are playing that week.

We try to create strong internal support throughout our department. When I first came to Texas, I had a meeting with the staff of our women's athletics department. Feelings between the two departments had been strained, and I wanted to shoot straight with the women's staff and coaches. In the 2000–2001 season at Texas, the total budget for men's and women's athletics was

$52 million. Of that total, football generated $42 million, or 80 percent of the money. I wanted them to understand how important it was for us to succeed, and I explained that we needed their support. Throughout both departments, we now have a common purpose. On Fridays, everybody wears orange, and we have support buttons unique to the opponent of the week.

When you hire creative people, let them do their jobs. Our media-relations staff is the best in the country. They have divided their staff to take care of a large media base. The University of Texas is the state's largest educational institution, so we draw tremendous coverage not only from our home in Austin but also from Houston, Dallas-Fort Worth, and San Antonio—3 of the state's 10 largest cities. Over 58,000 Texas alums live in Houston alone. Every television appearance by the staff or by our players is a promotional opportunity.

The media-relations staff, working with their own excellent publications department, produces award-winning media guides that serve recruits and fans as well as the press. They make sure to meet the basic needs of the media, but those books sell our program as nothing else can.

Through our life-skills program, we reach out to the community in many ways. Players visit schools and serve as tutors to young kids, and we make weekly visits to our local children's hospitals. Those visits not only help the people we are trying to help but also make great media opportunities. When our kids are doing something that positive, we want to let people know about it.

Besides calling on the talents of your own staff, look to those in your community who have expertise in the areas of promotion. In Austin we are lucky to have one of the nation's most successful advertising companies in GSD&M. They handle accounts like Southwest Airlines and Wal-Mart. One of the founders, Roy Spence, is a former high school quarterback, and the partners in the company are all Texas graduates. They have been a great resource for us. They helped us set up our Internet site and produce inspirational banners for the team. So my advice is to think outside the box. You may not have a GSD&M in your town, but I promise that you have people willing to help.

At Texas we formed a partnership with Host Communications of Lexington, Kentucky, to handle all our marketing and radio and television business. By involving a major company like Host and giving them all the ad sales, we were able to take advantage of a multilevel corporation partnership that helped sell everything from game programs to ad space in the coaches' shows.

Most of all, use your coaches in a positive way. Don't ever take them from their primary duties of recruiting or their coaching duties with your team, but trust them to speak for you when you can't handle all the requests. Just make sure that you and your entire staff are on the same page before people go out to speak.

Cleve Bryant, an outstanding coach and now our associate athletics director for football operations, handles all speaking requests. In our first season at Texas I had over 700 requests for personal appearances. Obviously, I couldn't do them all. I had to make time to do even the ones that involved our Longhorn clubs around the state. So we developed a system in which an assistant coach would combine a recruiting trip with a speaking engagement. This approach has worked out well.

At the student level, we have a group of female students called the Texas Angels who help us with recruiting weekends and assist with other duties in the office.

In three other areas it is important for you to get people involved. The first concerns your lettermen. At Texas, for a variety of reasons, our lettermen felt separated from the program. Coach Darrell Royal, one of the great legends in our profession, was one of the main reasons I came to Texas. He built a tradition in the late 1960s when I was a college player, and through the years I had remained a great admirer of his. You may not have a Darrell Royal at your school, but don't be afraid to reach out to tradition. It is a sign of insecurity not to embrace it. If you don't have a tradition, involve others to start developing a theme that will reflect one.

In the spring of our first year, we started a football letterman's reunion and golf tournament as an event surrounding our spring game. Through the help of Joe Jamail, a highly successful attorney and one of our biggest supporters, we started a golf tournament and named it for Mike Campbell, who was Coach Royal's long-time assistant. We put David McWilliams, who had coached at Texas and was the captain of the 1963 national champion Longhorn team, in charge of all our lettermen.

Your lettermen can be your biggest asset. Nobody has more invested in the program than they do, and nobody actually knows the challenges of the game as well as they do. Involve them in every way you can. Obviously, NCAA rules limit what they can do in recruiting, but when it comes to promoting your program, you can have no better friends. Understand that people will be asking them about your program, so the best thing you can do is make them feel a part of it. Because they will be talking about your program, you need them saying positive things.

I have found it important to identify a small circle of your university's top supporters to use as a sounding board for advice. The people I am talking about are not the stereotypical folks who try to run your program. Instead, I want to work with men and women who have been tremendously successful in their own fields and who understand that there is more to a job than may meet the eye. Educate them. They must know the challenges you face and the progress you are making in order to help your program.

The final involvement is obvious—your fan base. When we came to Texas, people told me that the fans had been fickle and critical, so from the beginning I tried to be positive with them. Folks said that our fans showed up fashionably late to games, weren't loud, and that they left before the game ended. Our color is burnt orange, which is not considered the most fashionable color, so our fans didn't wear it much. One lady told me, "I look awful in burnt orange." I asked her to do me a favor and humor me for three and a quarter hours each Saturday.

So we started our time here with a slogan: "Come Early, Be Loud, Stay Late, and Wear Orange With Pride." It caught on. By our fourth season, our home stadium, Darrell K. Royal Texas Memorial Stadium, was a sea of burnt orange. The crowd was tremendously supportive. They even made up T-shirts with the slogan on it.

We turned our spring game into an event, and by our fourth spring, 35,000 people were coming for what was basically a scrimmage. But we reach out to them when they come. We set up an autograph session, and some of our star players and I have spent as much as four and a half hours signing autographs. We put in a long day, but the worst thing you can do is offer something and then take it away. The little kid who has waited in line for three hours only to be told he won't get to meet that player or get that autograph will remember the hurt forever. Meeting with fans is the least we in college athletics can do to repay the support we get.

We also asked the fans to meet the team when the buses arrive at the stadium, and 4,000 regularly show up to do that. At every opportunity, whether it is on our coaches' show or a radio show or a public appearance, we make a point of thanking our fans, and we always include our students and the Longhorn band. Not only did the fans turn the stadium orange, they created one of the best home-field advantages in the country. What we do is *interact,* a fourth *I* that relates to *involve.*

Now, with all that said, let's make sure we understand one thing: when it comes to promoting a program, the most important thing you can do is win. We are in the education business during the week, but we are in the entertainment business on the weekends. Nothing entertains like winning. All of that wonderful support we are talking about—55,000 season tickets sold, over 60 luxury suites with a 50-person waiting list—comes when people are having fun, and they have a lot more fun winning than losing. I know. I've tried it both ways.

In the world of advertising there is a story about a dog-food company that spent thousands of dollars on a marketing campaign for a new product. They used television, print ads, and even special coupons at the store. This all seemed to work at the beginning, but then they discovered something that destroyed the whole thing. The dogs didn't like the food, and they wouldn't eat it, so the company eventually discontinued the product.

That story contains a moral for anybody in business (and we are in the business of college football). Build your program with sound principles of relationships, so that people will like you and understand what you are trying to do with your program. In our first two years at North Carolina, we went 2-20. Only because we'd formed good relationships and because people believed us did we survive to go 21-3 over our last two seasons.

Most of all, keep in mind what you are trying to promote. Make a good impression of who you are, imagine what can be rather than settling for something less, and involve people in your journey. The game of college football isn't about you. It's about kids. You are just there to help them find their way to make a difference in this world. And if you can't promote that, then there's not much that's worth promoting.

PART IV

Innovative and Effective Practice Sessions

Ron Schipper

Football commentators love to talk about how decisions made in the heat of battle win and lose games. Yet the scoreboard more typically reflects what your team has accomplished Monday through Friday. I believe that success in any job depends on our ability to develop and execute what I call the three Ps to success—your plan, your people, and your preparation.

You must have a plan of action. This plan includes every goal you hope to reach and how you intend to get there. You must have the right people to execute the plan, and you must take the time and make the effort to prepare properly. Success will come only if you believe in your plan and sell it to everyone involved in your program, find and develop the people to make your plan a reality, and plan perfect practices to prepare your players.

This section includes a plan of action for every phase of team preparation. We cover the complete physical, mental, and emotional preparation of all the people who call you Coach. This section can help you plan a drill for a grueling morning practice in August, prepare for the emotion of that big game in October, and find ways to succeed in the cold wind and rain of a gray afternoon in November. Our goal is to help you develop a specific plan of action for your program that will allow each of your players to maximize his talents and become the best football player his ability will allow.

Some coaches cannot wait until game time. To them, practice is simply unavoidable and a means of passing the time until kickoff. Others recognize the importance of practice but go through the motions of performing a few drills without purpose. But I am a coach who thoroughly enjoys practice. The practice field is my classroom. To me, a successful coach believes it is his responsibility to prepare a young man fully for the big game and for life. That mission must take place on the practice field.

Practice provides you an opportunity to teach, to help your players develop and grow. But practice also gives you a chance to get to know your players. What are their work habits? How tough are they physically and mentally? Are they students of the game, or do they need direction every minute they are on the field? Taking on these challenges is why I have found so much pleasure on the practice field.

I am convinced that more coaches fail because of poor organization than they do for any other reason. The coach must have a plan to cover every phase of the game. For most football coaches, offensive, defensive, and special-teams game plans are the most obvious. Most coaches are eager to work on these plans but find it difficult to develop a crisp, thorough practice session.

To develop the ideal practice plan, you must first define what practice really means to you. My definition is that practice is the place where a group of young men become a team. This transformation occurs through one-on-one drills that allow players to develop physical and mental toughness as well as through small-group drills in which individuals learn to work together as a unit. It happens through seven-on-seven drills, during which players master the basics of pass offense and defense through repetition. Finally, it happens through a controlled team scrimmage, when the entire offensive and defensive units come together with the purpose of coordinating the execution of their individual skills and techniques into a successful play.

More simply, practice is the time when players learn, drill, and refine individual skills and techniques. Players discover who they are and what they are capable of doing. A football game lasts just 60 minutes. You must plan every minute of practice if you hope to achieve success on game day. This section can help you prepare the perfect practice for your football program.

Gene Stallings has planned practices for some of the finest players in the game. He's done so both as a position coach and as a head coach responsible for the preparation of the entire team. Although individual coaches' practice plans may differ, Coach Stallings believes some aspects are integral in planning each of your practices, such as identifying the specific phases of the game to stress on a given day of practice each week. Coach Stallings identifies the essential elements of an effective practice. He tells you how to maintain efficiency in each session. And he teaches you how to break down and assemble various positions into individual, group, and team drills.

Joe Tiller has fun coaching football. He finds that real enjoyment comes from seeing a player perfect the skills and techniques of his position. But before that can happen, Coach Tiller believes you must get to know your players, understand who they are, and develop a strong player-coach relationship. Few are better at that than Coach Tiller.

Coach Tiller is on a continuous quest for discovering better methods for teaching a particular skill to his players. He provides an inside look at the unique instructional approaches he's created to help players grasp the techniques and tactics that make his system successful. But he also stresses the importance of getting players to believe in what you are teaching. You must have your players' respect and the ability to command their undivided attention on the practice field. You must continually reinforce proper execution and eliminate errors.

The dream of every football coach is to have a team capable of playing the entire game at full speed. Coach Mike Bellotti outlines a program designed to help each athlete take the field in peak playing condition.

A total conditioning program requires more than physical training. Being in optimal playing shape requires mental and emotional preparation as well. Athletes with higher levels of motivation and determination are more likely to produce their peak physical performance. And athletes who are better conditioned will play with more confidence.

Coach Bellotti emphasizes that the key to any successful conditioning program is a focus on quality workouts and goal setting. He offers a detailed year-round training plan that stresses agility training as well as speed and strength training.

Every coach will face adversity sometime in his coaching career. You may not be able to develop a specific plan of attack for every problem you'll face, but you do need a method of dealing with those situations. Hayden Fry has always been known as a coach who enjoys doing the unexpected. His willingness to be different has often led him to use adversity to his advantage, rather than just react to it. Life and coaching would be much simpler if everything went according to plan. But extreme weather conditions, injuries to key players, strategy changes by opponents, and other surprises may force you to abandon a thoroughly prepared game plan. Coach Fry explains how to handle the unpredictable situations you'll encounter and identifies what a coach can do to prepare a team for such situations.

14

Planning and Conducting Productive Practices

Gene Stallings

The old saying "Practice makes perfect" is not correct at all! Perfect practice makes perfect. Every team in the country has good Xs and Os. The difference is in performance, and good performance comes from lots of research, hours of planning, and proper use of time.

It is important for everyone to use the same terminology. Both the offense and defense should use the same names for plays, coverages, formations, forces, alignments, stunts, techniques, and personnel. To reduce confusion, the offensive and defensive coaches should use the same name in speaking to any combination of players.

Many coaches do not require this consistency from their staff members. The result is that coaches have trouble communicating with the other side of the ball during practice or a game.

Important Points to Remember

■ Football players win games by making plays. A player cannot consistently make good plays if he's confused.

■ Players must use techniques properly. Learning to do this is what practice is all about.

■ Never send your players off the field in a bad frame of mind. Find something positive to say.

■ Stay on schedule.

■ Being loud does not make you a good coach.

■ Good assistant coaches are good on-the-field coaches.

■ There is no substitute for knowledge.

■ You cannot coach well without some enthusiasm.

■ Your players take on your personality.

■ The game is for the players.

■ The best-coached teams usually win.

Efficient planning and organization require that you group strategy situations. For example, in a practice when you say, "We will be working on run situations," everyone should know that you mean run situations of first and 1 to 10 yards, second and 5 yards, and second and 6 to 9 yards. I do not mean to imply, however, that the opponent will never pass in a run situation or will never run in a pass situation. For efficiency, categorize pass situations (second and 10 or more yards, third and 3 to 5 yards, third and 6 to 12 yards, and third and 13 or more yards) and short-yardage situations (third and 1 to 2 yards, and fourth and 1 to 2 yards) as well.

Every time I organize a practice, I want to accomplish something. Table 14.1 shows a sample weekly practice plan with a list of goals for each day.

Rehearsing substitutions is extremely important. The wrong personnel in the game at crucial times can cost you a game. Here's an example of the way I practice substituting.

I begin by saying, "We are working on offensive substitution." Then I go over every possible scenario, as in these examples:

- "It's first and 10. Give me diamond personnel." (Diamond personnel run onto the field.)

- "It's third and 1. Give me short-yardage personnel." (Diamond personnel run off the field, and short-yardage personnel run on.)

- "It's first and 10. Give me standard personnel." (Standard personnel run onto the field.)

— TABLE 14.1 —

Sample Weekly Practice Schedule

Day of the week	Practice goals
Monday	• Introduce run-situation runs and run-situation passes to both offense and defense • Work on punt protection • Work on kicking game: extra point, field goal, and rush
Tuesday	• Introduce more run-situation runs and passes • Introduce pass-situation passes • Work on blitz and blitz pickup in run situations • Work on kicking: extra points, field goals, rush, and punt block and return
Wednesday	• Work on field-goal, extra-point, and punt protection • Work on run-situation runs and passes • Work on pass-situation runs and passes • Work on blitz and blitz pickup in run situations • Add short-yardage and goal-line situations
Thursday	• Introduce more run-situation runs and passes • Work on pass-situation runs and passes • Work on blitz and blitz pickup in run situations • Work on short-yardage and goal-line situations • Add blitz and blitz pickup in pass situations • Work on kickoff returns
Friday	• Rehearse all phases of the kicking game • Rehearse offensive plan on field and call plays by substitution • Rehearse defensive plan on the field and substitution in all strategy situations

As I call for different personnel, the coaches check to be sure that the proper people are running onto the field. After six or seven minutes of this, we put the defensive players on the field and go over defensive substitutions. I say something like the following:

- "The opponents have yellow personnel. Give me 4-0 personnel."
- "They have standard people. Give me regular personnel."
- "They have goal-line personnel. Give me goal-line defense."

We go through all substitutions with defensive personnel against the opponent's offensive personnel as well as substitutions for strategy situations.

I never allow talking during this time. If a player is not on the field physically, I want him to be there mentally.

We then check the depth chart for all phases of kicking-game substitutions. We call the first team on the field with their backups behind them and rehearse substitutions for punt protection, punt blocking, extra-point and field-goal protection, extra-point and field-goal blocking, kickoff and kickoff returns, and onside kicks and onside-kick defense.

We always know exactly what we want to accomplish during each two-a-day practice. I ask the coaches on my staff what they want to put in during the morning practice for offense, defense, and special teams and again for the afternoon practice schedule.

I try to coordinate what the offense and defense work on. When the offense works on wide running plays, the defense works on end-run forces. The offense and defense can then work against each other, not against just the scout team. Table 14.2 shows other examples. Although making out this kind of schedule requires more work for the head coach, the benefits are worth it.

A good defensive team can always adjust to an unusual formation and movement. Making the adjustment, however, it is not always easy. A team needs practice time to learn how to anticipate. Every day for five or six days, I put in a period that lasts about 15 minutes. The number-one offense and number-one defense work on the field while the rest of the team watches

TABLE 14.2

Coordinating Offensive and Defensive Practice

When the offense works on . . .	The defense works on . . .
Goal-line offense	Goal-line defense
Run-situation offense	Run-situation defense
Pickup blitz	Blitz package
Short-yardage offense	Short-yardage defense
Pass-situation offense	Pass-situation defense
Plus-territory offense	Plus-territory defense
Backed-up offense	Backed-up defense
Last play of the game	Last play of the game

the play at their positions. I ask the offense to huddle and call a formation that includes some kind of movement. The movement could be a halfback in motion, a divided tight end, or a wide receiver moving from flip to standard or standard to flip. I want every possible formation and every possible movement.

The offense calls the formation and movement, goes to the line, gives the defense a look, goes through the movement, and snaps the ball, but they do not run a play. The offensive coaches see that the players line up properly and get the proper movement.

The defense calls a defense, adjusts to the formation, and calls the forces and pass coverages. When the offense starts the movement, the defense signal caller calls out the proper ad-

Courtesy of University of Alabama/Athletic Dept.-Kent Gidley

justment. The strong safety adjusts the coverage properly, and the players responsible for the proper end-run force call their forces. The defensive coaches watch their players and correct them if the adjustments are incorrect. The players not on the field watch their positions and mentally carry out their responsibilities.

After a few days, offensive players can get into any alignment they want with movement, and at the same time the defensive players have confidence that they can line up correctly against any formation and adjust to any kind of movement.

All defensive coaches must be on the same page because it's possible to adjust more than one way. When a player asks a question, I want all defensive coaches to give the same answer. We spend a lot of time in meetings deciding exactly how we will adjust, what the coverage will become, and what the force will be. I do not want two coaches giving two different answers.

I always insist that our defense be able to adjust to any unusual formation and handle any movement that could come from it. When your players are confident and prepared, they will play better.

In organizing a practice session, it's important to understand that your players improve more when practicing against good players. Your players can learn assignments, run proper adjustments, and fake properly against a scout team. But if you want them to make great strides, the first team must go against the first team some of the time.

Twice a week, I have the best offense, minus wide receivers, against the best defense, minus cornerbacks. The offensive team can run what it wants to run. I ask only that the team make four yards or better. The defense can run whatever it wants. I ask only that it stop the offense. This session usually lasts 9 to 12 minutes, and I hold my breath hoping that no one gets hurt. We do the same thing for third-down situations, except then we run the entire third-down offense team against the entire third-down defensive unit.

We work with chains and the down marker. I give a situation, such as third and eight. We set the chains, and the offense must make nine yards. The defense has to stop them. The game plan has nothing to do with this drill. I simply want the offense and defense to improve.

These drills never last long. We schedule 10 to 15 minutes, and I usually cut it short, always after a good play by the side that needs a boost in confidence.

One drill we do every day is to kick extra points and field goals, and practice rushing those situations. Before the drill is over, I ask the offense to fake the kick and pass instead. I want the defense to expect a pass on every situation. The defensive player needs to know his responsibility.

At least once a week, I have the field-goal kicking team on the sideline and say, "18 seconds, no timeouts, clock running." Then I send the players in from the sideline running full speed to their positions. They get in position and snap the ball. We have never done this in a game, but we are ready if the situation ever presents itself.

At times in a game you must do some unusual things, and you must rehearse these situations. For example, your team may need to give a safety during a game, and they should know when and how to do it. This play requires practice. You should practice other unique situations such as using the clock and knowing when to call timeout and when to take a penalty, taking the last snap of the game, and fair catching a punt for a free kick.

I believe that more teams are overworked than underworked. Time is one of our most valuable commodities, and we must use it wisely. Time on the field will vary according to the day of the week, especially on Mondays and Fridays. Practice time on Tuesday, Wednesday, and Thursday may vary by only 10 to 15 minutes. A typical Tuesday, Wednesday, or Thursday practice might look something like this:

- **Specialty period (20 minutes).** During this period anyone who handles the ball can get some extra work. All kickers, punt catchers, and kickoff receivers receive supervised instruction. The quarterbacks can rotate snappers, and the coach can work on kicking into the wind, kicking with the wind, or whatever needs the most attention.

- **Exercise and stretching period (15 minutes).** You can do this as a team, by offense or defense, or by position. I prefer team exercises because they are similar to pregame exercise and stretching time.
- **Group work (20 minutes).** During this period each individual coach takes his players to a particular area and works on what his group needs. We discuss these needs in the staff meeting while going over the practice schedule. The head coach needs to know exactly what each group will cover.
- **Extra points and field goals (10 minutes).** The players work on extra points, field-goal kick and protection, and extra-point and field-goal rush. I do this every day.
- **Run-situation runs or run-situation runs and passes (20 minutes).** Depending on the day of the week, both offense and defense will work on these situations.
- **Team offense versus defense (10 minutes).** Team offense minus wide receivers works against team defense minus cornerbacks, practicing good players against good players to improve. We usually did this on Tuesday and Wednesday.
- **Blitz and blitz pickup (15 minutes).** Work in this period usually focuses more on run situations than passing situations.
- **Passing situations (20 minutes).** This period includes blitz and blitz pickup.
- **Kicking game (10 minutes).** In the middle of practice, work on some phase of the kicking game.
- **Goal line (20 to 25 minutes).** Depending on the day of the week, devote 10 minutes to goal-line situations and 10 to 15 minutes for run-situation runs and passes.
- **Protection (10 minutes).** In the early part of the week, use this time for punt protection.
- **Conditioning (10 to 12 minutes).** Conditioning can take numerous forms, but we keep it in the 10- to 12-minute range.
- **Closing (5 minutes).** When practice is over I always try to find something positive to say before I send the team into the dressing room. Then I send everyone in except the snappers, who have to execute 10 perfect snaps before they go in.

When working on practice time, it's important to remember the time allowed by NCAA rules. You must not exceed this time limitation.

All areas of your practice field should have a name or a number. For example, you may split the field into field A (left, middle, and right) and field B (left, middle, and right). Or you may want to divide the field according to what part of the game you practice there (for example, sled field, kicking field, offensive field, and defensive field). Then give a name, number, or letter to different areas of each field. A system like this eliminates confusion, and coaches and players know exactly where they are to go.

In planning practice, it is important to keep your players hydrated. How and when you choose to make water available to the athletes is up to you, but you must build water breaks into your schedule.

A head coach should be an expert in all phases of the game. He should not rely entirely on his coordinators. The head coach should know what kind of offense, defense, and kicking game he wants. He needs good people who can coach the techniques properly.

The coach should ask for ideas and strategy from his staff, but he should make the final decisions. Everywhere I've been—Texas A&M, St. Louis, Phoenix, and Alabama—I've made out the practice schedule, but I've always asked each assistant coach to list on the chalkboard what his players needed to work on. The offensive-line coach might want some work on team pass protection or picking up stunts. The linebacker coach might want to spend time on zone drops or covering a back man-to-man. The secondary coach might want work on open-field tackling. I'll try to include drills they've suggested, but I also have to keep in mind what's in the best interest of the entire team. The head coach must make those decisions.

15

Maximizing the Ability of Players

Joe Tiller

We use a number of methods to build our football team. We try to identify ability levels, develop trust within the team and the coaching staff, set daily expectations, be perfectionists, and do the little things right.

Coaching is teaching, and to teach, you need to identify exactly where the student is with his physical ability and knowledge. We never assume that any of our athletes can already perform or understand what we're trying to teach. We must identify each athlete's capabilities by determining current strengths and weaknesses. Therefore, we perform an initial evaluation to determine the athlete's physical and mental ability.

After we do the evaluation, we try to raise the level of ability through technique and skill work on the football field and with classroom work off the field. If a quarterback has a footwork problem, then we try to improve it with specific footwork drills and technique. If arm strength is lacking, we have specific drills for that. If the player needs to increase his knowledge, we spend more time in the classroom watching videotape.

We try to enhance trust between the coaching staff and players so that the players believe what we tell them. With that trust, players understand that we're not doing something just to be doing it but that we have the athlete's best interest in mind. To maximize performance, players must understand what we expect from them. We must lay down our criteria and expectations, and we must be consistent in enforcing the criteria. Coaches can't apply different rules for each player. We strive to create an environment in which the player with the least playing time feels that he's as much

173

a part of the group as the best player on the team. Find a responsibility for each player and a role for every player.

We try to have high expectations as coaches, and we set daily, weekly, and season goals. Once we reach a goal, we re-evaluate and then reset the goal. We constantly talk to our players about setting a level of performance, and although we as coaches try not to harp on reaching a goal, we are constantly setting a level of expectation. In every practice we try to hold them to their goals and prevent them from backsliding.

We have a saying that "You're either getting better or you're getting worse, but you are not staying the same." That is one of the ways that we help the player understand that he needs

Courtesy of Tom Campbell/Purdue University

to get better every time he is out on the practice field, that we as a team need to get better, and that everybody needs to push. Whether the player is a starter or number five at his position, he should be pushing the other players.

I think our focus on competition helps a lot. We try to create more competition by having a level of expectation and asking the players to reach it not every once in a while, but every day of the week. We have an expectation for that day, and unless they achieve it, they may slide back in the depth chart.

We coach the little things—doing things the right way, being on time, giving 100 percent. We don't like guys loafing—we expect 100 percent on and off the field. We coach all players about what we expect from them and what they should expect from themselves. We coach them hard on the little things and try to make them better. They hear repeatedly that we expect consistency from them, so they must see that we coaches are consistent, too. We come to practice every day with the attitude of getting better. We don't take a day off, and we won't allow them to take a day off. They need to know that they can count on us. When players can count on coaches, as time goes by relationships develop that transform the team into a family. And in a family, each member is accountable to everyone else.

Getting Players to Learn

Learning is a step-by-step process. When a player arrives on campus, we assess his learning style to identify how he learns best. Everybody learns in a different way, and we need to present material in a way that allows each player to learn efficiently and effectively.

Depending on how players learn, we try to break down what we're trying to teach them and present it verbally, visually on the board, or in practice. Some kids learn by memorizing written material. Other kids learn visually and need to see it on the board. Other kids learn aurally; they will listen to you and understand. Some kids have to learn by hands-on experience or a walk-through. Others learn better when they see it at full speed.

When we go out onto the field, we demonstrate what we want and walk through it. Whether we are presenting drills or techniques, once the players have a foundation of what we want, we begin to pick up the tempo. We begin to drill those points and move at a faster pace. We film what we're doing, take it back inside, and watch the video. This is the time to make improvements, to start to coach the players and show them where they can improve.

We try to break down all our drills to the fundamentals. For instance, with defensive backs we never backpedal before we break. We start with stand there and plant, then plant and go. Then we do a couple steps backward, then plant and go. Then we try a slow backpedal, then plant and go. Finally, we pick it up and progress to where we can do it at full speed. I try to do that with every technique. You can keep building on the fundamentals if you have a strong foundation.

We prefer to present material in the classroom setting and then go out and walk through it. We try to break the material down into little bits and pieces and then show the players how it fits together. Our coaches do a good job of testing our players, giving a written or oral test so that the players have to repeat what they are trying to do.

For example, when we put in a new defense, we draw the defense on the board in our individual meetings. We then go to the practice field and walk through that defense during prepractice. Each coach describes the technique or responsibility for his players. We want the whole group to understand what is going on so that they know what we are trying to do as a unit. We also describe the strengths and weaknesses of that call and why we would make the call. We try to make our instructions explicit. Explain it, demonstrate it, and drill it. We never assume that everybody understands a concept the first time, the second time, or even the third time.

We cover everything in practice and allow players to make mistakes so that we can offer positive reinforcement in practice with the correction. Then on the game field, they already understand what they are to do. We try to make sure that we put them in every possible situation in practice.

We practice for a set time with a goal of what we want to accomplish in that practice. We accomplish it, and then we get off the field. Players would rather have an intense hour-and-a-half practice than a two-and-a-half-hour survival contest.

Getting Players to Believe

You must have a firm grasp of what you're talking about. A player can sense when you're not sure about what you're teaching. When I first started coaching, I was given things to teach I didn't totally understand. Consequently, I couldn't teach comprehensively.

You also have to believe in your system before your players will. Players are not stupid. They watch TV, and they know what the pros are doing. Players constantly question our system. You must be able to tell them why you use what you use and why your system is the best one for your team.

We teach things that other teams do, but we also teach things that others do not. There are always different ideas and methods for doing things. But I believe in what we do, and I think that comes across because I'm enthusiastic. I'm also consistent in what I teach. We don't teach one thing one day and something else the next. We are confident that our system works, and we believe in it. With that confidence comes the players' trust and belief that you are doing what you should be doing.

A challenge we faced at both Wyoming and Purdue was that our system was much different from the system that had been in place before our arrival. At Wyoming we were converting from a wishbone team to a passing offense. At Purdue we were converting from a standard two-back, 70 percent rushing attack into a 70 percent throwing offense. We introduced a different style, and that helped us because neither program had achieved a great deal of success before our arrival. The general attitude among the players was that they hadn't had success running the ball, so they might as well try something else. I think the newness of the system, running the spread offense, helped us some.

The head coach and the nine assistant coaches must all believe the same thing. We have always presented our system to the team as a unified group of coaches who believe in what we are trying to accomplish. At both Wyoming and Purdue our kids believed in what we did because we presented it in a positive manner with the intent of making football fun. They may not have believed that from the start, but they eventually saw the results.

Players like to have fun, and we've made the system fun here at Purdue. We use a system that involves all the players, and that is a selling point. Our system does not focus on a couple of star players. Combine that approach with an aggressive, attacking style, which players like, and making the sale is much easier. The players need to understand that you're in it to improve them, not only as players but also as people. We try to make sure that in the early stages we face a situation where the players have to trust me. Then we go to bat for them. The situation might occur in a specific practice, it might involve a social problem, or it might be something off campus. But somewhere we try to create a situation where we earn their trust. Then we try to create situations where they can count on us and we can count on them.

A method we use to get and keep the players' attention is to stress certain critical concepts. At the end of the day, if you are stressing creating turnovers or tackles for loss or whatever, pull out examples on video of guys doing it correctly. Show players what you want and expect. We don't talk about what we don't want—we talk about what we want. We emphasize why we like a particular play or call and show the players how to do it.

Reinforcing Learning and Discouraging Errors

Reinforcing learning, correcting performance, and discouraging errors is the essence of teaching. Make sure that you have a teaching progression. Provide a bit of knowledge and then reinforce it by praising the player who executes correctly. Rather than just continuing to add new plays, you need to teach two plays and make sure the player knows two plays well before you move on. I believe you do that through positive statements. Rather than focusing on a mistake, focus on what he should have been doing. Tell the player he needs to make an earlier decision or that he needs to understand the play to make a more informed decision.

A primary goal of coaching is to minimize mistakes. Coaching is based on reputation and being proactive in your approach with players to develop in them a constant desire to improve. Having better athletes is an advantage, but usually the team that makes the fewest mistakes will win.

One of the best incentives for learning is playing time. If players don't do something the way you want them to do it, they don't play. All players are motivated by their desire to get on the field.

Always Be Positive

When correcting performance, I try to sandwich a negative comment or a correction between two positive statements. We first give a player a little positive stroke, then share what he needs to improve on, and try to end with another positive stroke. Most players already know when they've made an error. I want to focus on the positive so that the players won't continue to hammer themselves by focusing on the negative.

Do not tell a player what *not* to do—tell him what *to* do. If we tell a quarterback, "Don't throw that out into the rolled-up corner," soon all he thinks about is throwing it into that rolled-up corner. We want to make sure that he knows what a rolled-up corner is and tell him how he should throw the ball versus the rolled-up corner so that he starts visualizing himself doing it the right way.

When we make a mistake or lose a game, we talk about how we are going to correct it and then we move on. We don't hold mistakes against a player—we just keep on moving on. We use the game of golf as an analogy to impress this concept on our players. If you make a bad shot at the beginning of your round and continue to think about it, the shot affects you for the rest of the round. We don't want to do that. If we make a mistake on the first play of the game, we correct it, move on, and get back into the flow as quickly as possible.

We understand that occasionally a player may just be out of sync. We have to replace him, but he can recover and come back. We let him know that he'll get another opportunity. You just have to keep working and keep trying to get better. It goes back to your teaching and evaluation techniques. From the first day of practice, we try to teach from a positive situation.

Expect Maximum Effort

One of the ideas we stress is that we want players to give 100 percent effort. We tell them that without 100 percent effort, they are not going to see the football field. We want to put guys on the field who not only do things right but also make plays. We reinforce the need by pointing out great efforts on film.

We also give our players an effort grade. At Purdue we want to be known by how hard we play. We post the effort grades, and everybody knows who performed well. The player sees himself within his position and knows the level he needs to bring himself up to if he wants to get out on the field.

We emphasize effort, technique, and assignment competency. We want to go out and play hard, use correct technique, and make sure that our players carry out their assignments. But we also want to be productive. A player may line up correctly, use good technique, and take care of his assignment but not make any plays. We want to do things right, but also we want to find guys who are playmakers or difference makers. We want guys who will score a lot of points for our defense, make tackles for loss, sack the quarterback, make interceptions, and recover fumbles.

We have a performance chart where we keep track of production points. We grade our players after the game on their technique, effort, and the number of plays made. We give production points for positive and negative production. We will always have players who rarely do anything technically right but still make plays. Those guys can have a huge number of production points. When a player sees his production points posted, he can tell what he needs to focus on. If he has minus 10 production points in a game, obviously he didn't play very well and made some mistakes.

Something I try to keep in mind is that although I live football 24 hours a day, these kids live it just 3 hours a day. I try to remember that the players, regardless of their failures or successes, are young and that it is my responsibility to mold them. I try to treat them as men and never back them into a corner where they feel the need to come out fighting. At times I have to give tough love by staying on them and trying to get them to do something that they don't realize they can do. If you treat players as men and you are fair, they will lay it on the line for you.

When we bring the players back to fall camp, I explain in a squad meeting what I expect of them and what they can expect of me. I try not to hide anything. I am honest with them, and I tell them I expect them to be honest with me. I think our players view me as a no-nonsense guy. They also know that I am not perfect and that they aren't either. We will make mistakes, but we live with them and go on. I think that I earn the respect of my players just by being honest with them and being the guy who's going to push them to be the best they can be.

Be a Mentor, Not a Buddy

To earn a player's respect, you need to respect him. I respect the rights of the players, try to treat them all the same, and care about them. But I have long felt that a player respects you more if you don't try to be his buddy all the time. I believe that coaches and players have a unique relationship in which the coach is a combination father, friend, and mentor, but not a buddy. We are not the same age or from the same generation. Because we come from different eras, we are not going to be best buddies. But players need to understand what the coaches are trying to do and that we are working toward the same goal.

We tell our players that our job is to get them to do what they don't want to do so that they can achieve their goals. You want them to feel good about coming to visit with you, but you must maintain some sort of distance or cushion between you and the players. Otherwise, when I get on them about something they did wrong, they think I don't like them.

Early each season, I sit down with the squad and lay out the basis of our relationship. As long as we are consistent with our philosophies and policies, the relationship will be strong. Kids are looking for people they can rely on. Even if they don't agree with every one of our policies, at least they understand why we conduct our program the way we do.

Be consistent. Like us, players don't like surprises. They don't like coaches who react in inconsistent ways. It's often said that teams take on the demeanor of the head coach. I think this is true. Our teams at Wyoming and here at Purdue like to have fun with football. I don't like surprises, I like things planned, and I want to know what's going on. But whether things are happening according to plan or not, I don't become flustered. I think you'll find that our team doesn't become flustered either.

We have an open-door policy. If a player has a problem and needs to talk about school, home, family, girlfriend, or whatever, we are always available.

Our players are our priority. If we are in a meeting and a player needs us, we'll stop our meeting and take care of the player. We want players to know that they are important. We are ready to listen and help. They may not always like what they hear, but they know that we'll be honest with them. If you show that you care about what is going on in their lives, not just what they do on the field, your players will respect you more. We try to make sure our players see us being active in their lives.

Conditioning for High Performance

Mike Bellotti

At the University of Oregon we have always taken great pride in our ability to field a football team that is in great condition year round and can play an entire football game full speed. We believe that the methods and techniques we employ are special and create a winning edge. I want to share them with you.

First, I'll discuss several concepts that define our program. The most important concept is that power or ultimate performance is made up of three components: strength, speed, and agility. I'll discuss both long-term and short-term goals for athletes and how to facilitate and use strength and speed improvements over the course of their careers. I'll provide a yearly schedule of our training regimens broken down into periods based on the various seasons in and around competition. I'll also provide a seasonal plan broken down further into cycles of training to develop power endurance. I'll include weekly objectives and daily breakdowns of activities and discuss specific viewpoints regarding workout rules, regimens, and the progressions and technical components necessary to improve change of direction, which we feel is essential to success on the football field.

Quest for Performance

Football conditioning is a quest for power and ultimate performance. We believe in the need for a total athletic development program that will still fit into the NCAA-mandated workout week. Workouts must accomplish more in less time while avoiding breakdown, injury, and overtraining. For the purpose of training football players, we define power and apply the formula shown in figure 16.1 to football athleticism.

$$P = \frac{F \times d}{t}$$

P = power (football performance)

F = force application (strength/impulse)

d = distance transition (agility/coordination)

t = time reduction (speed/acceleration)

Figure 16.1 This simple equation defines and illustrates power.

To apply more force (F), the athlete needs improved strength. Strength can be viewed as relative (proportional to body weight) and dynamic (strength with the application of speed). Reducing the time factor (t) requires accelerated movements.

Agility, the most-often neglected component, allows an individual to use strength with speed effectively. The coordination needed to make optimal distance transitions (d) has certain physical, proportional, and medical limitations. Agility training to enhance coordination should be just as important as strength training and speed training.

Goals and Objectives

In setting training goals for a football player, long-term goals stretch over the length of the athlete's playing career. Long-term goals revolve around explosive power, which includes applied strength, directional speed, and transitional agility. Our goal is to develop an athlete who can powerfully accelerate out of a stance to a specific point on the field, be forceful in engaging an opponent, and be agile enough to power away from that engagement—whether through the opponent or around him—to make whatever play is necessary.

Many people emphasize sheer strength, but applied strength, which we will discuss later, is the key to success. Individuals do not necessarily use their weight-room strength to become better football players. The same problem exists with speed. Athletes who are exceptionally fast straight ahead have great potential but are extremely limited if they are unable to use that speed in a multitude of directions. A third point concerns transitional agility, which involves change of direction. This change can be on the field from point A to point B and then on to point C. A change of direction may also occur in the most basic movement form—within the body. The posture and coordination that the body uses to make the transition from flexion to extension to rotation is the basis for all agile movements on the field of play.

Short-term goals for each training period (off-season, preseason, and so on) are the basis for acquiring the capacity to do a greater amount of quality work. Short-term objectives revolve around power endurance, which includes work capacity, recovery, and stamina. An increased ability to do quality repetitions will elevate the chances for developing skills applicable to the game, which involves many starts and stops. Exhibiting great power in football for only the first few plays of a series or game will not bring success. Interval work involving high speed and intensity with adequate recovery helps to create the stamina that can produce quality repetitions of powerful work.

Short-term goals develop greater capacity for quality work and decrease recovery time. Each is a stepping-stone for the next training phase, period, and year. We break down objectives so that we can work on them to improve the preparational, technical, developmental, and transitional aspects of conditioning, both long term and short term. Figure 16.2 shows a daily breakdown of the necessary areas.

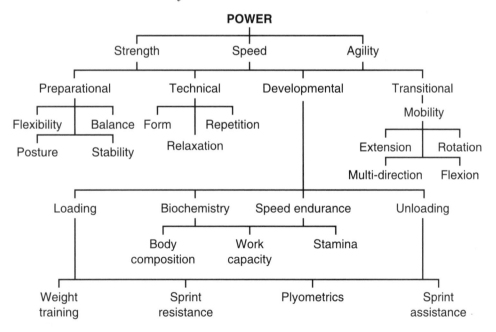

Figure 16.2 Breakdown of important training areas.
Adapted, by permission, from Radcliffe and Farentinos, 1999, *High-Powered Plyometrics.* (Champaign, IL: Human Kinetics, 159.)

As we watch a football game being played at any level, certain players stand out, usually those who make plays or put themselves into position to make plays. The ability to get quickly from a starting point to any other point on the field is more important than any other skill. Developing this ability requires a great amount of training. We can think of countless athletes who have great strength in the weight room; outstanding speed on the straightaway; and terrific ability to jump, catch, and hit yet are seldom able to display their talent because they cannot get into position to make the play. Our goal is to train the football athlete to exhibit greater mobility and agility.

Mobility is fluid movement through great range in all planes of direction. It is also posture, balance, stability, and flexibility involved in the flexion, extension, and rotation of the body at the most efficient speed possible. Agility is efficient movement transitions with changes in direction and, more specifically, the ability to make speed cuts and power cuts in a reactive manner. The breakdown in terms of percentage of application for a complete year according to training for health, development, and performance is illustrated in figure 16.3.

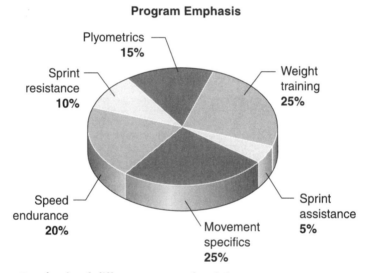

Figure 16.3 Emphasis of different areas of training.

Planning

Planning includes both an annual plan with the year broken down into periods and a seasonal plan with the periods broken down into phases.

In the annual plan we need to view training as it extends over the entire year so that our long-term goal of progressive development can overlap in a stair-step manner. Three or four different periods fill the year of the football athlete, one being the segment in which competitive games occur (figure 16.4). Performance during the in-season is the ultimate objective; therefore, specific strength, speed, and agility progressions should be at their planned peak. We work backward from this point through the preseason, off-season, and postseason. We begin the postseason with general training and progress to specific strength, speed, and agility techniques necessary for in-season success.

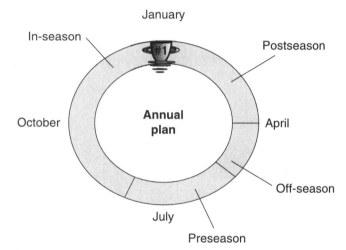

Figure 16.4 The annual training plan breaks the year into different seasons.

Seasonal plans should depict the goals and methods for strength, speed, agility, and the enduring effects of these qualities (power endurance) for every phase. Traditional lifting progresses through the postseason (winter) with longer buildup phases to increase joint range of motion, muscular endurance, and hypertrophy. Maximum strength phases, maintaining range of motion and technique, follow. Attention to power should begin in the postseason period and should be part of all training periods. Speed is more difficult to develop than muscular strength because speed requires more nervous-system involvement. If more powerful movement is desired, the training must include exercises of a more rapid nature.

The off-season period (spring) is segmented with a shorter muscular buildup phase, more maximum strength work, and continued speed development (figure 16.5). The preseason period is similar to the off-season period, with the majority of time spent in power development. By power development, we mean speed and strength specific to desired competitive skills. In preseason, training should mimic the specific movements of competitive play.

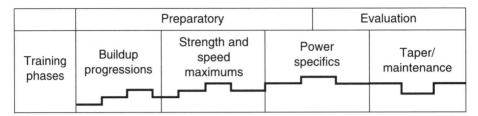

Figure 16.5 Training phases are further divided into preparatory and evaluation phases.

In all the training periods, at least one day per week should include sets of position-specific sprints (some coaches refer to these as metabolics). These sprinting reps are a series of starts, accelerations, and movements that completely mimic game play for a specific position, including routes by receivers and ends, drops and recoveries by defensive backs and backers, and get-offs with pulls, spins, swims, and so forth by linemen.

Start and acceleration training is of prime importance in postseason field training. Emphasis is on the technical components of starts from differing two-point stances and acceleration mechanics. Progressions of deceleration training follow. We work into and out of forward, lateral, and backward positions to develop the proper techniques for the various changes of direction. We will discuss the different change-of-direction mechanics in a later section.

Off-Season Training Objectives

The spring off-season segment progresses from acceleration to speed. Training takes movement patterns out to slightly longer distances and places more emphasis on drills that cover greater portions of the field.

We begin every training routine with warm-up activities that are movement oriented and emphasize core stability and mobility (calisthenics, gymnastics, and so forth). Exercises that are dynamic and explosive should precede those geared for absolute or relative strength. We train with higher intensities early, tapering to moderate or lighter percentages of load in the later part of the week.

General acceleration work starts the conditioning week, special speed work (sprint resistance or sprint assistance) is in the middle, and specific work capacities finish the week.

The preseason (summer) culminates field training with starts, accelerations, decelerations, and changes of direction in more of a speed-endurance setting. These summer training bouts train the work-to-rest ratio that matches game conditions and continuous play or no-huddle simulations. Table 16.1 shows an example of a preseason week.

TABLE 16.1

Sample Preseason Weekly Workout

Day of the week	Training program
Monday	Core work Dynamic lifts Plyometrics Starts and accelerations
Tuesday	Core work Strength lifts Run technique Position-specific speed and tempo
Wednesday	Rest
Thursday	Core work Dynamic lifts Plyometrics Sprint resistance and agility work
Friday	Core work Strength lifts Mobility Speed endurance

In-Season Training

Every training routine should begin with warm-up activities that are movement oriented and emphasize core stability and mobility. We stress work capacity early to aid recovery from the workouts of the previous week as well as to build a base for the new week of training. Midweek training should focus on position-specific conditioning and high-quality change-of-direction repetitions. We finish the week on Thursday by emphasizing efficient reactions and effective accelerations. This aspect will diminish as the season progresses. Figure 16.6 shows an example of an in-season practice plan.

Strength work is the focus early in the week. More dynamic lifts are used midweek, and elastic-reactive work (for example, snatch, squat jump, medicine ball plyometrics) will be used on the day before competition to aid in uploading the nervous system. Table 16.2 shows a sample training schedule for a competition week.

Opponent _____   Surface _____

Climate _____   Conditions _____

Period	Def. line	Def. backs	Off. line	Off. backs	Time
	General warm-up				10 min.
1	Agilities	Drops/releases	Get-offs	Ball handling	10 min.
2	No-huddle/hurry-up mock scrimmage				5 min.
3	Sleds/chutes	Coverage skills	Sleds/chutes	Route review	10 min.
4	Versus off. line	With LBs	Versus def. line	With QBs, TEs	10 min.
5	Inside drills	1 on 1	Inside drills	1 on 1	10 min.
6	Special teams versus opponent looks				20 min.
7	11 versus 11 scheme work				10 min.
8	Pass rush	7 on 7	Pass rush	7 on 7	15 min.
9	Team execution work				25 min.
10	Team or position or specialty conditioning				7 min.

Figure 16.6   In-season practice plan.

TABLE 16.2

Sample In-Season Weekly Workout

Day of the week	Training program
Monday	Core work Strength lift Practice Total team work-capacity conditioning
Tuesday	Practice Specialty or position conditioning
Wednesday	Core work Dynamic lifts Practice Total team agility conditioning
Thursday	Practice Tapered starts and acceleration
Friday	Core work Reactive lifts Walk-through
Saturday	Game day

The daily breakdown shows that we use a sequencing of workloads. Early in the week we condition as a total team. We then progress to specific position techniques including special teams. Finally, we do total team conditioning with an emphasis on change of direction and explosive power. The ultimate in-season conditioning package includes practice sessions that are mentally demanding and physically hard so that players perceive the games as easy.

We expect conditioning to occur during the flow of practice. Players run to and from all drills, resting only while in line. After sufficient warm-up we begin each practice session with a no-huddle or hurry-up series, pitting the offense versus the defense. This activity kick starts practice by simulating game-specific conditions in the most challenging mental and physical ways. Players must think, align, and react in a hurry-up mode.

We also believe in conditioning at the end of practice both for the obvious physiological benefits and to reinforce the concept of never giving up and always being able to overcome fatigue. Other aspects of physiological and psychological conditioning that need to be addressed include, but are not limited to, exposing the players to crowd noise, different game surfaces, temperature, wind, altitude, and the elements.

We rely on positive peer pressure as a tool to motivate athletes in the pursuit of optimal physical conditioning. Leadership and team chemistry

© Eric Evans Photography

are two essential elements for success in this area. We use all these conditions to help motivate athletes to have confidence in their durability and their ability to make plays in any situation.

Posture, balance, stability, and flexibility are prerequisites to using strength, speed, and agility in football performance. We use the same four components as evaluation tools to indicate progress from one exercise to a more difficult one. The ultimate goal will be to exhibit these qualities with functional strength, high speed, and efficient transitions in changing direction. Therefore, players must perform as much work as possible while on their feet because balance is crucial to success in football.

Workout Sessions

The reasoning for cycling workouts within each phase is to allow for recovery and regeneration. Although changes in phases and cycles of training promote development, we must abide by certain rules of consistent training. The following are the restoration credos we adhere to with our football athletes.

Rule 1: Warm Up

Players should perform a complete warm-up to begin a workout, maintain core warmth throughout, and adequately cool down after completing the workout. A general warm-up breaks a sweat and mobilizes the entire body. Core warming to strengthen and enhance mobility in the trunk (abs, low back, hips, and upper back) follows.

Players perform a specific warming by doing modified, low-stress versions of the pulling, squatting, pushing, running, jumping, and throwing activities. By using this approach, players work proper mechanics before placing any load on the system. If proper posture, balance, stability, and flexibility are not apparent in this portion of the workout, players must make adjustments before loading. Athletes must show that they can pull, squat, push, flex, extend, and rotate through a proper range of motion without limitations. Athletes will maintain warmth throughout the core of the body by following certain workout guidelines:

- The warm-up is followed by speed and dynamic work such as explosive movements (clean, snatch, jumping, and so on).

- The strength work occurs next (heavy multiple-joint movements such as squat, lunge, jerk, towing, sandpit, and so on).

- Isolated work such as lying or seated movements (bench, pulleys, and so on) follows multiple-joint work.

- The workout should end with mobility work that uses full, fluid body movements (jump rope, direction drills, partner stretching, and so on).

Rule 2: Plan Intense Workouts

For athletes to be able to observe rule 1, workouts must be short, concise, intense, and coordinated. We suggest a one-hour comprehensive menu. Athletes must move efficiently through the workout. Each workout is coordinated so that each athlete and his partner or group can complete the work with appropriate rest but without wasting time.

Athletes don't need workouts that last two hours or more. Long workouts generally include excessive rest, trips to the water fountain, idle conversation, and subsequent core cooling, thereby increasing the chance for breakdowns if intense work is attempted. Common sense dictates that it is more difficult to keep the core warm and maintain workout intensity for extended periods. Each workout or training session, whether it be in a weight room or on the field, can adhere to the stages referred to in figure 16.2 on page 183: preparational (dynamic core warm-up), technical (form running and lifting movements), developmental (all forms of loading, duration, and speed), and transitional (mobility and recovery). Table 16.3 shows a sample workout.

TABLE 16.3

Training Examples for Weight-Room and Conditioning-Field Settings

Time	Weight-room setting	Conditioning-field setting
:00	Dynamic warm-up (walk, lunge, crawl, jog, skip, shoulder roll, trunk twist, hip rotations, leg swings) Static stretch Core work (posture, balance, stability, flexibility)	Dynamic warm-up (walk, lunge, crawl, jog, skip, shoulder roll, trunk twist, hip rotations, leg swings) Static stretch
:11	Technical period Core specifics (postural pulling, squatting, pushing)	Technical period (form walk, skip, run, prance, gallop—forward, laterally, and backward)
:21	Developmental period (main lifting sequence of circuit, stage, general, maximum, dynamic, and elastic strength training)	Developmental period (main sequence of plyometric, sprint with resistance or assistance, and speed-endurance work)
:46	Mobility period (specific training involving resistance loads and footwork, squat jumps, medicine ball presses and throws, vibration work)	Mobility period (drills and games, speed cuts and power cuts, situation starts, timed change-of-direction drills, slide board)
:56	Cool-down (partner contract and relax and assisted isolated stretching)	Cool-down (partner contract and relax and assisted isolated stretching)

Rule 3: Plan Variety

We maintain variety in exercise mode and stimulus as a way of cycling workout stress and maintaining work intensity. Variety in exercise mode allows athletes to attack all workouts with vigor, intensity, and renewed enthusiasm.

When we plan a light workout or easy week, however, we do not want the athletes to confuse this with a low effort. We like to have high-intensity efforts, while at the same time cycling the stress of the work in a high, low, and moderate fashion (these also are adjustable). Downloading the workload from heavy to light can simply be a matter of adjusting the type or style of exercise within the methods we have planned.

For example, every weight-room workout will have a pulling, squatting, and pushing movement in the developmental portion, just as every conditioning workout will have a jump, bound, hop, and stride or sprint portion. By changing the type of squat, jump, or sprint drills, we can alter the stress it will have on the body and subsequent recovery. Table 16.4 shows more examples.

Changing the number of major joints employed in a movement, moving the barbell on the shoulders from behind the neck to the front, moving off both legs rather than one, and forcing athletes to be accountable for proper mechanics can unload or load the stress of the workout and the time of recovery from it. Yet every workout requires that athletes have the proper attitude and work ethic. Athletic advancement ceases if athletes do not exhibit the correct mental and physical approach.

TABLE 16.4

Examples of High-Intensity, Moderate-Intensity, and Light-Intensity Workouts

High-intensity (heavy)	Moderate-intensity (medium)	Light-intensity (low)
Cleans off floor	Cleans from blocks	Snatch pulls from hang
Back squat or lunge	Front lunge or single-leg squat	Overhead squat or lunge
Push jerk	Incline press	Dumbbell military
Bounding	Galloping	Prancing
Assisted sprints	Hill sprints (6- to 8-degree incline)	Gears (ins and outs)

Progressions

As mentioned before, applied strength requires that athletes be strong and powerful while correctly employing posture, balance, stability, and flexibility. Training progressions are designed to foster that.

Strength Progression

Core-stabilization exercises based on gymnastic movements use the athlete's own body weight to help him prepare. Exercises such as crawls, crunches, rolls, pedestals, balances, walkovers, reversals, handstands, and twists can accomplish this.

Strength-training work performed in the weight room falls into three main components—pulling, squatting, and pushing. That should be the order of their execution for training the modern football athlete. The key indicators are how well athletes exhibit posture, balance, stability, and flexibility through flexion, extension, and rotation. Without adequate performance in these areas, the technique involved does not foster the mobility necessary for true skill improvement.

The workouts in pulling progressions for introductory training phases (for beginners, players returning after long breaks, rehabilitating athletes) are pulls past one or two major joints. Initial pulls should be to the top of the knees or pulls from the hang position past the hips. If attention to the technical components is improved and maintained, then progressions to multiple-joint transitions (high pulls, cleans, and so on) can occur. Do simple exercises emphasizing range of motion in the lower back and hamstrings, such as good mornings, back extensions, and deadlift progressions. Transition into exercises using a more expanded torso (thigh, hip, shoulder), such as clean-and-snatch progressions. These exercises are irreplaceable for the simple fact that they are one of the most difficult athletic endeavors in any sport. The modern football player must be able to produce great force and center-of-gravity projection through extension and recovery thousands of times in a competitive event.

Squatting is the technical and developmental work designed to facilitate the mobility of a low-hip power position. On squatting and lunging movements, we use bar placement overhead, to the front of the shoulders, and to the back of the shoulders. We squat with feet approximately shoulder-width apart and toes slightly outward for optimal hip mobility and knee tracking. Lunges start with straight-ahead repetitions, progressing to reps at 45-degree angles and then lateral reps. Next in the progression are single-leg exercises from squat to jump status, leading to truly elastic reactive (plyometric) exercise movements. This single-leg power progression is extremely important.

For all players, true skill is the ability to avoid, redirect, and distance themselves from an opponent or to pursue, adjust, close, and engage. The ability to get maximum hip extension and projection and then properly reaccelerate the whole leg back onto the ground requires the mobility and power assessed and developed by drills such as single-leg step-downs, step-ups, squats, and hops.

Hopping correctly can be the ultimate tool to improve these skills. The problem is that hopping is difficult to master without two main components—correct technique and quality repetitions. Without those and the proper progressions into the hopping sequence, hopping can be more detrimental than helpful because it is very demanding on the lower leg. The squat-to-jump-to-bound-to-hop movements progress into landings that are transitions to starts, cuts, and direction changes.

In squatting progressions, the athlete starts with the overhead squat. This may require the athlete to use a stick or empty bar, because for the bar to remain balanced over the feet the posture must be strict. The feet must be balanced and flat and the torso stable, and there must be flexibility in the shoulders, hips, and legs. This technique will allow the athlete to descend into a full range of motion. The hips need to rotate when they descend below knee level. The ability to perform the overhead squat correctly fosters progressions to front squats and lunges.

The same principle applies to pushing movements. Technical and developmental progressions from the traditional lying and sitting presses transition to standing presses, which are more functional from a mobility standpoint. Progressions move from slow, controlled presses to involvement of the legs and hips in more dynamic endeavors such as the push press, push jerk, and split jerk.

Pass and push movements involving medicine balls, logs, and sleds are next on the list but are usually reserved for linemen. Dynamic pushing aids hip projection in the skilled football player because the ability afforded to project the hips in a desired direction and to control them in transitions (direction changes) is optimal. Because football is played on the feet as opposed to lying or sitting, we emphasize standing presses exhibiting posture, balance, and stability while progressing in dynamics.

Conditioning progressions are similar. Plyometric work begins with simple, two-foot, in-place takeoffs progressing to more complex alternating or single-leg landings and takeoffs that travel. Sprinting foundation work begins with mechanics that consist of walking, then skipping, then running. Keep in mind that changing the speed of a drill changes the drill. Work-capacity drills that develop form and relaxation progress to resistance drills that help refine acceleration mechanics. If technique is good, then assistance drills follow, but not at the expense of acceleration mechanics. Speed endurance follows speed development.

Speed Progression

We start with technical and developmental exercises that involve setting the hips in a back-arched, full-foot ground-contact stance to foster the ability to push off with both feet with knee extension and to project the hips in any direction. Stances include squared, staggered, open-step (laterally), and drop-step (in the backward direction) positions from a two-point stance.

For the skill positions, two-point stance work is the norm, but occasionally we use three-point work with fullbacks, tight ends, and linemen. We then progress to what we call balanced starts, or one-point stances. These are get-offs from a set position on one leg, settling into the stance from a staggered or open step. By setting the hips and maintaining posture and stability with the balanced stance, we can develop three components:

1. The necessity to set the hips, stressing posture, arched back, tension in the thigh, and full-foot contact with weight over the instep

2. The need to get the other foot in a dorsiflexed position (with the toe up and heel above and ahead of the opposite knee) to be immediately accelerated back down onto the ground with a positive shin angle

3. The importance of pushing off with both feet when that luxury exists

Developmental starting drills can progress through the use of resistance with a partner or sleds strapped on the hips to emphasize projection, or through the use of assistance with elastic tubing or bands to emphasize hip projection and aggressive foot plant. Situation starts are the next phase, using dilemma positions such as on the knees, sitting, or lying. The use of soft surfaces such as sand is helpful for the two-point starting as well, because the softness accentuates the negative mechanics and problems if technique is incorrect.

The final phase of starting is from movement, such as shuffles, skips, backpedaling, and hopping. Preceding an open or drop step with a shuffle is a breaking down of the actual movement players use most of the time. Working on the plant step with single-leg hops is great work for an offensive player seeking to develop better route breaks. A crossing step over the hop leg accentuates the ability to speed cut, and an open step away from the hop leg trains the power cut.

Acceleration includes the technical progression of mechanics beginning with a walk tempo, then a skip tempo, and finally a run tempo. We cover movements in forward, lateral, and backward directions. Developmental progressions of sprint mechanics include the use of resisted and, in special cases, assisted methods. Sprint work involves hills, partner pushing and towing, sled towing, stride ladders, and elastic bands. Emphasis is on ground preparation, in terms of proper foot, ankle, and shin placement, and extension angles to push or project the hips down the field from all starting positions.

We also address the technical progression of deceleration mechanics. These mechanics return us from the extended acceleration positions into flexion postures, a dropping of the hips, and fuller foot contact to regain the positions that create smoother transitions to change direction. Duck walking, over and under hurdle or elastic-cord maneuvers, balance boards or beams, and sandpit work aid in the development of deceleration, direction change, and reacceleration transitions.

Agility Progressions

Speed cuts include the use of technical progressions that lead to the ability to cut off the inside leg at increasingly greater angles (usually greater than 90 degrees). Eventually, speed-cut breaks need to be reaction oriented. Players sprint toward a certain direction and then react to a stimulus to cross over the inside step to redirect.

Power cuts involve technical progressions that lead to the ability to cut off the outside foot (figure 16.7). This technique is usually a necessity at angle changes of less than 90 degrees, but most athletes use the power cut in many situations whether they need it or not.

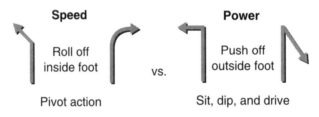

Figure 16.7 Speed and power cuts.

It is important to use a power cut without false stepping (stepping out away from the direction change). False stepping indicates a lack of posture, balance, functional leg strength, and stability. Quick directional changes result from the ability to make the cut over the plant foot to distance the hips from the break point, which is in fact the ultimate goal.

Finally, the culmination of training the modern football athlete is playing one-on-one or going man-on-man for a series of movement sequences within certain constraints, such as hands behind the back, within a five-yard sideline, around a circle or ring, and so on. Training this ability is hard but enjoyable work; it is technically sound and extremely productive as a conditioning tool.

Although track-and-field training techniques are extremely valuable, football is a game of starting, accelerating, decelerating, changing direction, and reaccelerating, unlike track and field. Olympic lifting and absolute strength exercises have a place in football training, yet Olympic lifters and powerlifters do not necessarily make great football players. Training, rehabilitating, and developing football power has a place of its own. Football is a survival sport. The more we learn, apply, mold, carve, and develop its training, the better our chance for long-term endurance.

Resources

Bompa, T. 1983. *Theory and methodology of training: The key to athletic performance.* Dubuque, IA: Kendall Hunt.

Dick, F. 1984. *Training theory.* London: British Amateur Athletic Board.

Fox, E.L., and D. Mathews. 1981. *The physiological basis of physical education and athletics.* Philadelphia: Saunders.

Harre, D. 1982. *Principles of sports training: Introduction to the theory and methods of training.* Berlin: Sportverlag.

King, I. 1993. Plyometric training: In perspective, part I. *Science periodical on research and technology in sport* 11(5).

Lamb, D.R. 1984. *Physiology of exercise, responses and adaptations* (rev. ed.). New York: Macmillan.

Radcliffe, I.C., and R.C. Farentinos. 1999. *High-powered plyometrics.* Champaign, IL: Human Kinetics.

Sale, D. 1991. Testing strength and power. In *Physiological testing of the high performance athlete* (rev. ed.), ed. I.D. MacDougall, H.A. Wenger, and H.I. Green, 21–106. Champaign, IL: Human Kinetics.

Schmidtbleicher, D. 1992. Training for power events. In *Strength and power in sport,* ed. P.V. Komi, 381–395. Oxford: Blackwell Scientific.

Sift, M., and Y. Verkhoshanski. 1996. *Super training: Special strength training for sporting excellence* (2nd ed.). Pittsburgh and Johannesburg, South Africa: Sports Support Syndicate.

Stauber, W. 1989. Eccentric action of muscles: Physiology, injury, and adaptation. *Exercise and Sport Science Reviews* 11:157–185.

Wilson, G.J., R.U. Newton, A.J. Murphy, and B.J. Humphries. 1993. The optimal training load for the development of dynamic athletic performance. *Medicine and Science in Sports and Exercise* 25(11):1279–1286.

Vorobyev, A. 1978. A textbook on weightlifting. *Athletic Journal* 2(76):89–90.

Adjusting for Weather, Injuries, and Opponents

Hayden Fry

"Scratch where it itches" has been my primary football philosophy through-out my head-coaching career. It means taking advantage of whatever comes your way and doing whatever needs to be done. This philosophy applies to weather, injuries, and opponents.

This chapter is devoted to some of the unpredictable factors every coach faces. Life and football would be simpler if everything went according to plan. However that is not always the case. I am not aware of any coach who has all the answers as to making the right adjustments for weather, injuries, and opponents. The information in this chapter is based on what I thought to be the best adjustments during my coaching career.

Adjusting for Weather

The most important thing you can do when the weather turns bad is have a team celebration. Why? Because you have practiced in the spring and fall for exactly this kind of weather on game day. Your players and coaches should have a positive attitude because they are prepared to execute in all weather conditions.

The team doctor, trainer, and strength conditioning coach are leaders in coordinating bad weather practices. Our advantage over opponents was that we practiced every week for the bad weather game. Obviously, you are not going to play in the snow early in the season, but look at your schedule for possible games in the snow. Call your coaching friends in snow country and get their advice on shoes, heaters, and windbreakers. Be like the Boy Scouts—be prepared!

Other severe weather elements—heat, rain, wind, and so on—will happen out of season or during spring or fall practices. Take advantage of these opportunities to build individual and team confidence by practicing in the elements.

The coaching staff must sell to players the idea that the team is going to be better prepared for the elements on game day than the opponents. We'd practice quarterback-center exchanges, handoffs and pitches, passing and receiving, and all phases of the kicking game in the rain and wind. We cut back on our running game practice time in order to give priority to the passing and kicking game. This builds great confidence and a positive attitude in our players.

During the season, if it hadn't rained during practice that week, we would have wet ball drills for 10 minutes on Thursday. Before each snap, punt, pass, or kick the manager at each drill wiped the ball with a wet towel. We conducted these drills at the end of practice and extended practice time if the execution was not acceptable. Players came to realize that we could pass with consistency in the rain. Snappers, punters, and kickers also gained confidence in their execution.

Passing and Kicking in Bad Weather

We strongly emphasized throwing the ball deep, as most of our opponents did not believe we could throw the ball deep during a rainstorm. We were playing a rainy bowl game against a team that had led the nation in total defense for eight weeks during the regular season. We passed for six touchdowns. Our opponents did not believe we could throw with accuracy during a monsoon. Our receivers knew where they were going and the secondary defenders had to adjust in slippery conditions. Our game plan was to always force our opponents to make adjustments.

Windy days also present an excellent opportunity to practice all phases of the kicking and passing games. In the spring and during two-a-day practices, readjust your schedule to take advantage of windy days. At that practice, cut back on the running game. Emphasize punting and kicking into the wind, with the wind, and from the hash marks. Practice kicking off into the wind and line-driving the ball low to the deep open spot. Practice the bloop kickoff into the wind by kicking the ball high across the field with kickoff team coverage.

We had an automatic onside kickoff against certain kickoff return alignments. If we saw a particular kickoff return alignment, the kicker made the call to the kickoff coverage team when the coach signaled an onside kick.

Windy days also present a great opportunity for the snapper to learn to keep snaps low to the punter. The punter learns to hold onto the ball and to place it on his foot, not drop it. The wind changes the ball's position before the punter makes contact. Through the years our tight punt formation was most valuable during games played in wind and rain.

We used the pro formation with the quarterback in his normal position behind the center and our punter nine yards deep. The ball is snapped between the quarterback's legs to the punter. The punter takes a rocker step back and forward with his left leg and punts the ball with his right foot.

The tight punt formation is great for punting or quick-kicking into the wind or as a surprise punt on third down to eliminate the normal

Courtesy of University of Iowa AV Photo Service

punt return and punt block schemes. It is also valuable to use as a no-huddle punt or fake punt and pass. This formation is also excellent for taking a safety with the wind in your face late in the game. Obviously you want to be ahead by four points or more unless only a few seconds remain on the clock.

On a windy day, the passing game is limited going into the wind but opens up with the wind at your back. Practice throwing the ball deep. You could get a completion or defensive interference call. Regardless of the results of deep passes, you are going to have a better chance of completing short passes after throwing several deep passes.

A sound offensive strategy for going into the wind has these three objectives:

1. No turnovers or penalties—protect the football.
2. Make a minimum of three first downs before punting when you take over the ball inside your 20-yard line
3. Run as much time off the clock as possible each play.

Defending in Bad Weather

When defending punts on a windy day, it is best to rush the punter when he is punting into the wind. The ball will not go too far and someone probably will have to make a fair catch. Try to block the punt, but be sure that you do not rough the punter.

In a windy or rainy game, defensively load up or blitz on first down as much as possible. Try to put your opponent in a long-yardage situation on second and third down.

Most close games are determined by turnovers. Games played in extreme heat, cold, or rain or in windy conditions present an excellent opportunity for your defense to create turnovers. Schedule turnover drills for stripping the ball, recovering fumbles, intercepting passes, and blocking punts and field goals. These drills can provide the winning edge against a superior opponent during a bad weather game.

Preparing for Bad Weather

On the Sunday before each game, get a long-range weather forecast for the game location. This will help you make your practice and game plans. Get an updated forecast for game day the day before the game. Share this information with the team the night before the game. When you arrive at the stadium, check the wind velocity and direction. Give instructions to all kickers, punters, passers, receivers, and return men. Continue to monitor the wind during pregame warm-up.

At the conclusion of the pregame warm-up, briefly meet with your staff on the field and decide what you prefer for the opening kickoff. The pregame warm-up will have provided a chance to observe the opponent's kicking and passing game as well as the execution of your kickers and passers. You should know whether or not the bad weather will continue throughout the game or clear up by halftime. Consider all of these factors when making your decision whether to kick off or receive. If you decide to kick off, be sure your captains select the end of the field that will put the wind at your back.

Preventing Heat-Related Injuries

Every football team in America is subjected to practicing and playing in excessive heat. Nothing is more important than educating the entire football staff as well as athletes about how to prevent heat-related injuries. Many of the suggestions the follow are recommended by the AFCA and National Athletic Trainer's Association. Other recommendations have come from various publications that educate athletes in preventing heat-related injuries during the summer and two-a-day practices.

The coaching staff, team physician, trainer, and strength conditioning coach must unite to educate team members about how to stay at their best during summer and two-a-day workouts and how to avoid heat-related injuries.

Encourage athletes to begin conditioning at least one month before two-a-days. The strength conditioning coach is permitted to supervise summer conditioning. Inform the players in the spring that they will be tested on the first day of fall practice. If they fail the conditioning test, they will have additional running the next two weeks following practice. This motivates athletes to report in top physical condition.

A sports drink containing a six-percent carbohydrate solution, such as Gatorade, can be absorbed as rapidly as water. But unlike water, a sports drink also provides energy, delays fatigue, and improves performance. Place information in the players' playbook on fluid guidelines for two-a-days. It is imperative to replace fluids immediately after a training session or game. Our trainers weigh athletes before and after practice. Research shows that for every pound of weight lost, athletes should drink at least 20 ounces of fluid to optimize rehydration. Sports beverages are an excellent choice.

Athletes should warm up in the shade, if possible, and return to the shade during breaks. Cotton-blend, loose-fitting clothing helps promote heat loss. The general rule is the less clothing, the better.

Coaches, managers, or trainers should always have a cell phone and be familiar with emergency numbers. Ice and iced towels should be available during each break.

The coaching staff has no more important duty than making sure that their athletes maintain their health during practices in excessive heat. Each position coach should check his players' weight loss and fluid intake following each practice. The trainer must notify the coaches about any player who is not properly hydrated. Fluid loss must be replaced before permitting the player to practice. Some signs of dehydration and heat illness are thirst, irritability, headache, weakness, dizziness, cramps, nausea, and decreased performance.

Delegating Responsibilities

It is very important to assign all assistant coaches specific liaison responsibilities with the medical staff, strength and conditioning coach, equipment manager, and academic advisor. Their job is to inform the football staff during daily staff meetings about everything that can help create a healthy and winning environment for the athletes.

I also had a grass coach and a weather coach. The grass coach was responsible for making sure that the maintenance people kept our practice fields and stadium fields in great shape. The weather coach reported on weather conditions for each practice and also the projected weather for game day.

The weather coach and the equipment coach should work together to ensure the correct equipment is provided to the players whether the weather is hot, cold, or wet. Junior high and high schools should seek help from booster clubs in providing sideline heaters, hand warmers, fans, rain gear, and so on. This is one great way a booster club can contribute to your team's success.

Adjusting for Injuries

One of the most important strategies for winning football games is preventing injuries. Since football is a contact sport, it is impossible to keep everyone healthy. Injuries are going to happen, but I believe that many injuries can be prevented and the number of injuries can be significantly reduced by following a few precautions.

Reduce the number of full-team scrimmages for veteran players. Your experienced players do not need to prove anything by participating in full-speed contact in fall practice, and they risk injury if they do. A short "get the cob webs off" scrimmage in the fall is adequate for veteran players. Reserve the emphasis on full-speed practice for reserve players and freshmen.

I eagerly anticipated the first fall scrimmage at the University of Arkansas after I accepted the offensive backfield coaching position on Coach Frank Broyles' staff. I inherited an All-American running back named Lance Alworth. I couldn't wait to see him perform. As the coaching staff walked to the stadium for the scrimmage, a heavy rain began to fall. I asked one of the older assistant coaches if he thought we would scrimmage in the rain. He said, "Yep—but don't get the stud in the mud." I am confident that if Lance Alworth had injured himself before our first game, my coaching career would have been less enjoyable.

Later in my career as the head coach at Southern Methodist University, I had the opportunity to ask athletic director and legendary coach Matty Bell how he was so successful. Without hesitation he said, "I never let Doak Walker or Kyle Rote get tackled in practice." Both players were All-American running backs, and they were not tackled too many times in games.

Here is one last story to get the message across. Coach Bum Phillips was going to his first practice as head coach of the Houston Oilers. As he entered the stadium a group of reporters asked him, "Coach Phillips, when have you scheduled your first scrimmage?" Bum said, "Just a minute." He reached in his jacket, pulled out the schedule for the Houston Oilers, and said, "I don't see the Houston Oilers on our schedule." Then he walked off to practice.

Eliminate all full-speed blocking and tackling below the waist in the fall for veterans. Eliminate all full-speed drills involving more than five players. Analyze and evaluate each drill from a safety standpoint. Do not permit full-speed drills that have a history of producing injuries. Require offensive and defensive linemen to wear knee braces.

Analyze and evaluate the strength and conditioning program. Most college football programs today require year-round conditioning and heavy weight training. Remember that the body and mind need a vacation from time to time. Be sure to schedule rest and recovery time.

Also remember that all motivated players want to get back into action after an injury as quickly as possible. Many players return before their injury has had time to heal. Certain injuries require more time to heal properly. Your doctor or trainer knows what is best for your injured players. Please follow their advice and see that the injured player receives the medical treatment he needs to fully recover. The AFCA has done an outstanding job providing injury statistics and information that can assist the coaching staff in reducing injuries to the players.

I strongly recommend that the head coach and the injured player's position coach follow up on every injured player. If a player is injured in practice or during a game, the head coach should go with the trainer immediately to check on the injured player. After the practice or game, the head coach should check with the injured player in the training room or hospital. If the injury is serious, the doctor or trainer must call the injured player's parents. A few words to the parents from the head coach should be standard procedure. The personal attention by the coaching staff will be greatly appreciated by all of the players, parents, and fans. Do it because it is the right thing to do!

Because injuries are inevitable, it is important to prepare a backup game plan before injuries occur. The coaching staff should organize a plan in the spring for the replacement of key personnel. Position coaches should rotate individual players from the second team to the first team and permit individual third-team players to participate some on the second team.

I have found that the quality of play is usually much improved in practice when a player is elevated to the next team. The player recognizes his additional value to the performance of his new team and becomes a better player. Upgrading reserves in the spring and early fall camps is a great team motivator and also gives the coaching staff the opportunity to evaluate the new player's strengths and weaknesses. This is particularly valuable at the quarterback and running back positions. A sense of urgency and an attitude of "I can help us win" is created immediately. It also helps the other members of that team accept the reserve as a member of their unit. It is extremely important that team members accept the replacement starter in practice as opposed to the reserve being thrown into combat during a game after an injury to the number-one player.

Ironically, injuries to key personnel sometimes lead to better team performance because the coaching staff has to make adjustments for the anticipated dropoff in the ability of the substitute. Through the years, key injuries have necessitated adjustments in our team's techniques, alignment, and assignments. Many of these adjustments were beneficial to our execution and became our standard way of operating.

Injury prevention is the reason we stand up our tight end. We lost our two tight ends to injury so rather than eliminate the tight-end position, we moved a wide receiver into the tight-end position. He was much smaller and not nearly as strong or tough as the injured players. Therefore, we let him stand up to keep him from being injured by the big defensive tackle, end, or linebacker. We simplified his blocking responsibilities to two blocks. He had a smother block, where he laid on top of the first player to his inside when we ran the option or off-tackle. On the power sweep, he had an entertainment block on the defensive man lined up on him or outside. He used his quick feet and balance to help the defensive player go in the direction he wanted to go. The ball carrier keyed the defensive player and simply ran away from him inside or outside. It's simple, and it became a great play in our offense.

However, the other benefits were even better. Having our tight end stand up required the defensive player who normally played against a tight end in a three-point stance to change his defensive technique in only four practices. Our tight end now became the periscope in helping the quarterback read various secondary coverages, blitzes, and stunts. His vision and verbal communication greatly helped eliminate bad plays. He also could flex more outside or trade to the other side of the formation. He could quickly go in motion across the formation or outside. We discovered all this because injuries necessitated personnel adjustments.

If your quarterback goes down to an injury, hopefully number two can continue to execute at the same level of performance. You should always have a backup plan for the quarterback position. I have seen great teams lose their outstanding option quarterback or super passing quarterback to injury. The replacement was not able to give a winning performance. It is critical to evaluate the strengths and weaknesses of your number-two and number-three quarterbacks before fall practice. Design a game plan that the new quarterback can execute successfully if the number one quarterback is injured. Don't wait until it happens. You can't win many games if you have to install a new offense after the season has started.

One season, my number-one quarterback was an excellent runner and passer. We enjoyed an exciting run-pass offense. Then he fell to an injury that knocked him out for the season. Our number-two quarterback was an excellent passer but was very slow. Fortunately, we had created an injury game plan for key positions in the spring and practiced what we would do if we lost our number-one quarterback. We eliminated a few running plays and featured the quarterback in the spread or shotgun formation. Since we had practiced in the spring and during two-a-days, the transition was easy and we had a successful season.

One of the biggest adjustments has to be made if the punter, field goal kicker, or deep snapper is injured. Design a game plan and practice it in the spring and fall with the replacements. You cannot let injuries demoralize your team. Explain what will happen if one of these players is injured, and practice with the replacement before the injury occurs. This is extremely valuable in facilitating team acceptance and execution.

It is imperative that you evaluate the strengths and weaknesses of the replacement player in practice. Position coaches must know the replacement's limitations and what he executes best. Always emphasize his strengths and eliminate his weaknesses by not requiring him to do something that will not result in a winning performance. You don't have to tell the team the various offensive and defensive plays that will be eliminated. Just don't call them in a game.

One rule that I believe is extremely valuable is that no player or coach discusses an injury to a player. The head coach should be the only spokesman regarding injuries to team members. The head coach will give out information only on players who definitely will not play in the game that week. The general public and ticket-holders are entitled to know if a player will not play. It is obvious without going into detail why you should not discuss the injured player's condition if there is a chance he might play. The safety and well-being of your player is more important than telling everyone, including the opponent, that he is injured and missing a few practices.

Adjusting for Opponents

Each football season presents new, exciting challenges to the coaching staff. The new season requires in-depth evaluation of your team's strengths and weaknesses as compared to the strengths and weaknesses of the opponents on your schedule.

Our game plan for offense, defense, and the kicking game was dictated by what we had to do in order to defeat the top three teams on our schedule. This required designing offensive and defensive schemes based on all the scouting information we could gather. I enjoyed creating a football philosophy based on scouting reports on the opponents. Coaching my personnel to execute the game plan developed from the scout reports always presented the biggest challenge.

Through the years, I realized that rather than attempting to make specific adjustments each week for different teams, we needed to present different looks while remaining fundamentally sound. Our philosophy was to keep adjustments to a minimum and make our opponents adjust to us. This required base offensive and defensive schemes that were different and diversified but could still be executed by our personnel.

Our own base offense and defense were designed to defeat the best three or four teams on our schedule. This obviously allowed us to be flexible, but it also kept our adjustments for the "big game" to a minimum. Using this system and philosophy means that the opponent has to be prepared for all of the various offensive and defensive schemes they have scouted in previous games. In other words, the opposing team has to be prepared for everything because they don't know what you will emphasize against them.

We shortened our offensive and defensive game plans each week to our best attacks and best defenses against the opponent that week. Our preparation created many problems for the opposition. They had to be prepared for a multitude of offensive formations and defensive alignments. We used a lot of window trimmings—shifting, jumping formations, motioning different backs and receivers—to disguise our bread-and-butter runs and passes. Defensively we attempted to bait the opposing team to run or throw at our strengths by aligning our defense to show an obvious weakness. When the ball was snapped, we tried to take away the apparent weakness whether it was the run or the pass.

The players enjoyed being involved in creating the game plan for the top teams on our schedule. Each spring the coaching staff analyzed the film and scouting reports for the teams on our football schedule. We requested that players study the reports the same way they would study the notes for one of their academic courses. They would be tested throughout spring training and two-a-day practices. This approach in preparing for our opponents gave us added emphasis and knowledge prior to the week of the game.

Once the season began, we updated the spring and summer scouting report on our upcoming opponents. This greatly reduced the number of last-minute adjustments necessary to win the game. We short-listed our game plan each week for that specific opponent, keeping adjustments to a minimum and forcing our opponents to adjust.

I had the good fortune to be seated between Coach Paul "Bear" Bryant and Coach John McKay at the AFCA convention my first year as a college head coach. I got up the nerve to ask Coach Bryant about the most important thing he had done to be a winning coach. What he said had a lifelong impact on my coaching philosophy. He said, "Son, just remember if the other team can't score, you can't come out worse than a tie." My next question was, "How do you do that?" Coach Bryant said, "Get your defense to stop or slow down their bread-and-butter plays. Make them do something that they don't like to do. On the offensive side of the ball, don't beat yourself." Coach McKay was listening and he said, "That pretty well sums it up—go get 'em, Coach!"

I have always been highly motivated to study all phases of the game of football. It is an exciting, intriguing, adventuresome, constantly changing game. Football has all these aspects and more because of the men who coach it. To truly understand an opponent's offense, defense, and kicking game, you need a sound understanding of the coaches who call the offensive and defensive plays. Gather information about their football philosophy and their play-calling tendencies in critical-down situations. This requires a disciplined study of their football experiences as players and coaches. The research on each opposing head coach and offensive and defensive coordinators was one of the most beneficial and enjoyable projects I had in college football. I created my "Bible on Coaches" and added or deleted changes each spring and summer before the season. I referred to it prior to organizing of our game plan. I never told my assistant coaches about my personal "Bible on Coaches." They only knew that I had knowledge from film and scouting reports. This insight into the personalities of the opposing coaches greatly assisted me in creating the right mental approach for the coaching staff as well as the players in critical-down situations.

Preparation for the strengths and weaknesses of each opponent requires that you be disciplined and keep adjustments to a minimum. Therefore your offense, defense, and kicking game should be diversified so that few additions will be necessary during the season. It is imperative to spend time in the spring and during two-a-day sessions preparing for your toughest opponents. By dedicating specific practices and special drills to specific opponents, you impress on your players the importance of that particular game. Also players begin building their confidence. Following a normal practice, we added the "fifth quarter" segment and dedicated it to one of our toughest opponents.

The mental aspect cannot be over emphasized in preparing for the best teams on your schedule. Following practice in the fall prior to the first game, encourage your captains with a statements such as"Let's run five more cross countries" for a specific opponent.

Adjustments for specific opponents were done during our "shine and polish" segments of practice. Having practiced most of the bread and butter plays and defensive schemes in the spring and early fall, the players execute their responsibilities much better during practice the week of the game.

Another very important thing is the quality of the organization and decisions your coaching staff makes during the half time intermission. I always had outstanding coaches who utilized the halftime to analyze the first-half results and make a game plan for the second half by eliminating or adding specific coverages, stunts, runs, and passes. Most of the emphasis in adjusting our game plan was given to critical-down situations because this is where the game is won or lost. Our entire organization and the way the coaching staff operated was discussed in our team meetings so that the players fully understood what to expect and why we were doing it. Each position coach prepared specific suggestions relative to his players' performance during the first half. At the conclusion of the first half of play, we met as a staff for the first five minutes and made decisions on our game plan for the second half. Then each position coach lectured his players on the adjustments and corrections to be used for the second half.

Relax and Have Fun

I always had a lot of fun coaching. Once "all the hay was in the barn," I thought it was important to help our players relax prior to the kickoff. Many of the pregame jokes and stories helped relax our players and were repeated to me years later. The hard work in preparation for the game and the pressure to win was somewhat relieved by laughter during our last meeting prior to pregame warm-up. I also enjoyed telling jokes to the opposing head coach in pregame warm-up. This always helped me to relax. Perhaps this closing story will get across the message that football is truly a game to enjoy. We were ranked number one in the nation, and we were playing the number-two ranked team. In pregame warm-up I had our centers and guards change position for the punting game. The opposing head coach came down to talk with me, and he began watching our guards snap the ball on the ground and over the head of our punter. After a few minutes of observing he said, "You are not going to let those guys snap the ball during the game are you?" I said, "Coach, we don't plan on punting," and I turned and walked away. Have fun, and keep the faith. Always remember, "The sun doesn't shine on the same ol' dogs' rump every day!"

PART V

Individual Skills and Team Tactics

Dick Tomey

This section, some would say, is the meat and potatoes of football—the Xs and Os, the guts. Our contributors are a marvelous collection of career coaches who have won consistently at the highest level. Our coaches will share their thoughts about a phase of the game in which they have particular expertise.

Barry Alvarez of Wisconsin will outline the strong commitment to run offense that has made the Badgers the most successful Big Ten program of recent years.

LaVell Edwards, the legendary BYU coach, will tell us that it was his knowledge of the single wing that got him a job at BYU in the early days. BYU's later emergence as a national power that relied on the pass is well known. Lavell will share his pass offense with us.

To be a good football team you must be able to stop the run. In R.C. Slocum's career at Texas A&M, his "wrecking crew" was known as a difficult team to run against every year.

No coach in college football has done a better job over the last 10 years than Sonny Lubick of Colorado State University. Sonny's teams play in the pass-oriented Mountain West Conference, so to be successful their pass defense must be sound, well taught, and multifaceted. And it has been.

Virginia Tech's Frank Beamer has built a reputation as a winner and as a coach who has given his team a better chance to win because of his special-teams approach. Coach Beamer's thoughts will have an effect on you.

These five coaches are at the top of their profession. We admire their expertise and are fortunate to have them share it with us.

Although running the ball and stopping the run are still cornerstones to winning, the game has changed in many ways over the last 30 years. Special teams have become more appreciated, and techniques and schemes have been improved incrementally. This, along with improved training of punters and kickers, makes the kicking game a place where your team can make a difference. Pass offense and pass defense have changed more than anything else because of the influence of pro football, the training of quarterbacks and wide receivers, the use of innovative formations, and football rules. To keep up, defenses have countered with man-to-man defenses, the zone blitz, and better pass-rush training, including training in martial arts.

Despite all these developments, the most important things are giving a great effort and continuing to rely on fundamentals. It is still true that winning the turnover battle wins games and losing the kicking game loses games.

Coaching has not changed much. The best coaches are still the ones who can create the right environment for learning and have a passion for excellence and unselfishness that translates into outstanding individual and team performance. This section will be a buffet for all who hunger for football insight. Enjoy!

The Running Game

Barry Alvarez

Questions always arise about the largest contributing factors to the success of a prominent program. We point directly at two things—the ability to run the football and the ability to defend the run. The compatibility of these processes has been the benchmark of how we approach the game. Historically, running teams have enjoyed continued success. We do not live by the theory "every time you throw a pass, two of the possible three results are bad," but we start with the run.

Establishing a successful running game is the key to developing a complementary and equally successful passing game. These ideas should always take into account the perspective of normal down and distance. No offense can achieve success in abnormal situations.

Deciding to Run

As we looked at our situation and evaluated our program, certain factors were evident. Many of these are common to most programs.

The first factor we looked at was locale. Why would location have an effect on the type of team you have? Where you live and the attendant features strongly affect the available ingredients for success. A major factor of locale is weather, not just during the season but throughout the entire year. What effect does weather have on the type of athletes who live

Contributions by Jim Hueber, Run Game Coordinator

relatively nearby, in areas where we could be prominent? In our case, in the upper Midwest the most plentiful type of player was going to be the big, tough, physical player with a great work ethic. Guys in snowshoes and people in snowmobile suits, who move more like offensive tackles than wide receivers, usually do not win the sprint races. Since 1993 we've had 14 first-team all-conference offensive linemen and three consensus all-Americans, two of whom were Outland Trophy candidates.

A historical look at the Big Ten, even since the inclusion of Penn State, would show that successful programs were able to run the ball, especially late in the season as the weather changed. To be sure, there have been exceptions, but close study will show that they are rare and that their prominence is fleeting.

Next, we made a philosophical decision. What type of team did we want? We wanted a tough, hard-nosed, and physical team on both sides of the ball. Combining all the factors gave us an answer—run the ball!

Last, we had to decide how to run the ball. What type of offense would best fit our situation? Our coaches came from varied backgrounds. Some were from one-back teams, some from split-back or I-formation teams. We even had some expertise in option football. The answer for us was contained in our profile. The most readily available talent pool was going to be made up of big, physical, tough, hard-working linemen. Reasonable deduction told us that we would not have much finesse. The model we chose to follow would comprise a combination of zone runs and off-tackle plays common to successful NFL teams.

We decided that we were going to run the ball and use action passes based on the prescribed runs to establish our offensive identity, our foundation, and ultimately our success. A result of this approach was the ability to defense runs. Hence, our basic mandate was "run the ball, stop the run."

Inside Runs

Figure 18.1 shows an inside zone at TE run. The objectives of this play are to attack the defense at the playside tackle, make the defense move to defend that point, block the backside pursuit, and "run where they ain't!"

Zone-blocked plays are just that—plays designed so that the offensive lineman can block any defender who aligns or moves to his zone.

The simplistic premise of blocking areas with big bodies appealed to us. Little did we know of the discipline and hard work involved. We would need both to get first downs. We will try to dissect these plays and give the most pertinent coaching points.

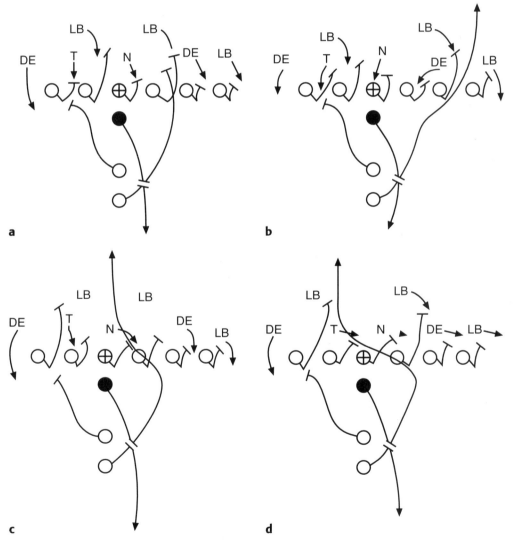

Figure 18.1 Inside zone at TE.

Here are the rules for the inside zone at TE:

TE: Deny inside penetration. Cover defender. Pester and at a minimum keep him on LOS.

PT: Aim at outside breast of defensive end. Block him at LOS. Deny penetration. If inside, move zone up to LB and cover defender you block.

PG: Step in playside gap. Peek at DE. Be prepared for inside move—if it occurs, block it; if he plays outside, find LB in your zone. Cover defender you block.

C: Block man on or playside gap. Be sure to attack playside breast of defender. Cover up defender.

OG: Be sure your head is inside. Block man on with offensive tackle. Double LOS defender to LB.

OT: Push to get inside man on offensive guard. Double LOS defender to LB. Important coaching points: know where your zone is and cover any defender you block (take away opposite color for RB to see his read).

FB: Step away from hole number. Block through B gap. Step penetration or trail from end of LOS defender (block inside-out to ensure gap protection).

TB: Open and run at inside leg of PT. Read defender on PT—if he goes out, bend inside. Find next defender on LOS and run opposite him. Important coaching points: run on feet of offensive lineman; do not attack LOS full speed—have something left to cross LOS; cut to a hole—don't cut back. Buzz phrase: speed *through* the hole, not *to* the hole. Patience is helpful.

QB: Drive the ball as deep as possible to TB. Handoff comes out opposite of hole number on play-action fake. Get ball to TB as soon as possible.

WR: Work to block secondary defenders closest to formation.

Figure 18.2 shows the inside zone away from the TE with a lead blocker. The objectives behind this run are to attack the defense at the playside tackle, make the defense move to that point, block the backside pursuit, and run where they ain't! The rules for the inside zone away from the TE with a lead blocker are the following:

PT: Aim at outside breast of defender. Block man on and widen the hole.

PG: Aim at outside breast of defender. Take him any way he wants to go.

C: In combination with OG, double-team nose to backside LB.

OG: In combination with C, through inside A gap, double-team nose to backside LB.

OT: In combination with TE, stay inside DE and look for fold from outside LB.

TE: In combination with OT, run to get inside DE. Eye outside LB for key to stop on him or push under DE with fold.

FB: Attack B gap. See man on guard and enter opposite him. Block playside LB and cover him up.

TB: Open and run at inside leg of PT. Read defender on PG. Run opposite him if he goes out. Find next defender on LOS. Important coaching points: run on feet of offensive line; do not attack LOS full speed—have something left to cross LOS; cut to a hole—don't cut back. Buzz phrase: speed *through* the hole, not *to* the hole.

QB: Drive ball back to TB as deep as possible. Handoff comes out opposite hole of number on play-action fake.

WR: Work to block secondary defenders closest to formation.

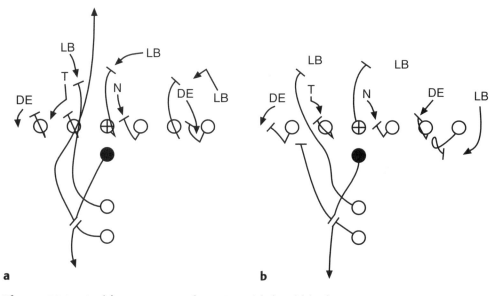

Figure 18.2 Inside zone away from TE with lead blocker.

As you look at these plays, you can see the emphasis on man blocking (one-on-one) at the point of attack. Varying abilities of players caused us to add a tighter, quicker-hitting play that takes advantage of defensive movement, a play we call the tight zone (figure 18.3). We still zone block this play, but the tighter, quicker landmark by the tailback will allow the ball to cut sooner and easier behind moving defenders. For the tailback, his landmark is now the inside leg of the playside guard, and his read is the A gap to the offside. The tempo and coaching points are the same as they were for zone. The tailback must speed *through* the hole, not *to* the hole.

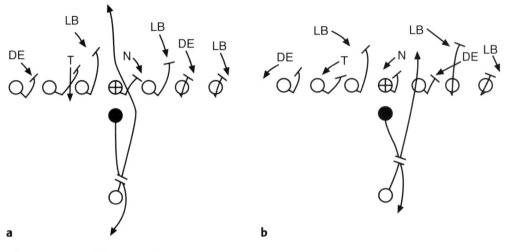

Figure 18.3 Tight zone.

In 1993 this subtle change allowed us to beat Michigan and propelled us to our first Rose Bowl in 31 years. We were able to find many seams versus Michigan's angle defense, and we successfully moved the ball and controlled the game. Since 1993 these three plays (inside zone to TE, inside zone away from TE, and tight zone) have been our inside running game. They have been the basis for seven top 25 rushing teams, based on NCAA statistics, and provided the impetus for eight consecutive 1,000-yard rushers, three Rose Bowl MVPs, and a Heisman Trophy winner.

Outside Runs

The zone-blocked complement to the inside play is the stretch (figure 18.4). The ability to put the ball outside or over the tight end with similar blocks and at least similar initial steps by the tailback is important in building a successful running game.

Once the tailback has the ball, his coaching points remain the same. Essentially, his goals are to attack the landmark, get up on the feet of the offensive lineman to make the cut, have something left to break across the line of scrimmage, and speed *through* the hole, not *to* the hole.

Note that the tailback's first step should be similar to his first step in inside zone. His shoulder turn should give the illusion that he could go to either landmark.

The objectives for this play are to attack the perimeter of the defense, make the defense defend the field, block the playside force, and run around or through defenders.

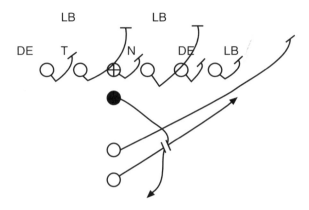

Figure 18.4 Stretch.

On the stretch, the landmark stays very wide—one yard deep and three yards outside the tight end. The play is designed to go around the corner of the defense first, but by isolating defenders at the point of attack, the available running lanes are magnified by overpursuit or by defenders coming under blocks.

Remember, this design is to go outside the defense, but the tailback should have something left at the point of attack to attack the goal line.

For the outside zone at TE (figure 18.5), the fullback will be responsible for blocking the strong safety area, leaving a defender unblocked away from the play. To slow the pursuit of that defender, the quarterback must naked fake every time he hands off.

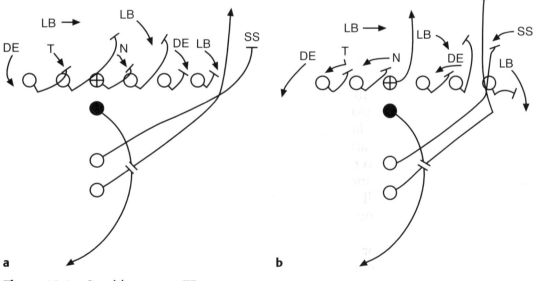

a   b

Figure 18.5 Outside zone at TE.

These are the rules for the outside zone at TE:

TE: Most important rule is to keep defender on LOS. Initial position is to fight to reach defender. If not possible, pester him and cover him up.

PT: Aim for the outside armpit of DE. Run to reach him and block any movement in your path.

PG: Block the outside gap and block any movement in your zone. Attack the outside breast of LB. Cover him and run him by the hole, if you must.

C: Reach hard to playside gap. Block any defender at any level along your path. Work your head to the play side.

OG: Flat reach step—look for defensive lineman to rock you. Be prepared to block it! If nothing is on your path, continue to next level. Block LB and get your head to the play side.

OT: Flat reach step—look for defensive lineman along your path. Be prepared to block it! If nothing is on your path, continue to next level. Block LB and get your head to the play side. Important coaching points: no matter where the defense moves, cover it up; take color away for back to read; keep defenders on LOS at a minimum.

FB: Lead step directly outside (sometimes this could happen off motion). Attack the SS area. Block force (cover up and take away color, head on outside breast, inside foot on inside foot).

TB: Open and run at LB (one yard deep, three yards outside TE). Do not overcoach this! Run outside the defense first. If anything crosses your face outside or upfield, plant your outside foot and run hard at the goal line through the defense.

QB: Drive the ball deep and wide. Get it to TB as soon as possible. The naked fake is urgent!

WR: Work to block defenders over you.

This outside play was a favorite run of our initial one-two punch—Brent Moss (Big 10 and Rose Bowl MVP) and Terrell Fletcher (two-time 1,000-yard rusher and Hall of Fame Bowl MVP)—who gained 5,000 yards rushing combined over a two-year period.

As we continued to evolve offensively, defenses began to attack the stretch aggressively. We started to see penetrating players in the B or C gap. We began to see the outside linebacker upfield to force the ball inside. Coincidently, at almost the same time, our type of running back changed. We went from quick, slashing runners (Moss and Fletcher) to bigger, stronger, more deliberate runners (Carl McCullough, our third 1,000-yard rusher, and Ron Dayne, who never had a season with less than 1,200 yards and won the Heisman Trophy). These two occurrences caused us to explore new ways to attack the defense, and we decided on the handoff (figure 18.6).

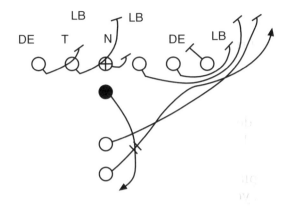

Figure 18.6 Handoff.

We combined the element of the outside stretch but relied more on scheme blocking in the offensive line than our standard zone blocking. The handoff was a good choice for us because the principles for the quarterback and fullback remained the same.

We altered the landmark of the tailback to running directly at the tight end, but we did not change the coaching point of "speed through the hole, not to the hole." The primary coaching really comes from the playside guard, tackle, and tight end. The decision was to cut the defense to define running lanes and defeat penetration and movement.

The objectives for the handoff play are to attack the defensive perimeter, stop defensive penetration and movement, force the defense to cover all gaps, and run where scheme allows. The rules for the handoff are as follows:

TE: Block down on DE. Expect penetration or movement at you.

PT: Pull—run to reach outside LB. If he penetrates, kick him out.

PG: Pull to get outside first. If you cannot, take first entry attack and cover up playside LB.

C: Reach hard playside gap. Block any defender at any level along your path. Work your head hard to the play side.

OG: Flat reach step—look for defensive lineman along your path. Be prepared to block him. If nothing is in your path, continue to next level. Block LB and get your head to play side.

OT: Flat reach step—look for defensive lineman along your path. Be prepared to block him. If nothing is in your path, continue to next level. Block LB and get your head to play side.

FB: Lead step directly outside (this could happen off motion). Attack the SS area and block force (cover up and take away color).

TB: Open and run directly at TE. Read the area and puller's blocks. Run outside defense or plant and run back at LOS under any block on LOS.

QB: Drive the ball deep. Get it to TB as soon as possible. Naked fake is urgent.

WR: Work to block defenders over you.

This change in philosophy has given us many big-hit runs of more than 10 yards over the past five years. Without a doubt, this is the favorite play of Ron Dayne, the all-time leading rusher in NCAA Division I history.

Off–Tackle Runs:
The Power and the Counter

The last components to our run package are what we call track-blocked plays, in which the playside blockers block down on imaginary tracks and an offside puller leads the play through the point of attack (figure 18.7).

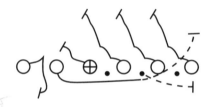

Figure 18.7   Track blocking.

The objectives behind this method of blocking are to attack the defense with gap-blocked play, sometimes with misdirection. We force the defense to defeat gap blocks as opposed to zone blocks, thus creating more defined running lanes for the running back. We use this kind of blocking in all short-yardage and goal-line situations.

These plays blocked on tracks are toughness plays, which create basic looks at a run for the tailback.

The play side of both the power and the counter are blocked the same way. The kickout and lead blockers change assignments, but the initial aiming point and reads for the tailback are the same.

The standard rules for the power and counter (see figure 18.8a) are the following:

TE: Block inside gap through any defender to next level. Block offside LB.

PT: Block inside gap through any defender to next level. Block offside LB.

PG: Block inside gap through any defender to next level. Block offside LB.

C: Block back on LOS through off gap to down defender.

OT: Close inside gap and funnel any defender outside.

WR: Block most dangerous defender closest to formation.

The rules for the power (see figure 18.8b) are the following:

FB: Lead blocker. Step directly at outside leg of PT. Run hard at this landmark. Get your feet across LOS or out of hole depending on how defender plays.

OG: Escort blocker. Think pull over PT. If closed, go around outside. See playside LB along the pull. Attack LB and block at his level. Get feet out of hole.

QB: Drive ball deep to TB. Drop back to show play-action pass.

TB: On power, drop step the opposite foot and run at PG. Pace should keep you behind escort blocker. Read blocks on LOS for first entry. Attack LOS.

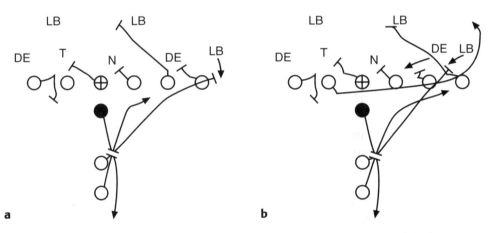

Figure 18.8 Power and counter: (*a*) standard blocking, (*b*) power blocking.

Here are the rules for the counter (see figure 18.9):

OG: Pull. Look in backfield for penetration first. Run directly at defender. If he closes, hook naturally. If he goes upfield, kick out and get your foot out of the hole.

FB: Escort blocker. Think entry over the PT. If he closes, go around outside. See playside LB along the pull. Attack LB and block at his level. Get feet out of hole (FB could be offset or motion away from hole).

QB: Open away from hole called. Drive ball deep to TB and move away as play-action pass.

TB: Step quickly away from hole called, then get back on power course. Pace should keep you behind escort. Read blocks on LOS for first entry. Attack LOS.

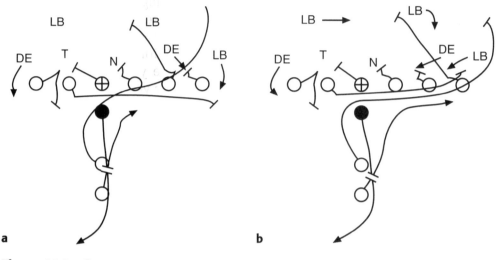

Figure 18.9 Counter.

Conclusion

This short synopsis gives you insight into our approach to the running game. The formula and principles used in the decision-making process are sound and provide answers that will guide you in your choices.

In this chapter we stressed individual accomplishments (a Heisman Trophy winner, 1,000-yard rushers, bowl MVPs, and all-American offensive linemen), and we touched on the success of the team in Rose Bowl victories.

The overall team accomplishments that resulted from our basic approach to running the football have been tremendous. Before listing the team records most associated with rushing the ball, we would like to offer a few notes about where our passing statistics fall. Demonstrating our ability to diversify, quarterback Darrell Bevell holds the school record for both most yards passing and most completions in a game, in a season, and during a career. Bevell also holds the school record for most consecutive completions. Darrell is the all-time completion percentage leader in each category and has the most passing touchdowns in a game and in a career.

Matt Nyquist holds the school record for most receptions in a game by a tight end; Chris Chambers holds the record for most receptions by a wide receiver. Tony Simmons, a wide receiver, holds the record for most career touchdown catches at any position. So within our philosophical mandate, a need to be stubborn never overshadowed our ability to throw the ball.

Referring to team accomplishments, the University of Wisconsin is the only team to win two Bowl Championship Series games. The Badgers are also the only Big Ten team in history to win back-to-back Rose Bowl games. Since 1990 Wisconsin has the best winning percentage of any team playing in at least five bowl games, and we are one of only seven teams in Division I-A that have won a total of 30 games in the last three years.

The sound principles involved in our preparation have allowed us to produce six top-25 rushing teams in the last nine years. Since 1993 the average rushing total has been over 2,800 yards per year, an average of 250 yards per game.

Our perception of how to play and our sound physical approach to football, offensively and defensively, have brought us tremendous pride as we've realized our goals. Our defensive accomplishments have been equally impressive. Reflection on either set of facts would still bring us back to the same philosophical approach—run the ball and stop the run.

19

The Passing Game

LaVell Edwards

Over the years, young coaches who want their teams to throw the football have written me to ask about the best way to get started. My professional advice never includes my personal secret, knowing the single wing. In 1961 BYU appointed Hal Mitchell as the head football coach. Mitchell wanted to bring the single-wing attack back into college football. I think Princeton was the only Division I school running it at the time. After Hal's first year, a coach left the staff, and Hal began looking for a replacement. Because I was probably the only Mormon in the country coaching the single wing, I was offered the job.

The single wing didn't work, so Hal left two years later, and BYU hired Tommy Hudspeth. Tommy came with a new approach and enthusiasm. Fortunately for me, he kept me on his staff, and in the second year we won the first conference championship in school history. We were only 6-4, but we won the right games primarily by throwing the football with a quarterback named Virgil Carter.

After Virgil graduated we got away from passing the ball again. After the 1971 season Tommy left, and I was appointed the head coach. How or why I got the job is still one of the great mysteries of the profession. In 18 years of coaching (8 in high school, 10 at BYU) I had been associated with only 4 winning seasons. In 47 years of football BYU had averaged a little over three victories per year, had won one conference championship, and had never been to a bowl game.

In a situation like that, you have to think outside of the box a little and be more creative than usual. My concern was not whether I would be fired, but when. That had been the pattern for many years. I figured that because

I probably wasn't going to make it anyway, I might as well try something radically different. I decided to throw the football, not just the normal 10 or 15 times a game, but 35 to 45 times per game, on any down, from our own end zone to the opponent's end zone. The only success we had ever had at BYU was when Virgil Carter was our quarterback. In addition, Stanford had just won back-to-back Rose Bowls with Jim Plunkett and Don Bunce throwing the ball.

Ironically, in that first season we had a running back, Pete Van Valkenburg, who led the nation in rushing. Picked to finish last in the conference, we tied for second place. The second year we started our passing game with a quarterback named Gary Sheide and had our only losing season. In light of the success we had in that first year, it would have

Courtesy of Mark A. Philbrick/Brigham Young University

been easy to abandon the pass and stay conventional. The third year we started out 0-3-1. We then won seven straight and never looked back. That year we won the conference championship and played in the Fiesta Bowl, the first bowl game in school history.

Philosophy

The BYU pass offense is based on a timing system. We design quarterback drops, route depths, and protection schemes so that the quarterback can throw the ball in a specific timed sequence. If the defense and coverage will not allow us to execute our rhythm or timing, then we convert our attack with route adjustments. We want to throw the ball up the field by attacking the vertical seams created by coverage and the horizontal seams created by using our running backs in a flare-flood control concept. By doing these things, we can still be a ball-control offense and take advantage of what the defense is giving us. Big plays come from misalignments or mismatches that we are able to create with formations, personnel groups, and motions. Big plays also occur with the receiver's ability to run with the ball after the catch.

We have five basic tenets in our passing philosophy. First, we must protect the quarterback. Second, we want to play ball-control football, primarily with the forward pass. Third, it is important to incorporate an effective running game with the passing attack. Fourth, we will take what the defense gives us. Fifth, we as coaches must constantly KISS the offense (KISS being an acronym for Keep It Simple, Stupid).

Protect the Quarterback

The success of any offense primarily depends on effective performance by the offensive line. Each individual on the line has a single task to perform, and the collective performance of the players directly affects the success of the offense.

The BYU passing offense starts with pass protection. The quarterback must have adequate time to read the defensive coverage, locate the appropriate receiver, and deliver the football. The receiver must have time to run his pass route at the proper depth, make his proper break, and then receive the pass. To accomplish this, the offensive line (and backs and tight ends, when necessary) must provide maximum pass protection.

Many talk about cup protection, meaning you block defensive people on the line of scrimmage in a cup formation to give the quarterback enough room to throw. We talk in slightly different terms. For many years, Roger French has taught our linemen what he calls mug protection.

The word *mug* emphasizes staying square to the line of scrimmage. Our center and guards are responsible for locking up their blocks so that the quarterback has room to step up if he needs to. We ask our linemen to get three-foot splits, lengthening the distance that an outside rusher has to run to get to the quarterback. Although we ask our tackles to be patient and let the defense come to them, we still emphasize keeping the shoulders and hips square to the line of scrimmage. What you end up with is a pocket shaped more like a mug than a cup. If our tackles get their shoulders and hips turned, the pocket will close like a cup, usually meaning that the quarterback has less time to throw the ball and less room to maneuver in the pocket.

Without spending too much time on individual blocking technique, we have four "nevers" that we teach offensive linemen. First, never go forward. If you go forward, you are going to lose the battle. We fire forward on our three-step game and play-action passes, but we never want to go forward on our five- and seven-step passes. Most of the time, a lineman who lunges forward ends up in a footrace to the quarterback. Second, never cross your feet. This is a big one. It is impossible to stay square to the line of scrimmage with crossed feet. Third, never drop your head. Once you drop your head, people get behind you. Fourth, never be beaten inside. By not giving up the inside, we force the defender to take the long way to the quarterback. If we can use good splits and protect the inside, we force the defender to take an even longer path to the quarterback.

Ideally, the simplest way to protect the quarterback is to make each offensive player responsible for a defensive player. Then you know exactly which player is responsible if a breakdown in protection occurs. This approach is possible versus an odd front, but against even fronts it is also necessary to zone block. If the defense rushes six defenders, we will block six. If the defense rushes seven defenders, we will block seven. We devote a lot of practice time to identifying blitz-pickup assignments and individual pass-protection techniques needed to carry out the blocks. Defenses might be better than we are athletically, but we will always try to protect the quarterback schematically. If we decide to use a hot route, we use a hot route that incorporates the unblocked defender. Whoever that unblocked defender is, we simply include his name in the play call so that everyone knows off whom we are hot.

Control the Ball With the Forward Pass

Much of our success over the years has come about because we ask our quarterbacks to complete simple throws. Even though we throw the ball often, simple passes allow us to control the clock and be as aware of time of possession as anyone.

Incorporate the Run Game

We always strive to have an effective running game. It is difficult to win football games if you cannot run and throw effectively. We want to employ play-action passes that look just like our best run plays. Later in this chapter I will talk about the path that our halfback takes in our H option route, which he should disguise to look exactly like the path he takes as he goes to block the whip in our draw trap.

Take What the Defense Gives Us

The idea to take what the defense allows seems to have become a cliche in football, but it remains true nonetheless. A defense can rarely cover the entire field. But the sophistication of defenses today makes it difficult for us to determine exactly what blitzes or coverages they are running over the course of a game. What we try to do is take a portion of the football field, the weak flat for example, and attack that area until we figure out what the defense is trying to do. Once we figure out the intentions of the defense, we attack the coverage we see.

KISS the Offense

Our coaches have always agreed that you have to KISS the offense. KISS is a common coaching acronym meaning Keep It Simple, Stupid. Although this may be another cliche, it is essential to our success. We have only about 10 passing plays and 5 running plays, which we run from multiple formations, personnel groups, and motions. The result is an attack that looks more complex than it really is. One of the biggest mistakes we make as football coaches is trying to do too much. It is always interesting to see how much time we spend practicing new plays, how few times we use them, and how we come back to the basic plays that we have run for years.

Oblique Stretches

Everybody understands horizontal stretch routes and vertical stretch routes. At BYU we have tried to develop oblique stretches, or triangles. This is a basic strongside pattern for us (figure 19.1). The Z executes a streak route and must release outside the cornerback to prevent him from being able to take away the tight end's route. The tight end runs a 15-yard sail route. We try to get the tight end in the imaginary spot behind underneath coverage where the three-deep zones meet. Versus man-to-man coverage, the tight end will square out at 15 yards, putting a good man-to-man move on the defender covering him. The X will run a post on the back side trying to occupy the free safety. The playside back checks his protection responsibilities and then runs an arrow route to the strong flat.

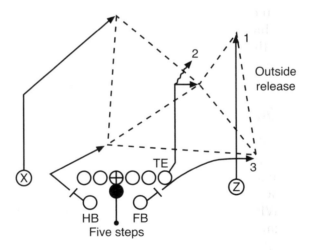

Figure 19.1 Oblique stretch to strong side.

The quarterback's progression is deep to short. Versus cover 3, we will peek at Z as #1. The X on the backside post and the tight end on the sail route are simultaneously #2, and the fullback in the flat is #3. All we have done is create triangles depending on how the defense plays us. If the free safety comes down to take away the sail, we might have a shot at the post. In a true cover 3, the post route should occupy the free safety, and we progress from the tight end to the flat. If the strong safety hangs to take away the sail, we should have a high-percentage throw to the flat. Versus man-to-man coverage, the possibility of taking a shot at Z on the streak route increases. If not, it becomes important that the tight end execute a good man route.

Another possibility versus man coverage using the same pattern is to call the fullback on an option route (figure 19.2). The option route changes the halfback's route to an arrow to create more room for the fullback to work. If the strongside linebacker rushes, the fullback is hot and turns out right away. If the strongside linebacker plays the fullback man-to-man, the fullback sets him up in one direction and gets open by breaking the opposite way.

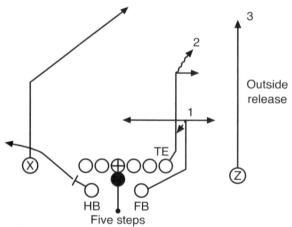

Figure 19.2 FB option.

Here is another idea based on the same basic pass pattern. If the defense is rolling the zone over to the strong side and taking away the sail hole, we call the same play from a one-back, doubles formation and end it with the word *Wanda* (figure 19.3), which we use to designate the weakside linebacker (or nickel) as the defender we cannot block. If Wanda rushes, we become hot. The quarterback's progression then changes from deep to short. The hot route is #1, the tight end is #2, and the Z is #3. If Wanda does not rush, we have created the same triangles as before, but we now have our X receiver in the spot that the strongside linebacker vacates if he goes to take away the sail route.

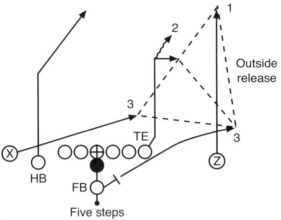

Figure 19.3 Wanda.

Using Running Backs in the Passing Game

Running backs play two key roles in the BYU passing offense. One is pass protection. As mentioned previously, we spend a lot of time making sure that our running backs are prepared to fill their role in the protection scheme, whether they are blocking blitzers or hot releases or executing a screen. We have to block the blitz or attack the blitz. The second role running backs play in our passing attack is that of receiver. Running backs are critical in creating the stretches necessary to beat zone coverage, whether it is a horizontal stretch, vertical stretch, or an oblique stretch in which we are trying to stretch a zone at an angle.

We also like to get our running backs involved versus man coverage because we can often match up a good athlete against a linebacker. Because most quarterbacks like to throw deep or always think the deep guy is open, we have added terms to our basic plays that help remind our quarterback to read from short to deep. This approach gets our backs and tight ends more involved in the passing game. On the FB option mentioned previously, the quarterback's reads go in reverse. The fullback's option route is #1, the sail route by the tight end is #2, and the Z on the streak is #3. If the blitz comes from the strong side, the fullback turns out and the quarterback throws it hot immediately. We want the quarterback's focus to be on throwing a short, high-percentage pass. If our fullback can break a tackle or shake a tackler, we have a chance to make a big play with a short, high-percentage throw.

Using the same pass pattern, we use the F angle to create another wrinkle (figure 19.4). As the fullback executes his arrow route to the flat, he plants his foot in the ground and returns into the hole where the strongside linebacker was. This can be an effective play if the stud is getting back to take away the intermediate throw to the tight end. The angle is also good against man coverage because it creates a difficult matchup for a linebacker.

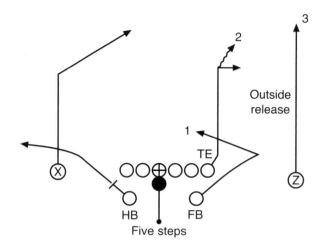

Figure 19.4 F angle.

We also add terms that do not change the quarterback's progression but still emphasize in his mind that the running backs might offer an easy completion. For example, we can put the fullback on a delay route (figure 19.5). The quarterback still goes through his normal reads from deep to short. The term *delay,* however, reminds him that if the strongside linebacker drops to take away the sail route, he can dump the ball to the fullback running the delay route.

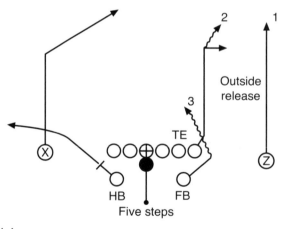

Figure 19.5 FB delay.

We also attack the weak side of the field using the same oblique stretch or triangle concept (figure 19.6). This now puts X on the streak route with an outside release. The tight end pushes upfield and executes a crossing route that ends up in the weakside sail hole. The tight end must get over the middle linebacker as he crosses the field. The halfback executes an arrow route stretching the weak flat. The Z now executes the backside post to hold the free safety from taking away the tight end. The quarterback still reads deep to intermediate to short, just as before.

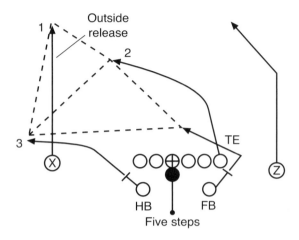

Figure 19.6 Oblique stretch to weak side.

Halfback Option

From the weakside stretch, we add a halfback option (figure 19.7). This play is one of the best ways for us to get the ball to a good receiver who can run after the catch. First, it is important to evaluate personnel and pick a halfback who can execute the option route versus man-to-man coverage. He must be able to separate at the move point. Although coaching this route is essential, we have found that some players have a feel for it and others do not. A guy who doesn't have a knack for it will have difficulty running it correctly. When we add the term *HB option,* the quarterback's reads change from short to deep. The option route becomes #1, the intermediate route by the tight end is #2, and the streak by X is #3.

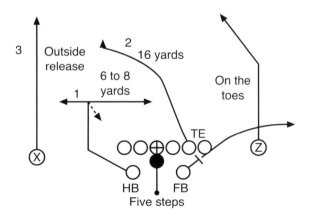

Figure 19.7 HB option.

The first element in teaching the HB option route is alignment. We can run this route only from split backs. Therefore, the halfback can line up no tighter than the inside leg of the tackle. The release should be an arc that gains a little bit of width. We train our halfbacks to make this look exactly like the path we take to block the weak outside linebacker in our draw trap. We want to make it look the same to the whip so that he cannot recognize the difference. We also run a play-action pass in which we fake the draw trap and run X on a 14-yard curl. The halfback takes the same path that he would on the option route or draw trap and then executes an arrow route.

If the whip blitzes as the halfback releases, the halfback is hot and should execute a swing route. The proper technique is to plant the foot in the ground and push hard for width. We emphasize getting width for two reasons. First, we want to get away from the zone blitz. If a defensive end peels or a defensive tackle drops out, we want to push hard to the sideline and separate. Second, we need to get rid of the ball quickly so that the free safety cannot disguise a blitz by staying high. Precision is required for the quarterback to get the ball quickly to the halfback at the correct width. If we get the bailout to the halfback before the free safety or dropping lineman can get there, we expect to make a tackler miss and possibly make a big play. We could also turn our protection against the blitz to avoid having the halfback become hot. But then we have to peek at the other side for new blitzers and hot people.

If the halfback releases and reads zone coverage, his route becomes almost like those of playground football. We teach our halfback to get to the hole in the zone with his feet. If the corner drops deep and the weakside linebacker drops wide, the hole will be between the weakside and middle linebackers. As we get to the proper hole, the halfback should plant his foot and get his head, shoulders, and hips around immediately. The quarterback should throw the ball as the halfback plants his foot so that the defense is unable to squeeze us. If the defense does squeeze the option route, we have the tight end coming over the top and the quarterback will throw behind the defenders who are squeezing.

The most common mistake made on this route is that the halfback sometimes wants to fishhook or bend as he turns to receive the ball. He must stick a plant foot in the ground, snap the head around, and turn directly back to the quarterback as the ball arrives. If the halfback sees cover 2 or a roll weak look with the weak corner in the flat and the whip dropping straight back, he should attack the hole where the whip dropped. It now becomes even more important not to fishhook. We also teach our halfbacks to crouch and become small after the catch so that they are harder to tackle.

Finally, if the halfback sees man coverage, he pushes upfield six yards, makes a move, and works inside or outside to get open. The most difficult part for young players to learn is patience. Most young guys hurry too much. We teach our option runners to get to the move point, shake, put on a definite move, and push to separate out of the break. We practice this route every day with our quarterbacks in a drill that helps the quarterbacks recognize what the back is going to do before he makes his break. The right halfback executing this route properly can be a real equalizer. The players gain a lot of confidence when they get a feel for it. Our halfbacks love the chance to be one-on-one versus a linebacker and have some grass to work with.

Mesh Pattern

Another example of a basic pattern that can be easily adapted with formations and motion into numerous variations is our mesh play. Some people refer to the mesh as a pick or cross (figure 19.8).

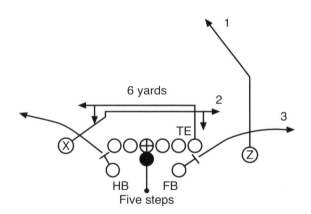

Figure 19.8 Mesh.

This play is good for several reasons. First, the pattern works against almost any coverage. The quarterback should be able to find a high-percentage completion. Second, this is an excellent red-zone pattern because it is low risk and excellent against man coverages, which the defense is likely to use inside the 20-yard line. Third, we can run this pattern effectively from multiple formations and motions using variations on the route of the receiver not involved in the mesh (figure 19.9).

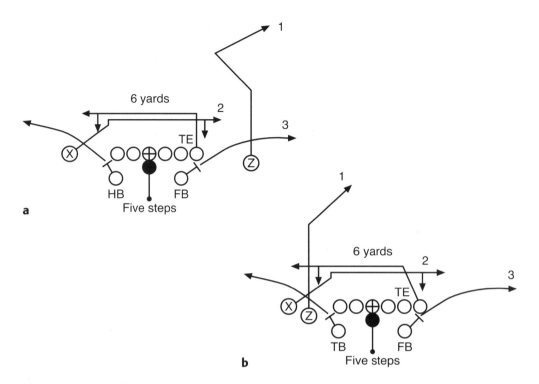

Figure 19.9 Variations of mesh patterns.

The most important coaching point of this play is the mesh itself. The tight end is responsible for obtaining a depth of six to seven yards, and the X is responsible for the mesh. If the tight end gets knocked around a bit and crosses at only five yards, X should be rubbing shoulders with him at four yards. If the tight end is at eight yards, then X should be at seven. Essential to the mesh is that both players move horizontally at the mesh point. The tight end should push upfield, put his foot in the ground, and come flat at six to seven yards deep. The X should cut down his split and locate the tight end at the snap. The X can and probably will release at an angle aiming for the mesh. Once he locates the tight end, X should stair climb his defender and break flat so that he can move horizontally through the mesh point. Versus man coverage the X must mesh tightly with the tight end, forcing his defender to climb over the top to catch up.

The quarterback's progression is from deep to short. It starts with a pre-snap look at how the safeties are playing. If the single safety or safety nearest the Z is cheating up, the quarterback can take a shot at the post route. This possibility is particularly common in the red zone as safeties crowd up. The receiver should run the post route on the defenders' toes, and the post may look like a slant route inside the 10-yard line. We might also call Z on a corner route inside the red zone. If the post does not look good, the quarterback's eyes should come right to the mesh. The X is most likely to come open because the tight end is setting the pick. Against zone coverages both receivers involved in the mesh should sit in the next hole past the mesh point. The quarterback then reads the flat defender. If the flat defender squeezes the mesh, the quarterback throws the arrow route in the flat. The backs check their protection responsibilities but get moving once they know they can release. The horizontal stretch by the backs is what creates space for the mesh to be effective.

Conclusion

This chapter presents some of the ideas that have worked for us over the past 29 years. I believe that it is important to base your philosophy on your personality. Woody Hayes once said that it is all right to try to emulate traits and concepts of others, but it does not work to try to imitate them. To pass the ball successfully, you should develop a philosophy and stick with it. Perhaps the most important characteristic you can have as a coach is to be consistent. Consistency develops honesty, which in turn develops trust. Without these things, execution will be inconsistent at best. In the BYU passing offense, we cannot win with an inconsistent performer, regardless of how well he throws the ball. But we can win with a player who has an average throwing arm if he is consistent and runs the offense.

20

Run Defense

R.C. Slocum

It is a great honor for me to be asked to submit my ideas on run defense. The defense of the run is one of the foundations of football. Without a solid run defense, it is difficult to stop any type of offense.

I have never been as concerned about a team completing a pass on us as I have about a team running successfully against us. We always have the hope that on the next play we will pressure or sack the quarterback, the passer will throw a bad pass, or the receiver will drop the pass. But when a team can line up and run the football at us and knock our line of scrimmage back, it is demoralizing. In every game, a time comes when you must be able to stop the run if you're going to prevent the team from scoring or making a first down. For this reason, the foundation of every defense must be first to stop the run.

Even teams that display prolific passing attacks recognize that at times they must be able to run to be successful. All the great offenses that I've encountered over the last 30-plus years at the major college level have been able to run the football effectively, and all the great defenses have been able to stop the run.

Football is a tough, physical game. To have an effective defense, a coach must be able to mold his defensive unit into a tough, physical presence. A hard-hitting defense, besides creating problems for your opponents, has a tremendous effect on the personality of your offense. If you have an effective run defense, your offense becomes tougher and more able to run the football. This combination allows you to develop a physically and mentally tough football team, which is a requirement if you want to be a championship-caliber team.

The starting point in playing effective run defense is persuading your players to play hard. That is something every player can do regardless of ability. Over the years I have had coaches tell me that they're not very good this year because they don't have this player or that player or they don't have much ability. I have often wanted to tell them that until they get their team playing hard, they're never going to have a top-notch defense. You get what you demand in terms of effort. You should never accept anything less than all-out effort. This does not come easily. Effort is something that you must drill and work on daily.

We normally start defensive practice with a pursuit drill (figure 20.1). In this drill, the coach steps in the huddle and calls the defense. The defense breaks the huddle and hustles to their alignments. The coach gives the back a direction and pitches him the ball, and the entire team must take their proper pursuit angle and chase the football. If one man does not give all-out effort, the whole group has to come back and do it again. We videotape this drill each day, and the staff grades it. We also show the tape to the team. The point we are trying to make is that the starting point for playing great defense is making all-out effort and taking proper pursuit angles.

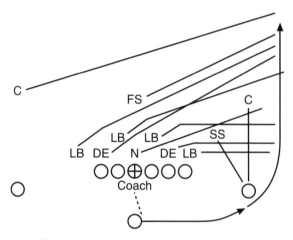

Figure 20.1 Pursuit drill.

Playing good defense against the run must be a team effort. Every player has a responsibility to make it work. A good opponent will inevitably block players from time to time, but with an all-out team effort and a swarming defense, someone can cover for the blocked player to hold the opponent to a minimal gain. If the entire team gives maximum effort and takes the proper angles, the offense should never be able to produce a long run.

In reviewing practice and game tapes with the team, coaches must emphasize effort and pursuit angles. Coaches often watch tapes hurriedly and do not spend enough time grading the elementary essential of playing good run defense—great effort. I cannot emphasize this too much because without effort, nothing else matters. A defense will be doomed to mediocrity without all-out effort. On every play, every player has an assignment, and he must carry it out with great effort. Nothing demoralizes an offense or a runner more than team pursuit and gang tackling.

Find a Base Defense

In defending the run, a team must have a base defense in which they believe strongly. I have seen great defensive teams over the years that have employed the 3-4, the 4-3, or an 8-man front. For those teams, it was not the defensive scheme that made them great but how they played it. You should have a base defense in which you feel you can line up and stop any run. You can complement your base with movements and blitzes, but I don't think you can be effective unless you have a base that you can execute and in which your team has confidence.

When a team is effective with its base defense, then movements can create some helpful disruption. You can use movements and the blitz to your advantage in anticipation of a particular play, but it is difficult to play effective defense if you have to trick or outguess the offensive playcaller throughout the game.

Courtesy of Texas A&M University

Another important aspect of playing run defense is playing situational football. Players must understand down and distance and what the opponent is likely to do in particular situations. The person calling the defenses must have a thorough understanding of the opponent's tendencies in the various down-and-distance situations and must call defenses accordingly. I have never felt that you could defend everything on every play. The coach must anticipate what he is likely to see based on down and distance and then call the most effective defense for that situation. To stop the run, the coach must often create a numerical advantage over the opponent. The objective is to have the best defensive alignment at the anticipated point of attack and get more people in that area than that opponent can possibly block. I'll address this topic later in the chapter.

Now I would like to begin a discussion of our base 3-4 defense and what we do with it to stop the run. First, why the 3-4? Over the years I have coached a number of defensive schemes (figure 20.2). In the 1970s we ran the college 4-3 and the pro 4-3 (6-1). After a few years we added the 6-1 under. In 1981 I went to the University of Southern California to work for John Robinson. They had been a 3-4 defense, and John wanted to blend in some 4-3 principles. We did that and led the Pacific-10 Conference in total defense in 1981.

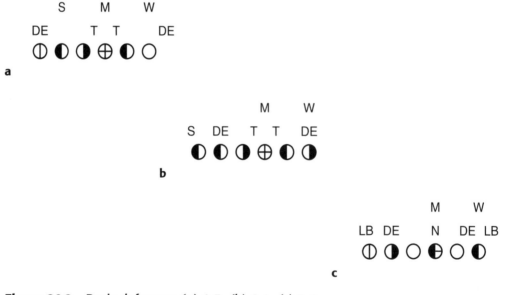

Figure 20.2 Basic defenses: *(a)* 4-3, *(b)* 6-1, *(c)* 3-4.

When I came back to Texas A&M in 1982, we ran the 4-3 and some 8-man front. Before the 1983 season, the defensive staff and I visited several NFL teams that were running the 3-4. At the time I felt that our personnel was much more fitted for the 3-4 defense, and I liked the element of having a four-linebacker defense. From a recruiting standpoint I felt that more linebackers than defensive linemen were available. In addition, I thought we could take the big, strong safety-type athletes, who might not be quite fast enough to play in the secondary at our level, and play them at linebacker, thereby adding speed to our defense.

We had a number of those players who came to us as safeties and became great linebackers in our "wrecking crew" defense. Johnny Holland was a two-time all-American who later played for Green Bay, and William Thomas was an all-American who also had a great professional career, with the Eagles and Raiders. By getting more speed on the field with players like these, I felt that we were better equipped to defend the run, especially against the option-oriented teams that we saw often in the Southwest Conference. In my opinion, having a stand-up linebacker on the end of the line of scrimmage to defend against the quarterback in an option scheme was better than having a down lineman trying to come up out of a stance and take the quarterback.

After visiting with several NFL teams that used the 3-4, we came back and wrote up the defense we have used now for approximately 18 years—the 44 cover 3 (figure 20.3). Like all teams, we have added some wrinkles here and there over the years, but the foundation of the defense has remained the same. I think that this scheme allows us to have a base defense that is effective against the run and, with the speed at the linebacker position, allows us to disrupt runs by various movements and blitzes.

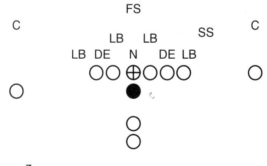

Figure 20.3   44 cover 3.

Now I would like to discuss our base 3-4 defense. To play his position, each player must understand several elements. Players must understand and execute these points regardless of the defensive scheme played.

- **Assignment:** Each player has a specific assignment or job on every defense, for example, to control the B gap. A player can never leave the huddle without knowing his assignment.

- **Alignment:** Each player has a precise alignment on each defensive call. To facilitate learning these, we talk in terms of numbered alignments (figure 20.4), for example, a 3 alignment or a 5 alignment. We also give specific definitions of each alignment; for example, a 3 is an outside-crotch alignment, which means the defender's inside leg splits the offensive linemen's crotch. A 4 alignment is an inside-track alignment; the player's tracks, his feet, are just inside the opponent's feet. For linebackers lined up off the line, we use the same numbers but add a zero, for example, a 30 alignment. Players must learn precise alignments, and the coach must emphasize correct alignment on every down. If a player must move because of motion, he should move to a precise alignment. The player's ability to carry out his job depends on his taking the proper alignment. If a defense is to be gap sound, all players must align precisely.

Figure 20.4 Alignment responsibilities.

- **Stance:** On every play each player should use a particular stance. To be able to carry out his assignment, the player must distribute his weight properly and place his hands, feet, and eyes in the right position.

- **Key:** Because the eyes control where the body goes, it is extremely important that a player know exactly where his focal point should be. He must develop the discipline to direct his eyes so that he will get the proper key. Achieving this often requires a lot of coaching and repetition. The coach should take a position that will allow him to observe the eyes of the player. No guessing should occur, although players can sometimes guess right and make a big play. To be consistent, the player must be disciplined in reading keys. In professional football, an older player who has lost some speed can still play effectively because he has become extremely disciplined in reading keys. He doesn't take false steps and therefore is always heading in the right direction. He plays quicker than his ability would indicate.

- **Reaction:** The name of the game on defense is reaction. The essence of coaching defense is putting a player in a situation enough times that he can make the proper reaction.

- **Technique:** In reacting to circumstances, the player must learn specific techniques that allow him to carry out his job. Many coaches spend a lot of time on scheme and alignments and fail to drill the techniques that allow a player to execute his assignment. Coaches must give constant attention to developing technique in taking on blocks, getting off blocks, and tackling. Coaching run defense involves repetitiously emphasizing the proper technique so that players can carry out their assignments.

Each player on defense must thoroughly understand each of these elements. The coach should regularly ask the player to recite to him, in the proper order, each of the essential elements. The object is to develop consistency of performance by each player so that when the group comes together, the defense will be consistent. Players must understand that each of their assignments is interrelated with the other positions and that the overall performance of the defense requires each player to do his job.

Base 3–4 Defense

In discussing our base 3-4 defense, I will define each of these six elements for each position. First, the huddle call would be 44 cover 3. To assist in the learning process, all calls for defenses, stunts, and coverages should be as descriptive as possible. Players will learn more easily if the defensive calls are well thought out and presented so that the players can relate one call to other calls they might hear. In this way, the whole defensive package does not involve total rote learning.

For example, in the 44-front call, the first 4 is to the end to the strong side. The second call is to the other end. The nose understands that he shades to the strong end. After the offense is aligned, the Mike linebacker will make the call strong left or strong right. The front will then align accordingly.

The coach from the sideline can also make the determination by making a field call. In that case, the Mike linebacker would call "Field left." The second part of the call, the 3, refers to the coverage and tells the secondary that it's a three-deep coverage. Calls should be brief so that they can be transmitted to the huddle and given easily. I don't like the signal caller to step out of the huddle to get the call and then step back into the huddle to give it. I prefer him to give the call as he receives the signal from the sideline or reads it from a wristband.

Nose

The assignment for the nose is to control the strongside A gap. His alignment is a strong shade, which means his inside foot will split the center's crotch. He uses a three-point stance with his inside foot staggered approximately six inches back.

His key is the center, and he will feel the guard. His technique will be to take a short power step with his inside foot keeping his pads down and thrusting his hands toward the center's breastplate. He should have his thumbs up and try to grab the cloth of the center's jersey with his fingers. If he should miss on the first try, he should keep grabbing with his hands until he gets a firm grasp on the center. If the center is trying to reach block him, he should escape fast and laterally down the line of scrimmage to the outside. If the center is trying to zone through his inside shoulder, he should hang on to the center with both hands and try to work laterally in the direction the center is going.

If it's a zone block and the guard is trying to overtake him, he should keep his focus on his primary key—the center—and hang on to him for as long as possible. He should make every effort to keep a strong inside shoulder and not let the center off on the linebacker. If the center blocks flat down the line, away from the nose, the nose should anticipate the counter and immediately look for the off guard pulling in his direction. He should then try to get penetration upfield to beat the down block of the strong guard. As he gains penetration, he should try to disrupt the pulling guard and tackle.

End

The end's assignment is to maintain the B gap. His alignment is a 4 alignment, or inside track on the offensive tackle. He uses a three-point stance with the outside hand down and the outside leg staggered back approximately six inches.

His key is the offensive tackle, and he will feel the offensive guard. He will react based on the release of the tackle. The technique he should use is to step with a short outside step and read on the move. If the tackle is releasing to his outside, he should thrust his hands to the breastplate area of the tackle, and, keeping his pads down, try to grab cloth with both hands working to the inside V of the neck of the offensive tackle. He should work hard to maintain a strong outside arm and work his outside hip squarely down the line to the outside.

At this time, he should feel the guard to determine whether he is involved in a zone-blocking scheme. If the guard is not coming, he should anticipate trap, immediately release the tackle, and work hard back inside to wrong shoulder any trapper. If the guard is coming to the end in a zone-blocking scheme, he should continue to focus on his primary key—the tackle—and try to hang on to keep the tackle off the linebacker for as long as possible. If the tackle takes an inside release or cutoff angle, the end should work fast down the line in the direction of the cutoff.

This is one of the beauties of the defense in terms of stopping the run. The end should never be cut off, and he should hit any cutback by the back.

Outside Linebacker

The outside linebacker's assignment is to read the release of the tight end and work C gap to D gap, depending on the block of the tight end. His alignment is a 6 alignment with his tracks just outside the tracks of the tight end. He uses a two-point stance with his feet close to parallel.

His key is the tight end. His reaction should be to step to the tight end with his inside foot and react to the tight end's block. If the tight end blocks down, he should gain ground slightly upfield and to the inside, keeping his pads parallel to the line in trying to close the distance between himself and the defensive end. If the tight end reach blocks, the linebacker should thrust his hands to the breastplate of the tight end, grabbing cloth and keeping his pads square. He should keep an outside presence while keeping his eyes inside to see if the ball is committed inside or out. If the ball is committed inside, he will be late help in the C gap. If the ball is outside, he will be a D-gap player.

He must keep his hips and pads square. If the tight end attempts a base cutoff, the linebacker will work across the tight end's face to take the C gap or drive the tight end's butt into the hole. If the outside backer has no tight end over which to align, he will align over an imaginary tight end or where a tight end would be if one were on his side. His key will then be the triangle of the offensive tackle, quarterback, and tailback. He should look through the tackle, see the quarterback and tailback, and get a flow read from them. If he gets a flow-away read, he should shuffle straight down the line and play any cutback into the C gap. If he gets a flow read to him, he should spill the ball to the outside or contain, depending on the coverage being played.

Mike Linebacker

Mike's assignment on flow to him is C gap; on flow away, he has the off A gap. His alignment is four and a half yards deep with a 30 alignment on the offensive guard, an outside crotch alignment. He uses a two-point stance with his weight on the balls of his feet. He should be in a comfortable position so that he does not have to bob up or down to move.

The first thing I look for at the start of a play is to see whether the linebacker has to lower or raise his body position before moving. If he does, he has an improper stance. He should be in a stance that wastes no time or action in getting on the move.

His key is the tailback, and he should underkey the guard in seeing the quarterback. So his point of vision is somewhere between the guard and the tailback. Again, we talk about seeing the triangle of the guard, quarterback, and tailback (figure 20.5). Mike should get a flow, or directional read, from reading his keys.

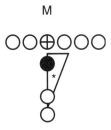

Figure 20.5   Triangle key for the Mike linebacker.

Mike and Will are tied together and should react in the same direction on running plays. If Mike gets a flow to him, he should shuffle laterally and then work hard downhill into the inside of the C gap to his side. If he gets a flow-away read, he should shuffle laterally and work hard downhill to the off A gap. He should take on blocks explosively, using his hands and working into the blocker with leverage while exploding upward.

Will Linebacker

Will's assignment is onside C gap with flow to him and onside A gap with flow away. His alignment is head up to the offensive guard and four and a half yards deep. His stance and key are the same as Mike's. His reaction on flow to him is to shuffle to the outside and attack the C gap hard downhill. On flow away, he should read whether there is a potential cutback runner to the A gap. If so, he should read the guard and angle the guard's block. If the guard is straight ahead, Will should attack him aggressively downhill with his inside arm free. If the guard takes an aggressive cutoff angle, Mike should come downhill to the backside V of the neck of the guard and try to knock him past the hole.

Mike and Will should be reading the same key against an I-formation (this would normally be the tailback), and Will should also underkey the guard. Mike and Will have the same keys and should work together as if they were attached to a string. On any given run play, they initially should be shuffling in the same direction (figure 20.6).

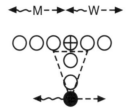

Figure 20.6 Linebacker read and shuffle.

The philosophy of the 44 defense is to tie up the interior five offensive linemen with the three defensive linemen. This approach allows the four linebackers to use their speed to make plays. In addition, we want to force the ball sideways by aligning with five defenders between the offensive tackles. A popular play from the I-formation is the tailback counter (figure 20.7), which is a good play to show how the assignments of the 44 defense should work.

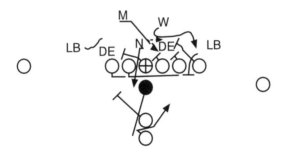

Figure 20.7 44 defense versus TB counter.

The outside linebacker to the play side must do a good job of getting his hands on the tight end, working upfield, and staying square while taking on the pulling guard. We would like him to take away the inside running lane, but we do not like to talk in terms of wrong shouldering the guard. We would like for him to squeeze the hole, keep his hat inside the guard, but attack with both hands and keep his pads square. Mike should shuffle and retrace as he picks up the offside pulling guard and then come downhill hard in the C gap, forcing everything to bounce outside to the strong safety.

From base 44, a number of individual movements can give the offense a change-up. Instead of playing a base technique, the nose can have a nose-strong or nose-weak stunt in which he moves on the snap. In addition, we like to have the strong end do an out move.

At times we slant the whole front three linemen either strong or weak, for example, 44 strong slant (figure 20.8). This is a way to get more people at the point of attack to stop the run. If we expect a strongside run, we use the strong slant to gain an advantage at the point of attack. We could also move the line the other way.

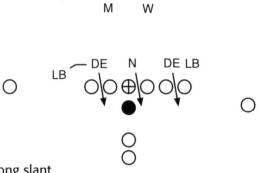

Figure 20.8   44 strong slant.

Another way would be to overshift the front before the snap, which we do quite often. We call this 53 (figure 20.9). In other words, the strong end plays a 5, the weak end plays a 3, and the nose shades to the 5 side. The linebacker over the tight end also widens his alignment to 9 alignment with his inside foot splitting the tight end's crotch. We overshift our defense to the strong side, which gives us an advantage on strongside runs. We could go a step further by calling 53 G and moving our nose over the frontside guard (figure 20.10).

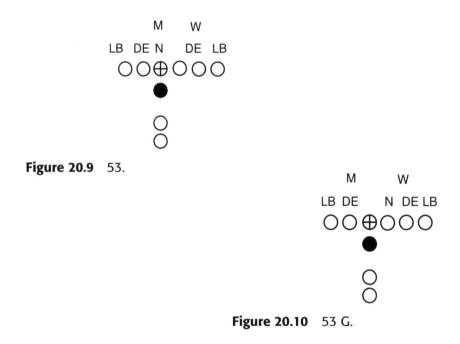

Figure 20.9   53.

Figure 20.10   53 G.

Most teams have a marked tendency to run to the strong side, or tight-end side, and normally do not have prominent weakside running attacks. Some offenses, however, have the ability to attack the weak side of the defense. When a team is good at running both strong and weak, we need to find a way to get an additional defender involved with the front. One of the ways we do this is to bring a safety down to linebacker level. We can overshift our front to the strong side to help the run defense there and then bring the free safety down to the weak side to help the defense there. In effect, this gives us a true eight-man front.

We can give the free safety a couple of different run responsibilities depending on what we did with the front. One way to do this is with what we call the 53 joker (figure 20.11). The free safety holds his alignment as long as possible but moves down late in the cadence to the weak B gap. He is responsible for any cutback, which frees up the Will linebacker to fast flow strong without any responsibility for the weak A gap. On any flow weak, Will could aggressively attack the A gap and force the ball to bounce outside to the free safety.

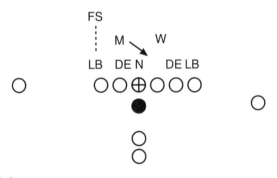

Figure 20.11   53 joker.

Another call might be 53 G weak in joker (figure 20.12). Again, the safety moves down late to the weak B-gap area. We stunt the weak end into the weak A gap. On flow strong, Will again is a free runner with no responsibility for cutback. The free safety handles the cutback. On flow weak, Will attacks any ISO or lead into the weak B gap aggressively inside out and forces the ball to bounce to the free safety. To compensate for the free safety's coming down, we play our weak corner in an inside halves technique and play quarter-quarter on the strong side.

Another defense in which we involve the safety to get an eight-man front uses our strong safety as a run defender and plays a man-free concept behind it in the secondary. We call this 44 jack (figure 20.13). We use this to help the strongside run defense. It also helps the weakside run defense because it frees up Mike to be a free player to the weak side on flow away.

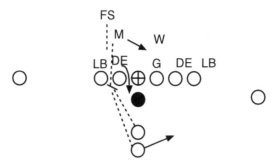

Figure 20.12 53 G weak in joker.

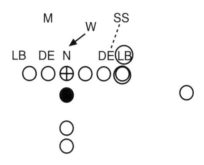

Figure 20.13 44 jack.

We give the cutback responsibility to the strong safety. We show our quarter-quarter-quarter-quarter look in the secondary, and the strong safety moves down late to take the cutback in either the B or C gap according to the strong end's alignment. With the strongside end in a 4, the strong safety has the C gap on cutback. The outside linebacker has coverage on the tight end. This also helps on the strongside ISO because Mike can now take on the fullback from the inside and force the ball outside to the strong safety and, at the same time, allow Will to stay backside for the cutback (see figure 20.14). We could also use the jack concept while playing our 53 front or 43 front.

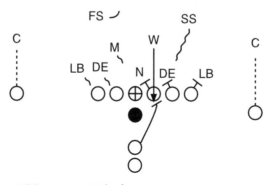

Figure 20.14 Strong ISO versus 44 jack.

Against one-back sets, the 3-4 scheme allows the flexibility of having athletes at the outside linebackers. These defenders can cover down on a removed receiver and at the same time maintain a presence in the front defense, thereby outnumbering the offensive blockers (figure 20.15).

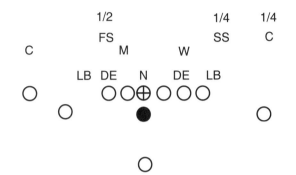

Figure 20.15 44 versus one-back set (zone).

We could do this with a quarter-quarter-half coverage or by locking the strong outside linebacker on the tight end and using a man-free concept. The free safety would cover the removed #2 to the weak side (figure 20.16).

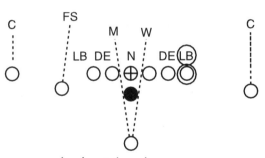

Figure 20.16 44 versus one-back set (man).

In defending against the run versus a four-wide set, we could play 44 or 54 and have our backers loosen to the #2 on their side while still keeping a presence in the run front. We can do this by playing a two-deep coverage or three-deep coverage (figure 20.17).

As one can see by the diagrams, the 3-4 allows tremendous flexibility in adjusting to different formations while still maintaining a strong defense against the run using base personnel. Modern offensive football uses formations and personnel groupings to spread the defense in hopes of getting substitute players on the field, thereby weakening the run defense.

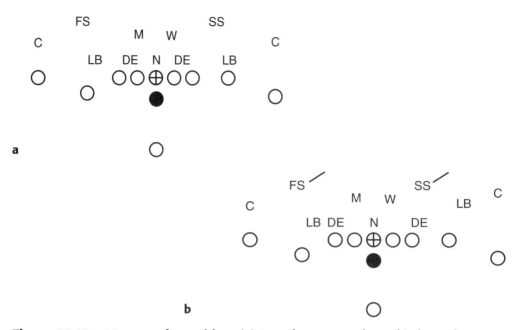

Figure 20.17 44 versus four wides: *(a)* two-deep secondary, *(b)* three-deep secondary.

As down and distance and tendencies dictate, a run defense must be on the field regardless of the formation. Base personnel can use any number of individual movements, stunts, and blitzes to disrupt the running game. As the situation dictates, we can put additional pass defenders on the field when tendencies indicate that a pass is likely. Even the most sophisticated passing teams, however, recognize the importance of the running game and make strong attempts to run the football. To be successful, a defense must have a way to stop the run when the situation dictates.

In closing, I would like to reemphasize that the most important elements of playing good run defense are having a sound base package, playing gap control, using great technique, having relentless pursuit of the ball, and gang tackling. In addition, you must be able to strengthen the defense by changing alignment and by properly using a player from the secondary to gain numerical superiority over the opponent at the point of attack. In addition, supplementing the base package with individual movements and a sound blitz package gives the defense a great chance to defend against the run and force the offense into a one-dimensional attack. I recognize that these ideas are not the only way to stop the run, but my teams have used these concepts for many years with a fair amount of success.

21

Pass Defense

Sonny Lubick

Throughout my coaching career I have had the good fortune to learn from some of the best coaches in the business. Nearly every aspect of the coaching philosophy I've developed reflects in some way the ideas of the many coaches I've had the pleasure of knowing.

For more than 25 years I emulated many of the ideas and schemes brought forward by Monte Kiffin, currently the defensive coordinator of the Tampa Bay Buccaneers. His influence and intelligence have benefited me immensely. One of the primary areas in which Coach Kiffin influenced my coaching career was in making me aware of the need for a solid concept for defensive football. Another trait that I admire in Coach Kiffin is his ability to discuss openly his theories with any coach who is willing to listen.

Such influence is apparent in the success we've enjoyed at Colorado State over the past eight seasons. One of my finest moments as a coach came during the opening game of the 1999 season. Since 1998 CSU and the University of Colorado have played one another in Denver, first at Mile High Stadium and beginning in 2001 at Invesco Field at Mile High. In 1999 CSU entered the game as a heavy underdog but won 41-14. The defensive schemes that our staff learned from Coach Kiffin helped us dominate a team we had not defeated since 1986. In that game our defensive unit had three interceptions, including one that we returned for a touchdown. We caused four fumbles and set a new school record by sacking the quarterback eight times. We could never have had that sort of success without studying and learning from Coach Kiffin. All of us must pursue learning daily. To this day I routinely call Coach Kiffin for advice. He keeps me abreast of the latest defensive schemes and coaching techniques.

I use that example to show that a coach needs to stay informed about the latest trends in football. Had our staff not taken advantage of studying and learning from the best, I know that we would not have had the success we've enjoyed at Colorado State.

Another individual who has had a great effect on my coaching career is Tom Osborne. Over a 10-year period I attended spring football practices at the University of Nebraska. Whenever I was present, Coach Osborne was always gracious and generous in sharing his insight and information. Coach Osborne helped me formulate my ideas about practice organization and my approach to maintaining continuity in my coaching staff.

Courtesy of Colorado State University

I have been fortunate at Colorado State to have consistency among the assistant coaches. I still have five members of my original coaching staff from nine years ago. Assistant coaches who have left our staff have done so because they had an opportunity to enhance their coaching careers.

For many years Tom Bass served as my mentor in all phases of technical secondary play. Formerly a defensive coordinator of the San Diego Chargers, Tom helped shape my philosophy in the technical aspects of football, especially in the techniques of secondary play. As coaches, we know the value of teaching and learning.

Philosophy

"Do the little things right" is a motto that we adhere to daily. It means paying attention to detail. Doing the little things is often the difference between success and failure, between winning and losing. This axiom applies particularly to coaching and playing the secondary. We prefer to use three or four base coverages and limit our blitz package to no more than five or six for the entire season. We categorize our coverages into run-pass coverages and our blitzes into run-pass blitzes.

By limiting the number of base coverages and blitzes we use, we maximize our repetitions. The increased number of repetitions helps us prepare for all the variations that an offense might present. We have time to iron out any wrinkles, limit our mistakes, and concentrate and prepare for the variations that can arise during a game.

This defensive coaching philosophy helps players develop a sense of confidence in performing and executing coverages. The morale of the team—especially the players in the secondary—grows stronger with each practice. Through constant repetition, players sense the improvement they are making.

Consequently, as their performance improves through repetition, players play with greater confidence. Each player is comfortable performing at his position and has confidence in his teammates. Confident play in the secondary improves the morale of the entire defense and the rest of the team. Players develop a sense that they can overcome the adversity that occurs in every game because they have a strong foundation built through repetition.

Simplicity, execution, and consistency are important pieces of overall defensive philosophy, especially in the secondary. So is discipline. Discipline is vital to the success of secondary play. During the 2000 season we were the least-penalized team in the conference and one of the least-penalized teams in the nation. In 2000 the secondary committed only six penalties in 12 games, a statistic we are extremely proud of. We feel that this performance results directly from the confidence that the players had in executing the coverages in our system.

This philosophy was evident during Colorado State's Liberty Bowl game in 2000 against the University of Louisville. We knew we were playing a talented, explosive offensive team—a team with a solid offensive scheme and one of the nation's better quarterbacks. Our plan entering the game was the same as our plan was all season: don't commit foolish penalties, play with discipline, and play the same scheme we had been using. We knew Louisville had four weeks to prepare for our defensive coverage in the secondary, in which we primarily used cover 2 and forced the offense to earn what they could.

Sticking to the same philosophy that helped us reach the Liberty Bowl proved to be successful. The Rams enjoyed one of their finest defensive games of the year. We held Louisville more than 100 yards below their season average and gave up less than 100 yards rushing. More important, we limited them to only 17 points, 14 fewer than their average. These statistics illustrate the importance of believing in a system and staying with it.

Personnel

When evaluating a defensive back, we look for four main traits: football intelligence, mental and physical toughness, quickness, and speed. We stress the importance of each of these qualities to our players. We have been fortunate to have players with these attributes. They also understood the importance of those assets and were willing to work toward a higher degree of success, performance, and achievement.

Six former defensive backs from our program are now on NFL rosters. Greg Myers, winner of the 1995 Jim Thorpe Award as the nation's most outstanding defensive back, now plays for the Dallas Cowboys. Greg's accomplishments also include being named academic all-American three times. Greg is an example of a player who uses intelligence and has the toughness to play every play with a determination to be the best player possible.

Each week in college football, the defense faces a different challenge. For example, Air Force runs the wishbone better than any other team in the nation. Consequently, this offense provides a stiff challenge for a defense. Greg epitomized the traits of a good defensive back more than any other player I have known. Many of our finest performances at Colorado State against the wishbone attack of Air Force came while Greg was playing safety. Greg was able to adapt to all the different looks he would see when playing against the wishbone. Because of that, we gave Greg a lot of responsibility.

On all option plays he was primarily responsible for the quarterback. That assignment taxed his quick thinking as well as his open-field tackling because in Air Force's scheme the quarterback can run as well as most tailbacks. Greg won most of the battles because he could anticipate and because he was mentally and physically tough. He persevered.

My first victory at Colorado State came in the second game of the 1993 season, when the Rams beat Air Force 8 to 5. Greg played a masterful game and made 18 tackles. He was instrumental in helping our defense stop the wishbone.

A few years later, using the same scheme in which the safety is responsible for the quarterback, Greg again played exceptionally well. Late in the game, with Air Force driving for what would be the winning score, he came up with a huge interception that preserved the victory.

Other outstanding former Rams now in the NFL are Calvin Branch, who plays for the Oakland Raiders, Ray Jackson of the Cleveland Browns, Jason Craft and Erik Olson, both of the Jacksonville Jaguars, and John Howell, who was drafted recently by the Tampa Bay Buccaneers. In every case these players demonstrated football intelligence, mental and physical toughness, quickness, speed, and a strong work ethic. Though each of these players was blessed with physical and mental attributes, they achieved success through persistence and hard work. All were dedicated to team success before individual attention.

Fundamentals

Tom Bass was one of the coaches who impressed on me the importance of being fundamentally sound not only in the scheme of a defense but also, and more important, in the technical aspects of each position. In teaching our players fundamentals, we design drills that focus on a specific aspect of their respective positions.

For example, to teach the proper stance for a certain position, we focus only on the stance. We cannot teach stance, start, and sprint all in one drill. We must break down the position and design drills for a specific function.

To play in the secondary, a player must have the desire to be the best at his position. He must report in peak condition and maintain his conditioning throughout the year. He must know his responsibilities and concentrate completely on doing his job.

Technique training begins with the stance. The defensive back stands with his weight on his front foot, his front foot ahead of his nose, and his shoulders ahead of his front foot. He starts his run by pushing off with his front foot, stepping back with his back foot. He should allow his shoulders to come up naturally. To sprint, he lifts his heel and steps backward, keeping his shoulders in front of his hips and his feet under his hips. His arms move normally.

The basic technique all defensive backs must master is the backpedal. The ability to backpedal at maximum speed, adjust body position without crossing the feet, and change direction quickly is essential to the success of players in the secondary. The defensive back steps backward, keeping his shoulders in front of his hips.

If the defensive back doesn't start by taking a step backward with his back foot, he will seriously handicap his ability to cover the receiver. He must push off with his front foot and step back with his back foot. He should not be in a hurry to get his shoulders up. If the back foot comes up, the defensive back will lose two steps in coverage and will have to get out of his backpedal much sooner.

While running backward the defensive back should not push with his feet but should reach back with each step and pull his body over his feet, as if he were running forward. He must learn to bend his knees so that his feet extend back past his hips. He must keep a slight forward lean with his shoulders and move his arms in a normal, relaxed running motion.

Now that he's running backward in a straight line, his next step is to change the angle of his run without crossing his legs. To maintain the backpedal while changing direction, he must swing around with the leg opposite the direction he wishes to go. This movement is difficult to master and will require a lot of practice. When the defensive back learns this technique, however, the offensive man will be unable to turn him.

When the defensive back is forced to leave his backpedal, he must roll over the leg in the direction he wants to go. He throws his hips and shoulders in that direction, rolling over the leg. He should never push off the foot away from the desired direction.

Remember, in zone pass defense the ball will take the defensive back to the man; in man-to-man pass defense the man will take the defensive back to the ball.

Man-to-Man Pass Defense

A defender must be psychologically ready to play man-to-man. He must know and accept the five priorities of man-to-man coverage:

1. Force incompletions (top priority).
2. Never miss a tackle.
3. Remember that third-down completions that don't gain a first down are a victory.
4. Eliminate the long touchdown pass.
5. Go for the ball whenever possible.

Fundamentally, the defender must know the proper way to run backward. He must be able to recognize patterns and know the breaking and interception point. To avoid penalties, he must understand the importance of the cushion. He must be able to focus on the receiver and look for the ball. Finally, he must know when his teammates are in position to help him and where their help will come from.

The man-to-man pass defender must have mastered all the elements of a good backpedal: stance, start, sprint, change of direction, and roll to run. Next, he must know the basic patterns that the receivers can run:

- Outside receivers: quick out, hitch, slant, out, in, comeback, hook, shake
- Slot back: straight, short, delay, out, in, look, cross, hook, corner, go, post
- Offensive backs: hook, close, curl, wide, flat, short, in, out, corner, go

The defensive back's knowledge of these basic patterns and his ability to recognize each pattern quickly are essential if he is to be successful in covering his man.

After he can recognize each pattern, he must learn where the receiver will usually catch the ball. This point, called the interception point, is usually six yards in front of the receiver when the defensive back recognizes the pattern (figure 21.1).

After recognizing the pattern the defensive back drives to the interception point. After locating the interception point the defensive back moves there in a straight line, usually arriving ahead of or at the same time as the ball. The defensive back who cannot recognize the interception point will always be a follower on patterns he should be able to cover.

In man-to-man coverage the defensive back must always see the man he is covering as he looks for the ball. He should never look away from the receiver to find the ball. If the receiver is going to catch the ball and the defender has no chance to intercept or deflect it, he should tear away the receiver's upfield arm, the arm farthest from the flight of the ball. An incompletion is the same as a running play that fails to gain a yard.

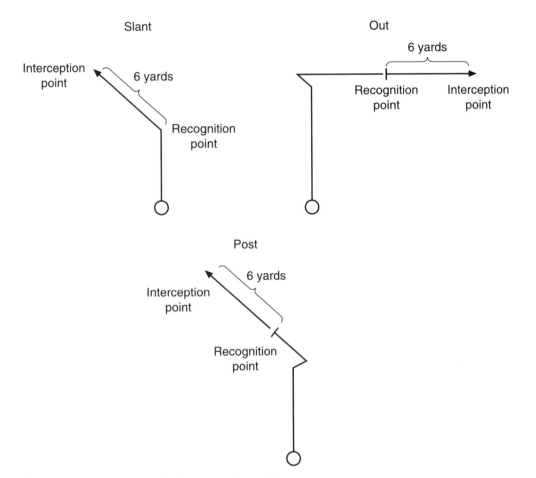

Figure 21.1 Locating the interception point.

If the receiver is so far away that he cannot reach the receiver's upfield arm as the ball arrives, then the defensive back must make the tackle. He should hit the receiver with as much force and strength as he can, but he must be sure to make the tackle. Hard, clean, aggressive tackling will discourage some receivers from making receptions.

Pass Rushing

In any discussion of pass defense it is critical to note the importance of a fierce pass rush. The combination of a great rush and great coverage downfield is what produces a successful pass defense. The better the pass rush, the easier it is to play in the secondary.

When I was the defensive coordinator at the University of Miami in 1989 and 1990, we seldom blitzed. The front four, which included Russell Maryland, Jimmie Jones, Cortez Kennedy, Shane Curry, Willis Peguese, and Greg

Mark, put plenty of pressure on the passer. Having those guys up front made coaching the secondary much easier.

In 1990 the University of Houston came to play the Hurricanes in Miami. At the time Houston was capable of putting a lot of points on the scoreboard. They had scored more than 70 in their game the week before. During the previous season Houston commonly scored 40 or more points a game. Their prolific attack concerned us, and during the week leading up to the game we deliberated about the best approach to slow down their offense.

We decided to play our base cover 2 and hope that our front would pressure the quarterback enough to assist the secondary. The front four did a masterful job of pressuring the quarterback. As a result we played the entire game with one coverage—cover 2—and our players up front dominated the line of scrimmage. Houston did not score until less than a minute remained in the game, with Miami comfortably ahead. The game was proof that a great rush definitely can slow down a passing team.

A secondary will usually be only as effective as the rest of the defense. Conversely, good coverage by the secondary can help the front with quarterback sacks and traps.

A defensive team cannot be effective against the pass unless they have pressure on the quarterback. Pass defense is the combination of a great pass rush and a solid, well-devised play in the secondary.

Colorado State's game with the University of Arizona in 1994 illustrated the importance of a pass rush. During the preseason *Sports Illustrated* ranked Arizona as the top team in the country. In the early 1990s Arizona boasted one of the nation's top defenses. The Colorado State program didn't have much tradition at the time, and not many observers gave the Rams a chance in that game. But both teams played great defense, and it was a low-scoring game. Late in the game, Colorado State nursed a narrow lead, but Arizona was driving for the go-ahead score. On a pass play one of CSU's linebackers, Garrett Sand, pressured the quarterback and knocked the ball loose. Defensive end Sean Moran scooped it up and returned it 77 yards for a touchdown to seal the victory for Colorado State.

Fans still refer to that play as the biggest play in CSU football history. The play and the game not only gave CSU instant national credibility but also put the program on a winning course that we've maintained ever since. The solid defense and great pass rush of that 1994 team allowed them to create a turnover that launched an entire era.

Moran was one of two great defensive ends on that team. He and teammate Brady Smith have played in the NFL for the past six seasons. Both still rank among the top career players in school history in quarterback sacks. Their presence, along with the rest of the front four, was a critical part of our pass defense.

Strategy of Pass Defense

In planning pass defense in the secondary we have developed a staff philosophy with definite strategies for specific coverages. Our defensive philosophy is to disguise our coverages to help the secondary gain an advantage. We generate all our coverages from a cover 2 shell to create indecision in the quarterback's mind. Such indecision by the quarterback gives the defense an advantage.

Coaches and players should know the strengths and weaknesses of each coverage. Cover 2 is a five-under, two-deep zone coverage that is adequate against the run and good against the pass. We use cover 2, our best pass coverage, more than any other coverage. We call this coverage whenever we feel that the opponent is in a passing situation. We also like to use it in third-and-long situations (six or more yards). But we must be able to play cover 2 in run situations occasionally to avoid becoming too predictable. Figure 21.2 shows the use of cover 2 versus a pro formation and against a slot formation.

Against the pro formation the corners line up 4 yards deep with an outside shade on the wide receivers. The safeties line up 12 yards deep, 2 yards outside the hash marks. The weakside, middle, and strongside linebackers line up 4 yards deep.

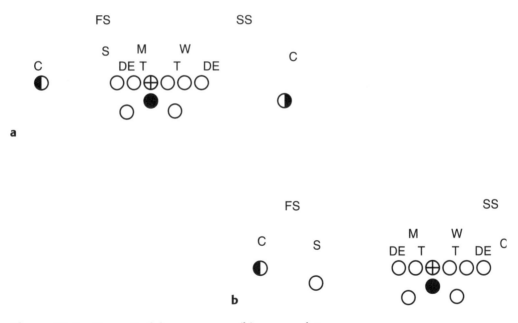

Figure 21.2 Cover 2: *(a)* versus pro, *(b)* versus slot.

Against the slot formation the strongside corner lines up 2 yards deep and 2 yards wide of the tight end. The weakside corner lines up 4 yards deep with an outside shade of the wide receiver. The strong safety lines up 9 yards deep over the tight end. The free safety lines up 12 yards deep, 2 yards outside the hash mark. The weakside, middle, and strongside linebackers line up 4 yards deep.

Cover 3 and 1 free are coverages we employ when we expect the opponent to run the ball. Cover 3 is a three-deep, four-under zone concept and includes an eight-man front alignment. Both cover 3 and 1 free involve eight-man fronts, so we are more apt to call them in normal situations (first and 10, or third and 4 or fewer yards to go). As a change-up we call cover 3 or 1 free in a passing situation to avoid predictability. Figure 21.3 shows cover 3 against the same pro formation and slot formation. Just before the snap of the ball the safeties move from a cover 2 look into a cover 3 look.

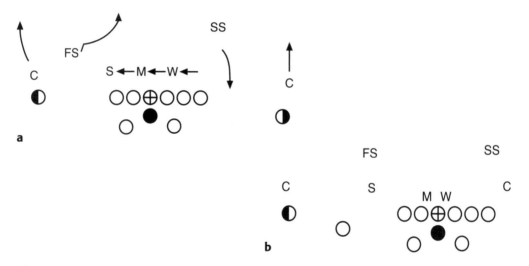

Figure 21.3 Cover 3: *(a)* versus pro, *(b)* versus slot.

Against the pro formation the corners loosen 8 to 9 yards deep. Before the snap the strong safety walks toward the line of scrimmage until he is only 5 yards deep. As he does, the weakside, middle, and strongside linebackers slide away from the safety. The free safety shifts to the middle of the formation about 13 yards deep.

Against a slot formation cover 3 reverts to cover 2. The strongside corner lines up 2 yards deep and 2 yards wide of the tight end. The weakside corner lines up 4 yards deep with an outside shade of the wide receiver. The strong safety lines up 9 yards deep over the tight end. The free safety lines up 12 yards deep outside the hash mark. The weakside, middle, and strongside linebackers slide away from the strongside corner.

The other base coverage that we use, 1 free, also comes from the cover 2 shell. Rather than playing a three-deep zone, the free safety rotates up. This formation gives us an eight-man front, and we play man-to-man coverage with a safety in the deep middle of the field. Figure 21.4 illustrates moving from a seven-man front to an eight-man front and playing a tight man-to-man coverage.

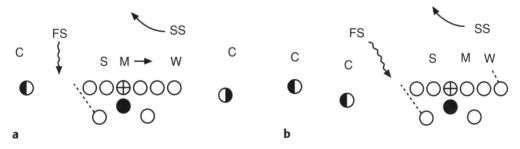

Figure 21.4 1 free: *(a)* versus pro, *(b)* versus slot.

Against a pro formation the corners line up 9 yards deep with an outside shade of their wide receivers and play man-to-man against their receivers. The strong safety lines up 13 yards deep in the middle of the formation. Before the snap the free safety walks toward the line of scrimmage until he is 5 yards deep over the offensive tackle and plays man on the #2 back. The weakside, middle, and strongside linebackers slide away from the free safety as he walks toward the line of scrimmage. The weakside linebacker plays man against the tight end.

Against a slot formation both corners line up on the weak side. The inside corner lines up 5 yards deep and plays man against his receiver. The outside corner lines up 9 yards deep with an outside shade on his receiver and plays man against him. The strong safety lines up 13 yards deep in the middle of the formation. The free safety walks toward the line of scrimmage until he is 5 yards deep over the offensive tackle. He plays man against the halfback. The weakside linebacker plays man against the tight end.

Just before the snap all three coverages—cover 2, cover 3, and 1 free— look alike to the quarterback. Once the ball is snapped the quarterback must adjust his reads and the receivers must adjust their routes on the move. The defense thus gains an advantage.

Another part of our defensive philosophy involves how the offense attempts to attack the various coverages. For instance, cover 2 is a good coverage against teams that use quick, three-step hitches. Cover 3 and 1 free, by comparison, are weak against those types of routes. If an opposing offense feels we are playing too much man-free coverage, they will run crossing routes that can hurt that coverage. Changing from cover 2 takes away the hitches and crossing routes; the offense cannot get comfortable in their route selection.

Cover 2 with rolled-up corners (figure 21.5) eliminates the three-step hitch. This coverage, however, is vulnerable to quick slants and option routes. The ability to move from cover 2 to man-free on the snap allows the defense to take away the slant route by jumping the wide receiver and closing the window.

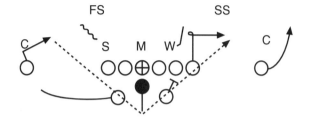

Figure 21.5   Cover 2 with rolled up-corners.

Cover 2 with rolled-up corners makes the option route difficult to defend. The tight end pivots away from the linebacker. The quarterback has an easy window to throw to. In addition, the slant is a high-percentage completion against cover 2.

Another tactic we use is to take away the tight-end option route by jumping the tight end with our linebacker (figure 21.6).

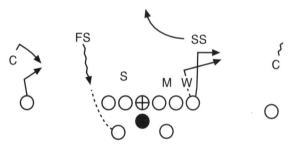

Figure 21.6   1 free versus option route and slant.

The purpose of using different coverages is to create indecision in the quarterback's mind with the hope that he'll hold the ball a second longer. An interception or a trap can result. Unless we confuse the quarterback, he will often find the weakness of a defense and exploit a particular coverage. Defensively, we prepare for specific formations and down-and-distance situations, helping to raise player confidence.

Part of our defensive philosophy is to match secondary coverages to offensive formations. Because 1 free is a good coverage against the run, we avoid using it against an offense that employs a four-wideout passing game (figure 21.7).

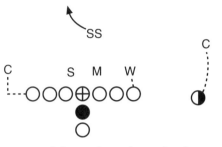

Figure 21.7 1 free versus two tight ends and two backs.

Against two tight ends and two backs, the outside corner lines up nine yards deep with an outside shade on his receiver. The inside corner lines up two yards deep and two yards outside the tight end. The strong safety takes responsibility for the middle one-third of the field. The free safety lines up seven yards deep over the tight end and plays man against the first back to the weak side.

Matching the coverage against the formation allows players to see the same plays repeatedly for maximum repetition. Most important, we don't spend all our practice time working on the exceptions. We practice the exact situation that we will encounter on game day.

From a specific formation the offense can execute a limited number of passing plays. With that in mind, we don't try to play every coverage against a two-tight-end formation. Instead, we concentrate on using one coverage to stop the run and prepare for the one or two play-action passes that the offense can use from that formation. By planning in this manner we are able to get the most out of our practice time.

Practice Organization for the Secondary

Coaches by nature devote hours teaching the various techniques required for a specific position. For instance, a cornerback in our system must master a variety of techniques. To master those techniques, we must perform adequate repetitions.

To succeed as a cornerback at Colorado State, a player must be proficient in these techniques:

- Cover 2 zone: roll up and reroute the receiver
- Cover 3 zone: play at a nine-yard depth and secure one-third of the field
- Cover 1 free: play at a nine-yard depth and play man-to-man on the receiver
- Cover 1 free press: play man-to-man from a bump-and-run position on the receiver

Playing the cornerback position is physically and mentally demanding. A cornerback must master both the physical and mental aspects of the position. Once the cornerback understands the physical aspects required to play the position in our system, the emphasis shifts to include the mental aspects. Likewise, safeties in our system must learn a number of techniques. When a player masters the physical techniques and becomes comfortable with the mental aspects, his confidence grows dramatically and he takes a more aggressive approach to executing the defense

Within our daily practice plan we implement a special-category section designed to sharpen the skills of our players in game situations. During each practice we devote two sections to special categories, including the following:

- Normal: first-and-10 situation—run, play-action bootleg
- Third and long: 7 or more yards for a first down—drop-back pass and screen pass plays
- Second and long: 8 or more yards for a first down—drop-back pass plays and some draw plays
- Third and 3 to 5 yards for a first down—run or pass plays
- Red zone: inside the 15-yard line—run and pass plays
- Two minutes: last two minutes of a half or game—pass plays, draw plays, screen plays

By emphasizing the special categories we can better prepare our defensive backs for situations they will encounter in a game.

In a normal-situation period we call only certain coverages. This approach allows players to play with more confidence. The players must be ready to stop the run, knowing that a play-action pass or a bootleg play is always possible.

By comparison, during a third-and-long period, players expect open formations, such as those that use three or four wide receivers. Offenses will usually drop back and pass in that situation. Our players know that we will use only one or two coverages and that the offense will be trying to gain a first down. With that in mind, the drops by the defensive backs will be deeper. Players must also be prepared to defend against trick plays and screens.

As we devise our defenses, including our coverages, we want to ensure that the different coverages complement one another. Cover 2 and 1 free are great examples of complementary coverages. For instance, cover 2 is successful against spread formations. We like this coverage in long-yardage situations (third down and seven or more yards to go).

Against the same formations, 1 free is an excellent coverage, but we are more likely to call 1 free when the offense may run the ball, such as when they face a third down with three to five yards to go. Cover 1 free provides an eight-man front that is solid against the run. By playing an eight-man front with our free safety coming up, we cover all the gaps and take care of the cutback. Cover 1 free provides better coverage than cover 2, which can be vulnerable in that situation (figure 21.8). The seven-man front in cover 2 doesn't allow us to cover all the gaps.

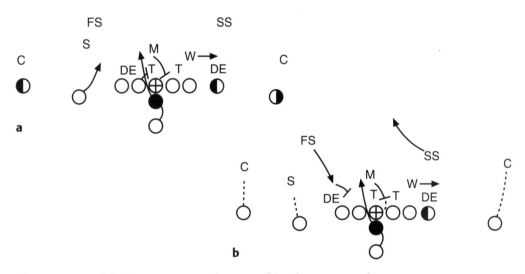

Figure 21.8 *(a)* Cover 2 versus the run, *(b)* 1 free versus the run.

These two coverages—cover 2 and 1 free—complement each other in passing situations. Cover 2 provides solid coverage against crossing routes, whereas 1 free is vulnerable to natural picks that happen with crossing routes (figure 21.9).

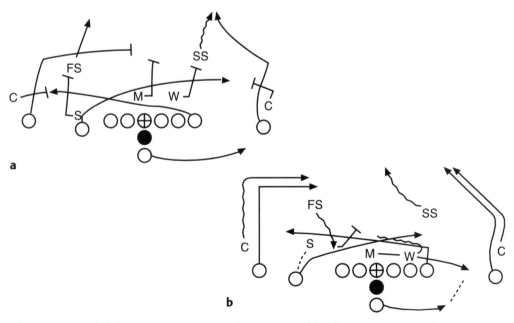

Figure 21.9 *(a)* Cover 2 versus crossing routes, *(b)* 1 free versus crossing routes.

In cover 2, the corners have the responsibility to cover the shallow, crossing receivers. The linebackers have the deep crossing routes, and the safeties cover the post routes. Defenders can cover these routes effectively with cover 2.

In cover 1 free, crossing patterns can produce some natural picks that can cause the defender to lose his coverage. Those routes are effective against man-to-man coverage. By having both coverages available, we can change between them, creating indecision in the minds of the quarterback and receivers.

Other routes that are difficult to defend in cover 2 include the option and smash routes. In 1 free, we feel we can take these routes away through design and execution (figure 21.10).

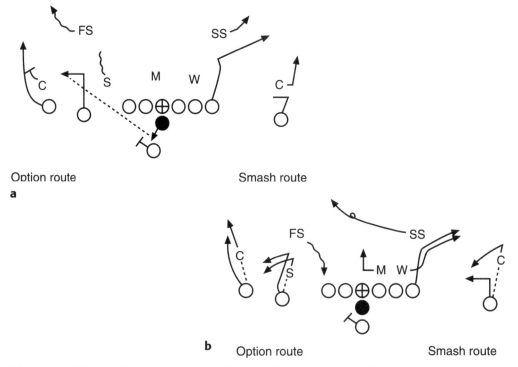

Figure 21.10 *(a)* Cover 2 versus option and smash routes, *(b)* 1 free versus option and smash routes.

In a smash route the quarterback tries to read the cornerback. If the cornerback gains depth, the quarterback tries to hit the wide receiver with a pass that will gain about six yards. If the cornerback plays tight against the wide receiver, the quarterback tries to throw to the tight end in the sweet spot for a big gain. Defending the smash with cover 2 is difficult.

Cover 1 free gives the defense a distinct advantage against the smash route. In this coverage the defense jumps all receivers and plays tough, man-to-man coverage. The weakside linebacker overplays the tight-end route, knowing that he has help inside from the strong safety.

The option route is effective against cover 2 because the quarterback reads the strongside linebacker and tries to complete a pass for about an eight-yard gain. If the linebacker gains any depth in this coverage, it's an easy pass-and-catch play for the offense. The option route to the wide field is a high-percentage pass against cover 2.

Cover 1 free eliminates the option route because as the slot settles to catch a pass at about eight yards past the line of scrimmage, we jump the receiver with our strongside linebacker. The receiver must then adjust his routes on the move. Cover 1 free allows the defense to overplay the option route with the strongside linebacker, who knows he has help deep from the strong safety.

Cover 3 is our other base coverage. It complements both cover 2 and cover 1 free. When we include cover 3 in our defensive secondary scheme, we have ample coverages to face nearly every situation.

Cover 3 evolves, as do our other coverages, from the cover 2 shell. Cover 3 is an eight-man front similar to cover 1 free. But cover 3 gives us an eight-man front while we play a three-deep, four-under zone coverage.

Like cover 1 free, cover 3 is a call we usually make in a run situation (figure 21.11). We feel that in this coverage we will be effective against the run by using the eight-man front.

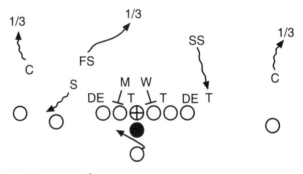

Figure 21.11 Cover 3 versus the run.

In cover 1 free coverage, we walk the free safety down to provide the eighth man in the front. In cover 3, we walk the strong safety down on the opposite side of the formation to provide another complementary eight-man front. With this eight-man front we cover all the gaps making us strong against the run—no cutback lanes.

A strategic part of our defensive play calling is matching our three basic coverages not only to the formation but also to the down and distance. By mixing our coverages during a game, we avoid becoming predictable to the offense.

By using these three coverages in the secondary, we can use our practice time to perfect techniques and understanding of the defense. We have sufficient time and opportunity to cover nearly every situation that can arise during a game.

22

The Kicking Game

Frank Beamer

When you talk about the kicking game, you are dealing with big yardage, momentum, and scoring. When you start on your own 20-yard line, you have 1 chance in 30 of scoring. If you're on the other 20 going in, it's 1 out of 2. If you start on your 40-yard line, you have 1 chance in 8 of scoring. If you start on the other 40, it's 1 out of 3. It's all about field position, and the greatest way to get field position is to be good in the kicking game.

In this chapter I will talk about the punt-block-and-return team, which I will call "pride and joy" from here on. If you can block a kick, you can change the momentum of the game, gain yardage in the situation, and maybe score. The same is true if you can return a kick. I'm going to give you some of my thoughts about the pride-and-joy team later. First, though, I'd like to talk about making the kicking game important.

I think all coaches feel that the kicking game is one-third of their football program, with offense and defense forming the other two-thirds, but I don't think everyone treats it that way. I'd like to show you how you can make it important to the players so that they take it seriously and want to be on the kicking teams. If you treat the kicking game as an extra part, not equal to offense and defense, then players will treat it the same way. You will have a hard time convincing your good players to be on a special team. Their participation is crucial.

Our best players are on our special teams at Virginia Tech. Think about it. The skills involved in special-teams play call for exceptional athletes. Players must be athletic and have good hand-eye coordination to block kicks. Blocking someone in the open field requires an athletic move. Making tackles in the open field calls for skill. If you put average players on your special teams, you will be average. If you put good players on your special teams, then you have a chance to be good.

People tell me all the time that teams must spend a great deal of time practicing special teams. We don't. I seriously doubt that we practice special teams longer than most other teams in the country, but we do go to great lengths to make our special teams important.

Become Involved in Special Teams

Active participation of the head coach in special teams sends a message to the players. When I first started at Virginia Tech, I assigned an assistant coach to head up each special team. It was his team, and he was responsible for it. As I lost a couple special-teams coaches, I decided to take over that team. In the end, I think the players believed that because the head coach was involved, it must be important. That was the message I wanted them to have.

Because I spent more time on special-teams preparation, our offensive and defensive staffs had more time to work on their game plans. I've always placed such great emphasis on special teams that I would, for example, tell my defensive coordinator to make sure he did his special-teams work first before starting on the defensive game plan. But when I was able to take over his punt-protection team, he had more time to get started on his defensive game plan. I think this approach works well.

I spend up to four hours on our pride-and-joy game plan, an amount significantly greater than a position coach would probably be able to spend. I come up with one new rush each week. When you play Virginia Tech, you will see a rush you've never seen before, no matter how much video you study. During the week, when every minute is precious, the most efficient way to operate is for the head coach to spend time with special-teams game plans, for the defensive coordinator to spend time with the defensive game plan, and for the offensive coordinator to spend time with the offensive game plan.

Your special-teams players often stand off to the side until it is time to kick a field goal. Only then are they with the football team. I like to spend the first four periods of practice with our special-teams players. I work with the punters, charting the operation time, the hang time, and the distance. Our two field-goal kickers compete against each other to see who'll win the kicking contest that day. We get our kickoff guy and chart his hang time and distance. We work on onside kicks. We work on poocher kickoffs. I like spending time with the kickers. After all, you generally call on them in a critical situation, and they need to feel as if they are part of the football team.

I try to convince players—and this is something I really believe—that developing a special-teams skill just might help their pro careers. For example, being a good cover guy on punts or returning kickoffs or blocking a kick might be the edge a player needs to make a 53-man squad in pro football. Many pro teams want to keep guys who are good on special teams, so I tell our players that being good on special teams in college might help them in pro football.

In trying to make special teams important, it is critical that you never ask them to do extra work. If you ask your players to come before practice or stay late, you are punishing them. You are telling your team that kicking is not important enough to work on in practice. We do offense and defense in practice. If kicking is truly a third of the game, treat it that way.

If you come to our practices, you will see a brisk tempo. We perform drills quickly. People move fast. The only time we stop everything is in the middle of practice for kicking. We come to one field where everyone can watch, and we take care of our kicking then. This is another way of saying that special teams are important. We are sending a message to our players.

We don't punish our players by bringing them in before practice or keeping them after practice. Instead, we give them privileges for being on special teams. For example, during conditioning if the pride-and-joy team is making perfect punt returns against the scout team, I make sure the pride-and-joy team is off the field before conditioning is over. I want them to be able to run by the conditioning group as they head out the gate. By being on the pride-and-joy team, they get to leave the field first. On Tuesday of each week in game preparation, we work on punt protection and coverage versus pride and joy. During conditioning that afternoon, we require two fewer sprints from anyone who is on either special team. Virginia Tech players get benefits by being on special teams.

I want to make sure that we have the same awards for offense, defense, and special teams. If we have a player of the game, it is in all three areas. If we have a big hit, it is in all three areas. I like to do the kicking-game big hit in front of the whole team, which is appropriate because we have members of both the offense and defense on special teams. Defense does their big hit in a defensive meeting, offense does theirs in an offensive meeting, but special teams' big hit is in front of the whole group. We are sending a message with that approach. We have a goal chart for offense, a goal chart for defense, and a goal chart for special teams. Just as I review the offensive goals and defensive goals that we've reached that week, I also review the special-teams goals that we've reached that week. We treat them all the same.

Setting meeting times for kicking teams is difficult, but I think it is important that special teams meet just as the offense or defense would. We do this on Monday by taking 10 minutes with each team to go over the video from Saturday's game and to distribute the scouting report and game plan for the upcoming opponent. During the week we videotape each kicking period, and in a Friday meeting we review the week's work. I think the best way to learn is through video, and to make video of kicking and never see it doesn't make good sense. You wouldn't do that with offense or defense, so don't do it with your kicking game. Show that video. Learn from it.

Blocking Punts

Next, I want to spend some time on punt blocks, which offer a great opportunity to change the momentum of a football game.

Teams would probably try to block more kicks if they weren't afraid of roughing the kicker. We stress several points so that we feel confident that we will not rough the kicker.

First, the landmark, the point a yard and a half in front of where the punter kicks the ball, is critical. The player must put his body through that landmark. That way, the player reaches out to block the kick. The body is never on a collision course with the punter. Anytime a player is past the landmark, he pulls off. He is not going to block it this time. He should not take a chance on roughing the kicker. Players are better off being short of the landmark than long. If a player is short, he can redirect to the punter. If he is past the landmark, he is on a collision course with the punter. If he doesn't get the punt, he might rough the kicker.

Let's say the landmark is 8 yards from the ball. When we line up, every punt blocker should see the landmark (eight yards from the ball). To block kicks, players must go full speed through the blocking area. If a player hits the landmark, he will never rough the kicker. This method builds confidence. Players must know the landmark and never try to block a kick when they are past it.

A player should never leave his feet to block a kick because he may not be able to control what happens. As long as his feet are on the ground, he can adjust himself and redirect.

Another point in blocking a punt is to take a proper angle to the ball. If the player is coming from the side, he should come across the kicker, reach out, and put his hand on the kicker's foot. If he is coming up the middle or right at the punter, he should always come off to the punter's kicking foot. In other words, if the punter is right-footed, the player should come off to his left. If the punter is left-footed, the player comes off to the right. If the player does the opposite, he puts himself in a collision course with the punter.

If the player is knocked more than one step off his course, he should stop, work outside, and make sure that the ball is kicked. We want only one person free at the block point. If we have more than one, we may run into each other and as a result rough the kicker.

Players who are blocked should work to the outside for several reasons. If a teammate blocks the kick, the player will be there to pick it up. Alternatively, if the punter realizes that the ball will be blocked, he may pull it down to run with it. The player will be there to make the tackle.

Punt-Block Principles

Now that we've covered points that prevent us from roughing the kicker, let's go to our punt-block principles.

First, we want to make block and return look the same. In other words, a protector should never be able to tell by our stance whether we are rushing or returning. We don't want to give them a pre-snap read.

Second, we want to crowd the ball, to get as much of the football as possible. We teach players to put their hands down right in front of the ball. By keeping their heads behind their hands, they know that they are onside. Now they're free to read the key. Some players, however, feel more comfortable with their heads past their hands. If that is the case, the hands have to come back away from the ball as far as the head is past the hands. The goal is to be as close to the football as possible. Every inch matters in blocking a kick.

Third, players should key the ball to get a jump on it. The snapper's hands, fingers, and knuckles tighten in the split second before he snaps the ball. That action tells the defenders that he is about to snap the ball. Getting a great jump is necessary in blocking kicks.

Fourth, players should accelerate out of the stance. This point seems obvious, but players often want to see if they are going to come free before they really accelerate. They must come out of the stance with the idea that they are going to come free, just as a sprinter would. He comes out low and accelerates.

Fifth, players should not put their hands up until the last second. Many people put their hands up early in the punt-blocking process, sacrificing a good deal of speed. Players should run like sprinters, and only at the last second should they take their hands from their running position to waist high to block the kick. Moving the hands is a simple move at the end of the process.

Sixth, players must look at the punter's foot and keep their eyes open. Many people have trouble doing this, but it is essential to blocking a kick. Players should try to put their hands on the punter's foot, which in turn puts their hands on the ball.

Finally, against zone protection, players should stay low and turn their shoulders sideways. By using this technique, the player offers the protector little surface to get his hands on. Most protections I've seen are half zone—zone on one side and man on the other. Many protection schemes use zones on both sides, so players should turn sideways and stay low.

Drills for Blocking Punts

In the first drill we take a ball and put it right on the tip of a line. The punt blocker lines up with his hand as close to that line as possible. The snapper snaps the ball to the coach behind the punter. The punt rusher can then get a true sense of the ball being snapped. He can see the tightening of the fingers, which allows him to get that great jump. He accelerates out of his stance, takes a proper angle to the landmark, and puts his hands on the kicker's foot. As you can see in figure 22.1a, the punt rusher is coming up the middle so he will come off to the left of the right-footed punter.

In figure 22.1b, the blocker is coming from the side. He accelerates to the landmark, comes across the punter's foot, and takes the ball off the punter's foot.

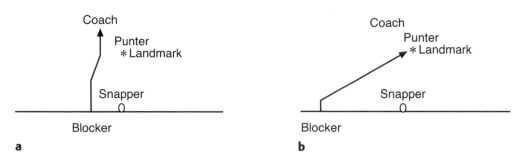

Figure 22.1 Punt-blocking drill: *(a)* up the middle, *(b)* from the side.

When we do this drill, we align our guys in their positions on the pride-and-joy team. We go one at a time, alternate back and forth, and accomplish a lot in a short time. To avoid beating up our hands in blocking kicks, we take some of the air out of the balls that we are punting.

The next drill involves half line. Again, we start with the ball on a line so that the players can get the correct alignment (figure 22.2). After a while, we take it off the line so that we can line up getting all the ball we can regardless of where it is.

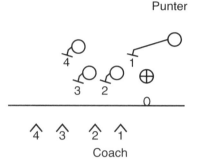

Figure 22.2 The half-line drill.

We use specific blocking assignments for the protection team. The personal protector takes the first guy, the guard takes the second, the tackle the third, and the slot the fourth. This is the procedure for both sides.

This drill begins with the coach standing behind the punt-block team, telling the protection team who should go free. In the case illustrated below (figure 22.3), the coach tells the block team that #2 should go free. The guard who was to block him now doubles #1 with the personal protector. Following his blocking rules, #2 goes free to block the kick; #1, #3, and #4 are blocked. These players start to slide to the outside, and when the kick is blocked, they react to it. Whoever is closest to the ball picks it up. The others turn and block an opposite-color jersey.

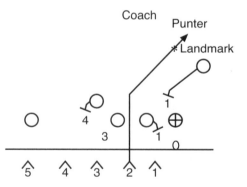

Figure 22.3 Coach chooses #2 to go free.

I like this drill because it teaches people to come off the line expecting to go free. If they are not coming hard off the line, you can see it right away. Next, we see if people are working to the outside when blocked and if they are reacting quickly after the kick is blocked.

In figure 22.4a, #1 goes free following his blocking techniques, so the personal protector would double on #2. I should see #2, #3, and #4 working to the outside and then reacting to get the ball to the end zone.

We also want to incorporate the event when #5 comes off the headhunter. As you can see in figure 22.4b, if #5 is the guy who will come free, everybody just blocks his man. After coming free, #5 comes across the kicker's foot, hitting his landmark and reaching out to block the kick. As he does that, #1, #2, #3, and #4 work to the outside. The lead person picks the ball up; the others turn and block an opposite-color jersey.

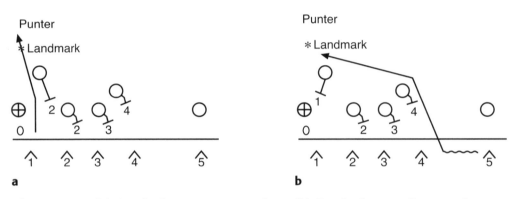

Figure 22.4 *(a)* Coach chooses #1 to go free. *(b)* Coach chooses #5 to go free.

Rushing the Punt

Now let's turn our attention to a team punt rush. Generally, people block zone to one side and man to the other. If we are trying to attack a zone side, we want to work to the edges of the zone to stretch it as far as possible (figure 22.5).

Here #6 rushes over the guard's inside foot, which stretches the center's zone as far as possible. To stretch the guard's zone, #7 is over the inside foot of the tackle. We tell #8 to go upfield until the tackle cannot touch him, then bend hard, almost running away from the slot to stretch that zone. We

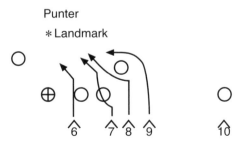

Figure 22.5 Working against zone blocking.

tell #9 to go upfield to where the slot cannot touch him, then bend hard to the landmark to stretch the slot zone. Everything starts upfield and then bends hard to the landmark. Working upfield for the first three or four steps really stretches the zone. If a player comes free, he bends or redirects to the landmark.

In figure 22.6 we are attacking man protection. We hope to cause confusion in their numbering, thus getting a blocker free.

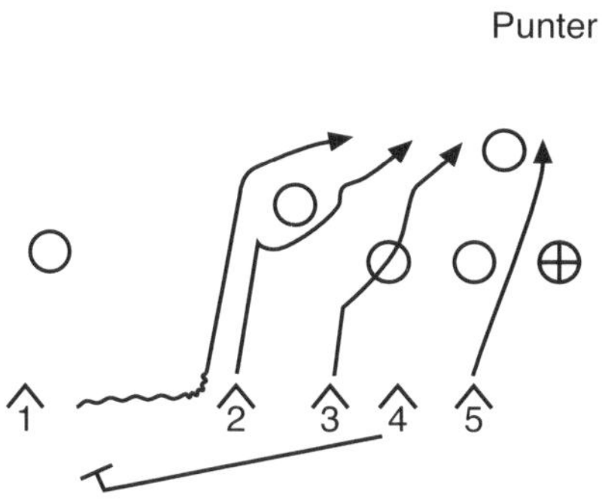

Punter

Figure 22.6 Working against man blocking.

Punt Returns

Now let's go to a basic return. Figure 22.7 shows a basic return left that we use. My main objective is to keep people out of our punt returner's face so that he can get started.

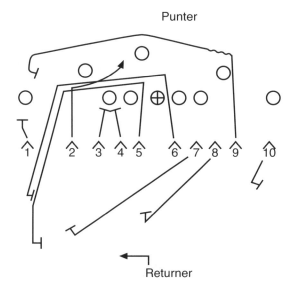

Punter

Returner

Figure 22.7 Return left.

As you can see, #1 and #7 whirlwind the headhunter. I don't particularly care which way the headhunter goes. My main objective is to prevent him from getting down the field where he can distract the punt returner. Whoever is not on the headhunter should stay about five yards away so that he can get on him when he comes off the other guy. If the player gets too close, the headhunter may beat both players and then it is just a footrace to the return man. As #7 goes to the whirlwind, he checks the slot for a fake.

We give #2 an opportunity to block the kick, which also serves the purpose of occupying that slot. If the slot is chasing #2, then he is not getting down the field to cover the kick.

We want #3 and #4 to whirlwind the tackle. They stay shoulder to shoulder and let the tackle take a direction, right or left, but never let him split #3 and #4 and beat them both. Let's say the tackle comes off to the left. When the tackle chooses left, #3 takes him and #4 comes around, keeping his distance, getting ready to pick up the tackle when he comes off #3.

After giving the appearance of a rush, #5 goes directly to the wall. When setting the wall, we would rather have too much width than not enough. The goal is to keep everyone inside.

Like #5, #6 gives the appearance of a rush, coming down the line of scrimmage and looking at the punter to make sure that he kicks the ball. Then #6 goes to the wall.

The first responsibility for #8 is to check the personal protector for a fake kick. If there is no fake kick, then approximately 25 yards down the field he blocks the first dangerous cover to the side of the punt return.

Because he is contain rushing, #9 checks the slot to his side for a fake, makes sure the ball is kicked, and then comes around to the wall.

We want to keep the headhunter to the outside away from the return, so #10 is on an island on the headhunter. Our return guy takes a couple steps to draw the coverage to him if he has time. He then goes to his left for what we hope will be a great return.

Figure 22.8 shows a combination rush and return. I like this play because it keeps the pressure on, and as I wrote earlier, we want only one guy free to block the kick. Here we have a chance to do that. By rushing and returning to the same side, we keep that side of the protection in. The kicking team has to protect hard, preventing them from getting downfield quickly, which allows us to get a punt returner started. We rush from the left with our basic zone rush; #2 and #6 follow rush principles, and #7, #8, #9, and #10 follow return-left techniques.

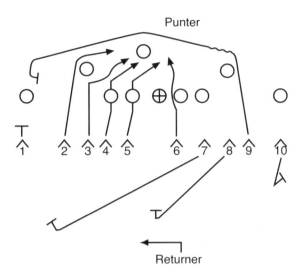

Punter

Returner

Figure 22.8 Rush left, return left.

Coaching the Kicking Game

Let me describe what we do during a week of practice to improve our kicking game. We call our protection team "pride" and our punt-block-and-return team "pride and joy."

On Monday we always start with what we call a converge period, including screens, delays, draws, reverses, and halfback passes. We want to start practice with a fast pace.

We move from that to a field goal versus field-goal rush. This session puts the kicker in front of the whole team. The more times your kicker has a chance to kick in pressure situations, the greater his chances for success on Saturday. I don't like to go full team on field-goal rush in practice. We allow only three people on defense to rush. Everybody lines up and takes his first three steps with a sense of urgency, but only three come. That way we don't have people falling over each other, but we still get good work on protection and rush.

On Tuesday we stop practice in the middle, and our pride team goes against our pride-and-joy team. The first rep is a protection for pride and a rush by pride and joy. The next rep is the return, but we divide it into two segments.

Let's go back to a return left (figure 22.7). First the headhunters and anyone responsible for the headhunters (#1, #7, #10) go. Next the remaining seven coverage people and anyone responsible for them (#2, #3, #4, #5, #6, #8, #9) go. Video review is valuable here because you see your headhunters and the people responsible for them. Next, you see the seven coverage guys. Videotape will clearly show whether players are keeping their proper coverage lanes, and the tape may tell you if the return team is blocking properly. Video review is a great way to evaluate and teach.

We then turn that drill around and do another protect and a protect and cover.

On Wednesday we stop practice again in the middle, but we work different teams. I intentionally start talking louder and faster because practice has stopped and everyone is looking. I want the players to feel the intensity and importance of the kicking game.

We start the period with our pride going against pride and joy. Next, we get a field goal versus field-goal rush, again getting the kicker in front of the group. Third, we get another pride versus pride and joy. Fourth, we do an onside prevent. We call our hands team out, get our onside kicker, and kick a different onside kick each week. The onside kick is a crucial play in a game—we want to make sure we practice it. Our fifth play is another pride versus pride and joy. Sixth is field goal versus field-goal block. The seventh play is pride versus punt safe (defense plus punt returner). Our pride team tries to kick the ball inside the 10-yard line. Both sides need to practice this important play. Our last play is for our kickoff-return team. We give them either a squib or poocher kick. I like to run teams on and off the field to simulate a game. We do it quickly and with urgency. We put white grid lids over our helmets so that we can distinguish who is on which team.

Another thing we do on Wednesday is have a specialty period. I do this not so much for the first-team punter or snapper but for the backups. Your backup kickers, punters, snappers, and punt returners must get work during the week. This is an excellent time to accomplish this task. We also have everyone come through the first drill for blocking a kick (figure 22.1). To be effective in a ball game, players need experience being around the punter. The more times we have the experience of blocking a kick, the better we will react in a game.

We also do some poocher or popup kicks to our kickoff-return people.

Thursday's practice involves kickoff return and kickoff coverage. We also have a five-minute period in which I do the second drill for blocking punts, the half-line drill (figure 22.2). We use the rushes that we are going to use that week with one guy coming free. I'll say again that the more times players can block a punt in practice, the more confidence they'll have when they get that opportunity in a game.

Kicking is the main emphasis of practice on Friday. We call each team out, and then we call out their backups to make sure we have our personnel right. We also cover different situations with each team. For example, with our pride team, we do a poocher kick to get the ball inside the 10, we put the ball at the 1-yard line punting out, we kick with under 5 seconds on the 25-second clock, we kick versus an 11-man rush as if it were the last play of the game, and we take a safety. With pride and joy, we practice the ball being blocked (the punter throws the ball to the ground either behind or past the line of scrimmage) so that the pride-and-joy team can react accordingly. We also practice a short kick in which the punt returner must get everyone away from the ball.

You get the idea. We want to cover unusual situations that might come up in a ballgame.

In this chapter I have offered some ideas about how to make the kicking game important, explained the principles of blocking a kick, and described some of our basic rushes and returns. The most important point of this chapter is to make the kicking game important so that you get good players on special teams. If you do that, you will block and return some kicks. Being good in the kicking game can go a long way toward winning football games.

PART VI

Game-Winning Strategies

Bill Mallory

In the next five chapters the authors present their philosophies and approaches to strategies that will help you win football games. These head coaches have had excellent success with their programs and will give you some ideas that can make the difference between winning and losing.

Phil Fulmer presents the scouting program at the University of Tennessee. Their method of studying upcoming opponents has been instrumental in the success of the University of Tennessee football team. Coach Fulmer states that scouting opponents has evolved through the years into one of the most important areas of preparation. As a coach, you must know your opponents thoroughly—their personnel, tendencies, trickery, strengths, and weaknesses. Quality scouting is where it all starts in preparing to win a game.

As head coach at the University of Arizona, Purdue University, and West Point, Jim Young developed programs into winners, champions, and bowl participants. Coach Young presents his approach to developing players and building winning programs. Jim believes that creating a mental edge is the key to developing players and programs to be winners. He offers excellent ideas that will help you improve your program.

Frosty Westering, head coach at Pacific Lutheran University, and his son Scott Westering, offensive coordinator, present their thoughts concerning offensive play calling. Frosty and Scott cover different aspects of their offensive system. They discuss their play-calling procedures, play scripting, play calling in various areas of the field, their audible system, and dealing with key situations such as the two-minute drill. This chapter presents ideas that can be helpful in preparing your game plan and managing various game situations when they occur.

Jerry Sandusky writes about calling defensive plays during pivotal game situations. During Coach Sandusky's tenure at Penn State he established an excellent defensive tradition and was considered one of the best defensive coordinators in college football. Coach Sandusky writes about planning. Planning starts with evaluating your own personnel and the defenses you used in the previous game. Which defenses were productive and which ones faltered? This evaluation combined with a breakdown of the opponent's tendencies make up a game plan. Coach Sandusky then moves to preparation. Players and coaches prepare for the game together, beginning in the meeting room with scouting reports and videos of the opponent's previous games. Preparation then moves onto the practice field. Coach Sandusky finishes by discussing the game. When it's time to play, coaches and players should be alert, not tense. Good preparation leaves a team feeling confident and ready to play agressively, unafraid of failure. Players and coaches should be confident enough to play the game with their hearts as well as their minds.

Ken Sparks, head coach at Carson Newman College, discusses his approach to evaluating his players' performance in the classroom, on the field, and off the field. He believes in developing the total person. To be productive, your players and team must make continual improvement. You must have a thorough evaluation process. The old saying is that you either get better or you get worse—you never stay the same. Ken presents some excellent and unique ideas concerning player and team evaluation.

Scouting the Opposition

Phil Fulmer

Scouting is the foundation on which we build our game plan, so we must be certain that we do it without making mistakes. If our analysis is sloppy or filled with typing errors, we get a distorted view of our opponent's tendencies.

In-season scouting of our opponent begins on the Tuesday 11 days before the game. Exchange film arrives at 10:30 A.M., and we immediately make a copy for the graduate assistants to break down. We keep tape of every opponent's game we get for three years. We thus have an extensive library of tape to pull from for different ideas on coaching schemes. We also save our self-scout tapes forever. We constantly go back to look at what was successful for us in the past.

We start on breakdowns right away so that when questions arise we can answer them quickly and work through the puzzles. Generally, we break down four games for the cutups. We study certain situations from all games: goal line, short yardage, trick plays, two-point plays, and plays that we do not see in the four-game breakdown. We feel that these situations are important enough to study from the entire year.

Coordinators pick the four games that go in the cutups. Sometimes they choose the four most recent games; other times coordinators opt to trade a recent game to see a team that runs a similar offense or defense. Sometimes we use last year's game against the upcoming opponent in the cutups.

To break down a game, the graduate assistants draw the plays by hand. They give them to the defensive coaches, who then have both graphic and written descriptions of each play. We name the plays to ensure uniformity. The offense does not draw their plays, but they have a system of checks in place to ensure that plays are named correctly.

Graduate assistants break down the games and enter the information into a laptop computer using the scouting software FLEX. We have used FLEX for eight years and really like it. FLEX gives us the opportunity to customize our reports. Even in midseason, we can change or add reports on opponents.

We want to be sure that we enter the data correctly. We check every piece of data for typing errors. If the coverage 1-Robber is entered 1-Rob, 1Rob, or 1Robber, the computer will recognize these as three distinct coverages even though they are the same. We must weed out mistakes to produce an accurate report.

After we enter the data and check for mistakes, we match it with the video in the PINNACLE computer system. We have had PINNACLE (or AVID as it was called before the companies merged in 2000) for seven years. We like PINNACLE because it gives us instant access to anything that an opponent does. We also have the ability to change any cutup or create new ones.

The first three of the four games that we break down are in the computers by Friday morning. We can then run a test set of cutups to make sure that we are on the right track. If we have any problems, we have time to correct them.

The last game arrives Sunday morning. We immediately copy the last game and give it to the graduate assistants for breakdown. The coaching staff finishes grading the self-scout game from the previous game, while the support staff works hard on the opponent's game. When the coaching staff finishes grading the self-scout game, they watch the opponent's game from the previous day. After that we start on the cutups.

We break down special teams while all this is going on. We use the same concept of the last four games with special teams. We go back and look at all the games, and we pick out and save any tricks, such as returns for touchdowns, blocked kicks, onside kicks, and deceptive or unusual kicks. We save these on tape for a year on special-teams study.

The special-teams coordinator makes a meeting tape for each special team. This tape has four to six kicks showing tricks, blocks, or what we plan to do for the next game.

Scouting the Opponent's Defense

When we as an offensive staff begin to scout an opponent, we approach it from a number of areas. Obviously, you are much more familiar with the teams you play each year, but you should approach them with the same basic questions in mind. The more information you can gather about your opponent, the better you will know them and the better idea you will have of how they will react in pressure situations.

We gather all the film and video possible from the previous season, and we often go back two years. If the opponent has a new coach on the defensive staff, we go back to his previous school and get their game films. We also have student workers check the Internet throughout the year for articles or interviews from players and coaches that may provide clues about anything new or different we may see in the coming season.

The three primary areas that we study and examine when scouting an opponent are their personnel, their scheme, and the background and personality of their coaches.

Before going too much further in this discussion, I must mention that we must know as much as possible about ourselves. We do self-scouts every week to discover any tendencies we may have, and we do an extremely thorough study during any open dates during the season. These self-scouts include breakdowns by down and distance, field position, and situations in a game, such as two-minute drills and stall offense. In addition, we try to be realistic about the ability of our own players. This assessment becomes vital when we start trying to evaluate personnel matchups with our opponents.

One of the first areas to look at in breaking down an opponent is to do a thorough study of the other team's players. What are the real strengths of their defensive team? What are their defensive weaknesses? Once we determine these things, we can decide how they coincide with the strengths and weaknesses of our offense and how best to attack them. In addition, we want to know exactly how we will match up with them in pure ability. We want to decide if their players are as good as ours are. We look hard to find which matchups are going to be a problem, especially in the offensive and defensive lines as well as with our receivers versus their defensive backs. We also want to know if someone on their defense demands special consideration such as double-team blocking in the run game or in passing situations.

Courtesy of Gary Moor Photography

We try to evaluate the overall speed of the defense to determine what type of plays we need in our game plan that week. If they are a fast defense, we need to attack with misdirection plays, counter-type plays, and schemes that attack downhill and straight ahead. If their team speed is not equal to ours, we need to get on the perimeter and make them run. We try to put our athletes in space versus their guys and allow our speed and athletic ability to take over. We also want to study how well their front seven plays with pad leverage. This point is especially critical when we start developing our goal-line and short-yardage plan.

The second primary area we look at in scouting an opponent is their defensive schemes and tendencies. We begin by identifying their base front and coverage packages. We try to get a good feel for what they want to accomplish. Then we look into the variations of their base package and how easy it is for them to get to those variations. For instance, some teams may take a defensive tackle out of the game and bring in another linebacker to go from a 4-3 front to a 3-4 look; another team may just stand up an end and bump out the tackle to accomplish the same thing. Do they bring in an extra defensive back in obvious passing situations, or do they have a linebacker they feel good about in pass coverage? Tendencies that indicate that they are changing from their base package have proved invaluable to our players in the past several years, both in their preparation and in the confidence with which they approach the game.

Another important element of their base schemes that we study is their secondary run-support system. We want to know whether they are supporting with their safeties or cornerbacks, whether they are supporting with both safeties, and whether this support is coming from the inside or from the edge of the defense. Each of these possibilities leads us in a different direction with the game plan. We also look for tips in the secondary presnap to give the quarterback clues about what coverage or support package he may see on each play. We often study the depth of the safeties or technique tips that give away a coverage or secondary blitz. Most teams we play have some tendencies we can pick up if we study diligently enough.

In the secondary we see a number of disguise looks, such as four across or a two-deep shell look. From those looks, defenses can work to a number of coverages and cause confusion in the offensive rhythm of the game. In studying tape of an opponent we look at what sets or personnel groupings can force the defense to show its hand or give away the coverage that they are rolling to. What effect do motion, down and distance, formations, and trades and shifts have on a secondary that is disguising its looks? Does the defense cheat or tip off from the disguise look what coverage it is going to roll to? In our study of the opponent, we ask and answer these questions and build them into our game plan.

Scouting an opponent requires a look at the defensive scheme or philosophy in certain areas of the field. The ultimate object in this game is to score points, so it is vital to get an understanding of the goal-line and short-yardage fronts they play. In the goal-line and short-yardage breakdowns, we look at every snap from that season. If we are playing early in the year, we refer to film from the previous years.

As mentioned earlier, it is important to see how the front seven play with pad leverage in goal-line and short-yardage situations. From their base scheme, what is the defense going to take away? Where in their base looks are they vulnerable? Where have opponents attacked them with success? With a number of snaps of goal-line or short-yardage situations to study, we look at what fronts we may see in our base short-yardage and goal-line personnel groupings.

You should go into the game with a simple plan that gives your players a chance to move the ball. When looking at an opponent's defense, it is important to see if they have a tendency to play the same front or come out with all-out pressure on the next down. Opponents often substitute in goal-line or short-yardage situations. We look at what they accomplish by substituting and what prevents them from subbing in those situations. We look to see if there is a place to insert a trick play or simple change such as a dummy snap count. By studying past opponents we are able to generate new ideas and incorporate them into our plans.

Since Buddy Ryan introduced the Bear defense, offenses have had to develop answers for the pressure defense. Within our breakdown of an opponent's schemes, we look at the Bear package and what they are trying to accomplish. We begin by identifying their Bear package and how they get to the Bear look in their different package groupings. From those different looks, we determine what type of pressure they bring and where they are out of position by playing that defense. As a staff we look at formation shifts, personnel groupings, field zone, and down and distance and their effect on a team's Bear package. What offensive schemes and plays can they not defend in that defense? Often we look at the extra defender they will bring in the box, their run-support ability, and the overall ability of the defense to cover the passing game. We look particularly at how their defenders will match up with our best players.

By playing Bear defense, do they put a lesser defender one-on-one in space against a better player? We study not only the individual Bear cutups but also each game to get a feel for when and where they play that look. We want to know if we must give special attention to someone or somewhere in that look, and we want to determine the effect the Bear look has on our run and pass blocking.

In looking at an opponent's defense, we look at the base, goal-line, short-yardage, and Bear defenses. Then we look into the various linebacker stunts and secondary blitzes the defense uses to bring pressure. We consider pressure to be any time a defense brings five or more defenders. In the individual breakdown of each game, the graduate assistant notes on each play the number of defenders brought by the defense. From the breakdown of the games, we look at pressure in five categories:

1. Pressure from linebacker stunts
2. Pressure from secondary blitzes
3. Pressure from a combination of a linebacker stunt and a secondary blitz
4. Zone-blitz pressure
5. Man-to-man pressure

We feel it is important to understand when and where the defense will bring extra defenders. We look at tendencies related to down and distance, formation, defensive front, offensive and defensive personnel groupings, and field zone. In the study of the opponent, it is crucial to understand and rank what the primary pressures are and what the gimmick pressures are for that week. In our self-scout study we look closely at what types of pressure have given us trouble and find answers to those problems. In studying our offense, our opponent may see a type of blitz or stunt that has given us problems and incorporate it into their package.

We attempt to anticipate the pressure a defense will bring and the new additions we may see. Inevitably, there are tips as to when and where a defense is going to come with pressure. In bringing pressure, a defense gives up a particular area or puts individual defenders one-on-one with no help. We look for where to attack a defense when they come with pressure, and we look at how teams have been successful in moving the ball when pressured. We want to go in with a plan that answers pressure and gives us a chance to make big plays when we see pressure.

In the study of an opponent's defense, we look at their personnel, their scheme, the coaching staff, and their tendencies by down and distance and field zone. Within our breakdown we look at the primary defenses by down and distance and what tendencies they have on any of the four downs. We then look at what defenses we will see in a particular part of the field. Are they a pressure team in the open field? Inside the 35-yard line, are they a man-coverage team? Then we look at tendencies by down and distance in a particular field zone. On second and 10 or more from midfield, do they bring pressure or only four rushers?

It is important to understand what defenses we can expect to see on any down and to know what tendencies they may have on that particular down in different areas of the field. When studying a defense we often see multiple fronts, stunts, secondary blitzes, and coverages. By studying an opponent by down, distance, and field zone, we often uncover definite tendencies that simplify what we are going to see from a defense in a particular area or down.

In studying an opponent we look at a number of different criteria. Every year we see defenses become more multiple in their looks and pressure packages. We try to study our opponent and understand them in the simplest terms possible. By studying a team by down, distance, and field zone, we simplify their tendencies. We take it a step further by studying the defense by their tendencies versus offensive personnel groupings. How do they play two-back, one-tight-end sets? If we are playing a team that is extremely multiple, does the two-tight-end, two-back set force them to play a basic defense? Does staying away from certain personnel sets eliminate particular looks that may give us trouble? By studying personnel groupings we can often eliminate or simplify the defenses that we will see. By simplifying the opponent's defense, our study and game planning becomes manageable and easier to understand. Our players can more easily understand what they will see from that particular opponent.

Scouting the Opponent's Offense

When scouting our opponent we need to know whom we are coaching against. We look at the members that make up their offensive staff. We find out as much as possible about the play caller—his tendencies, his philosophy, and his approach to attacking us or teams similar to us.

This analysis gives us insight into what techniques the opposing coach will teach his unit. If we face this opponent every year, we look at scouting reports from previous seasons. This information provides us great insight into how they plan to attack us and what areas we need to focus on as a defense.

During the summer we spend time as a defensive staff discussing the general issues that pertain to our side of the ball and what we may see. In general terms we evaluate the strengths and weaknesses of the team. Last, we discuss matchups against that particular opponent. Those matchups may pertain to personnel or schemes.

Again, one of the most important issues when scouting is to know ourselves—the strengths and weaknesses of our personnel, our schemes, and the stress points of every defense on paper. This may change from year to year based on the availability of players and their skills in the context of our defense. This analysis sets the dimensions of the entire defense.

During game week the first thing we discuss is the injury situation of our opponent. We also discuss the changes of personnel that have occurred in previous games. If a player is injured a team may be unable to run certain packages. Our opponent may focus more on another part of its game. By identifying injuries and the status of personnel, we can develop a greater idea of what we will see in the game. Doing this groundwork helps to narrow the scope of our preparation.

As a staff we watch the last four games of the opponent. If we play the opponent yearly, we also watch the previous year's game and review the notes from that game. We assess their personnel, their strengths, their recent tendencies, and their stress points. After watching those games our staff engages in detailed conversation on the defensive matchups. This discussion encompasses scheme, personnel, strengths and weaknesses, and down and distance as our defensive unit relates to our offensive opponent. We address the positives and the concerns throughout the week leading up to game day.

Among the defensive staff, each coach has a certain area that he concentrates on when developing an opponent's scouting report and breakdown. The secondary coach is in charge of the passing game and trick plays. The defensive tackle coach is in charge of inside run and pass protection. The defensive end coach is responsible for the outside run. The defensive coordinator is in charge of goal-line and short-yardage situations.

After watching the previous four games we break down the opponent and study three categories—field position, down and distance, and personnel. We collect this information and put into a computer program, which gives us a statistical report to use for more detailed breakdown and analysis. After looking at the four games we look at what the opponent has done well for the season and if they have changed any of their philosophy of attack over the course of the season.

Our first focus is field position. What is their philosophy, and what do they tend to do in particular situations? The second focus is personnel grouping. We assess what they like to do with certain personnel groupings and what threats they possess. Then we study down and distance, evaluating how and when they tactically use their offense. Finally, we combine all three and look for tendencies.

Next, we study the personnel in categories of formation in each grouping. Formation studies show what offensive plays a team runs with one tight end, two tight ends, and so forth. This personnel study also helps to uncover tendencies within each formation. We do the same with field position and down and distance.

Before we leave on Sunday we watch all the goal-line and short-yardage situations. In this film study we look for tendencies in personnel, field position, and down and distance. We assess the strengths of the opponent in goal-line and short-yardage situations and discuss the matchups for both sides.

If our opponent has a balanced attack, we evaluate their running and play-action passing attack. We break down the run game by personnel, field position, and down and distance, looking for tendencies. In the running game we look at all matchups and determine where we match up best. We also look at the play-action passes that will usually complement the run game.

We also break down the passing game by personnel, field position, and down and distance. We look at formations and the personnel within each formation. Afterward, we study the routes and the protections, and we tie in the screen and draw game.

We always look for alignment tips or stance tips that indicate certain plays.

In scouting our opponent we look at their history against us and against opponents with similar defensive schemes over the past few years. We want to know the opponent's history in key situations. What does the opponent do on fourth downs—fourth and long and fourth and short—when they have to make it? What is the history of trick plays?

We look at different scenarios and enter them into the computer. These scenarios include what the opponent does when behind in the fourth quarter, when ahead by more than a touchdown in the fourth quarter, and if tied in the fourth quarter and in need of a field goal to win.

On Monday we present the team with goal-line and short-yardage situations. We devote Tuesday to the running game and play-action passes. On Wednesday we cover drop-back passes, screens, and draws.

Finally, we talk to coaches who have previously played our opponent to get their assessment of what they would do differently or would continue to do—their evaluation of personnel, strengths and weaknesses, and what they felt they had to focus on to be successful.

Getting the Competitive Mental Edge

Jim Young

Getting a competitive mental edge on the opponent has always been the goal of successful coaches. Success in any football game depends on the physical abilities and mental attitudes of the players involved. A coach has the ability to influence the mental attitude of his team. Doing so in a positive way can be the key to victory. Achieving that goal is difficult, however, because it is impossible to have complete control of your own mental and emotional makeup, let alone that of a team made up of many individuals.

Coaches use various methods to motivate a team and achieve the proper mental edge. Each successful coach has his own method of motivating his team. The ideas presented in this chapter are just one coach's way of attempting to gain that elusive mental edge. Other approaches may be equally successful. The ideas presented here concern not only how to motivate your team but also how to motivate yourself. You must do both to be successful.

Developing a winning mental edge is not a pep talk, it is not gimmickry, it is not a one-week effort—it is an all-consuming mission. The proper mental edge involves developing pride, poise, and a team attitude in yourself, your coaches, your players, and your support people. It all starts with the head coach, and it involves your philosophy, leadership qualities, understanding of the concept of personal responsibility, and use of proper organizational guidelines.

301

Coaching Philosophy

Having a sound philosophy is key to developing the mental edge and becoming a successful coach. Every coach has a philosophy, whether he knows it or not. This philosophy should be built around leadership, motivation, flexibility, goal setting, visualization, and personal responsibility.

Let us first look at forming a philosophy. The number-one principle is to be your own person. Individuals often look at successful people and try to copy them. Doing this is a mistake. You should study their good traits but then work the traits that you can use into your personal style. An individual builds his philosophy by trial and error. Keep the good and drop the bad.

A coach also needs to expose himself to many different situations and individuals. Coaching clinics, discussions, and looking to other fields can all help a coach absorb new ideas and information. Over the years, I obtained many of my ideas from the business world, the field of psychology, Eastern philosophy, self-help courses, and other areas unrelated to football.

Personal thinking time alone is key to improving all aspects of coaching. We tend to become involved with many things that pull us in different directions and do not allow time for thinking. Allow yourself some time alone to think and to develop new ideas for yourself and your program.

I developed a personal coaching philosophy that includes six key principles. My number-one personal philosophy is to be myself.

Second, I believe that you can achieve what you decide to emphasize. The key is deciding what is critical to your success. You cannot achieve an unlimited number of goals, so limit your program to the basic keys for its success. You will need a lot of study, meetings, discussion, and thinking time to get to identify few key elements of your program.

Third, I am responsible for the success of my program. I win or I lose, not someone else. If you as a coach feel that way and then transfer that belief to your players, your team will become a hard team to defeat. No one passes the buck, and everyone sees himself as personally responsible for the success or failure of the team. This is what you want in a winning organization.

The next key is single mindedness and focusing on the mission. You must believe in what you are doing. This belief must be so strong in your mind that it has already become a reality to you and you will accept nothing less than your goal. You must then add the total effort (work) to put it into action. A great amount of work is required for any successful venture. Belief plus action equals success. I always felt that it is OK to burn your bridges, which is another way of saying that you and your team are totally committed to the mission. A coach must also keep his priorities in order if he is going to focus on the mission. If your mission is not your top priority, you will not accomplish it. The best way to accomplish your mission is to approach it with a desperate outlook, not a contented outlook. As individuals become successful, they tend to become contented. This attitude develops unless a coach makes an effort to keep it from happening. I always wanted my team to approach a game confidently but from the underdog position, if at all possible—confident that they could win but feeling that they must put everything on the line to defeat their opponent. That kind of team is hard to beat. The same attitude is important with a coaching staff. One year I told the coaching staff that we needed to coach as if our jobs were on the line that year, not as if we had three more years on our contracts.

The fifth key is to prepare. The team will respond. It was my responsibility to get myself ready for the season and for each game. I did not feel I could ask my team to make a total commitment if I did not do the same. I always set physical and mental goals to toughen myself for the upcoming season. I expected my players to report in top shape for the start of the season, so I made my own physical commitment to the football season. One year it was to run 78 straight days at 5:30 in the morning, and one year at West Point it was to participate in the Plebe March and Infantry Week. During the season I used visualization to prepare myself to call plays in the game. I put in many hours of thought as a personal commitment to my team and our success. Playing and coaching require the same dedication. I wanted us to have nothing left mentally, physically, or emotionally after a game. A coach who is totally into the game is able to pass this belief on to his team.

I grew up in an environment where the head coach called the offensive plays, and I believe that this helps a coach be completely involved. I realize that calling the offensive plays is difficult because of all the demands placed today on a head coach. It goes back to keeping your priorities in order and deciding what is most important to you. Calling plays would still be a top priority for me.

The last personal key is to be positive a high percentage of the time. Good coaching is correcting mistakes and demanding execution, but a coach must not allow his coaching to be on the negative side. No one can be positive all the time, and there certainly is a need

Courtesy of USMA Media Relations

to correct mistakes. A coach must demand execution and may at times become angry. When you correct a mistake, however, always tell the player what he did wrong and how he can correct it. A coach must make the effort to be positive most of the time if he wants his team to develop into a functioning, winning unit.

Leadership

Now let us turn to leadership. As the coach, you are responsible for the success or failure of your team. You must use your power so players will respect you as their leader. Players must perceive that you have empathy for them. Leadership is the ability to make decisions and make them sooner rather than later. Leadership is the ability to create and change for the better.

Share your philosophy with your team. Repeat your key beliefs and key goals for the season. Once you decide what key points to emphasize, present them repeatedly to your team, using different ways to get your point across. You will know you have been successful when your players start expressing your thoughts to the press and thinking that they are their own.

A coach can make some crucial mistakes in the realm of leadership. If you want to be a head coach, you must grow and prepare for that leadership position. For example, do not study just one side of the ball. If you must stay on one side of the ball for a time, you can still make the effort to study the other side. You must expand your knowledge. Set personal goals and visualize where you want to go.

Once you are a head coach, focus not on your team weaknesses but on your team strengths. At West Point, we felt that focusing on our strengths was a key to success. We had great mental ability in our football team. Our players were smart overachievers who would never quit. They were mentally tough and had great discipline. The wishbone offense fit perfectly with the mental strength of our team. We did not use the physical excuse that our players were not as big or as fast as our opponents were. We did not ignore the physical aspects, of course, and we tried to improve that element in every way possible. But our focus was on our mental strengths, not our physical weaknesses.

If your school has a tradition, use it. It is a mistake not to make your players aware of your school's football traditions. You may have to go back years, but all schools have had traditions that you can use with your present players. When we got to West Point we found the players unaware of, or in some cases intimidated by, Army's great football traditions. We made all our players aware of the honor of playing football at a school with a great tradition. We used old highlights, talks, letters, and anything we could to emphasize our past traditions and the great effort needed to carry on those traditions in the present era.

A coach today must strike a balance between an autocratic leadership style and a democratic one. Doing that is tough. The coach who has empathy for his players, is totally involved with them, is an up-front leader, and is willing to make the tough decisions can be an outstanding leader.

At Bowling Green State University I had the opportunity to play and coach for Doyt Perry, a great Hall of Fame coach. He had 11 coaching principles, which I used in my coaching. I feel that they still apply to coaching today. I later added three more.

1. Always be fully prepared for a day's work before you go on the field.
2. After practice, check each player's attitude, effort, and accomplishments.
3. Morale is our most important objective. It starts with you and is largely stimulated by individual effort.
4. To do a good job, you must teach physical aggressiveness (toughness) as well as technique.
5. Never loaf or allow players to loaf in any football activity. If you are too tired, rest.
6. Use professional courtesy, but never fail to talk with any coach involved about anything that will aid our football team.
7. Be constantly aware of rules violations. Do not allow them on the practice field.
8. The important factors are why and how, not just seeing a mistake.
9. Each coach is responsible for the mistakes of his position players.
10. Act, don't talk, on the field. Talk in meetings.
11. Do not bluff—know what you are doing.
12. Constantly build and emphasize pride, poise, and team.
13. Constantly look for better ways to motivate and teach your players.
14. Repetition is the best form of learning, provided you can keep it from being too boring.

Organization

So far we have dealt with the coach and how his leadership and philosophy affect the mental outlook of his team. We will now look at four basic organizational concepts and how they help develop the competitive mental edge.

Develop a Team Attitude

The first idea is the development of a team attitude. Develop a belief in the program. This starts with you, your coaches, your seniors, and your team. I never believed in saying anything about rebuilding a program. I went into four losing situations, but in each case I said that we expected to win in the first year. It is a mistake to indicate to your present players that they are not good enough and that you need to rebuild before you can win. A coach does not win with players who he has already said are not good enough to win. We were not always successful in our first year, but never because we said we were rebuilding.

It is human nature to go into a new situation and be critical of the previous program and staff. The less said about the previous program to your team and the press, the better. Seniors are always the hardest to sell on a new program because they have been accustomed to a different way of doing things for the longest time. Sell the seniors, and you sell your program.

Everything we did in practice and meetings was intended to sell the team concept. Handouts, talks, videos, cookouts—every item and activity emphasized the team. The head coach must provide direction for the team. Otherwise, the coordinators of each phase will emphasize their own areas. Before each game coordinators went over their game plan in front of the whole team. At halftime units met separately at first and then came together for a team meeting with the head coach. These are a few examples of what we did to emphasize the team. If you don't emphasize the team, you will not have a team—you will have an organization of individuals and units.

For a team attitude to develop, discipline must be fair and consistent. Players will respect the coach if they feel that they are all equally important and if the coach treats them that way.

In all the years I was a head coach, we elected team captains before the season only once. Army had a great tradition of electing a team captain, and I maintained that tradition the first year. But the next year I went back to having all the seniors be game-week captains throughout the year. I believe strongly in having game captains with all seniors participating. Game captains are responsible for game-week motivation and speaking at quarterback meetings. All seniors serve as team leaders throughout the season. Before the last game of the season, the team voted on the captains for that year. Voting at the end of the season gives you the true leaders of the year and allows all seniors to participate in the leadership of the team. All seniors on our team knew that they were responsible for the leadership of that particular year. One year the seniors felt so strongly about this that they did not want to elect any captains at the end of the year. The 1984 Army team captains were simply all of the seniors.

From my days as a high school coach I always felt that a conditioning and strength program produced more than just physical benefits. A team develops mental toughness and togetherness in a good off-season program. The coaches and seniors should provide leadership in this program rather than just turn it over to a strength coach.

A coach should meet and talk with his players individually. I learned a great deal about our program from the players in these individual meetings. Players must feel free to bring problems and ideas to you. I also liked to use unsigned questionnaires to find out what my players were really thinking. The year we put the wishbone in, 80 percent of the players stated after spring practice that they liked the new offense. I knew we were moving in the right direction.

At one of the major colleges where I coached, a player told me that the scout-team players did not feel as if they were part of the team because of the way the lockers were numbered. I asked him what he meant, and he said that the lockers were marked with either red or black numbers—red numbers for the scholarship players and black ones for the walk-ons. The equipment manager used that system to know which lockers to put good equipment in. We quickly changed that practice and treated the whole team equally with all red numbers and good equipment. The change had a positive effect on our walk-on players. I would have never known about the situation without getting input from each player in our program.

One year I felt that I had not done a good job of coaching, so I asked my departing seniors to evaluate my coaching for the past season. They agreed that I had not done a good job. Their assessment was tough to take but helpful to know.

At the start of the season we give all players their own notebooks. Offensive players get offensive notebooks, defensive players get defensive notebooks, and special-teams players get special-teams notebooks. For the last 15 years I coached, we also gave each player his own team notebook.

The team notebook had all the general information a player needed, but the main purpose of the notebook was to develop motivation and team attitude. The notebook contained no plays or defenses. We had a different theme for each year, and the notebook was made up of articles and quotes that emphasized the theme. For example, one year we filled the notebook with quotations by Sun Tzu, a Chinese military philosopher, and explained about how his ideas applied to our football team. I used the team notebook every night of the preseason when I met with the team.

I also had team members speak on various football subjects in these nightly meetings. This practice helped develop our team attitude. Players express themselves in a different way than a coach might express himself. Having a player talk to the team about gang tackling, sideline discipline, or the importance of defense (sometimes by an offensive player) can make for a stimulating team meeting. Players love to hear their teammates talk.

One memorable talk was by a sophomore fullback who asked to speak one night. In front of the team he said, "If you ever need one yard and a first down, call on me!" In the Army-Navy game that year we had the ball on our own 23-yard line, fourth and inches. I took time-out, called Ben over, and asked him if he remembered the talk he gave the team in the preseason. We got that first down.

One of the most important elements in developing a team attitude is to have team goals or objectives. For many years we had unit objectives for the offense, defense, and special teams. I decided that if we were a team then we needed team objectives, not unit objectives. We discussed the key team objectives that applied to all units. We decided on the following five:

1. Win the turnover battle.
2. Win the kicking game.
3. Win the critical situations (sudden change, hurry-hurry, coming out, going in).
4. Win the conditioning battle (fourth quarter).
5. Win the mental battle (belief plus action).

We started using these team objectives in 1973 and never changed them. The only chart in the locker room on objectives was the team-objective chart. Winning three or more of these objectives meant winning the game.

Many years ago I wanted to promote individual effort within the framework of a team concept. We started a motivation club on the high school level in the early 1960s, and it remained basically the same ever since. The club has been known by many different names over the years: Red Devils, Scalpers, Victors, Bear Down, Hammer, and Ranger Club.

This club develops consistent season-long play in combination with outstanding weekly individual play. Club members get their names on a locker-room plaque, a decal on their helmets, ranger jerseys in practice, and trophies at the end of the year for those who were members for 8 out of 11 weeks. Qualifications for admission to the club were

- always giving a winning effort in practice and games,
- knowing all assignments,
- being hard-nosed at all times in practice and in games, and
- being willing to come out early or stay after practice to work on self-improvement.

Week-to-week admission depended on the previous qualifications and being personally responsible for a key play leading to a victory, being a member of an offensive unit that scores 30 points or more or being a member of a defensive unit that holds an opponent to 7 points or less, and having an outstanding all-around game. Offensive and defensive players must have played 20 plays, and specialists must have played 10 plays.

A player could lose membership if he committed these infractions:

- Being responsible for a fumble, pass interception, penalty, missed tackle, or missed assignment that was the turning point of the game
- Not giving winning effort in a practice or the game

- Losing his temper or behaving in an unsportsmanlike way
- Missing a game or three days of practice during the week of a game
- Performing poorly in the game

Over the years, in many different schools, players have taken to this club and felt honored to receive a trophy at the end of the year. The coach should make attaining membership tough and equal for all. A player can have a great game, but if he missed practice that week or received an unsportsmanlike-conduct penalty in the game, he is not in the club for that week.

For most years the only trophies we gave at our season-ending banquet were for membership in the team club and for one other award—our Champion of the Year, given to the best scout-team player of the year. Each week we had scout-team awards to recognize the effort put forth by the scout players in practice. We always tried to honor our scout-team players so that we could have quality practice time during the week. Some years we took the weekly scout winners on our road trip, and some years we played them on the kickoff-receive team for that week's game.

In 1960 we started using helmet awards for great individual plays, such as interceptions and outstanding run. We copied this idea from World War II pilots who put small flags of shot-down enemy planes on the fuselage of their planes. In some programs we put the award on the player's helmet. In other programs we put the award on the player's locker.

The most important thing we did, however, was tie most of the awards to our team objectives. Everyone on the offense received an award if the offense had no turnovers in an entire game; every offensive player received an award for being part of a 12-play offensive drive that led to a score; every defensive player received an award for forcing a turnover inside the 40-yard line that led to a score; everyone on the defensive team received an award if the defense scored a touchdown; and so forth. This way the reward system recognized not only outstanding individual play but also outstanding unit play that led to the achievement of the team objectives and victory.

Develop Pride and Poise

Development of pride and poise is the second key organizational concept. An organization must have pride and be able to handle stressful situations if it is to achieve success. The coach is responsible for creating an environment that will foster these two key elements.

Individuals and teams learn to handle stressful situations by practicing gamelike situations without the full stress being in effect. Scrimmaging suits that purpose well. We always tried to scrimmage the key situations that would help us achieve our team objectives, such as sudden change (unexpected turnover in the red zone), hurry-hurry (two-minute drill), and other key game situations.

We also made our players aware of the challenge of these crucial situations by going over the statistics of past challenges. We disclosed the percentage chance of being successful and then tried to beat that percentage. We kept these challenges constantly in our players' thoughts.

A coach can do many things to improve the pride factor of his team. Going first class in every way possible will help. Of course, you do not want to waste money, but you can make best use of what you have available. Allowing the players to get on a charter plane first and sit wherever they want to sit rather than letting alums on the plane first and having them take the front-row seats is a good example of treating your players in a first-class way.

Think like a winner, act like a winner, and you will become a winner. Keep your locker-room signs and charts few but repetitive of the goals that you want to achieve. Our two key signs, which we first used at Lima Shawnee High School in 1960, never changed. They read "Pride, Poise, Team" and "Those who stay will be champions."

A coach's work habits are important to team members. Your team must always feel that you are outworking everyone and that the success of the program is your number-one goal. You cannot expect players to have pride in the program if they do not have pride in the head coach.

We always made an effort to teach our players the basic concepts of the program—our offensive theories, defensive theories, and special-teams theories. Players are more likely to have pride in a program when they understand what the program is trying to accomplish.

I always liked to compare a football team with the 101st and 82nd Airborne Divisions. The soldiers in those units parachuted into Normandy in 1944, but they landed many miles from their assigned zones. They could not tell where they were in the dark, confusion reigned supreme, but small groups formed and took the battle successfully to the enemy. Their training had developed the pride and poise needed to carry them through to victory. The same thing happens to a football team. A team practices all week against a certain defense, but in the game the opponent plays a different defense, or the man over a player is much stronger in the game than the player whom he had practiced against all week. Training must prepare the team for the unexpected.

This sort of circumstance is called organized confusion. It occurs in war, and it occurs in football. The unit or team that has developed the most pride and poise will win when the unexpected hits them.

Develop a System

The third concept is to have a sound but flexible system. No matter what type of offense or defense we had, we wanted one that was simple for our team to operate but looked complicated to our opponents. A coach must be able to adjust his system to his personnel rather than trying to adjust his players' talents to one set system.

A coach must be willing to change and take a chance. This does not mean that you change just to change, but that you change to improve your team. One type of creativity is seeing the old in a new way. In many ways that is what change is all about. When we decided to go to the wishbone offense we did not invent it or copy it; we created the Army wishbone.

But do not just go with the current trends. Use ideas that fit your program. When you add something to your program you must also subtract something. Otherwise, you soon find yourself trying to do so many things that you cannot emphasize the key points. Each year evaluate the program and make an effort to "plus" your program. By proper research, study, and creativity a program can be plussed. A program will not stand still; it will go backward if it is not plussed.

Apply Motivation, Organization, and Learning

We have already touched on the fourth key organizational concept, which is the proper application of the basic principles of motivation, organization, and learning. A well-organized, planned practice that moves at a fast tempo does wonders in getting your players' attention, saving time, and motivating them to action. A good coach is also aware of the importance of changing the routine. This is particularly important when you are winning. I never liked to change the routine when we had a win streak going, but that is the very time that a change of routine can stimulate your team and keep them from just going through the motions. A coach must be willing to change—the practice approach, the meeting approach, or his coaching approach—if he wants to renew his team's enthusiasm.

A coach should use his gut feeling to motivate his team. In general I used what motivated me to motivate my team for any given game. Don't be afraid to try gimmicks if your gut feeling tells you they will work. We have tried many things over the years—tug-of-war between players and coaches, a hamburger drill with the head coach, player-coach parties, taking pregame warm-up and spelling out "HIT," placing signs or sayings on each player's locker, and many other unusual motivational aids. Most worked and some did not. The biggest mistake was trying to use a success motivation gimmick twice. Come up with a new, unique idea.

In approaching player learning, we had several important principles. Spaced repetition is the best way to teach as long as you can keep it from becoming boring. Once a coach has decided what points he wants to emphasize, he must repeat them in the winter and spring, in summer letters, and throughout the football season. The method of presenting the key points will change but the key points themselves will not.

We make game plans and adjustments early in the week. As a staff we are going to work very hard on our game plan Saturday night and Sunday, and we have it done on Monday. Giving your players a good game plan they can practice for the whole week is better than giving them a great plan on Wednesday that they don't have much time to practice.

When I was a position coach, I gave my players adjustment sheets before each practice. These sheets covered the previous practice mistakes, corrections, new adjustments, and some motivational thoughts. They contained what a coach would usually put on the chalkboard during his prepractice meeting. I did not have to take the time to write on the chalkboard as I was talking, and I used the adjustment sheets to cover what I wanted to go over in the position meeting. The players had a copy of the key points to work on, which they could take with them and look over later.

We also practiced what we called flexible learning early. Exposing individuals to the same ideas over time is a much better method of teaching than giving them several ideas at once and expecting them to pick up everything quickly. For example, let's say we were going to meet a wishbone offense for the first time in the eighth week of the season. We did not want to wait until the eighth week of the season to work on our wishbone defense. In spring practice we would expose our team to the wishbone defense. In summer letters we would write about that defense. In the preseason we would again expose our players to the wishbone defense. What our players learned before that eighth week helped them pick up the defense. They did not have to learn something totally new in the eighth week.

Position coaches used walk-through learning whenever possible. It is much better to have your players on their feet going through assignments rather than sitting in their chairs listening to the coach go through assignments. This approach is particularly good for offensive-line adjustments and defensive-backfield adjustments. We also used player tests and player talks to check knowledge.

If you want improvement, then you must emphasize improvement. You must talk about improvement, about either getting better or getting worse, about how individual improvement leads to team improvement. If each player and coach can improve by about two percent each day, unbelievable improvement will occur in the total team.

The type of staff you have plays an important role in developing a winning edge. A football staff should be made up of mostly young coaches, not yes men. Coaches should be able to give and take, be willing to work, and be able to relate to players. A good staff needs several coaches who are creative thinkers.

It is the responsibility of the head coach to put all assignments in writing, to plan the staff meeting before the meeting, to meet with the goal of accomplishing things (not just to meet), to involve his assistants as much as possible (to call on all staff members in meetings, not just the ones who always speak up), to keep the organization moving forward, and to avoid separating himself from his staff or players. A head coach should be removed but not remote, involved but not a buddy. Each spring and fall, we had a coach's clinic in which each coach went over his area of responsibility with the rest of the staff.

In a good player-coach relationship, the coach provides discipline, interjects humor, and keeps the lines of communication open. Treat your players as individuals and treat them fairly. Do not make a negative judgment too early in a player's career or it will become a self-fulfilling prophecy. Never criticize players in public. Give players a sound, hard-working, well-organized program in which they can have pride, and the player-coach relationship will be successful.

Visualization and goal setting are two important methods of gaining a competitive edge. I have always used visualization myself, and I presented the techniques of visualization to all my teams. The ability to visualize and to practice in your mind successful techniques or situations can be a great aid to an individual and to a team.

The use of goal setting for both individual goals and team goals gives proper direction to both the individual and the team. It is hard to accomplish a mission unless you know what the mission is and how to accomplish it.

We have looked at both external and internal motivation. External motivation is important for short-term motivation. To motivate his team, a coach should use weekly awards, gimmicks, pep talks, changes in routine, signs, and so forth. External motivation, however, is temporary, and a coach must come up with new ideas to keep it going.

Internal motivation is the best way to achieve a permanent competitive mental edge. You can build the framework for permanent team success by emphasizing self-responsibility and self-accountability, by letting players talk and determine team goals, by making all seniors captains, by emphasizing team togetherness, by getting player feedback, and by using key words, thoughts, and beliefs until the players see the words, thoughts, and beliefs as their own.

All areas of a football program are important in developing a competitive mental edge. Philosophy, leadership, organizational structure, creativity, and proper motivation techniques are essential to the success of a football program.

The challenge for the coach today is even greater than the challenge coaches faced in the past. Players in today's society grow up believing that individuality and self-expression are more important than putting the team first and being together as a unit. In football, team importance has always been number one, and a coach must strive to keep it that way. Present-day coaches must accept this challenge if they want to attain the competitive winning edge.

25

Offensive Play Calling in Key Game Situations

Frosty Westering

Vince Lombardi once stated that a football game normally includes 160 plays but only 3 or 4 plays make a difference in the outcome of a game. The challenge is that you never know when those plays are coming. Although Lombardi's statement related to an all-out effort on every play, we can apply it to specific play calling in key game situations.

Before discussing offensive play calling in key game situations, we must first talk about some of the various offensive philosophies and offensive systems in football today. Coaching philosophies range from the approach of a riverboat gambler to the mind-set that the most effective play produces three yards and a cloud of dust. Play calling in a game results directly from the philosophy—the offensive systems and styles of play—of the offensive coaching staff.

Coaches develop their offensive systems based on their background knowledge and basic philosophy of the offensive game. All offensive systems have a basic philosophy in attacking the defenses they will face, and play calling results directly from this. Football today embraces many outstanding systems and styles of play.

* With contributions from Scott Westering, PLU's outstanding offensive coordinator for the past 20 years.

Coaches need to realize, however, that their systems must be flexible enough to take advantage of the talent of their players. The system should put the players in the best position to use their talent. The ability of the coach to use the talent of his players within his offensive system is the key to developing a play-calling philosophy. At times, the player makes the play go. At other times, the play itself is the key to its success. Whether they use the West Coast, wing T, power I, veer option, run and shoot, or spread, all coaches try to use the talent of their players within the system. Offenses can incorporate multiple sets, shifting, and motion to take advantage of key personnel and create mismatches or misalignments for the defense. Understanding this concept is the basis used by every offensive coaching staff as they develop their systems, styles of play, and play calling in all game situations.

Field Position

We break the field down into zones, as do many coaches. Position on the field, to a certain extent, affects play calling. Coaches give these zones various names or colors.

The backup zone is from our own 10-yard line to our goal line. In this zone, we limit our play-calling possibilities to give us the best chance of gaining yards without turning the ball over. Sometimes you can roll the dice and go for the big play, but you have to be sure to protect your quarterback and send out fewer receivers than you would in the open field.

Courtesy of Pacific Lutheran University Photo Services

The three-down zone is from our 10-yard line to our opponent's 35. Play calls here are wide open with the basic understanding that on fourth down, we will punt the ball. The exception is late in the game when we are behind and need to score. Then we go for the first down or a touchdown.

The four-down zone is from our opponent's 35-yard line to the opponent's goal line. In this zone, on fourth down we will either go for it or kick a field goal.

The green zone is from the opponent's 20-yard line to the goal line. Many coaches refer to this as the red zone. For us, the term "red zone" is a defensive way to view it. The color red typically signifies "stop." However, for the offense, it is the green zone—green typically signifies "go" and we are in the go mode, the scoring mode. In the green zone, we use our goal-line package in varying degrees to dictate play calling.

Every offensive coach uses these zones or some variation of them to package their play selections for maximum effectiveness. There are exceptions to these; the key is to know when to make them.

Scripting

Bill Walsh, Hall of Fame coach of the three-time Super Bowl champion San Francisco 49ers and one of the most innovative coaches of the modern era, developed the art of scripting, play calling, and game planning to a much higher level. We employ much of Bill Walsh's system in scripting and game planning. That system has made our offensive game planning and play calling much more effective and productive.

We develop a master play list for each of our formations. Each week, we select from this list the first 24 first- and second-down plays for our script (figure 25.1). We also list play choices for third down, long yardage, and short yardage. We then list 24 other plays that we can call on first, second, or third down, or other situations.

We start by studying our opponent's defenses, possible alignments, adjustments to our formations, and how their personnel play their system. We note tendencies on specific downs, distances, and field position. We then precall the opening 24 first- and second-down plays for the game. For third down, we list three or four play choices (run or pass) based on yards to go, hash mark, field position, and game tempo.

The scripted game plan includes other key game situations including goal-line situations, two-point plays, the two-minute drill, and overtime. Our quarterback uses a wristband that has the basic script on it, and we signal plays from the sideline. Sometimes we send the play in with a player. It's important to have all key play calls on the wristband to avoid confusion at crucial times during the game.

Being able to set up big plays comes from developing play series. A series is a set of plays that start and look similar on the snap of the ball but then attack the defense in other places.

Figure 25.2 shows a basic series. The plays would be run in this order:

1. Basic play
2. Fake basic play, run to same side
3. Fake basic play, run to opposite side (counter or reverse)
4. Fake basic play, play-action pass or bootleg (figure 25.2)

1. 1st	9. 1st	17. 1st	Opponent
2. 2nd	10. 2nd	18. 2nd	Date
3. 1st	11. 1st	19. 1st	Comments
4. 2nd	12. 2nd	20. 2nd	
5. 1st	13. 1st	21. 1st	
6. 2nd	14. 2nd	22. 2nd	Key thoughts
7. 1st	15. 1st	23. 1st	
8. 2nd	16. 2nd	24. 2nd	

Third down		Goal-line offense (inside 10-yard line)	
2 to 4 yards	12 to 15 yards	Run	Pass
5 to 7 yards		Short yards (1 to 2)	
	15 or more yards		
8 to 11 yards		Special plays (run and pass)	
		Situation plays	
Blitz situations		Two-point plays	

Figure 25.1   Offensive game script form.

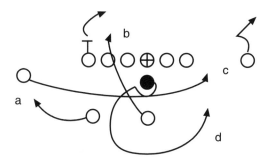

Figure 25.2 Basic series of plays. *(a)* Pitchout, *(b)* FB offtackle, *(c)* reverse, *(d)* bootleg pass.

Audibles

Every offensive system needs to be flexible enough to allow a change of play on the line of scrimmage. We coach quarterbacks to read for defensive alignment, blitz tip-offs, and secondary coverage. By taking advantage of any of these, the quarterback can run the play called or audible to a new play that has a better chance of success.

Teams use various audible systems (color, snap count, huddle call, automatic numbers). Our audible system follows the KISS principal—Keep It Simple and Short. We have a quick-hitting running play for each hole and two or three pass plays to take advantage of the defense (figure 25.3). We also add an audible play or two for specific opponents. We use the "check with me" system: no play is called in the huddle or we don't huddle at all. We practice audibles regularly, which keeps our execution at a high level.

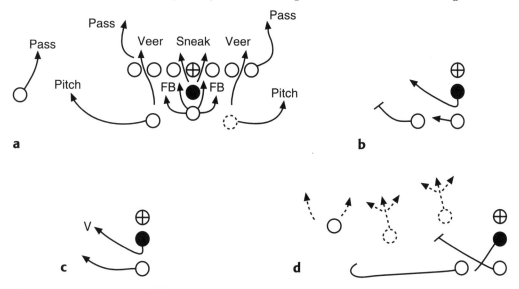

Figure 25.3 Basic audible system. *(a)* Pre-snap look—take advantage of opponent's defensive alignment (open gaps, blocking angles, passing lanes), *(b)* lead option, *(c)* speed option (one back), *(d)* ISO pass.

The ability of our quarterback, receivers, and running backs to read defenses is vital to the success of our offense. Our linemen also learn to read basic defensive alignments for checkoffs and blitz tip-offs. Formations and motion can force a defense to tip off many blitz situations. The zone blitz, however, presents a different challenge, because we must read it after we snap the ball.

Formations

A coach may use various offensive formations and motions to change alignment before the ball is snapped. We are a multiple-offense team that uses various formations with some shifting and motion. This approach allows us to run similar plays in a number of different ways. Our formation alignments determine the players' positions (figure 25.4). We are able to run many of our basic plays from these formations. Adding shifting and motion forces the defense to think and adjust, and we try to take advantage of this. The use of shifting and motion keeps the defense off balance.

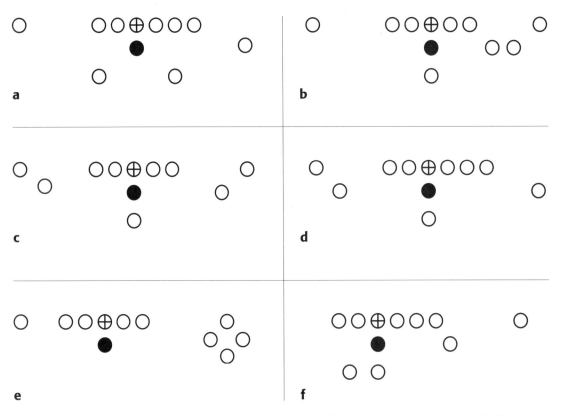

Figure 25.4 Offensive formations: *(a)* pro, *(b)* spread, *(c)* spread and shoot, *(d)* tight-end spread and shoot, *(e)* diamond spread, *(f)* unbalanced line.

Before calling a play against any defense, the offensive coach must know and identify the strengths and weakness of the opponent. The opponent may use different fronts, coverages, and blitzes, but they still have a basic defense that they play most of time. Different teams, however, may play a given system in different ways, depending on personnel and philosophy. One team may play cover 3 and have an aggressive run-support free safety. Another team may have a free safety who plays cover 3 deep and conservatively. Other considerations you have to look for include the following:

- What blitz packages does the defense use? Do they zone blitz?
- How aggressively does the front play?
- Do the linebackers attack or read?
- How big are the cornerbacks? Do they flip-flop?
- Does the secondary support the run, or do they play in strong pass-coverage mode?

After looking over this information, a coach should bring out the plays that have been successful against those types of defenses in the past—runs, counters, play-action passes, drop-back passes, or sprint-out passes.

You may need to adjust your key plays to take advantage of defensive weaknesses. For example, do you want to attack their free safety with a post or a drag route? You also need to consider what plays and formations appear to cause problems for your opponent's alignment or matchups.

The key to creating the offensive edge is to keep the defense off balance by calling and executing plays at the right time.

Key Situations

A useful idea we have borrowed from the business world is the 20-80 rule, which states that 20 percent of what you do produces 80 percent of the results. Therefore, for maximum efficiency, learn what the 20 percent is and spend 80 percent of your time there. In coaching football, the secret is to define key game situations (that 20 percent) and put a high percentage of your time there.

In six key situations, play calling can make a difference in the outcome of the game: third down, at the goal line, after a turnover, the final two minutes of the half or the game, when the game is on the line, and overtime.

Third Down

Third down, considered by most coaches the most important down in football, is a key situation. You need to prepare for and practice third-down plays. We break down third-down plays by yardage and plays. Play calling should focus on plays that enable you to get specific yardage. We look at plays that in theory should get us anywhere from 2 to 4 yards to 12 to 15 yards or more.

Another consideration you must keep in front of you is how you will deal with pressure. Some typical options are to keep in extra blockers (tight ends or running backs), to move the pocket by rolling the quarterback out, or to spread out the defense with four or five receivers.

In dealing with pressure, don't be afraid to use the shotgun. Remember that no matter how good your quarterback is, pressure changes everything. Many third downs never have a chance because the quarterback ends up running for his life. We have certain plays in our offense that we call blitz friendly. These plays allow our quarterback to anticipate the blitz and remain calm, staying with the play call. If the defense blitzes, he is ready; if they fake and drop into zones, the play call is still good. You have to look at what options make sense for you, your offensive system, and your players.

Goal Line

Goal line is obviously a key situation in any game. Scoring is imperative. Play calling is critical, and you cannot waste downs. We take the goal line and divide it into two areas—from the 10-yard line and from inside the 5-yard line. The closer you get to scoring, the more likely it is that the defense will change its philosophy. You have to be aware of such changes and how they affect your play calls.

Most coaches resign themselves to running the ball at the goal line, and only between the tackles. We believe you have to be equally committed to the passing game, especially the play-action passing game. This offensive approach creates a dilemma for the defensive coordinator about what coverage to play. You need to have pass plays that exploit both man and zone.

Overall, your goal-line package of play calls should cover the continuum from the quarterback sneak to the option or pitchout, from the bootleg pass to the fade.

After a Turnover

Turnovers occur in almost every game. The possibilities that come with a turnover make it a key situation. These sudden-change situations often catch coaches unprepared, so they just call a basic play. The first play following a turnover may not be the time to go for it, but we believe you must be ready.

Such a situation presented itself in one of our national championship games. We recovered a fumble on our opponent's 35-yard line and had a specific play ready to go. We executed it perfectly and scored. Those kinds of situations have the potential to change the momentum of a game.

Two Minutes

The final two minutes of the half or the end of the game can be a key situation. The clock is paramount. Play calling should consider the various ways to stop the clock.

The standard approach is to use out routes that gain moderate yardage and stop the clock. But remember that most defensive coaches remind their players not to get beat deep, so you should consider crossing routes and seam routes. Shorter passes can provide significant yards after catch (YAC), and your quarterback can always get the team up and spike the ball following a play call that isn't designed to get out of bounds.

Using basic personnel groupings and formations allows your quarterback to call several plays without much change or huddling. Don't lose sight of what you want to gain—a field-goal attempt or a touchdown. If you want to put yourself in position to attempt a field goal, then a specific yard line and hash mark are the goals in play calling.

Game on the Line

You have to be prepared for the ultimate key situation—the call with the game on the line. Usually, it's a fourth down or a time-restricted call. It may be a fourth and one or a second down on the 18-yard line going in to score with three seconds left. As a coach, you must have already thought through the situation and be ready with your best shot. Keep in mind your answer to the question, "If the game were on the line, who would you want to have the ball?"

Remember that your opponent is also studying what you do in key situations. You have to decide whether to do something new or commit to outexecuting the opposition with a play you usually run.

Overtime

Overtime creates another challenging and exciting dimension to offensive play calling. Most teams who win the coin toss in overtime choose to play defense first, giving them the advantage of knowing whether they need to score a touchdown or a field goal to win or tie the game. Look at the opponent's green zone (the defense calls this the red zone) tendencies during the game to help you with play selection. Consider using plays, formations, motions, or shifts that weren't used during regulation. It's vital, however, to continue to take advantage of your best players and your best plays.

Successful play calling in overtime requires a basic plan. Your entire team must know, understand, believe in, and practice the plan. Then they will be ready to give it their best shot with confidence, poise, and execution.

Key Plays

Now let's talk about those three or four plays that Lombardi referred to. Those plays can be big momentum changers. They can give confidence to an offensive team and be a key factor in winning a game. Remember that those plays can also come from the defense or special-teams as in the case of a safety blitz or a fake punt.

Most people think that the key play calls come near or at the end of a game, and at times that is true. But they may occur at other points in the game and really change the momentum, giving a team control of the game. Momentum (Big Mo) is a powerful catalyst. Teams that learn what it is and how to capture it have a decisive edge.

Several years ago we were playing in the third quarter of a tight game. Our opponent was blitzing a lot on first down. With the ball on our 20-yard line, we called a screen pass. Our quarterback read the blitz, stayed with the play, and it went 80 yards for a touchdown. Big-time momentum. We went on to score twice more in the fourth quarter, but the game breaker was the screen pass.

In a national playoff overtime game in the 2000 season, we called a key play that backfired. Rain had fallen steadily through the entire game, but we were playing on artificial turf so the footing was good. Our opponent had just scored. We moved the ball down to the 9-yard line and faced first and goal. We have an effective end sweep from our unbalanced formation and a halfback pass from the same action on the sweep. We hadn't used the halfback pass all year, but in that situation we believed it could score. The pass was intercepted near the goal line, however, and the game was over. Hindsight is always 20/20, and we should have stayed with our regular goal-line play calls to try to score.

We have had many game situations in which a big play has changed the momentum of the game. In a big triple-overtime game, we scored the winning two-point play with a little wrinkle. We called an option play in which we shifted our best back to be the pitch man. We had never done that from that formation. Putting the ball in the hands of our best back paid off as he went into the end zone standing up.

Late in another game we were driving for the winning touchdown. We anticipated an inside blitz with man coverage. Our play call was a double drag over the middle. We passed to the short drag man, and he outran his defender down the sideline for a touchdown. No defensive help was available on the play because our other receivers ran off the safeties and corners, who had our receivers man-to-man. The risk of blitzing and playing man can backfire on the defense with the right play call.

In another playoff game we were struggling on offense in the fourth quarter. We had put a play in just for that game to take advantage of a specific defensive coverage and blitz. This was a high-risk play for protecting our quarterback, but we blocked well and it played out just as we drew it up—touchdown. That score changed the momentum of the game, and we went on to win.

We have a psychological edge called the big five—scoring two touchdowns within five minutes on the game clock. The sequence begins on the kickoff following our touchdown and conversion. Our entire crowd and team stand with their arms and fingers extended over their heads. This ritual builds on the momentum of scoring and inspires our team. Many times our defense has been able to score by a fumble recovery, intercepted pass, blocked punt, or punt return. In other cases, they have forced our opponent to kick the ball and then our offense has gone on to score. This sequence presents a potential key situation in play calling. Momentum shifts can play a major role in the game.

Momentum does make a big difference. Timely, aggressive, risk-taking play calling in key game situations is crucial to creating Big Mo and giving your team the winning edge.

Regardless of what a coach's offensive play-calling philosophy is, all coaches need to remember six basic keys:

1. Use the talents of key players in specific down-and-distance situations.

2. Understand the defense's strategy in the different zones of the field.

3. Create a simple, quick hitting and passing audible system that can take advantage of personnel mismatches, defensive alignment, and secondary coverages.

4. Use various formations, shifts, and motions to cause defenses to adjust.

5. Have several misdirection runs, play-action passes, and special plays that you can execute at a high level for key times in a game.

6. Understand the importance of momentum in a game and how plays called in six key situations—third down, goal line, post-turnover, last two minutes, game on the line, and overtime—can affect it.

Remember, momentum can play a *major* role in the outcome of a game. Big plays in key game situations create momentum for your team.

Making Defensive Calls

Jerry Sandusky

Many factors go into making defensive calls in key game situations. Is it easy to come up with the best call for the critical moment? You and I know that it isn't. In one sense, though, it is easy, or, I should say, "EZ." The letter E represents efficiency, the ability to organize, prioritize, and focus on the most significant factors that influence the decision. The Z stands for *zygarnek*, a German term that means the compulsion to succeed, strong will, and the undying spirit that drives you forward regardless of the circumstances. Most good decisions spring from the traits expressed by these two letters.

Decisions are a by-product of in-depth analysis, experience, and gut feeling. Analysis—of yourself and your players—begins shortly after the previous game is over and ends with the 25 seconds you have to make the call. The coach should have a feel for what he has done in similar situations and for the capabilities of his players. He should know what the opponent has done in previous games. Players also must be mentally and physically prepared. Player feedback is an important factor in a decision. If a player has an opinion, the coach should at least consider it. The success or failure of any play comes down to the players: the way they execute the defense, their ability level, their motivation, and their trust.

In my coaching career, there were many times I didn't know what to call but had to make the decision. During most of my career, I felt good about being able to make critical calls and prided myself on having the poise to handle such situations. One exceptional game I remember was our national championship contest against Miami. When game day finally came, I was relieved and relaxed. I was determined to enjoy a beautiful night and a memorable experience. For 98 percent of that game I was relaxed. On their last drive, Miami went for it on fourth and long, and made a first down. Since we had won so many close games over a two-year period, it entered my mind that the law of averages might catch up with us. I suddenly became tense.

Miami moved down the field as the game clock wound down. My next-to-last defensive call of the game used a lot of words to call. Although it was a simple defense, it included a number of adjustments to formations. I gave the defense to Jim Williams, and he signaled it. Now Miami had one play left. This was it. We had put great effort and energy into winning the championship. I had to make the call, but nothing came out of my mouth. Finally I mumbled, "Same defense, Jim. You can signal it." Forget the analysis, forget all the planning. The key call was "Same defense, Jim."

Planning

Planning for the next game begins with an evaluation of the previous game. We begin by reviewing the game video. During this session, staff members evaluate our personnel, execution, and defensive scheme. We identify problems and try to come up with proper solutions.

When evaluating our personnel we assess execution and productivity. Each player is given a plus or minus on every play based on his alignment, assignment, and reaction. If he did his job, he receives a plus; a breakdown in any of these three areas results in a minus. Credit is given for being a positive factor during the play—making or assisting with a tackle, harassing or sacking the quarterback, making a tackle for a loss, causing a fumble, tipping a pass, making it possible for someone else to make a play, or making a critical play. Bonus points are given for recovering a fumble, intercepting a pass, scoring a touchdown, or blocking a kick. An initial performance score is derived by dividing the number of pluses by the number

Courtesy of Penn State University

of plays. An adjusted performance score is determined by adding the number of positive factors and double the bonus points to the initial performance score.

Personnel evaluation is a constant process. We have to ask ourselves many questions. Are we playing the right people? Are our expectations of the players realistic? Should we be doing something to take advantage of the strengths of our best players? Do we have the right chemistry? We try to be as objective as possible, but much of evaluation comes down to subjective decisions.

While evaluating players, we also evaluate the defense. We track down and distance, yard line, hash mark, defensive call, offensive play, and yards gained or lost. If the offense succeeded on the play, we chart the reason for the defensive breakdown—improper technique, mental errors, missed tackles, poor pursuit, poor effort, bad judgment, lack of toughness, a personnel problem, a great offensive play, a poor defensive call, or misfortune. Our goal is to identify any problems and take steps to resolve them. Have we become too predictable? Are we in the right defensive scheme? We discuss personnel and defensive strategy constantly, trying to make the best use of our players and trying not to put them in situations that they can't handle.

As soon as possible, we begin to analyze our upcoming opponent, starting with an in-depth study of their game videos. We always look at the most current games. In addition, if a video is available, we like to look at a game when a particular team did a good job defending the upcoming opponent. We also review our previous games against the opponent.

As we watch the videos, we make notes such as "they like to run the ball more than usual on third and long," "we must be alert for big splits," "last year we stopped them in short-yardage situations by pinching everyone to the inside," "they like to throw deep coming out," "they seem to run plays based on their backfield sets," "we need perimeter pressure," "we must have a way to force the quarterback to pitch the ball against the option," "we should pressure them on a pass down," "don't let the quarterback get into a good rhythm," and "we need a special coverage to handle their tight end."

Other staff members compile a scouting report that includes a page on the opponent's personnel, formation hit charts, run blocking schemes, pass protection schemes, and goal-line plays. The scouting report also includes an offensive summary (see figure 26.1) that covers an assessment of the team highlighting the most significant factors contributing to their wins and losses; strengths and weaknesses; key players; an overview of their offensive style; the most important plays to stop; go-to plays they like in key situations; huddle formation; cadence information; top formations; motions and shifts; personnel usage; and key short-yardage, goal-line, and pass plays.

We may watch tapes of entire games, or we may create and view specially edited tapes that break down key game situations from several games. We like to review the team's coming-out plays, which are run from their

Offensive overview	Huddle	Cadence
Notre Dame is a very big football team that runs a very concise offense. Their big play man is #81, Tim Brown. Brown is a threat as a WR and as a RB. He is 5th in the nation in all-purpose yards. Beuerlein likes to throw deep off of play-action. They ran 8 reverses in 4 games, all to Brown. Their backs are big and run hard but aren't exceptionally quick. To beat this team, we must take it to them.	TE QB FB TB FL SE T G C G T	Set, color, #, color, #, hut. Cadence is fast. Linemen use large splits.

Top formations

Formation	# of times	Percent
1. Twins I	91	29
2. Pro I	66	21
3. Wishbone	56	18
4. Double TE I	35	11
5. Spread twins	26	8
6. Double TE wishbone	23	7

Top run plays

Play	# of times	Percent
1. Option	70	26
2. ISO	43	14
3. Toss	27	9
4. Counter option	11	4
5. Power	11	4

Motions

Motion	# of times	Percent
1. Motion to Pro to Twins	5	2
2. Motion that doesn't change the formation	4	1

Top pass plays

Pass action	# of times
1. Play action	24
2. Drop back	22
3. Roll out strong	18

Favorite patterns
1. Quick screen
2. Screen to TB
3. Up
4. Out

Shifts

We have not seen any shifting.

Trick plays

1. Toss Sally
2. Option Sally
3. Jump pass on goal line

Short-yardage plays

1. Double TE I/ISO 5×
          /Dive 2×
2. Double TE wishbone/option 2×
         /counter option 2×
3. Double TE wing I/ISO 2×
* TB will jump in short-yardage situations.

Personnel usage

Notre Dame will use a variety of running backs in many situations.

Top run plays

1. Double TE I/option 3×
         /ISO
         /toss
         /counter
2. Double TE wishbone/option 3×
         /counter dive
         /jump pass
* TB will jump at goal line.

Games scouted

1. Notre Dame vs. Pitt (10/11/86)
2. Notre Dame vs. Air Force (10/18/86)
3. Notre Dame vs. Navy (11/1/86)
4. Notre Dame vs. SMU (11/9/86)

Backfield sets vs. run or pass

Backfield set	Run	Pass
1. I backs	141	56
2. Wishbone	73	7
3. One back	4	26

Figure 26.1 Sample offensive summary.

goal line to their 15-yard line. Pass downs are used in situations such as second down and seven-plus yards to go or third down and five-plus yards to go. We review short-yardage situations: third and one to two yards, fourth down and one. Intermediate zone passes are passes they attempt from their opponent's 30-yard line to their opponent's 16-yard line. Coming-in plays are run from their opponent's 15-yard line to their opponent's 4-yard line. Goal-line plays are run from their opponent's 4-yard line to the goal line. Finally we look at plays run with two minutes left—all the plays at the end of the first half and all the plays at the end of the second half—taking special note of situations in which the teams were tied or our upcoming opponent was behind.

Before coming to any final conclusions regarding what we will do in key situations, we review the tapes. We look for tendencies, especially favorite plays. We examine their run blocking schemes (figures 26.2 and 26.3) and their pass protection schemes. What plays in our defensive package are best suited to handle what we expect them to do? Do we have to adjust? Do we have to come up with something special?

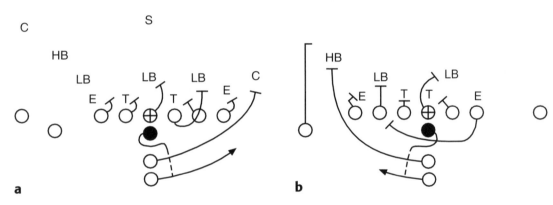

Figure 26.2 Run blocking schemes—the toss.

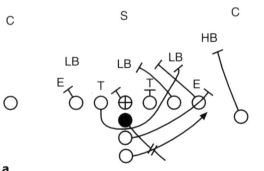
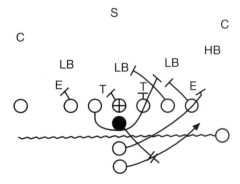

Figure 26.3 Run blocking schemes—power.

In one important game I remember, we were playing a team that liked to use a pick pass play on the goal line. The goal-line package with man-to-man coverage that we were using made us vulnerable to this play. We decided to create a special defense to counter it.

We began the second half by fumbling the opening kickoff on our own 4-yard line. On first down, we held them to a short gain. We knew they would run their pick play, so we called the special defense. We covered the pick play perfectly, but the ball was thrown high and the receiver made a fantastic catch.

Toward the end of the game, we again had our backs against the goal line as they tried to punch it in. On that play, even though we were misaligned, we threw them for a loss and won the game.

The positive outcome from that misalignment made me wonder about the value of all the planning that we do. However we continued to plan, and I feel that you must. If nothing else, planning helps players feel mentally prepared to handle key situations.

The game plan is created using the data collected and your own instinctive feelings about the opponent. First we consider our basic defenses and how they stack up against the opponent's offense. We must determine how much emphasis to place on our run and play-action base defenses as opposed to our pass package, including substitutions. For instance, if we were playing a strong running team such as Wisconsin, we would emphasize our basic package. However if we were playing a predominantly passing team such as Purdue, we would emphasize our pass package. We ask ourselves, how do we look against their best plays? Do we need to consider creating something special?

Usually we start with the run game and look at our perimeter play first. How are we going to handle down blocks? Who has contain? How is our secondary support tied to the front? Do we need pressure from the outside? What are our option responsibilities?

Next we analyze our interior defense. Do we need people to come down from the outside? Can our down people benefit from an out move? Do we need to plug linebackers? What run twists would be effective? Do our down people have enough variation (ins and outs)?

Then we focus on their passing game. What pass coverages are best suited to handle their favorite passes and their pass protection schemes? We create diagrams, such as those shown in figure 26.4, based on the tendencies evidenced in their game videos. Do we want to emphasize zone or man-to-man? How much pressure can we get from our standard rush? Philosophically, do we want to be more conservative or reckless? What pass blitzes would be most effective? What is best against their drop-back game? How do we handle their sprint, play-action, and misdirection pass games? What pass rush twists would be most effective? How can we conceal our pressure package and coverages? We always try to disguise everything as much as possible.

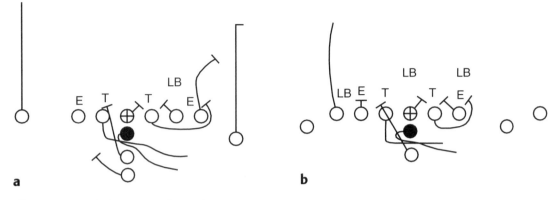

Figure 26.4 Pass protection schemes.

Finally we go over our adjustments and make sure that we'll be sound against multiple formations. The degree of emphasis we put on adjustments depends on our opponent's style of offense. If a team uses base formations most of the time but occasionally shows something out of the ordinary, we likely will audible against the unusual formation. Our thinking is to have a variety of defenses against their base formations but not to spend a lot of time planning to defend the unusual play. We want to be sound, but not necessarily flexible, against odd formations. However if multiple formations are a significant part of their plan, we want to have different ways to handle these formations.

This information is pulled together to create a game plan. The game plan includes alignment rules; adjustments and calls against no huddle, no signal, garbage formations, and third-down punts; special considerations such as formation or backfield adjustments; our defensive audibles and disguise package; our two-point defense; and a listing of all defenses with adjustments to formations.

Thoughts about key situations can occur anytime. An idea could come to you while you're working out or even sleeping. One year I awoke at 3:00 A.M. thinking about a two-point defense against Notre Dame. I couldn't go back to sleep; I kept thinking about what we should do. I had tremendous respect for Lou Holtz's play calling. He liked to do the unexpected. At 3:30 I decided that if we were faced with a two-point play, we would show a defense, take a look at their offensive set, then call time-out. Sure enough, the game ended on a two-point play that we were able to successfully defend.

The last sheet developed is the defensive call sheet. The call sheet includes a list of the base defenses (run and play-action pass defenses), our defensive audibles, short-yardage defenses, pass down selections, coming-in choices, and goal-line plans. I carry this sheet with me on game day. It is attached to my belt so that my movement and signaling capabilities are not inhibited. Most of the time, I go over the sheet between series to review situations or possible calls. On rare occasions I make the call directly from the sheet. I have found myself relying on the sheet more often when our opponent enters our red zone. I try to go over these situations thoroughly enough that I don't have to refer to the sheet much during the game.

Preparation

Players and coaches prepare for the game together. Preparation starts in the meeting room. The scouting report is given to the players, and an overview is presented. Players and coaches look at the opponent's game videos.

Throughout the week, position coaches show game videos, selected cutups, and our practice videos. The cutups help us concentrate on a particular area of concern. The particular cutups we study varies slightly according to the opponent. When we observe practice tapes, we check alignments, assignments, and techniques and evaluate the defenses.

Two days before the game, everyone comes together. Now the focus is on game tapes. I call a defense before the play, and the players visualize what they would do. The day before the game, we review. Throughout this process, I assess our opponent and my calls, trying to solidify the plan in my mind. I discuss the calls with the defensive staff and, sometimes, the players.

Practice prepares players and coaches for the game. Players hone the skills and techniques they need to perform, work on play recognition and reactions, and develop the mental and physical toughness they need to succeed. Practice gives the coaches an opportunity to evaluate the plan. What can we handle? How well are we executing?

I always draw the play for group and team periods. This gives me an opportunity to learn and evaluate what problems we might have. At times I draw plays that are challenging for the defense or that remind them of a specific point of emphasis (for example, a flare responsibility on a blitz). When conditioning is the primary purpose of practice, I attempt to beat the defense. Later in the week, I am more concerned about our confidence and want to see the defense succeed.

We work different aspects of the defense during practice periods. At alignment and stunt practice, players execute their assignments against formations without plays. We practice adjustments against odd formations, allowing us to check assignments without running plays. During practice on perimeter plays, we emphasize outside plays with some play-action and sprint passes. Interior play practice focuses on inside plays such as isolations, traps, and counters, with an emphasis on cutbacks. A special emphasis period covers key runs and play-action passes. We practice short-yardage, coming-in, and goal-line situations, including defending two-point plays. Game thud works on conditioning—two teams run plays against one defense at an extremely fast pace, forcing the defense to practice without a huddle. Game thud also can be used to work on game situations and substitutions in various situations such as first down, coming out, short yardage, pass down, coming in, and goal line. Players are under pressure to perform well in every period. We try to create an environment that is as similar to the actual game as possible.

Most of the decisions are made as early in the week as possible. Our game plan is completed on Tuesday, and the defensive call sheet is finished on Wednesday. At the end of the week, we may make some minor adjustments. The defense's experience and the players' comfort level affect our decisions to add or subtract defenses and make adjustments.

Finally we develop a philosophical approach for the game. How do we want to start? If everything goes as planned, what will we hold for later in the game? Do we have anything we want to hold on to until a critical situation arises? What can we expect from our offense, and how will our offense approach the game?

The Game

Often key decisions are called into question on game day. As scientific as we try to be in planning and preparation, many of the things that happen during the game influence calls.

The weather can be a big factor. Field conditions, wind, rain, snow, and the temperature are important variables that can influence defensive calls. If it's hot, we must be prepared to substitute. What limitations should we consider when we substitute? We might want to consider playing more zone and less man coverage on a wet day. What do we do if we lose one of our key players?

Our mood that day might determine what we do. A memorable moment for me was the morning of the first time we played Michigan. Following my game-day routine, I picked up a group of kids involved in our Second Mile program and took them to the game. After dropping everyone off, I returned to the car to retrieve my defensive call sheet. Having found it, I began walking toward the locker room, looking over my notes to make sure I had everything I needed. Someone had parked a small truck nearby and opened the back end, which extended over the sidewalk. I walked directly into the truck and hit the corner with my forehead. I immediately ducked and went to a knee, afraid someone had hit me in the head with something and might do it again. Curtis Enis, a high school senior at the time, observed the situation with a smile. I picked myself up and went to the training room, where the doctor put five stitches in my head. The kids enjoyed every one of them, but I didn't. It may have been an omen; we went on to lose a very close game.

When it is time to play, players and coaches should be alert but not too tense. The preparation of the previous week should help everyone feel secure, able to play the game aggressively without fear of failure. Players should have the courage to take a chance. Coaches should not be afraid to be different or do the unexpected. We want players and coaches who are confident enough to play the game with their hearts as well as their minds.

As important as planning is having a feel for the game. Is the opponent playing as we expected? What is our offense doing? Are we putting enough pressure on the quarterback? Where are they hurting us? If necessary, we make adjustments. Most of the time, the changes are subtle, though occasionally we make dramatic adjustments. The best time to make significant changes is at halftime, when there is time to think about it and everyone is together.

Communication from the press box is very important. Prior to each play, we must know the down and distance, position on the field, and key substitutions. Between series, key information is provided: plays that are hurting us, hash mark tendencies, down-and-distance tendencies, run blocking schemes, pass patterns, and pass protection schemes. Someone comes down before halftime and puts this information on the board for the coaches and players to study.

The approach at halftime is predicated, to a large extent, on our performance during the first half. First, we collect our thoughts. We review what happened during the first 30 minutes, looking closely at the problems we had, the opponent's blocking schemes, and key passes. We attempt to correct what we did poorly and to give positive feedback for what we did well.

Following this review, our focus turns to what we expect our opponent to do in the second half. We want to make sure that everyone understands his role in the defenses we plan to use in the second half.

Most of what is said is a spontaneous reaction to the mood at that moment. If confidence is lacking, we offer encouragement. If our level of effort has been inadequate, we try to motivate. Every squad is different, as is every game. The time spent together at the half is important, and much of what you do and say will be intuitive, based on your understanding of people and your experiences.

Significant changes usually are considered only in difficult situations. I remember making up a blitz in the second quarter against the University of Pittsburgh after they went ahead 14 to 0. The blitz helped, but some individual plays by Mark Robinson and Roger Jackson turned the game around, and we were able to shut them out for the rest of the game. Our initial impulse in preparing to face Ohio State in the Fiesta Bowl was to go with a true two-deep zone coverage that we hadn't played for a few weeks. We tried it in practice, became discouraged, and dropped the idea. The first half did not go well for us. At halftime we decided to put in the coverage and disguise it. Our original thought was correct, and we were very successful during the second half.

There also were times when our first impression wasn't accurate. In 1994 we were undefeated going into a game against Illinois. I felt that their quarterback was not a great decision maker and believed we could give up some zones in order to pressure him. I was wrong! He seemed to find every open area, and Illinois ran the ball extremely well. The result was a 28-point first half for Illinois. At halftime, the defensive staff met in the locker room. We were shocked by what had happened. Finally, out of desperation, we decided to change to an even defense with our base coverage and to put in some perimeter pressure to help against the run and misdirection pass game. It worked; we were able to settle into a couple of defenses and let the players play.

It is important to let the players use their talents and play without confusion. Sometimes I got overly creative. In 1986 we were undefeated going into a game against Notre Dame. My thought was to start the game by using an audible system to switch from one defense to another. I did, and they went down the field and scored. Tim Johnson, an outstanding defensive lineman, came to the sideline screaming at me to just call one defense and let them play. When someone who weighs 255 pounds and runs a 4.9 forty screams at you, you listen. I screamed back at him, "I'll call it. You better play it!" I called it, and he did play it.

That game was a real battle. Notre Dame completed a long pass at the end of the game. I knew it was deep in our territory but couldn't tell exactly where. If it was inside the 5-yard line, I wanted to substitute and play a goal-line defense. With only a few seconds to make the call, I went with a goal-line defense. When everything settled, I realized the ball was near the 10-yard line. When Notre Dame came out of the huddle, we were misaligned. However they ran into the strength of the defense, and we threw them for a loss. Bobby White, a tremendous person and leader, sacked the quarterback on second down. On third down, they threw a pass into the end zone. I thought they had caught it for a touchdown. What I didn't realize was that one of our defensive backs had knocked the ball loose. Jim Williams asked me for the next defense. I replied, "What do you mean? We lost." He said, "No, we knocked it loose." The players were all signaling for a certain defense. My response was, "If they want it, give it to them, Jim." He signaled it, and we stopped them to win the game.

Experiences such as this one have taught me that there always will be something beyond our coaching ability that will determine the team's destiny. Yes, we must plan, prepare for key situations, motivate everyone to do their best, and instill a level of confidence. But often it comes down to a player's or a coach's will to win and the undying spirit of a team.

Throughout my life, I've observed that success in key situations always comes down to trust. People who believe in each another find a way to get the job done. People who are committed and play with passion find a way to succeed. People unite in times of struggle and rise to the occasion. Great plans are important, but plans alone aren't enough in key situations. Great people—courageous, cooperative, committed, consistent, caring people—must be part of the plan.

27

Evaluating Performance

Ken Sparks

Of all the things a coach does, nothing is more critical than evaluating player performance and team performance! First, if you are to have a chance to win, you must play your best players and those who are performing the best. Players must be able to block, tackle, and execute well. The guys on the field must do that because coaches do not get to play! All coaches can do is to put the best players on the field.

Probably more important than getting the players on the field who physically do the job best is getting players on the field who have the trust of both coaches and teammates. When you do not do this, when trust does not exist, then other players do not feel good about being on the team. Attitude is a key factor in building a team.

Players today should know how you will evaluate them. Furthermore, they should have input into how that evaluation process will work, so a tremendous amount of communication must occur between coaches and players. Although not every player will play, players must understand how coaches make decisions about playing time. Players will understand the process only if they and the coaches work together. If there is an adversarial relationship, players against coaches or coaches against players, then from the outset you have a fragmented team. You will have difficulty motivating the team to accomplish what you want to accomplish. Players must understand the communication system in the evaluation process. Coaches must understand it as well so that they can encourage kids to do better and raise their level of performance.

Performance evaluation tends to focus on physical evaluation. Although that is important, so too is the underlying factor of how a player feels about himself, about the program, and about the way he is treated. Kids today want to know that someone cares about them. They are not interested so much in what people say but what people do. Coaches are frequently caught in this trap. I heard long ago that reputation is what you are in public and character is what you are in private. The trend among players today is that they want to know that someone cares about them as people, not just about what they can do to make the coach look good. Players occasionally put a coach in a situation to see if he really cares.

Our job as coaches is not merely to motivate guys on the field but to inspire them to live life fully, to get all they can out of life, and to put something back. When this happens, you also get more from players when they are on the field. When we evaluate players, we want them to improve not only on the football field but also in life.

Using the right standards in evaluating performance is important. Principles that are real, lasting, and absolute should be the basis of the standards. In society, criteria may change with every whim, but as coaches we must evaluate using principles that are right for life, not only for wins and losses. Players need to see coaches providing some real man guidance. There are many males and lots of male guidance, but not much man guidance. Many kids today are raised in homes that do not include a man; some are raised in homes with male influence, but that influence is often not that of a real man. Approximately 50 percent of the players on our team grew up in single-parent homes with no male role model.

Consequently, coaches have a great opportunity to affect young men. We must help them see that they are performing both individually and as members of a unit, a team. How we communicate and accomplish that goal is important. Furthermore, our concern cannot be only a seasonal thing or only on

Courtesy of Carson-Newman Media Relations

the playing field. It must be present on and off the field, and throughout the year.

Evaluation is difficult because coaches have recruiting and other responsibilities that limit day-to-day contact. That day-to-day contact, however, is what builds relationships with players. Many players start out thinking that the coach cares only whether they perform on the field. That attitude can undercut what we are trying to accomplish. If a player knows that we are trying to help him win the battle on the inside, then the battle on the outside will be much easier to win.

Many players today want to find real meaning in life and look to coaches to help them. When we separate football from life, we reduce the possibility of making a real difference in a player's performance. How we evaluate players relates directly to how we present ideas on how to live life. How we evaluate a player's performance on the field will determine the kind of relationship we have with him off the field. That system of principles is what he will use to make life decisions.

Individual Evaluation

If a player learns to live life responsibly and at a high level of performance, he can probably learn to play football. At our first team meeting in August, with all coaches, players, and parents present, we hand out a list of team responsibilities and opportunities. We give each player two copies, one to keep and one to sign and turn in, making a commitment to the team rules.

We tell players that if they really want to play, they need to look at three points. First, we play those who want to play. Second, we play those we can trust. If you can't go by the rules, you can't be trusted to play, and you will not stay eligible. Third, we play those who have the skills to play.

We go over the rules with the parents present, and they become part of the support and encouragement team. What does all this have to do with evaluation? Although a player may want to play, have an opportunity to play, and earn an evaluation that will permit him to play, he still must be able to be trusted. Consequently, team rules are important. Our team rules are academic, social, and commonsense:

- Academic—go to class; go to assigned study hall or tutoring; act like somebody in class; study and let others study outside of class.
- Social—abstain from drugs and alcohol; be honest (abstain from cheating, gambling, stealing).
- Commonsense—never miss or be late to practice or meetings; stay away from any place where people are doing drugs or alcohol; abstain from fighting, sexual immorality, and profanity; observe curfews; use common sense to control how you dress; wear no earrings in any team function or facility.

Those are some of our rules. I wish that everyone functioned on such a mature level that rules were unnecessary, but, realistically speaking, kids need to know where they are going and how to get there. If you don't know where you are, you can't get where you want to go. We try to make this clear. I believe that kids want direction. The problem is that they see so much specious authority in society today. What they want is authentic authority. Frequently, we misinterpret behavior as a lack of discipline when the real problem is they have not seen the real deal. This is where we as coaches can have a powerful positive effect.

If we expect players to perform and live at a higher level, many will respond to that expectation. That is why we have team rules with academic and social expectations. Expect a little; get a little. Expect a lot; get a lot. We don't just throw out rules to the players. We explain to the players, with parents present, why we have each one of these rules. We have academic rules because we want players to graduate from college. We provide many examples of students who have arrived without strong backgrounds but have made their experience in college successful. The same idea applies to the social and commonsense rules.

During fall camp, we bring in speakers to share their stories with the team, stories that relate to our rules. For example, during our 2001 fall camp, Jimmy Streeter spoke. He was a great player in college and in the Canadian Football League. He now struggles with partial paralysis and loss of one arm because he didn't follow the rules of life he should have followed.

In our opening session, then, we hand out a list of team rules and explain them in detail, with parents present. We ask each player to sign his commitment to follow the rules. If a player is not willing to do this, he should return home with his parents because that will ultimately happen anyway. From the outset, we want everyone involved with the football team heading in the same direction so that we can perform as we want to perform. Again, I don't think you can separate what happens on the outside from what happens on the inside.

Personal History

After the parents leave our initial meeting, we go to position meetings led by each position coach. They have a sharing time together. Players complete a personal history form that asks questions about a player's family, school experience, relationships, health, and other issues. The personal history form gives players the opportunity to write about themselves. After completing the form, the players gather with the coach in a circle so that the players do not view the coach as talking down to them. We do not want this sharing time to be embarrassing. It is a time for players to share anything going on in their lives. This session offers the coach another opportunity to evaluate the player and understand why he responds the way he does.

Player Leaders

Before we get on the football field to start any activities, we eat a meal together. We divide our players into huddles. We have 12 elected leaders on our team; thus, we have 12 huddles with 12 to 14 players in each group. At this meal, players sit together in huddles and get to know each other. They sit together at meals throughout camp.

As camp moves into the season, we ask players for their input into who should play. This approach contributes to getting the entire team headed in the same direction. I ask the 12 leaders questions such as, "Who do you want to start a game? Who do you want to have the ball when it is fourth and one? Behind which blockers would you like to see the ball carrier run?" The answers are revealing. Now, the players' judgments are not the final answer on who plays, but I listen carefully to their input. It's a good indicator about what is really going on inside the team. The huddle leaders know more than the coaches do because they sit in those huddle meetings.

All this has the goal of getting us on the same page. The total of the whole gets it done. If you get two or three complainers on the team, grumbling will spread. Sometimes the best players do not make up the best team. The best individuals do not always win. Those who play as a team win. So, when you are evaluating the team, it is not 11 times 1 but 1 times 11 that brings you the winning team.

As for other activities, we put the guys in a performance setting before they ever go on the practice field. For example, we'll load them up and go to the lake for a cookout. There, the 12 huddles will engage in activities that give them a chance to perform. An example would be getting every member of the huddle across a cove in the lake. A second example would be to play sand volleyball with coaches as referees. The coaches deliberately make some bad calls, such as calling a ball out when it is in, to see how a team will respond. At the end of the game, coaches bring the players together to explain what they were trying to teach, that during the year things will not always go our way. Bad calls or other negative things will happen. How are we going to respond? Another example would be a game of one-pitch softball with one team starting out behind 0-7. What kind of performance does this call for? How will players respond? Another example would be to tie players' legs together, put a blindfold on some, and put a gag on others. The question is how the players will get the task done with those impairments. Our time at the lake sets the stage for what it will be like when we put on the uniform and play a game. We let the players know what we expect of them.

These preseason events establish criteria for evaluation—team rules and responsibilities, personal history, and small groups. The 12 huddle leaders and the coaches establish the team rules and responsibilities before fall camp begins. So the rules are the players' rules. They know what we expect and how we will evaluate them.

Physical Evaluation

One thing we expect out of each player is physical performance. We use the shuttle run as our physical-fitness test. The shuttle run consists of a 300-yard shuttle performed twice with a five-minute rest between attempts. This is one of the ways we evaluate where players are physically. Consequently, we'll know how much conditioning to do. If some players come to camp not in condition, they are probably not going to help during the first game or two, so we will have to adjust. If they do not pass the shuttle-run test, they run it at 6:00 A.M. every day until they pass it. In a letter we send in the summer, we tell players that if they can't pass the shuttle run or a similar test that indicates readiness to play, they will not play.

Another thing we emphasize at the beginning of fall camp is that everyone starts even. A player may have had a good spring practice or a mediocre one. A player may have been on a backup unit or on the first unit. Regardless, in fall camp everyone begins on level ground. We feel this is important. Not having hope before beginning camp is a negative motivator. When we begin, we do not have a depth chart. We have a position chart and list each player alphabetically. We have no first, second, or third units at that point. In fact, we give names to each unit.

Observing NCAA rules, we wear no pads and do no contact work during the first three days. We have open competitions until our first major scrimmage. We go through three days in shorts and at least two or three days in pads before our first major scrimmage. The good thing about this is that everybody feels that they have an equal chance because they start even. Then we grade the first scrimmage as we would a game and assign players to units (see table 27.1).

We do not post a depth chart. We communicate with each player personally. In daily meetings, position coaches have players line up in a certain order or unit and then explain why certain people are lining up with certain units. Consequently, we have to communicate about performance. We constantly evaluate performance and communicate with players about our expectations.

After the first week of practice and after we place players in certain units, I ask position coaches to give an evaluation of each player at his position. We do this in writing on charts that we use to note areas where a player needs to improve. We use the threefold "want to play, trusted to play, and skilled to play" criteria.

Coaches talk to their position players about why they are on first unit, second unit, or third unit by telling them, "Here are three things you are doing very well and here are three things you need to improve." This approach prevents players from coming away down in the mouth. The coach isn't just telling players what they are not doing; he is also telling them what they are doing well. The player leaves this meeting with hope. He knows what the coach expects of him.

TABLE 27.1

Grade Sheet

	Play or defense	+/-	Effort	Comments
1				
2				
3				
4				
5				
6				
7				
8				
9				
10				
11				
12				
13				
14				
15				
16				
17				
18				
19				
20				
21				
22				
23				
24				
25				

This positive method of grading practice lets the player know what he needs to do. Again, the key is communication. At this time, the players also can tell the position coaches what they are doing well or what they are struggling with. This way the coach knows what he needs to do to help the players more. We create a "we're in this together" experience instead of an adversarial one.

After the first scrimmage I ask each position coach to list the top 25 athletes on the team. Just because these kids make the top 25 does not mean that they are the best players. Remember that 80 percent of who plays is determined by who wants to play and whom we can trust. This exercise is good for position coaches because it makes them evaluate the entire squad, not just the players in their areas.

Having several heads involved is always better than one, and this is especially true when it comes to evaluating players. We do not base our evaluation on one man's opinion because we all have blind spots. We can become involved in personalities and miss something good about another player.

I also ask position coaches to give me their top five in their areas. Because the key is to put the best 22 on the field, I occasionally make position changes when I think a player not in the top five at one position could be in the top five at another. I ask coaches for this information every day during early practices and in spring practice. Similarly, a player might be in the top five at one position but could be a starter in another position. The more quickly we make those changes, the better off we are. This ranking by the coaches is another way that we evaluate performance in early practices. I serve as a kind of clearinghouse for position changes to put players into the positions where they can play their best and contribute the most to the team.

We want to be sure that we are all going in the same direction. We are not a coaches' team or a players' team. We cannot be on different pages if we want to accomplish our goals. Communication is the key, both from coaches to players and from players to coaches.

Playing Time

We have talked about pre-fall practice and fall practice, and now it's time to talk about who gets to play in a game and how we grade individuals. The criteria we use to decide who gets to play are who wants to play, who has earned our trust, who has the skill, and who shows that skill to play.

It's easy to tell who wants to play. If a player wants to play, he hustles all the time. He is not an up-and-down player. He works hard to become a consistent player. He does everything he can to show that he wants to play. He doesn't have to be jump-started every day or be talked into working hard. Regardless of whether he is first, second, or third unit, he is all the way in. He shows by the way he practices that he wants to play. As a player performs in practice, so will he perform in the game.

The second criterion is whom we can trust. Can we trust him to play the technique we ask him to play, to play the gap responsibility we ask him to play, to do what he is supposed to do to make the whole unit sound? We must also be able to trust the player off the field and in the classroom. If he doesn't make good choices in those areas, our team will deteriorate from within because this player is not all the way in.

The third criterion is who has the skill to play. Who has the size, the speed, and the aggressiveness to use his speed? These attributes show that players have the skills. We are not interested in potential; potential is nothing. We look for the player who shows he has the skill to play the game.

Who plays in the game? Those who play are the players who demonstrate those three traits. We evaluate according to those criteria. If a player really wants to play, he will respond to the standards. If he wants to play, he will give a better effort consistently, and he will be more coachable. He will perform the techniques and assignments better and work to contribute solidly to the team. Even if we turn our backs on him, he will do the right thing on the field. Professors will not call to say that he is not attending class. Police officers will not call to tell us that he is not doing what he is supposed to be doing. We are going to play people we can trust. That's the bottom line.

The first two criteria make up about 80 percent of the standard. A player who may have less skill will play if he sacrifices and commits himself. A player who possesses more natural talent may not play if he doesn't show he wants to play or if we can't trust him.

I remind players of these three criteria so that they know the standard we are holding them to. When players know how it is, they are more likely to go in the same direction as the coach.

Academic Evaluation

Another part of the evaluation process concerns the performance of the student in the classroom. We do what we can to emphasize education. We tell players that if they leave college without a degree, they have likely wasted a key time in their lives. The bottom line is that we want them to get a degree.

We try to play a key role in the education of the players (although this varies according to the size of the school and the resources available to the athletic department). How can we coaches be all we say we are if we do not emphasize the other parts of life? Kids will play football for only a few years at most. What happens in the classroom will probably determine what happens with the rest of their lives.

Like it or not, if a kid does not get it done in the classroom, he can't play! Students have to maintain a specified grade point average and certain progress toward graduation. Therefore, coaches should be involved in evaluating players in the classroom. That concern is part of caring about those young men.

One thing we do is to send out evaluation forms to professors. We ask professors to list the player's current grade in the class, note any missing work and remaining tests, and indicate the number of absences the player has had. These forms help us know what is going on in the classroom. Preventing problems is better than having to cure them.

During position meetings, we give each player a calendar to write in his class schedule and his daily schedule, including time to study. As we help them see what it takes to be a successful person, they can see what it takes to be a successful football player. A player can either pay now and play later, or play now and pay later. If he makes the right choices and disciplines himself now, he will enjoy life to the fullest later. If he chooses to cut corners now, he will pay for his mistakes for the rest of his life. We stay involved in the education evaluation process through the forms sent to professors, the calendars provided to the players, and the work we do with the day-to-day application of getting an education.

Another way we encourage academic excellence is to have an ongoing position grade point average (GPA) contest. At the end of every grading period or semester, we calculate the position GPA. I challenge the players to produce the highest GPA at their positions, creating some excitement for those at the position with the highest GPA and a little shame for the group with the lowest. We have a board in the locker room where we show the position GPA and our individual GPA all-stars. We show a career average and a semester average. The performance of players in the classroom is yet another way we evaluate whether or not they are all the way in. We strive for them to understand that performance is not just on the football field but also in the classroom, in a restaurant, or anywhere. We do not want them to click it on when they are on the field and click it off when they go off the field. Performance is everywhere. If I care about a player as a football player, I care about him as a student, as a social being, and as a total person.

Evaluation of Team Performance

After personal player evaluation, we now come face-to-face with where we are as a team. Football is not about 11 players doing their own thing, but about 11 players working together to accomplish one thing. A good way to illustrate this is to compare the football team to an orchestra. Listen to an orchestra rehearse or tune up before a performance. As the musicians tune their instruments, the sound grates on the ears. After all the instruments are tuned, the focus shifts to the conductor, and the performers begin to play the assigned notes at the right time, creating beautiful music. We can say the same of a football team. We have the task of evaluating team performance so that we play as a team, not as a group of individual players.

Practice Field Performance Evaluation

The first step of team performance evaluation occurs on the practice field. We do this with each unit—offense, defense, and kicking—each day by viewing video of the previous day's practice. We watch ourselves both as individuals and as an offensive unit, defensive unit, or kicking unit. Something I've tried to do more lately is get the entire offensive unit in a room with all the coaches, the defense in a room with all the coaches, and the kicking units in a room with all the coaches. That way everybody knows what everybody else is doing and saying.

In this day of specialized football, the right hand sometimes doesn't know exactly what the left hand is doing. Sometimes we communicate poorly. We alleviate these problems by looking at video of each unit with all the coaches in the same room with the players. We make this a quick overview because we don't have much time. We must get to position meetings.

We conduct short, snappy practices with high intensity. I give awards on the field. For example, if we have offense going against defense on perimeter or skeleton situations, I may tell the offense that if they complete a certain number of passes, the defense does push-ups. When we struggled a bit with turnovers early one season, I said that any time the quarterback turned over the ball, Coach Sparks would do 10 push-ups. If the running back committed a turnover, the running-backs coach would do push-ups. We didn't do that long because I was doing all the push-ups! We've had some success with those approaches to getting players to think about their performance on the field.

We do something special for the nonplaying units, the scout-team players. These players cannot play for one reason or another, so they show us the offense or defense of the opposing team. They contribute a great deal to the effectiveness of our practices. We have Scout Players of the Week, two each on offense and defense, and we make a big deal out of it. We recognize the players in front of the whole team, and the team gives them a standing ovation.

We also have what we call a Monday Bowl for all the players who are not qualified to play or who dressed but did not play in the game of the previous week. They play a 40-minute scrimmage with coaches coaching them. We videotape, grade, and evaluate the scrimmage. The Monday Bowl gives those guys an opportunity to keep running our offense and defense, not just the offense and defense of our opponents. At the end of the season we have a Monday Super Bowl and give awards to the winners of the bowl (a T-shirt or something similar). Everybody knows how important scout teams are to the future of the team. We need to keep those guys involved in team performance.

Game-Day Performance Evaluation

Evaluation of our game-day performance is where the rubber meets the road. Emotions run high and low. Games present many teachable moments, so it is important to communicate in the right way. Players must know what you are thinking.

I take about 20 minutes each Monday after a game to explain the evaluation of what happened in the game. I ask the team what lessons they learned from the game. They often point out the same things I had on my notes. The process works much better when criticism comes from the players, from within, rather than from the head coach down to them. This approach has really been good for us and has laid the groundwork for us to improve.

I appoint four captains for the next game. I let the captains of the previous game talk about our last effort. They also talk about our theme for the game last week, which is usually based on scripture, not something I made up, but something God said. They end the meeting by talking about how well we lived up to our theme in the previous week. This, too, has been a good forum and useful evaluation.

We do not give game-day awards. We have team awards, but not individual awards. On offense, we have six goals:

1. We give position grades: wide receivers, 90 percent; tight ends, 80 percent; offensive line, 75 percent; running backs, 80 percent; quarterbacks, 85 percent. The goal is for everybody to grade out on offense or achieve the average grade at every position.

2. We want to score every time we get in the orange zone (inside the 20-yard line).

3. We do not want a penalty to stop a drive.

4. We want to win third down.

5. We want at most one fumble for the game.

6. We want at most one interception for the game.

If the offense reaches four of the six goals, they earn a team award, usually a T-shirt with a special theme printed on it.

We also have six goals for the defense:

1. Score or set up a score.

2. Force three turnovers.

3. Miss fewer than nine tackles. (As the season goes along, I lower that number.)

4. Win third down (the defense must win two of every three third and fourth downs).

5. Sack the quarterback three or more times.

6. Bat down five passes.

If the defense reaches four of the six goals, they each get a T-shirt. We feel that our system is a good way to evaluate performance.

Each kicking unit has its own goals. The punting unit has a goal to avoid having a blocked punt all season and to net 36 yards per punt. The punt-return unit has goals to average 10 yards per return and to block a punt or force a bad punt every game. The goal of the kickoff unit is to force the receiving team to start on average at their own 23-yard line or worse. The kickoff receiving team has a goal to start at the 32-yard line or better. All these are averages for the entire game. The point-after-touchdown, field-goal team has the goal to avoid having an attempt blocked, to be 100 percent on all extra points, and to be 75 percent on all field goals. The goal of the kick-block unit is to block five kicks during the season. They also receive T-shirts when they reach their goals. With each of these units, we strive to improve our performance from week to week.

Off-the-Field Performance Opportunities

Because the season is a busy time for coaches, we may forget that perhaps the best way we can teach these young men to perform properly off the field is to give something back. This is especially important today when a "me-first" or "get more" attitude permeates our society.

Heavenly mathematics says that what you keep you lose and what you give away you gain, and if you would be first, you must be a servant. Players don't hear this much, but it is truth. One of the things we do is provide a Thanksgiving meal for four or five needy families in our community. We have been in the national playoffs in 15 of the last 16 years, so we practice at Thanksgiving. The players give money to provide this meal and divide into groups to take meals to the homes. It's an unbelievable experience.

We have also gone to local schools to present the FCA program "One Way to Play." In addition, we participate in reading programs at schools and the "Character Counts" program.

We have an orphanage in our area, and some of the players have gone to work with children who don't have role models. Through these activities, our players have the opportunity to give. Our Christian approach gives us opportunities to speak or sing at local churches. The key is to help players learn how to maximize their lives by living from the inside out rather than the outside in. We must constantly put this part into the evaluation process.

I hope that some of these ideas will help you increase your team's performance both on and off the field. May God bless the performance of your team.

About the AFCA

Since its establishment in 1922, the American Football Coaches Association (AFCA) has provided a forum for the discussion and study of all matters pertaining to football and coaching. It also works to maintain the highest possible standards in football and the coaching profession. These objectives—first declared by founders Major Charles Daly, Alonzo Staff, John Heisman, and others—have been instrumental in the AFCA's becoming the effective and highly respected organization it is today.

The AFCA now has more than 8,000 members, including coaches from Canada, Europe, Australia, Japan, and Russia. Through annual publications and several newsletters, the association keeps members informed of the most current rule changes and proposals, proper coaching methods, innovations in techniques, insights in coaching philosophy, and business conducted by the board of trustees and AFCA committees. A convention is held each January to give members a special opportunity to exchange ideas and recognize outstanding achievement.

The association promotes safety in the sport and establishes strong ethical and moral codes that govern all aspects of football coaching. In addition, the AFCA is involved in numerous programs that ensure the integrity of the coaching profession and enhance the development of the game. The AFCA works closely with the National Collegiate Athletic Association, the National Association of Collegiate Directors of Athletics, the National Association of Interscholastic Athletics, the National Football League, the National Football Foundation and Hall of Fame, Pop Warner, and other organizations involved in the game of football. Indeed, one of the goals of the association is to build a strong coalition of football coaches—Team AFCA—who speak out with a unified voice on issues that affect the sport and profession.

The AFCA is the team of the football coaching profession. All current and former football coaches or administrators involved with football are encouraged to join. For more information about becoming a member of the AFCA, please visit the AFCA Web site **(www.afca.com)** or write to the following address:

American Football Coaches Association
100 Legends Lane
Waco, TX 76706

About the Coordinators

Don Nehlen

- Head coach at West Virginia University and Bowling Green State University (Ohio) and assistant at the University of Michigan over 33 years.
- National Coach of the Year in 1988.
- Posted 17 winning seasons, two perfect regular seasons, and a 146-92-4 record at West Virginia as part of a 202-128-8 career record.
- AFCA President in 1997.

Harold "Tubby" Raymond

- Head coach at the University of Delaware for 36 years after serving 12 years as an assistant coach under David Nelson.
- One of only four college football head coaches to win 300 games at the same school.
- Posted winning records in 31 of his 36 seasons.
- Claimed Division II national titles in 1971, 1972, and 1979.

Bill Curry

Courtesy of Bill Curry

- Coached at Georgia Tech, the University of Alabama, and the University of Kentucky over 17 years.
- Played in the NFL from 1965 to 1974.
- Named Atlantic Coast Conference Coach of the Year in 1985 and Southeastern Conference Coach of the Year in 1987 and 1989.

Ron Schipper

Courtesy of Central College

- Coached at Central College (Iowa) for 36 years.
- Amassed a career record of 287-67-3.
- Led the Flying Dutchmen to 36 consecutive winning seasons, a record 18 Iowa Conference championships, and the NCAA Division III national title in 1974.
- AFCA President in 1994.

Dick Tomey

Courtesy of University of Arizona

- Coached at the University of Arizona and University of Hawaii over 24 seasons.
- Tallied a 95-64-4 record in becoming the University of Arizona's winningest coach ever.
- Won the Fiesta Bowl in 1994 and the Holiday Bowl in 1998.

Bill Mallory

Courtesy of Paul B. Riley/Indiana University Athletic Dept.

- Head coach at Indiana University, Northern Illinois University, the University of Colorado, and Miami University over 26 seasons.
- Compiled a career record of 168-129-4 as head coach.
- Two-time winner of Big Ten Conference Coach of the Year (1986 and 1987) and Mid-American Conference Coach of the Year in 1983.

About the Contributors

Grant Teaff

Courtesy of Chris Hansen

- Retired from a 30-year coaching career in 1992 after 22 years as Baylor University's head coach.
- While at Baylor, won 128 games and took his team to eight bowl games.
- Coached 12 postseason all-star games.
- Named Southwest Conference Coach of the Year six times and National Coach of the Year once.
- Currently serves as the executive director of the AFCA.

Bo Schembechler

Courtesy of University of Michigan Athletics Archives

- Coached at the University of Michigan for 20 years after stops at Ohio State, Northwestern, Bowling Green University, Presbyterian College, and Miami University, where he had previously played offensive tackle.
- Amassed a 194-47-5 record at the University of Michigan while winning 13 Big Ten Conference Championships.
- National Coach of the Year in 1969.
- President of the AFCA in 1983.

Fisher DeBerry

- Air Force head coach since 1984 after serving as assistant coach at the Academy. Nine years of previous head coaching experience at Appalachian State University (North Carolina).
- Winningest coach in Air Force history with three Western Athletic Conference titles and 10 bowl games.
- National Coach of the Year in 1985 and Western Athletic Conference Coach of the Year in 1985, 1995, and 1998.

Courtesy of Air Force Media Relations

Jim Tressel

- Head coach for The Ohio State University since 2001 after 15 years at Youngstown State University. Also coached at Syracuse University and the University of Akron.
- Led Youngstown State to four Division I-AA national championships and appeared in 10 Division I-AA playoffs.
- While at Youngstown, posted a 135-57-2 record and had 12 winning seasons.
- Named AFCA National Coach of the Year in 1991 and 1994.

Courtesy of Ohio State Athletics Communications

Joe Paterno

- Has been coaching football at Penn State University for almost 50 years, the last 36 as head coach.
- Led teams to five undefeated seasons, two national championship titles, and 21 bowl game wins, a record in college football.
- His 300-plus victories rank first among active college coaches.
- Four-time National Coach of the Year.

Courtesy of Penn State University

Bobby Bowden

© SportsChrome

- Florida State University head coach since 1976 after six years at West Virginia University and four years at Samford University (Alabama).
- Second-winningest active head coach in the nation and only coach in Division I-A history to record 13 straight 10-win seasons.
- Holds NCAA record for 14 consecutive bowl wins.
- Has led Florida State to two national championships.

Tom Osborne

Courtesy of University of Nebraska

- Posted a 255-49-3 record in 25 years as head coach at the University of Nebraska after serving as an assistant at the school.
- Led his teams to three national championships, 25 bowl games, 12 Big 8 Championships, and one Big 12 Championship.
- National Coach of the Year in 1994.

Lou Holtz

Courtesy of University of South Carolina

- Since 1969 has been head coach at South Carolina, Notre Dame, Minnesota, Arkansas, North Carolina State, and William & Mary, as well as the NFL's New York Jets.
- His 233 career victories rate Holtz 11th on Division I-A win list.
- Won national championship and was awarded the National Coach of Year in 1988.

Bill Snyder

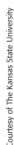

Courtesy of The Kansas State University

- Coached for 40 years at both the high school and collegiate level. Since 1989 has served as head coach for Kansas State University.
- Led Kansas State to eight straight bowl games and captured two Big 12 North Division championships for the Wildcats.
- Awarded numerous Big 12, Big 8, and National Coach of the Year awards including the Associated Press National Coach of the Year in 1998.

Larry Kehres

Courtesy of Mount Union College

- Head coach at Mount Union College (Ohio) since 1986.
- Compiled a winning streak of 54 games, the longest in football history.
- Guided his team to six national titles and 12 Ohio Athletic Conference championships.
- Named the Division III National Coach of the Year for a record six times in 2001.

Dick Foster

Courtesy of Dick Foster

- Coached 45 years at the high school and junior college levels.
- Only head coach to win two national junior college championships at two different schools (Fort Scott and Coffeyville).
- His 146-25-2 head coaching record is the highest winning percentage ever over 15 or more seasons in the NJCAA.
- Named National Junior College Coach of the Year in 1970 and has been inducted into the NJCAA National Hall of Fame.

George Curry

Courtesy of George Curry

- Berwick High School head coach since 1971.
- *USA Today*'s National Coach of the Year in 1983 and 1992.
- All-time winningest high school coach in Pennsylvania, including six state titles and 50 straight conference wins from 1987 to 1994.
- Led Berwick High to USA Today National Champions in 1983, 1992, and 1995.
- AFCA President in 1996.

Mack Brown

Courtesy of University of Texas

- University of Texas head coach since 1998 after head coaching positions at the University of North Carolina (10 years), Tulane University (3 years), and Appalachian State University (North Carolina) for one season.
- Has not had a losing season since 1989 and has led teams to 11 straight bowl appearances.
- Fourth winningest Division I-A coach since 1990.

Gene Stallings

Courtesy of University of Alabama/Athletic Dept.- Kent Gidley

- Retired after more than 39 years with coaching positions at the University of Alabama, Texas A&M University, the Dallas Cowboys, and the St. Louis Cardinals.
- During his time with the Cowboys, Dallas won seven division titles (1973, 1976–1979, 1981, 1985), three conference championships (1975, 1977–1978) and one Super Bowl (1978). The Cowboys also appeared in the 1976 and 1979 Super Bowls.
- Led the Crimson Tide to a perfect regular season (12–0) in 1992 and to five bowl games in his seven seasons as Alabama's head coach.
- National Coach of the Year in 1992.

Joe Tiller

- Head football coach at Purdue University since 1997 with more than 20 years coaching experience. Worked as an assistant coach at Montana State, Purdue, Washington State, and for the Calgary Stampeders, followed by a successful six-year run as Wyoming's head coach.
- Led the Boilermakers to four consecutive bowl games including the Rose Bowl in 2000.
- Won the Western Athletic Conference in 1996 and the Big Ten Conference in 2000.
- National Coach of the Year in 1997.

Mike Bellotti

- University of Oregon head coach since 1995 after six years as an assistant at the school, following five years as head coach at Chico State and seven seasons as offensive coordinator at Cal St.-Hayward and Weber State.
- Highest seven-year victory total in Oregon history. Led the school to six postseason berths in first seven years as head coach.

Hayden Fry

- Career head coaching record of 232-178-10, including 143-89-6 record at the University of Iowa, more wins than any coach at the school.
- Won three Big Ten titles and 14 bowl games. Named Big Ten Coach of the Year three times.
- AFCA president in 1993.

Barry Alvarez

Courtesy of University of Wisconsin

- University of Wisconsin head coach since 1990 after assistant coaching positions at the University of Notre Dame and University of Iowa.
- Has won three Big Ten Conference titles and two Rose Bowls in becoming Wisconsin's winningest coach ever.
- National Coach of the Year in 1993 and Big Ten Conference Coach of the Year in 1993 and 1998.

LaVell Edwards

Courtesy of Mark A. Philbrick/Brigham Young University

- Coached at Brigham Young University for 28 seasons, retiring with a career record of 257-101-3.
- National Coach of the Year in 1984, the season BYU won the national championship.
- Western Athletic Coach of the Year seven times. Won 20 conference championships.
- AFCA president in 1988.

R.C. Slocum

Courtesy of Texas A&M University

- Head football coach at Texas A&M University since 1989 after serving 16 years as assistant coach.
- Earned three Southwest Conference titles, two Big 12 South Division titles, and the 1998 Big 12 championship title.
- Coached his teams in 10 bowl games.
- Named to the AFCA Board of Trustees.

Sonny Lubick

Courtesy of Colorado State University

- Head coach at Colorado State University since 1993. Also served as head coach at Montana State University and assisted at Stanford University, the University of Miami, Colorado State University, and Montana State University.
- Led Colorado State University to five Mountain West Conference titles and six bowl games in nine seasons, becoming the most successful coach in school history.
- His 2000 team ranked 14th in the top 25 poll, Colorado State's highest-ever end-of-the-season ranking.

Frank Beamer

Courtesy of David Knachel/Virginia Tech

- Virginia Tech head coach since 1987 after six seasons as head coach at Murray State and eight years as an assistant at Murray State and The Citadel.
- Won three Big East Conference championships in becoming Virginia Tech's winningest coach ever.
- National Coach of the Year in 1999 and Big East Coach of the Year three times.

Phillip Fulmer

Courtesy of Gary Moor Photography

- Head coach at the University of Tennessee since 1992 after previous assistant coaching positions at that school as well as Wichita State University and Vanderbilt University.
- National Coach of the Year and SEC Coach of the Year in 1998, the season he led Tennessee to the national championship with a perfect 13–0 mark.
- Highest winning percentage in University of Tennessee history and quickest coach in SEC history to reach 50 and 75 wins.

Jim Young

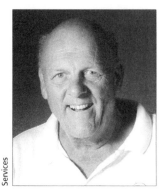

Courtesy of USMA Media Relations

- Head coach for 17 years on the collegiate level at West Point, Purdue University, and the University of Arizona. Also coached at Findlay College, Bowling Green University, Shawnee High School (Ohio), Miami of Ohio, and the University of Michigan.
- Retired from college coaching after posting a career record of 120-71-2.
- Led teams to 12 winning seasons and five bowl victories out of six attempts.

Frosty Westering

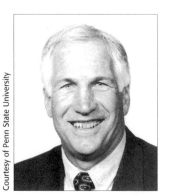

Courtesy of Pacific Lutheran University Photo Services

- Head coach of Pacific Lutheran University since 1972 after coaching at Parsons College (Iowa) and Lea College (Minnesota).
- Led the Lutes to the NCAA Division III national championship in 1999 and three NAIA Division II national titles in 1980, 1987, and 1993.
- Awarded Northwest Conference Coach of the Year in 1985, 1986, 1993, and 1998; AFCA NCAA Division III Coach of the Year in 1999; and NAIA National College Football Coach of the Year in 1983 and 1993.

Jerry Sandusky

Courtesy of Penn State University

- Coached at the collegiate level for 33 years, serving as an assistant at Penn State, Juniata College (Pennsylvania), and Boston University.
- Nine linebackers under Sandusky were awarded first-team All-American honors. Sandusky's defensive game plans helped win national championships in 1982 and 1986.
- Began his collegiate football experience as starting defensive end for Penn State from 1963 to 1965.

Ken Sparks

Courtesy of Carson-Newman Media Relations

- Head football coach of Carson-Newman College, his alma mater, since 1980. More than 34 years coaching experience.
- Led his teams to five national championships, 15 South Atlantic Conference championships, and 17 NAIA or NCAA postseason appearances.
- Awarded SAC Coach of the Year nine times.
- Member of the AFCA Board of Trustees.

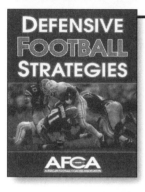
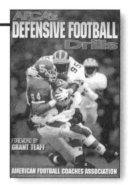
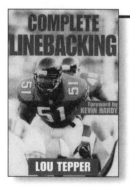

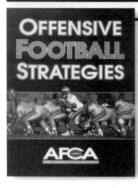
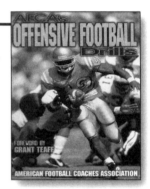